Irish/ness Is All Around Us

Language Revivalism and the Culture of Ethnic Identity in Northern Ireland

Olaf Zenker

berghahn
NEW YORK · OXFORD
www.berghahnbooks.com

Published in 2013 by
Berghahn Books
www.berghahnbooks.com

© 2013, 2016 Olaf Zenker
First paperback edition published in 2016

Library of Congress Cataloging-in-Publication Data
Zenker, Olaf.
Irish/ness is all around us : language revivalism and the culture of ethnic identity
in Northern Ireland / Olaf Zenker.
    p. cm. -- (Integration and conflict studies ; 6)
  Includes bibliographical references and index.
  ISBN 978-0-85745-913-8 (hardback) -- ISBN 978-1-78533-206-7 (paperback)
-- ISBN 978-0-85745-914-5 (ebook)
  1. English language--Dialects--Northern Ireland. 2. Group identity--Northern
Ireland. 3. Northern Ireland--Ethnic relations. I.
Title.
  PE2586.Z46 2013
  427'.9416--dc23

                                                        2012033494

British Library Cataloguing in Publication Data
A catalogue record for this book is available from the British Library

ISBN 978-0-85745-913-8 (hardback)
ISBN 978-1-78533-206-7 (paperback)
ISBN 978-0-85745-914-5 (ebook)

'And it can happen – to use an image you'll understand – it can happen that a civilisation can be imprisoned in a linguistic contour which no longer matches the landscape of ... fact.'

Hugh in Act II, Scene 1, of Brian Friel's *Translations* (1981)

To Julia and Nele who was to be

Contents

List of Maps, Figures and Tables

Acknowledgements ~ *Buíochas*

First, I wish to express my deep gratitude to Günther Schlee, Director of the Max Planck Institute for Social Anthropology in Halle/Saale, Germany, for intellectually and financially supporting my research project that ultimately led to this book. During my membership of Schlee's 'Integration and Conflict' Department at the Max Planck Institute, I benefited greatly both from his stimulating inputs and the exciting academic environment of the institute in general. I am also heavily indebted to Richard Rottenburg, professor at the Institute of Social and Cultural Anthropology, Martin Luther University Halle-Wittenberg, for creating the highly productive intellectual climate of his research colloquium. In the colloquium and during many other discussions, and also as a postdoctoral fellow of Rottenburg's Max Planck Fellow Group 'Law, Organization, Science and Technology (LOST)', I learnt a lot through his critical engagements.

Furthermore, I wish to thank (in alphabetical order) Brian Donahoe, Frank Donath, Julia Eckert, Thomas Hylland Eriksen, Dereje Feyissa, Markus Höhne, Richard Jenkins, Thomas Kirsch, Karsten Kumoll, Peter Loizos, Johanna Mugler, Boris Nieswand, Johnny Parry, Steve Reyna, Andrea Riester, Margreth Tolson and Julia Zenker for their intellectual contributions, inspiration and friendship. I am also deeply indebted to my informants and friends in West Belfast, who generously shared with me their views and concerns, let me participate in their daily lives and thus made possible my ethnographic research and, ultimately, this book. *Is mian liom buíochas ó chroí a ghabháil le gach duine i mBéal Feirste a chuidigh go fial leis an tionscadal seo.* I refrain from naming you individually – youse know who youse are.

In the process of reworking the draft manuscript into a book, the detailed comments by the editorial board members of the Berghahn Series 'Integration and Conflict Studies', Günther Schlee, John Eidson, Peter Finke, Joachim Görlich, Jacqueline Knörr and Bettina Mann, proved extremely helpful; many thanks to you as well as to three anonymous referees for further helpful suggestions. I am also very grateful to Jutta Turner for producing the maps and illustrations, and especially to Cornelia Schnepel for her invaluable assistance in the production of successive manuscript versions.

Some parts of arguments and materials presented in this book were previously published as articles; acknowledgements are due for: 'De Facto Exclusion through Discursive Inclusion: Autochthony in Discourses on Irishness and Politics in Catholic West Belfast' (*Paideuma* 52, 2006); 'Autochthony and Activism among Contemporary Irish Nationalists in Northern Ireland, Or: If "Civic" Nationalists Are "Ethno"-Cultural Revivalists, What Remains of the Civic/Ethnic Divide?' (*Nations and Nationalism* 15(4), 2009); 'Autochthony, Ethnicity, Indigeneity and Nationalism: Time-honouring and State-oriented Modes of Rooting Individual-territory-group-triads in a Globalising World' (*Critique of Anthropology* 31(1), 2011);

'On Prophets, Godfathers, Rebels, and Prostitutes: Distributed Agency in the Irish Language Revival of Northern Ireland' (*Zeitschrift für Ethnologie* 137(1), 2012).

Last but not least, I am very grateful to my family for their ongoing encouragement, interest, and support of my academic work. Finally, I wish to thank Julia, and Nele who was born in the middle of it all: it is youse who make it all worthwhile.

Olaf Zenker
April 2012

Glossary of Irish Terms, Local Expressions and Abbreviations

Aisling Ghéar	*Sharp Vision*; an Irish-medium drama company located in the *Cultúrlann*
Altram	*Fosterage*; an Irish-medium education agency
Amhrán na bhFiann	*A Soldier's Song*; the Irish national anthem
An Caife Glas	*The Green Café*; cafeteria in the *Cultúrlann*
An Ceathrú Póilí	*The Fourth Policeman*; bookshop in the *Cultúrlann*
An Coimisiún le Rincí Gaelacha	*The Irish Dancing Commission*; an organization operating under the auspices of the Gaelic League, responsible for collecting and standardizing Irish dances, certifying dance teachers as well as organizing and controlling Irish dance competitions
An Nasc	*The Connection*; an office building in Catholic West Belfast for Irish language organizations
An Siopa Síol	*The Bean Shop*; a small shop of fair trade, organic goods in the *Cultúrlann*
An Súil Aduaidh	*The Northern Eye*; an Irish-medium television production company in Catholic West Belfast
An Telelann	*The Tele-Place*; an organization offering media education through Irish
An tOireachtas	*The Assembly*; the annual Gaelic League festival, featuring various competitions in the Irish language, instrumental music, song and dance
Árdscoil	*High School*; the former headquarters in Belfast of the Northern Irish branch of the Gaelic League
Béarla	*The English language*
BIFHE	Belfast Institute of Further and Higher Education
Bréag	*Lie*; Irish-medium reggae band in Catholic West Belfast
Bunscoil Phobal Feirste	*Belfast Community Primary School*; the first Irish-medium primary school in Catholic West Belfast
caid	*Gaelic football*; see also *peil*
Caighdeán Oifigiúil	*Official Standard*; the standardized form of the Irish language

Cairde	*Friends*; a support group for the first Irish-medium primary school in Catholic West Belfast and the whole North of Ireland, *Bunscoil Phobal Feirste*
camán	*Hurling stick, hurley*
Castle Catholics	Local curse word for middle-class Catholics, reflecting the realities of the past when Catholics were hardly upwardly mobile unless they chummed up to the British establishment of Dublin Castle (the seat of British rule until Irish independence)
CCMS	The Council for Catholic Maintained Schools
céilí (pl. *céilithe*, anglicized: *céilís*)	(1) a social visit, a social evening; (2) a social dance event, sometimes also involving songs and performances; (3) a type of Irish dance
Céilí house	A private home where relatives, friends and neighbours frequently meet for social visits or 'céilís'; see the first meaning of *céilí*
Céilí-ing	Anglicized expression for paying a social visit, engaging in a social evening; see the first meaning of *céilí*
céilí mór	A big social dance event; see the second meaning of *céilí*
Ciorcal Amhránaíochta	*The Singing Circle* meeting in the *Cultúrlann*
Clár Ealaíon	*Arts Programme* of the *Cultúrlann*
Club Leabhar Choiscéim Feirste	*The Belfast Book Club*; book club of the Dublin-based Irish language publishing house Coiscéim, with regular book launches in the *Cultúrlann*
Coiste na nIarchimí	*Committee of ex-prisoners*; a Republican ex-prisoners support group
Coláiste Ollscoile Naomh Muire	*St. Mary's University College*; a local teacher training college for Catholic schools, with a strong focus on Irish-medium education
Comhairle na Gaelscolaíochta	*The Council for Irish-medium Education* set up by the Department of Education to facilitate and organize Irish-medium education in the North of Ireland
Comhaltas Ceoltóirí Éireann	*Gathering of Ireland's Musicians*; an organization promoting Irish traditional music; see *Fleadh Cheoil*
Comhaltas Uladh	*The Ulster Fellowship*; the Northern Irish branch of the Gaelic League
Comhrá	*Conversation*; also name of a type of Irish language class focusing on conversational skills

Conradh na Gaeilge	*The Gaelic League*; an all-Ireland organization founded in 1893 with the aim of reviving and promoting the Irish language
Cór Loch Lao	*The Belfast Bay Choir*; Irish-medium choir rehearsing in the *Cultúrlann*
Craic	*Crack*, fun, entertainment, a good time
Cultúrlann McAdam Ó Fiaich	*Culture Place McAdam Ó Fiaich*; an Irish language, culture and arts centre in Catholic West Belfast
Cumann Chluain Árd	*The Association of Clonard*; an Irish-only social club and branch of the Gaelic League in Catholic West Belfast
Cumann Lúthchleas Gael	*The Gaelic Athletic Association (GAA)*
cúpla focal	*A few words*; expression used to refer to a limited knowledge of the Irish language
Diddle-de-dee music	Local (sometimes derogatory) expression for Irish instrumental music
DENI	Department of Education for Northern Ireland
Dúch Dúchais	*Native Ink*; a design company, producing Irish language cards and calendars
feis	*Festival* or *competition* in Irish music and Irish dancing
Feis Cheoil	*Festival of Music*; an annual set of musical competitions, featuring largely non-traditional music
Fleadh Cheoil	*Festival of Music*; an annual All-Ireland competition in instrumental music, song and dance organized by the organization *Comhaltas Ceoltóirí Éireann*
Foinse	*Source*; a national weekly in Irish
Foras na Gaeilge	*The Irish Language Agency*; a cross-border body run by the Republic of Ireland and the United Kingdom, responsible for the promotion of the Irish language throughout the whole of Ireland
Forbairt Feirste	*Belfast Development*; an agency promoting Irish-medium enterprises and businesses
GAA	*The Gaelic Athletic Association*
Gaeilge	*The Irish language*
Gaeilge Bhéal Feirste	*Belfast Irish*; the variety of Irish typically spoken in Belfast
Gaeilge bhriste	*Broken Irish*; a mixture of Irish and English; see also *Géarla*
Gaeilgeoir (pl. *Gaeilgeoirí*)	*Irish learner and speaker*
Gael Linn	*Irish Pool*; an organization promoting the Irish language and arts, among others through producing Irish-medium records and CDs

Gaeloiliúint	*Irish language training*; an Irish-medium education agency
Gaelscoil na bhFál	*Falls Irish-medium Primary School*; the second Irish-medium primary school in Catholic West Belfast
Gaeltacht (pl. *Gaeltachtaí*)	*An Irish-speaking area*
Gaeltacht Bóthar Seoighe	*The Shaw's Road Gaeltacht*; a small neighbourhood in Catholic West Belfast where Irish is used as the first language in daily life
Géarla	Neologism for 'broken Irish' in the sense of a mixture of *Gaeilge* ('Irish') *and Béarla* ('English'); see also *Gaeilge bhriste*
Glór na nGael	*Voice of the Gael*; an all-Ireland organization promoting the use of the Irish language
IICD	Independent International Commission on Decommissioning
INLA	Irish National Liberation Army
iomáint, iománaíocht	*Hurling*
Ionad Uíbh Eachach	*Iveagh Centre*; a community centre in Catholic West Belfast offering Irish language classes
Iontaobhas na Gaelscolaíochta	*The Trust Fund for Irish-medium Education*, providing a financial foundation for the development and support of Irish-medium education
Iontaobhas ULTACH	*ULTACH Trust*; a cross-community Irish language agency promoting 'Ulster Language, Traditions and Cultural Heritage' (ULTACH) throughout Northern Ireland
IRA	Irish Republican Army (in recent decades usually referring to the Provisional IRA)
Jailtacht	A local pun, combining 'jail' and '*Gaeltacht*' in order to refer to prisons as Irish-speaking areas
Lá	*Day*; Irish-medium newspaper produced for decades in Catholic West Belfast
LGD	Local Government District
Meánscoil Feirste	*Belfast Secondary School*; an Irish-medium secondary school in Catholic West Belfast
naíscoil	Irish-medium nursery school
NICRA	Northern Ireland Civil Rights Association
NISRA	Northern Ireland Statistics and Research Agency
Oifig Fáilte	Tourist information point in the *Cultúrlann*
Oireachtas Rince na Cruinne	*The World Irish Dancing Championships*; an annual Irish dancing competition organized by *An Coimisiún le Rincí Gaelacha*

Páirc an Chrócaigh	*Croke Park*; the largest sports stadium in Ireland and headquarters of the Gaelic Athletic Association (GAA) in Dublin
PC	Parliamentary Constituency
peil, peil ghaelach	*Gaelic football*; see also *caid*
Pobal	*Community*; an umbrella organization for Irish language groups within the North of Ireland
PSNI	Police Service of Northern Ireland; the new name of the local police service
Radio Telefís Éireann (RTÉ)	The public television broadcaster in the Republic of Ireland
Raidió Fáilte	*Radio Welcome*; an Irish-medium community radio station broadcasting from the *Cultúrlann*
Raidio na Gaeltachta	*Gaeltacht Radio*; principal Irish language radio broadcaster in the Republic of Ireland
Rang Litridheachta	*Literature Class*; a type of Irish language class, focusing on Irish-medium literature
Roinn Cultuir	*The Cultural Department* of Sinn Féin, lobbying for the Irish language from a Republican perspective
RUC	Royal Ulster Constabulary; the former name of the local police service
Scannáin Aisling Ghéar	*Sharp Vision Films*; an Irish-medium television production company and spin-off of *Aisling Ghéar* located in the *Cultúrlann*
Seanchaí	*Irish storytellers*
sean-nós	*old style*; refers to a particular style of Irish singing, and also of Irish dancing
Seisiún an tSathairn	*The Saturday Session*; weekly traditional music session in the *Cultúrlann*
shebeen	An Anglicized expression (from the Irish word '*síbín*') for an illegal drinking den
sliotar	*Hurling ball*
Taca	*Support*; an Irish language lottery, raising funds for Irish language projects in the North of Ireland
Teilifís na Gaeilge	*Gaelic Television*; Irish-medium television channel (now TG4) in the Republic of Ireland
Tobar Productions	*The Well Productions*; an Irish-medium television production company located in the *Cultúrlann*

Prologue

Chapter 1
A Walk of Life
Entering Catholic West Belfast

On a Friday afternoon in September 2004, shortly before returning home from my ethnographic fieldwork, I took my video camera and filmed a walk from the city centre into Catholic West Belfast up to the Beechmount area, where I had lived and conducted much of my research. I had come to Catholic West Belfast fourteen months prior with the intention of learning about locally prevailing senses of ethnic identity. Yet I soon found out that virtually every local Catholic I talked to seemed to see him- or herself as 'Irish', and apparently expected other locals to do the same. My open questions such as 'What ethnic or national identity do you have?' at times even irritated my interlocutors, not so much, as I figured out, because they felt like I was contesting their sense of identity but, to the contrary, because the answer 'Irish' seemed so obvious. 'What else could I be?' was a rhetorical question I often encountered in such conversations, indicating to me that, for many, Irish identity went without saying. If that was the case, then what did being Irish mean to these people? What made somebody Irish, and where were local senses of Irishness to be found? Questions like these became the focus of my investigations and constitute the overall subject of this book.

One obvious entry point for addressing such questions consisted in attending to the ways in which Irishness was locally represented. Listening to how locals talked about their Irishness, keeping an eye on public representations by organizations and the media, and explicitly asking people about their Irishness in informal conversations and formal interviews all constituted ways of approaching this topic. But for reasons that will be discussed in the next chapter, my theoretical interests went beyond the level of representations. I wanted to come to terms not only with *'representational' practices* of Irishness but also with the realities of therein *'represented' practices* of Irishness, and finally with the interrelations between these two levels.

For this purpose, the Irish language caught my attention. Irish is one of six Celtic languages usually classified as a branch within the Indo-European language family, which is composed of several other branches such as the Germanic languages including English, to which Irish is only distantly related. Although Irish historically constituted the mother tongue of most of Ireland's inhabitants, it was increasingly replaced throughout the nineteenth century with English as the dominant first language (Hindley 1990; Purdon 1999; Murchú 2000; Price 2000; Schrijver 2000). Against this background, the Irish language experienced some local revival in Catholic West Belfast during the second half of the twentieth century despite its continued minority status in a predominantly English-speaking world. As I soon learnt during my stay, the Irish language was thereby represented by many locals as related to their Irish identity and also constituted a practice, the realization of which could be investigated in daily life.

My point of reference, therefore, narrowed down to the category of *Gaeilgeoirí* (i.e. Irish learners and speakers), with whom I could get in contact and hang around in various Irish language classes, groups and meeting places in Catholic West Belfast. While my research thus came to focus exclusively on local Gaeilgeoirí and on how they represented and practised the Irish language (and hence deliberately excludes the perspectives of non-speakers on both language and identity), I continued to ask both how these actors represented and practically experienced their sense of Irishness, and how language and identity were interrelated for them. Thus, if senses of Irishness were possibly but not exclusively found in representations and practices of the Irish language, where else could they be found? This question persistently stuck with me, and it was behind my idea of filming and later describing some of the impressions I had when walking in(to) my field. The following observations from my walk are therefore aimed at letting the reader participate in an initial search for local Irishness. At the same time, they are also intended as an introduction to the social field in which I conducted my research, thereby transforming this walk into a preliminary emblem of local walks of life.

Thus on that particular Friday afternoon, I left my place in Broadway and hailed one of the many black taxis that drive along the Falls Road to and from the city centre, as I had done so many times before when travelling within Catholic West Belfast. Established as a 'community' transport system in the 1970s when public buses for some time stopped serving West Belfast during the height of the Troubles, the classic black London taxis can be entered and exited at any point along their various routes. I got off in the city centre at the black taxi terminal, which was located in the basement of a parking block labelled 'The Castle Junction' in English and *'gabhal an chaisleáin'* in Irish ①.[1] I took out my video camera, started filming and slowly walked up to Divis Street the way I had just come.

During my stay, I had only rarely used my video camera. I had been afraid that extensively filming within Catholic West Belfast would nurture suspicions of me being a spy. I had consciously decided against a cross-community research setting and deliberately focused exclusively on the Catholic side of Belfast in order to reduce such mistrust from the very beginning. However, I had still encountered suspicions that I was a spy and was aware that some locals seemed unconvinced that I was only doing research; thus I did not want to further enhance their distrust. However, shortly before leaving, I felt that filming the Falls Road into Catholic West Belfast would be no big deal. I assumed that people would take me for a tourist, and indeed,

---

1. Encircled numbers refer to those landmarks that are marked through corresponding cyphers in Map 1.1.

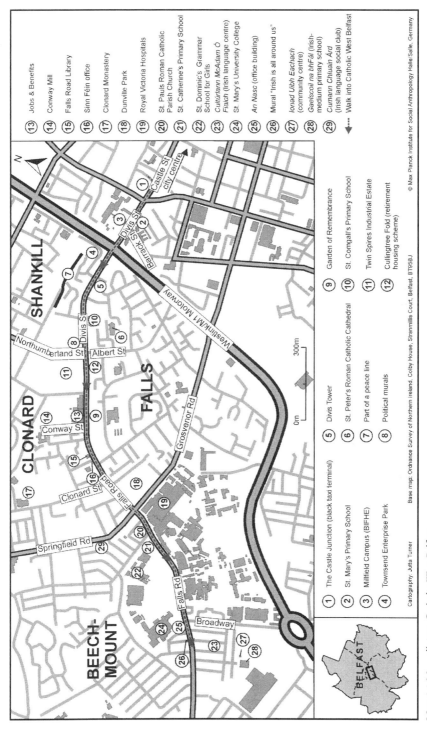

Map 1.1 My walk into Catholic West Belfast

① The Castle Junction (black taxi terminal)
② St. Mary's Primary School
③ Millfield Campus (BIFHE)
④ Townsend Enterprise Park
⑤ Divis Tower
⑥ St. Peter's Roman Catholic Cathedral
⑦ Part of a peace line
⑧ Political murals
⑨ Garden of Remembrance
⑩ St. Comgall's Primary School
⑪ Twin Spires Industrial Estate
⑫ Cullingtree Fold (retirement housing scheme)
⑬ Jobs & Benefits
⑭ Conway Mill
⑮ Falls Road Library
⑯ Sinn Féin office
⑰ Clonard Monastery
⑱ Dunville Park
⑲ Royal Victoria Hospitals
⑳ St. Pauls Roman Catholic Parish Church
㉑ St. Catherine's Primary School
㉒ St. Dominic's Grammar School for Girls
㉓ Cultúrlann McAdam Ó Fiaich (Irish language centre)
㉔ St. Mary's University College
㉕ An Nasc (office building)
㉖ Mural "Irish is all around us"
㉗ Ionad Uibh Eachach (community centre)
㉘ Gaelscoil na bhFál (Irish-medium primary school)
㉙ Cumann Chluain Ard (Irish language social club)
┅► Walk into Catholic West Belfast

Cartography: Jutta Turner   Base map: Ordnance Survey of Northern Ireland, Colby House, Stranmillis Court, Belfast, BT95BJ

© Max Planck Institute for Social Anthropology Halle/Salle, Germany

with the exception of some pupils who later jokingly asked what I was doing, no one paid attention to my filming.

Walking up Divis Street, I could see the ridge of the Black Mountain, which delimits the city of Belfast to the west. I passed St Mary's Primary School ②, which like many schools in Catholic areas was run by the Council for Catholic Maintained Schools (CCMS). At the corner of Divis and Westlink, the recently opened Millfield Campus of the Belfast Institute of Further and Higher Education (BIFHE) ③ rose into the partly cloudy sky.[2] There was quite a bit of traffic, with many cars entering the motorway. Those heading straight entered what a road sign indicated was 'Falls (Divis Street)'. Someone had added in yellow graffiti the letters 'HQ' on the sign, presumably standing for 'headquarters', thereby expressing a widespread perception that one was now entering a heartland of Irish Nationalism and Republicanism. There were also other boundary markers communicating a similar message: on a number of lampposts around the junction were attached flags. Some had appeared a couple of months earlier during the annual marching season of the Protestant Orange Order, while others were weatherworn and seemed older. Apart from the Irish tricolour, I could discern the remnants of a Starry Plough, a flag that was first used by James Connolly's socialist Irish Citizen Army in the early twentieth century. Featuring the constellation of Ursa Major (known as The Plough in Ireland and the U.K.) against a blue background, this flag has been used by various socialist and Republican groups. Another flag displayed the name 'Larsson' against a green and white striped background. Having spent a year in Belfast, I knew that it referred to the Celtic Football Club in Glasgow, and to its famous Swedish striker, Henrik Larsson. Larsson had just left Celtic for FC Barcelona in the summer of 2004 after having played seven years for the club with the emerald green and white hooped jerseys. As the saga goes, Celtic, whose emblem is a four-leaf shamrock, was founded in 1888 in Glasgow with the stated purpose of alleviating poverty among the local working class, many members of which were Irish migrants. Thus having an 'Irish dimension', as I was so often told, Glasgow Celtic had and continues to have a strong following among Irish Catholics in Ireland. The longstanding rivalry between Glasgow Celtic and the Rangers Football Club in Glasgow, whose supporters include many Protestants from Northern Ireland, has thereby transported and restaged religious, ethnic and political antagonisms prevalent in the North of Ireland.[3]

---

2. This is also the place where the *Árdscoil* ('High School') was once located. As we will see in Chapter 5, the Árdscoil was built in 1928 by the Northern Irish branch of the Gaelic League, *Comhaltas Uladh* ('the Ulster Fellowship'), as its headquarters and, before accidentally burning down in 1985, subsequently constituted one of the focal points for the local Irish-language scene (Mac Póilin 2006: 129).

3. In the politicized Northern Irish context, the use of words referring to the region is itself a matter of dispute, purportedly reflecting one's own ideological position on the conflict. Within the Nationalist/Catholic community, terms such as 'the North of Ireland', 'the six counties' or the 'occupied counties' are common currency, while Unionists/Protestants tend to speak of 'Northern Ireland', 'Ulster' or 'the province'. Given that I am concerned with a reconstruction of perspectives within 'Catholic' West Belfast, I will predominantly use the terminology of local Catholics.

Passing these boundary markers, I entered the Nationalist and Republican areas of Catholic West Belfast. Yet what is Catholic West Belfast? At the time of the then last Northern Ireland census in 2001, a total of 277,391 people lived in the city of Belfast as defined at the level of Local Government District (LGD).[4] Belfast is subdivided into four parliamentary constituencies: Belfast East, North, South and West. However, the figure of 87,610, indicated in the census as the total population of the parliamentary constituency Belfast West, is in a way misleading.[5] This is so because in 2001 the constituency Belfast West consisted of seventeen electoral wards, four of which on its south-westerly edge did not belong to Belfast but to Lisburn on the level of LGD.[6] In other words, only thirteen of the seventeen wards of the constituency Belfast West, with a total population of 70,447, also belonged to the LGD of Belfast (see Map 1.2).[7] Taking these thirteen wards as an approximation for what I refer to as 'West Belfast', a pronounced internal division between these wards can be observed in terms of the religious backgrounds of their inhabitants. In the 2001 census, a new variable, 'community background', was introduced, recording 'a person's current religion, if any, or the religion brought up in for those people who do not regard themselves as currently belonging to any religion' (see Northern Ireland Statistics and Research Agency [NISRA] 2003).

Distinguishing between 'Catholics' and 'Protestants' on the basis of their community background rather than their religious practices and beliefs, this variable is useful because some of my informants had become atheist or even strongly anti-Catholic and anti-religious in their lives despite (or even because of) their Catholic background. When talking about Catholics and Protestants throughout this book, I thus refer to peoples' religious backgrounds and reserve the terms 'practising Catholic' and 'practising Protestant' for those who describe themselves as religious. Thus, when one looks at dominant religious backgrounds in the thirteen wards of West Belfast as indicated in the 2001 census, a sharp division emerges. At the northern fringe, three wards – Glencairn (85.20 per cent), Highfield (94.01 per cent) and Shankill (94.34 per cent) – were predominantly Protestant, as the respective percentages indicate. In contrast, the remaining ten wards to the south were overwhelmingly Catholic: Falls (96.93 per cent), Clonard (96.09 per cent), Beechmount (92.19 per cent), Whiterock (99.04 per cent), Falls Park (97.72 per cent), Upper Springfield (96.90 per cent), Glen Road (97.19 per cent), Andersonstown (98.49 per cent), Glencolin (98.08 per cent) and Ladybrook (86.45 per cent). Against this backdrop, I refer to these ten wards with

4. See Northern Ireland Statistics and Research Agency (NISRA) 2006: Table KS01 ('Usually Resident Population').
5. See Northern Ireland Statistics and Research Agency (NISRA) 2006: Table KS01 ('Usually Resident Population').
6. See Northern Ireland Statistics and Research Agency (NISRA) 2006: Look-up Table (Ward to Parliamentary Constituency) KS.
7. This figure is the sum total of the resident population of the mentioned thirteen wards as indicated in Northern Ireland Statistics and Research Agency (NISRA) 2006: Table KS01 ('Usually Resident Population'), Ward Level.

a total population in 2001 of 57,327, of which a total of 95.85 per cent were of a Catholic religious background, as unambiguously constituting 'Catholic West Belfast' when presenting statistical data.[8] In everyday conversations, however, local Catholics tended to include with 'Catholic West Belfast' not only the above-mentioned four other wards in the south-west but also adjacent areas such as parts of Finaghy, which technically did not belong to West Belfast at all but were frequently inhabited by Catholics originally from West Belfast.

Map 1.2 depicts the distribution of religious backgrounds in 2001 for the whole of Belfast at the ward level, indicating the extent of religious segregation in the city. As Doherty and Poole (2000: 189) show, the current residential pattern can thereby be seen as the outcome of a ratchet effect whereby segregation since the nineteenth century has intensified, with precipitous increases following violent episodes and only slightly moderated in times of relative peace.

When I was crossing the Westlink, I was thus entering Catholic West Belfast. Yet the boundary markers I referred to above were political and possibly ethnic rather than religious. The flags seemed to mark some sense of Irishness as well as the political position of Nationalists and Republicans, both aspiring to independence from Britain and a united 32-county Ireland (i.e. including the six Northern Irish counties), though only Republicans endorsed violence as a legitimate means.[9] Was I not thus conflating political and ethnic with religious identifications? Can these three levels of identification be used interchangeably? In his account of contemporary Northern Irish society, Coulter speaks of '"two principal communal blocs" in Northern Ireland, one variously described as "Catholic", "nationalist" and "Irish", the other designated as "Protestant", "unionist" and "British"' (Coulter 1999: 10). In her analysis of self-ascribed ethnic identities among Catholics and Protestants, Trew (1998: 66) summarizes her findings in the following way:

> Protestants identify themselves as British, Northern Irish and Ulster but not Irish. Catholics identify themselves as Irish, Northern Irish or British but not Ulster. The majority of the population clearly identify themselves as either Irish Catholics or British Protestants but there is a sizeable minority who are Northern Irish.

This observation is supported by Coakley's recent analysis of all available public opinion data on the topic, in which he shows that 'religious background has been the most fundamental determinant of national identity in Northern Ireland'

---

8. See Northern Ireland Statistics and Research Agency (NISRA) 2006: Table KS07b ('Community Background: Religion or religion brought up in'), Ward Level.
9. In local discourse, the term 'Republicanism' typically refers to a more radicalized version of 'Nationalism', with both aspiring to unite Ireland. In contrast, 'Loyalism' constitutes a more radicalized form of 'Unionism', with both fighting for the maintenance of the United Kingdom. Throughout this book, I use the small-letter version of 'nationalism' to refer to an overarching analytical concept, while reserving the capitalized term 'Nationalism' for that particular strand among local nationalisms that aims for a united Ireland.

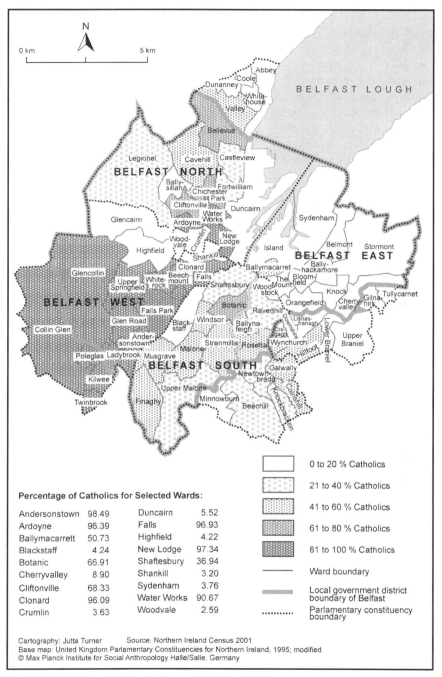

N

0 km   5 km

Percentage of Catholics for Selected Wards:

Andersonstown	98.49	Duncairn	5.52
Ardoyne	96.39	Falls	96.93
Ballymacarrett	50.73	Highfield	4.22
Blackstaff	4.24	New Lodge	97.34
Botanic	66.91	Shaftesbury	36.94
Cherryvalley	8.90	Shankill	3.20
Cliftonville	68.33	Sydenham	3.76
Clonard	96.09	Water Works	90.67
Crumlin	3.63	Woodvale	2.59

0 to 20 % Catholics

21 to 40 % Catholics

41 to 60 % Catholics

61 to 80 % Catholics

81 to 100 % Catholics

———— Ward boundary

Local government district boundary of Belfast

··········· Parlamentary constituency boundary

Cartography: Jutta Turner   Source: Northern Ireland Census 2001
Base map: United Kingdom Parlamentary Constituencies for Northern Ireland, 1995; modified
© Max Planck Institute for Social Anthropology Halle/Salle, Germany

Map 1.2 Distribution of religious background in Belfast (2001)

(Coakley 2007: 577). What this cursory overview indicates is that, in practice, there is indeed a considerable homology between 'Catholic', 'Irish' and 'Nationalist/ Republican', on the one hand, and 'Protestant', 'British' and 'Unionist/Loyalist', on the other, although some variations and cross-cuttings do exist and need to be explored.

However, while these layers of religious, ethnic and political identification do not often intersect in locals' actual self-ascriptions, this does not mean that they are not conceptualized by these actors as cross-cutting ties of affiliation. To put it differently, while there is a broad consensus in Northern Ireland about who has a Catholic or Protestant religious background, Catholics and Protestants have tended to disagree in terms of the ethnic identities they respectively ascribe to themselves as well as to associates of the other faith (and also about what political aspirations should follow from these ascribed ethnic identities). It is therefore convenient for researchers as well as for locals to use the labels 'Catholics' and 'Protestants' to refer unambiguously to the two blocs of actors, which have been largely self-reproductive given the high rates of endogamy on both sides (McGarry and O'Leary 1995: 186, 207). However, this pragmatic use of religious terminology is not meant to suggest that religion is the underlying source of conflict. In fact, this idea was strongly rejected by most of my 'Catholic' friends and informants, although they often also used this distinction as shorthand in conversations. Since the term 'Catholic' thus unambiguously refers to that category of actor with whom I exclusively conducted my research, I will continue to use this label throughout the book. But to reiterate, my pragmatic usage of the term 'Catholic' is meant to ascribe neither particular importance to religion/religious background in daily life and the local conflict in general, nor to Irishness in particular; instead the potential significance of Catholicism will have to be explicitly explored in subsequent chapters.

But back to Divis Street. To my right I could see Townsend Enterprise Park ④, adjoining the nearby Protestant Shankill area, which is separated by a so-called 'peace line' or protection wall from the Catholic Falls area. To my left, the multistorey residential Divis Tower ⑤ together with the twin spires of the nearby St Peter's Cathedral ⑥ rose above as the landmarks of an area that, like most of West Belfast, is largely dominated by seemingly endless rows of two- and three-storey terraced houses. But the area I was walking through had not always looked like this. During the 1960s, the Divis Flats complex of twelve medium-rise blocks and the Divis Tower were built, replacing the older poor housing in this Lower Falls area. After the outbreak of the Troubles in 1969 and the subsequent split of the IRA into the Official IRA and the increasingly dominant Provisional IRA in 1970, the Lower Falls area around the Divis Flats got a reputation for being a stronghold of the Officials and other dissident Republican groups such as INLA (Irish National Liberation Army) (Sluka 1989: 5; Patterson 1997: 140–79; Coogan 2002: 97). Despite their continued presence in the Divis Flats, in the late 1970s the British Army established a fortified base on the roof of Divis Tower, bristling with electronic surveillance equipment. With the demolition and replacement of the medium-rise blocks since the mid-1980s, all that remained when I was living in West Belfast was Divis Tower and the military base on its rooftop. It was to this situation that the phrase 'Demilitarise Divis Tower' referred, painted among other Republican slogans on a wall that I passed when walking up the gently inclined street.

In a way it is tempting to dwell further on local political history, which is associated with the area through which I was walking on that Friday afternoon. I could refer to the peace line ⑦ that I saw rising up behind some terraced houses. I could describe in much detail the political murals ⑧ up the road, which reiterated typical positions among Republicans: the ridicule of the allegedly reformed Police Service of Northern Ireland (PSNI) that for many locals was but a new name for the same old biased Royal Ulster Constabulary (RUC); the rejection of the recent war against Iraq started by President Bush, whose right-wing republicanism many local leftist Republicans had hastened to distance from themselves in conversations with me; and the support for and perceived similarity with other liberation movements in the Basque Country, Catalonia, Palestine, Turkey and elsewhere. I could draw the attention of the reader to the Falls Curfew of 1970, when approximately three thousand British Army troops for two days conducted a weapons search of approximately fifty small streets in this very area of the Lower Falls, and which, together with the introduction of internment (i.e. imprisonment without trial) one year later, strengthened rather than broke local support for the armed struggle (Coogan 1996: 128). I could go on to characterize the local Garden of Remembrance ⑨ dedicated to fallen IRA volunteers. For my friends, places like these indicated that the armed struggle had long ago ended – 'You only start to commemorate once a war is over', as one had put it – although it would take another year before the Provisional Republican movement would officially declare the end of its armed campaign and decommission what the Independent International Commission on Decommissioning (IICD) described in September 2005 as the 'totality of the IRA's arsenal' (IICD 2005). Or I could use the road sign, further up the Falls, pointing towards Clonard Monastery to indicate an 'interface area' (i.e. a border zone between Catholic and Protestant neighbourhoods) in which sectarian violence was particularly intense in mid-August 1969. Three-fifths of the houses on nearby Bombay Street were then burned down by a Protestant mob, one of the key incidents typically seen as marking the outbreak of the subsequent Troubles (Coogan 1996: 96–106; Fraser 2000: 36–47).

All of these political details could be important aspects for my search for local Irishness, but such a focus would be flawed in two ways. Firstly, such an approach would overemphasize the importance of politics at the expense of other equally important contributors to local senses of identity, thereby contributing to the misleading image that conflict alone defines daily life in Northern Ireland. Secondly, explicitly focusing on territorial inscriptions of political meanings can have the paradoxical effect of obstructing an equally important aspect of these political landscapes, namely, that local understandings and remembrances of these landscapes in everyday life tend to happen in a largely unnoticed and unconscious way, occurring as other activities are being consciously engaged in. This refers to Billig's distinction between 'waved' and 'unwaved flags' of 'banal nationalism' (1995). Although Billig (1995: 41) is surely right in pointing out that Irish tricolours in Belfast are generally more consciously perceived – or more 'waved' – than those hanging on public buildings all year round south of the border, these and other nationalist markers like murals are also considerably 'unwaved': 'they merge into the local landscape and while they remain notable to outsiders they may be virtually invisible to local residents' (Jarman 2007: 99).

Thus, turning towards less political but equally unnoticed landmarks, I saw a factory building when leaving behind Divis Tower. Situated opposite the derelict St Comgall's Primary School ⑩, the factory was possibly part of the neighbouring Twin Spires Industrial Estate ⑪, that faced an impressive building: *Teach Chrann Chuilin* ('Cullingtree Fold') ⑫. This expensive-looking complex was a retirement housing scheme that opened in 2000 and was run by the Fold Housing Association. The immediately surrounding neighbourhood stretching further up the road consisted of equally new and to my eye middle class housing blocks. Across the street, however, the Jobs & Benefits centre ⑬ was accommodated in an older-looking concrete building at the corner of Conway Street. This street branched off to the right, leading to Conway Mill ⑭, in which the Falls Flax Spinning Company operated from the mid-nineteenth century until the early 1970s as one of the biggest local employers in the by then decaying linen industry. In the early 1980s the vacated complex was then turned into a community centre.

These brief observations taken together are reminiscent of a phenomenon, which had fascinated me throughout my stay in Catholic West Belfast, namely, its class structure. West Belfast, East Belfast and most of North Belfast tend to be depicted in the literature as 'working class areas' (e.g. Murtagh 1996) and are typically contrasted with the 'middle class districts' of South Belfast such as the classy Malone Road and the upper stretches of Antrim Road in the north of the city (e.g. Coulter 1999: 39). The vast majority of local Catholics with whom I spoke described themselves as 'working class' and held corresponding views about the prevailing class nature of West Belfast. This spatial distribution of class is to some extent confirmed by data from the 2001 census. The census classifies occupations according to the National Statistics Socio-economic Classification (NS-SeC) (Office for National Statistics [ONS] 2005: 2). The census data in Table 1.1 is presented in the collapsed three-class version of the NS-SeC, providing a general overview of the distributions between the hierarchically ordered 'managerial and professional occupations', 'intermediate occupations' and 'routine and manual occupations' (Office for National Statistics [ONS] 2005: 15), which I will refer to as the 'middle', 'lower-middle' and 'working class'.

In 2001 within the whole of Northern Ireland, about 25 per cent of the working population belonged to the middle class and 20 per cent to the lower-middle class. The largest category, however, was the working class, composing approximately 40 per cent of all persons aged sixteen to seventy-four, excluding the long-term unemployed and full-time students, who made up about 7 and 8 per cent respectively.

Table 1.1 Percentages of three classes (collapsed NS-SeC classes) for all persons aged 16–74, by area and religious background[10]

	All persons aged 16 to 74	Distributions of 3 classes			Never worked and long-term unemployed	Not classified - full-time students
		Managerial and professional occupations	Intermediate occupations	Routine and manual occupations		
Northern Ireland	1,187,079	25.23	19.82	40.47	6.57	7.90
Belfast LGD	197,519	25.12	14.83	40.46	8.52	11.06
Protestants in Belfast LGD	97,461	24.92	15.19	45.01	6.81	8.07
Catholics in Belfast LGD	92,709	24.78	14.34	36.84	10.37	13.67
Catholic West Belfast (10 Catholic wards)	38,760	15.43	14.55	47.19	13.78	9.05
Clonard	3,003	10.52	12.99	53.57	15.02	7.89
Falls	3,292	7.15	9.53	52.52	21.51	9.30
Whiterock	3,419	8.39	8.83	52.50	22.61	7.66
Upper Springfield	3,868	9.31	10.45	51.78	19.78	8.69
Beechmount	3,845	17.27	14.41	47.17	11.34	9.80
Glencolin	4,862	16.46	15.47	46.85	13.22	8.00
Ladybrook	4,495	19.55	17.76	44.31	8.15	10.23
Glen Road	3,874	17.25	15.85	44.29	13.21	9.40
Andersonstown	4,088	20.59	18.24	42.53	9.27	9.34
Falls Park	4,014	23.12	19.11	40.23	7.68	9.87

These figures were echoed in the Local Government District of Belfast for the middle and working classes, while the slightly higher rates for the long-term unemployed (9 per cent) and full-time students (11 per cent) made up for the 5 per cent difference in the lower-middle class. Looking at the religious backgrounds of these classes, the middle and lower-middle classes were composed of Protestants and Catholics equally. However, Catholics were almost twice as likely as Protestants to be long-term unemployed, which, together with the higher proportion of full-time students, explains why Catholics (37 per cent) were underrepresented vis-à-vis Protestants (45 per cent) among the working class. These figures thus indicate that Catholic working class individuals enjoyed comparatively less access to the city's labour market.

Comparing the rates for Catholics in Belfast as a whole with the aggregated data for the ten above-mentioned wards of Catholic West Belfast, the figures show that the

---

10. These rates are based on the Northern Ireland Statistics and Research Agency (NISRA) 2006: Tables KS14a ('National Statistics – Socio Economic Classification – All Persons') and S349 ('NS-SeC By Sex And Community Background (Religion Or Religion Brought Up In)'), various levels.

latter area was indeed more 'working class'. Only 15 per cent of the local population belonged to the middle class, which is almost half the proportion of Catholics in that category for Belfast as a whole. While the percentage of local Catholics in the lower-middle class was nearly the same as at the city level (15 per cent), their local working class share (47 per cent) was considerably higher than the 37 per cent of working class Catholics in Belfast overall. In addition, in comparison to the 7 per cent of long-term unemployed Protestants in the city, the local proportion of long-term unemployed was higher (14 per cent) than the already high rate for such Catholics in Belfast (10 per cent). When combining the middle and lower-middle class rates, on the one hand, and the working class and unemployment rates, on the other, the picture becomes even more pronounced. A Catholic in Belfast was almost as likely to belong to one of the upper two classes as to be working class or unemployed; in contrast, two out of three people in Catholic West Belfast were either working class or long-term unemployed. This shows that Catholic West Belfast was indeed more working class and less middle class compared to the position of Catholics in the city overall.

Coulter (1999: 41) notes that before the Troubles started, the Catholic middle class was relatively small in comparison to its Protestant counterpart, and was engaged in a narrow range of activities, primarily providing services to their co-religionists as doctors, teachers, priests, publicans, and so on. As he further observes, the Catholic middle class has grown remarkably since the 1970s, facilitated both by growing post-secondary education and employment opportunities in the public sector due to Fair Employment Legislation, although Catholics have continued to be underrepresented in the upper echelons of many occupations (see Duffy and Evans 1997). However, the same period also negatively affected the Catholic working class because the decline in manufacturing resulted in higher levels of unemployment, which affected Protestants less than Catholics because the former had access to thousands of relatively lucrative positions within the security forces (Coulter 1999: 42).

Various authors have focused on this emerging Catholic middle class and have emphasized a pattern by which many of these social climbers have moved out of their working class neighbourhoods and into wealthier middle class districts that were formerly the preserve of wealthy Protestants (O'Connor 1993: 13–43; Coulter 1999: 39, 82). For Belfast, Cormack and Osborne (1994: 83) mention the expensive areas of Malone and Stranmillis in South Belfast, with their new suburban housing estates, as well as areas immediately adjacent to Catholic West Belfast such as Dunmurry and Derryaghy, as the target areas of such Catholic middle class relocations. These observations further contribute to the image of West Belfast as a continuing working class district from which the emerging Catholic middle class has been moving away.

Yet this is only half the story. As the respective distributions of class rates for the ten wards of Catholic West Belfast in Table 1.1 indicate, there was also considerable variation within this 'working class' area in 2001. Having arranged the wards in descending order according to their working class proportions, the figures shows that the first four wards – Clonard, Falls, Whiterock and Upper Springfield – exhibited an even more pronounced bias towards the working class and long-term unemployment than did the overall class structure for Catholic West Belfast, which in turn was largely echoed in Beechmount. However, the remaining five wards – Glencolin, Ladybrook, Glen Road, Andersonstown and Falls Park – were increasingly middle/lower-middle class and decreasingly working class than average. Within this gradually shifting class structure, the residents within the last ward, Falls Park, were thus not only considerably more likely to be middle and lower-middle class than the average inhabitant of Catholic West Belfast but also better off than Catholics in Belfast more generally: while comparable proportions belonged to the middle class (23–25 per cent), the ward rates were higher for the lower-middle and working classes and lower for long-term unemployment than those for Catholics in the city overall. This suggests that although 'Catholic West Belfast' can be characterized in relative terms as a working class district, there has been considerable variation between its constituent wards, which also has had a geographical dimension: the centre tended to be more working class, whereas the areas further from the centre to the south-west tended to be more middle and lower-middle class.

In such a context, it is interesting to note that not all of the above-mentioned locals describing themselves to me as 'working class' had working class jobs. To the contrary, my interlocutors worked in a broad range of occupations, including, for instance, professionals such as teachers, who are categorized as 'middle class' in the NS-SeC. This practice, I think, to some degree reflected their original working class background as well as their economic situation, which for many could not be described as affluent. However, it also expressed a general attitude, particularly prominent among older informants, according to which self-consciously 'middle class' Catholics were suspected of having sold out their 'own community' and become part of the pro-British establishment of the state. Such an attitude was occasionally articulated through the idiom of 'Castle Catholics', a local curse word reflecting the realities of the past when Catholics could not be upwardly mobile unless they denied their roots and 'chummed up' to the British establishment of Dublin Castle, the seat of British rule until Irish independence.

Against this background, I interpret my briefly sketched observations – the new and somewhat expensive-looking houses and elderly residential facilities, the Twin Spires industrial estate and the Townsend Enterprise Park as well as the mill-cum-community centre on Conway Street – as alluding to some economic regeneration that has occurred over the past few decades and particularly as a dividend of the peace process since the 1990s, when violence largely ended and Belfast as a city opened up again. Although Catholic West Belfast in general and the Falls area – through which I walked on that Friday – in particular have surely retained their working class character, some upward class mobility and internal diversification has occurred. While some of these new middle class Catholics have moved out of the area, others have stayed within their local community. In my experience, not a few of the latter have consciously decided against moving and following a route into potential 'Castle Catholicism', preferring instead to stay in the area, remaining committed to their personal background and their original 'Catholic', 'Irish', 'Nationalist' and 'working class' community. It was this commitment, I think, that together with often-aired sympathies with socialist politics found expression in continued self-ascriptions of 'working class' among many of those West Belfast people who could equally be described as having become middle or lower-middle class.

This class diversification within Catholic West Belfast was to some extent also apparent in the clothes that people wore. This brings me to a realization that, thus far, my walk had been unnecessarily void of people, even though I encountered quite a few pedestrians that day. To begin with, it was a Friday at around three in the afternoon, when the 'day' and 'week' ends in some jobs and most local schools. Pupils from the schools further up the road congregated, waiting for black taxis or local buses to pick them up. Given that school uniforms are compulsory in Northern Ireland, their clothes indicated little more than the particular institutions they attended. Apart from these students, I came across men in suits and ties; young lads wearing tracksuits, sneakers, baseball caps and soccer tricots of Manchester United or Glasgow Celtic or yellow jerseys representing the local County Antrim team in Gaelic games; a few elderly women and men, strolling along the road; and busy workers in boiler suits, to mention but a few. The clothes of some of these individuals indicated their occupations: manual workers wore boiler suits, and white-collar workers wore suits and ties. Apart from this, the main difference I noticed was between sportswear and 'ordinary' clothes. In a way, it is tempting to identify these two types of dress with class: sportswear could be reserved for the working class. Working class males I saw during my stay often had their hair short and gelled and wore gold chains, earrings, tracksuits, sport tops and sneakers. Working class females usually had long hair (occasionally dyed blond), wore big golden earrings and comparable sportswear or tight clothes. This caricature could then be contrasted with the 'ordinary' and somewhat more 'decent' clothes of the middle class: good-looking, higher quality shirts, pullovers and trousers, occasionally jackets, and leather shoes. Although it seems to me that there is a grain of truth in this ideal-typical classification, it is also grossly misleading, as local clothing also had a strong age component. A quick glance at my teenage informants revealed that youngsters from various class backgrounds wear sports apparel. In addition, Celtic or Country Antrim tops were quite common and not restricted to any particular class, age or gender group. Conversely, the 'decent', 'ordinary' look seemed to be more common with middle-aged and older people, regardless of class. All in all, distinctions in local clothing were thus not only indicative of variations in class but also more generally of differences in lifestyle, age and gender in line with Jenkins' (1983: 50) observations regarding Protestant working class youths.

Leaving Jobs & Benefits behind, the Falls Road led me to an area in which there were pubs, offices, shops and the like interspersed amongst the houses. I could see the Falls Road Library ⑮ in the distance. One of its walls facing me was adorned with a huge mural-like tapestry depicting the ten Republican hunger strikers from 1981 along an H-shaped 'table' reminiscent of both the Last Supper and the H-Blocks in the Long Kesh prison, where the strikers died demanding recognition as political prisoners. Just behind the library was the party office of Sinn Féin ⑯. I passed a few shops and offices, while down Clonard Street was Clonard Monastery ⑰.

At this street corner, I could see the social club of the Michael Davitt's Gaelic Athletic Club, one of the fifteen local clubs of the Gaelic Athletic Association

(GAA) in Catholic West Belfast. Up the road, there was the bar of another Gaelic Athletic Club, Seán MacDiarmada's. Both clubs were named after prominent Irish Nationalists, a practice not uncommon for clubs within the GAA. Founded in 1884, the GAA standardized the rules for Gaelic games and established an organizational structure for competitions, thereby (re)establishing 'Irish sports'. Such sports have been extremely popular among Catholics, while due to the long-standing identification of the GAA with Irish Nationalism, Protestants have tended not to participate (De Búrca 1999: 79; Sweeney 2004: 7–21).

The following stretch up to the junction of Falls, Springfield and Grosvenor Road was dominated by Dunville Park ⑱ to my left and various shops to my right, including one indicating its threefold purpose in Irish: *Sólaistí* ('Confectionery'), *Tobacadóir* ('Tobacconist'), and *Nuachtánaí* ('Newsagent'). This shop also displayed an advertisement for the local *Andersonstown* News, which together with the northern Nationalist daily, the Irish News, is quite popular in Catholic West Belfast. After crossing the junction with Grosvenor Road and Springfield Road, the Royal Victoria Hospitals ⑲ were on my left, while small shops continued on my right. This latter section also incorporated the Catholic parish church St Paul's ⑳, until it adjoined to the premises of St Catherine's Primary School ㉑ and the leafy park of St Dominic's Grammar School for Girls ㉒.

Both the schools and St Paul's were physical manifestations of the local influence of the Catholic Church. Education in Northern Ireland has largely remained segregated along religious lines, with 'maintained schools' under Catholic management predominantly catering for Catholic pupils, and the formally non-denominational 'controlled schools' run by the state attended mainly by Protestants. As data provided by the Department of Education in Northern Ireland (DENI) from the annual school census shows, in West Belfast in 2003/04 only 6 per cent of pupils in state schools were Catholic, while 80 per cent were Protestant, with the remaining 14 per cent consisting of 'other Christian', 'non Christian' and 'non-religious' pupils. In contrast, 98 per cent of pupils in schools under Catholic management were Catholic. Although so-called 'integrated schools' specifically designed to cater for both 'communities' did indeed educate more or less equal proportions of Protestant (45 per cent) and Catholic pupils (40 per cent), this sector composed only about 5 per cent of the total student population in Northern Ireland, thereby underlining continued educational segregation in general and the persisting impact of the Catholic Church on its 'community' via schooling in particular.[11]

---

11. These rates are based on the table 'Religion of pupils by school type and management type, 2003/04: Nursery, Primary, Post Primary and Special Schools' (DENI 2006). I have calculated the rates for state schools by combining the data for 'controlled' and 'controlled/voluntary' institutions. The overall figures for Catholic schools follow from the combined rates for 'Catholic Maintained', 'Catholic Maintained/Other Maintained' as well as 'Voluntary Schools under Catholic Management'. The rates for integrated schools include 'Controlled Integrated' and 'Grant Maintained Integrated' institutions. I have left out the data for 'Voluntary Schools under Other (than Catholic) Management' – catering for about 7 per cent (of which 71 per cent were Protestants) of the total student population – because these schools could not be easily attributed to any of the three categories.

The Catholic Church has of course also continued to exercise a considerable though somewhat contested influence through its religious beliefs and practices, to which local devotion has remained relatively high as the figures for self-ascribed 'religion' in the 2001 census show. While, as previously mentioned, 96 per cent of the local population in the ten wards of Catholic West Belfast indicated their religious background as Catholic, nearly the same amount – 89 per cent – identified as actively practising. This high rate of self-declared religiosity was not only echoed at various other regional levels for Catholics but also for Protestants, exhibiting an overall pattern in which rates for self-declared religion were persistently only slightly lower than the rates for religious background: in the city of Belfast (LGD) in 2001, 42 per cent of residents were practising Catholics as opposed to 47 per cent with a Catholic background; 40 per cent indicated their religion as 'Protestant (including other Christian or Christian related)' as opposed to 49 per cent with such a religious background. This pattern was exhibited at the level of Northern Ireland overall with, on the one hand, 40 per cent of the population being practising Catholics and 44 per cent of a Catholic background; and, on the other, 46 per cent of the population being self-declared Protestants and 53 per cent of a Protestant background.[12]

Besides denominational identification, other measurable levels of religiosity such as church attendance have also been remarkably high in Northern Ireland, especially when put into a comparative framework. Commenting on data from his survey conducted in 1968, Rose (1971: 264) notes that church attendance in Northern Ireland then was 'probably higher than anywhere else in the Western world – except the Republic of Ireland'. Subsequent surveys have shown that the proportions of local Christians attending church at least once a week dropped between 1968 and 1998 from 95 per cent to 67 per cent among Catholics and from 46 per cent to 29 per cent among Protestants (Rose 1971; McGarry and O'Leary 1995: 173–74). Nevertheless, religious decline has been considerably less pronounced in Northern Ireland than in the rest of the U.K., where between 1950 and 2000, Mass attendance dropped by 50 per cent in England and Scotland and by 40 per cent in Wales, while falling by only 10 per cent in Northern Ireland (Brewer 2002: 34). The North of Ireland thus still deserves its reputation as a religious society, although there have also been marked differences within. In West Belfast, for instance, decline in church attendance has been more noticeable than in other areas (McGarry and O'Leary 1995: 190), partly reflecting the ambiguous relationship between the Catholic Church and locally strong Republicanism. For despite some affinity with the latter's ideals, the Catholic Church has consistently condemned IRA violence and has sent conflicting political messages, for example, with its ambivalence regarding the burial of IRA volunteers on consecrated ground (Jenkins 1997: 118; Coogan 2002: 103). This, as well as the inherently conservative and 'pro-Establishment' attitude of the Church, reaching various accommodations with the Northern Irish regime (McGarry and O'Leary 1995: 206) while – as local perception goes – doing little to improve conditions for its own constituency, has resulted in a substantial alienation among Catholics. This has

---

12. These rates are based on the Northern Ireland Statistics and Research Agency (NISRA) 2006: Tables KS07a ('Religion') and KS07b ('Community Background: Religion or religion brought up in'), various levels.

contributed to a situation in West Belfast in which many of the practising Catholics I talked to felt somewhat alienated from the Church hierarchy and maintained an attitude nicely summarized by an elderly friend of mine and practising Catholic who proclaimed, 'We have remained Catholic *despite* the Catholic Church'.

Back on the Falls Road, the street passed the park of St Dominic's, opening up to a view of terraced houses. In the distance rose the verdigris-roofed, red brick tower of the former Broadway Presbyterian Church, which since the early 1990s has housed the Irish language, culture and arts centre *Cultúrlann McAdam Ó Fiaich* ('Culture Place McAdam Ó Fiaich') ㉓. Moving on, I passed the local branch of *Glór na nGael* ('Voice of the Gael'), an all-Ireland organization promoting the Irish language through a nationwide competition in which the achievements of local branches of the organization are rewarded. Leaving behind the 'Voice of the Gael', I was now approaching my own neighbourhood, situated near the junction of the Falls Road and Broadway, where I lived during my fieldwork in a flat shared with students. Some of my flatmates studied at St Mary's University College ㉔, which adjoined a row of terraced houses near the junction. St Mary's has been a teacher training college for Catholic schools since 1900. Offering courses taught in Irish since 1996 and hosting the Irish Medium Resource Unit for Irish-medium schools since 1998, St Mary's commitment to the language thus obviously did not stop at its gateway, where the name of the institution was also displayed in Irish: *Coláiste Ollscoile Naomh Muire*.

Located immediately at the junction with Broadway, two pubs – Caffrey's and the Red Devil Bar – faced one other on opposite sides of the Falls Road. Both regularly showed live football matches from the English Premier and Scottish leagues, as well as from European competitions. The Red Devil provided a venue for supporters of the English club Manchester United, the nickname of which gave the pub its name. Apart from sports, both pubs also offered weekly live music sessions with Irish folk, in addition to various disco nights and quiz evenings. The Red Devil Bar had recently been refurbished, and subsequently displayed its name in Irish as '*beár an diabhail deirg*' against its bright red walls. This was symptomatic of a recent trend within Catholic West Belfast towards bilingual inscription on shop and office signs. This was not surprising given that the neighbourhood accommodated a cluster of Irish language organizations and groups, including the economic development agency *Forbairt Feirste* ('Belfast Development'), which was engaged in a campaign encouraging local businesses and organizations to implement bilingual signage and services. Many of these language groups had their offices in the previously mentioned Irish language centre, Cultúrlann McAdam Ó Fiaich, or in the new office building *An Nasc* ('The Connection') ㉕.

Walking through an area that I had deliberately chosen as my 'base camp' for exploring representations and practices of Irish and Irishness among local Gaeilgeoirí, I reached another landmark that is the last focal point of this walk, namely, a mural ㉖ opposite the Cultúrlann (see Figure 1.1). Having been commissioned by the Irish language umbrella organization *Pobal* ('Community'), this bilingual mural proclaimed 'language rights' to be 'human rights' and demanded that 'the unique circumstances of the Irish language' be reflected in the 'Bill of Human Rights'. The mural thereby referred to the then ongoing process mandated by the Good Friday Agreement of 1998

Figure 1.1 Mural – 'Irish is all around us' (photo: Olaf Zenker)

of the newly established Northern Ireland Human Rights Commission to prepare a Bill of Rights for Northern Ireland, which would define rights in addition to those enumerated in the European Convention on Human Rights, reflecting the particular circumstances of Northern Ireland (Northern Ireland Office 1998: Section 6-II/III-§3-4). Against this backdrop, the mural underlined demands for specific language rights for which Pobal had continuously lobbied.

Throughout my stay in West Belfast, I passed this mural hundreds of times, and it repeatedly caught my attention, not so much because of its general human rights message but because of one particular slogan that directly appealed to and continuously reminded me of my own research interest. This slogan read: 'Irish is all around us'. In a way, I could immediately relate to this statement. Did I not constantly experience the plausibility of this representation in daily life given the manifold presence of Irish, be it in local language organizations and bilingual signage, or in the shape of local Gaeilgeoirí? Yet, as a political claim demanding more support for an endangered minority language, was it an accurate description of reality? In what sense did this slogan reflect the actual practice of the language, and to what extent was it simply a politicized claim with little substance in daily life? And by extension, given that people constantly linked the Irish language to their Irish identity, in what sense and to what extent was Irishness 'all around us', both in terms of representations and with regard to practical lived experiences?

Standing in front of this mural to which the main title of this book, 'Irish/ness is all around us', refers, I have brought you back to where this walk began. In narrating this journey, I have also briefly introduced the focus of this book, namely the interplay between representations and practices in the interrelation of the Irish language and Irishness among Gaeilgeoirí in Catholic West Belfast. This focus will now be specified in the next chapter before it finds its application in the remainder of the book.

Chapter 2

Framing the Research

Analytical Approach and Methodology

The North of Ireland or Northern Ireland constitutes, 'in proportionate terms at least' as Coulter (1999: 1) notes, 'the most researched region on the face of the planet'. It thus seems advisable to characterize briefly the place that the current study occupies within this vast field of research. First, this book is based on stationary ethnographic fieldwork and hence takes as its principal point of reference a locally and numerically restricted set of actors, namely, the Gaeilgeoirí of Catholic West Belfast. While most research on Northern Ireland has not been based on fieldwork and participant observation but rather on survey data, interview material, and other sources, a handful of ethnographies have been produced, focusing on localized community relations in the context of political conflict (Buckley 1982; Bufwack 1982); the role of paramilitary violence (Burton 1978; Sluka 1989; Feldman 1991); salient symbols of the conflict such as parades, political murals and flags (Jarman 1997; Buckley 1998; Bryan 2000); the intersection of local politics and gender (Whitaker 2001), age (Jenkins 1983) and class (Howe 1990); and the Irish language (Kachuk 1993; McCoy 1997; O'Reilly 1999). While Feldman, Howe, Kachuk, O'Reilly and Sluka conducted fieldwork in Catholic West Belfast in the 1980s and 1990s and thus provide important local background information, Kachuk's and O'Reilly's studies are particularly relevant to my own investigations as they deal with the Irish language.

This leads me to the second characteristic of this book, namely, its explicit focus on both the Irish language and Irish identity, which are distinguished analytically and investigated separately in order to develop a more comprehensive picture of their various interrelations. There is, of course, a considerable literature on the Irish language in general and on its special situation in the North of Ireland in particular, on which I heavily draw in subsequent chapters. Many of these texts make explicit reference to the role the Irish language plays in 'the politics of culture and identity' – which is the subtitle of O'Reilly's (1999) book. Nevertheless, these studies primarily concentrate on the Irish language, only tangentially addressing the relation of language and Irishness (Nic Craith 2007; McMonagle 2010; Muller 2010). Conversely, the literature on identity in the North of Ireland tends to make only passing reference to the Irish language (Nic Craith 2002: 121–24, 150–54 and 2003: 70–94).

A short description of some of the recent studies of local identities in the North will help to further specify the third feature of this book. Buckley and Kenney's *Negotiating Identity* (1995), for instance, looks at the continuous construction of Catholic and Protestant identities via the invocation of locally dominant symbols – e.g. the siege metaphor – and their ritual enactments in diverse interactional contexts such as parades and riots. Similarly, Harrington and Mitchell's *Politics and Performance in Contemporary Northern Ireland* (1999) explores the performative dimensions of identity by investigating how the realities of conflict are represented on the theatrical stage and how these conflicting identities themselves are symbolically staged in real life. Nic Craith's book *Plural Identities – Singular Narratives* (2002) is more concerned with deconstructing the prevailing paradigm of the 'two traditions' in Northern Ireland by showing how a much more heterogeneous past and present have been discursively essentialized. Also utilizing discourse analysis, Nic Craith's *Culture and Identity Politics in Northern Ireland* (2003) scrutinizes the relation between the recent 'cultural turn' in Northern Irish politics, on the one hand, and Unionist and Nationalist identity discourses, on the other. The 'cultural turn' in Northern Irish politics – that is to say, the official recognition and structural support of biculturalism by the British state – is also addressed in McCall's *Identity in Northern Ireland* (1999). However, McCall situates this change in political discourse and its implications for communal identities in the wider context of the European Union and thereby relates it to a general shift from a modernist to a post-modernist conception of politics. Finally, by analysing often overlooked materials such as films, biographies, popular fiction, and travel writing, Kirkland (2002) considers the increasing importance of local identities in political discourse in Northern Ireland.

While it goes without saying that the preceding brief presentation is anything but exhaustive, these texts are nevertheless to some extent representative of a contemporary focus on the representational side of identity constructions. While this is an important aspect of understanding identity, this study argues for a broader analytical framework that allows for the explicit investigation of the interplay between representational practices and therein represented practices of identity.

This last point needs further specification. The remainder of this chapter is thus concerned, first, with providing a detailed discussion of the analytical framework that will be used in the subsequent empirical analysis. The interplay between representations and practices will thereby be developed as the first of three dimensions constituting my analytical framework. In a second step, I will source-critically contextualize this work through some methodological considerations.

An Analytical Framework for the Study of Ethnic Identity (and the Irish Language)

'In social and cultural anthropology', Eriksen (2002: 1) observes, 'ethnicity has been a main preoccupation since the late 1960s, and it remains a central focus for research after the turn of the millennium.' Given the vast amount of literature and theoretical debate on this subject, as well as the limited space and purpose of this section, I will not attempt to provide a summary of the various developments within this field of research. I will also refrain from a general discussion of the various labels used within the literature to characterize divergent approaches such as 'primordialism', 'instrumentalism' and 'constructivism', because the usage of these terms is so inconsistent and, at times, even misleading (especially in the case of 'primordialism'[1]) that a detailed disentanglement would serve a history of the social sciences more so than my narrower aim of making explicit my own analytical framework. Instead, I will briefly propose my own usage and understandings of the key terms, and then move on with my argument. I will proceed by first distinguishing between 'naturalistic' and broadly 'constructivist' approaches to ethnicity, and then focus on three aspects in particular: first, the relationship between representations and practices of ethnicity, or – as this aspect is framed in the literature (e.g. Eriksen 2002) – between 'ethnicity and culture'; second, the relationship between individual agency and respective structural contexts; and third, the role of time and biographical histories in an understanding of ethnic identities in any ethnographic present.

At a very general level, notions of ethnic identity held by both everyday social actors and social analysts can be distinguished on the basis of whether or not ethnicity is primarily conceptualized as being determined by social practices. Those perspectives that posit non-social factors behind ethnic identities as dominant can be described as 'naturalistic'. Typically, such naturalistic approaches emphasize the importance of biology in one form or another. One variant of the naturalistic perspective consists of theories of race, which usually assume humankind to be subdivided into a limited number of races that are primarily defined by physical and visible differences. Members of a race are thought to share not only physical characteristics but also temperaments, abilities and moral qualities, which, in turn, are assumed to be transmitted biologically. Finally, such a position is often accompanied by assumptions about a hierarchical order of such races. Such theories of race are by now virtually extinct within the social sciences, given that biological and cultural variation within such defined categories has been shown to be greater than differences between them. Nevertheless, such a position may have support among, and hence inform the practices of, social actors under study, thus rendering 'race' – as an emic category – a potentially important field of investigation (Cavalli-Sforza et al. 1994; Jenkins 1997: 74–87; Eriksen 2002: 5–7; Fenton 2003: 13–24).

Within the recent literature, the vast majority of approaches – including my own – fall within the second category, primarily conceptualizing ethnic identity as the product of social practices. This perspective, which might be labelled 'constructionist', or 'constructivist'[2] in a broad sense, emphasizes that ethnic identities are continuously produced and reworked in social interactions, are primarily socially as opposed to naturally determined, and are not fixed or 'essential' in the sense of embodying an atemporal core; instead, ethnic identities are understood to be open to manipulation and change as the practices of social actors

---

1. Within the literature, the term 'primordialism' has been applied to such a broad and divergent variety of positions as to become largely meaningless (except, perhaps, as a straw man) and has also been used to utterly misrepresent the positions of the alleged founding fathers of 'primordialism', Shils and Geertz (see Fenton 2003: 73–90).
2. Both terms can be found in the literature. I use them interchangeably but generally prefer the label 'constructivism'.

develop over time. While endorsing such a very general position towards ethnicity, I concur with Fenton (2003: 87–88), who argues that 'the emphasis on what has been called "constructionism" in the sociology of ethnicity is nothing more than the good application of a standard sociological theorem: what is seen to be natural by actors is understood by sociologists as socially construed. No doubt there are many actors who also are not deceived.'

Thus departing from the very general and somewhat trivial assumption of a broad constructivism, I will now focus on the first of the three previously mentioned aspects of ethnic identity, namely, the relationship between ethnicity and culture. But first, a short qualification is necessary. Within the literature, ethnicity is often defined in terms of myths of common descent, on the one hand, and in terms of elements of shared culture, on the other. The problem with defining ethnicity in terms of allegedly shared descent and culture lies in the fact that it is not immediately conceptually obvious why these two elements should be linked. What is more, there are empirical cases in which a group of social actors understand themselves to share a collective identity with reference to a shared culture but not common descent, and vice versa. In the end, one is thus left with a choice: ethnicity can be defined solely with reference to either culture or descent, or the meaning of ethnicity can be restricted to only those cases in which both culture and descent are invoked together. For now, I opt for a broader notion of ethnicity based exclusively on shared culture, as I am interested in this study in the place that the Irish language occupies within 'Irish culture' in Catholic West Belfast. However, in Chapter 10, when I return to a theoretical discussion of ethnicity, 'shared descent' will be reintroduced into an expanded model of ethnicity.

In the preceding paragraph, I have implicitly made a distinction between 'ethnicity' and 'culture', thereby assuming that the two are not the same. Over the past few decades, this assumption has become one of the crucial and by now largely commonsensical foundations of the 'basic social anthropological model of ethnicity' (Jenkins 1997: 3–15). The *locus classicus* for this distinction is Barth's introduction to his edition *Ethnic Groups and Boundaries* (1969b), although – as Jenkins (1997: 3–24) shows – it can be traced further back to Leach, Everett Hughes and beyond. In the preface to the 1998 reprint of the collection, Barth argues against a then-contemporary and widespread though largely implicit assumption within anthropology that 'the world could be described usefully as a discontinuous array of entities called societies, each with its internally shared culture, and that this framed the issues of ethnicity' (Barth 1998: 5). In other words, the social boundaries of ethnic groups were assumed to correspond unproblematically to the boundaries constituted by internal cultural similarities and external cultural differences. Acknowledging that cultural variations in fact cross-cut each other in multiple ways that do not neatly correspond to the actual boundaries of ethnic groups, Barth defines ethnic identity as a matter of self-ascription and ascription by others, emphasizing that

> although ethnic categories take cultural differences into account, we can assume no simple one-to-one relationship between ethnic units and

cultural similarities and differences. The features that are taken into account are not the sum of 'objective' differences, but only those which the actors themselves regard as significant. ... some cultural features are used by the actors as signals and emblems of differences, others are ignored, and in some relationships radical differences are played down and denied. (Barth 1969b: 14)

This argument led Barth to the oft-quoted conclusion that '[t]he critical focus of investigation from this point of view becomes the ethnic *boundary* that defines the group, not the cultural stuff that it encloses' (1969b: 15 – emphasis in the original). In a way, this summary of Barth's argument can be read as the charter of a narrowly defined constructivist approach to ethnicity: actors 'construct' their ethnic identities in interaction with members and non-members by selecting and representing only a few and only those of their cultural practices as ethnic boundary markers that are shared within the group, while making members externally different from non-members. Such an approach not only generally assumes ethnic identities to be the product of social practices (i.e. the broad constructivist approach) but furthermore argues in a narrowly constructivist manner that the crucial process lies at the level of representational practices producing 'the ethnic boundary' rather than on the level of represented practices, 'the cultural stuff'.

The narrow constructivist approach subsequently developed into the dominant perspective within studies of ethnicity in anthropology (Royce 1982; Jenkins 1997: 17). Yet despite its undoubted benefits, this approach has created two related problems. First, the relationship between ethnicity and culture largely continues to be conceptualized *ex negativo* – in other words, in terms of what this relationship is not. Second, following Barth's suggestion, a dominant theoretical preoccupation with ethnic boundaries or representational practices of 'ethnicity' has emerged at the expense and neglect of the 'cultural stuff' or the therein represented practices of 'culture'. In fact, the implicit equation of representational practices with 'ethnicity' and represented practices with 'culture' perpetuates the notion that 'ethnicity' is solely confined to the level of representations.

Since the 1980s and the publication of *The Invention of Tradition* (Hobsbawm and Ranger 1983) and *Imagined Communities* (Anderson [1983] 1991), the prevalence of terms such as 'invention' and 'imagination' has further contributed to a theoretical preoccupation with discourses of identity. In his introduction to *The Invention of Tradition*, Hobsbawm distinguishes between 'genuine traditions', on the one hand, and 'invented traditions', on the other, with the latter referring to traditions that 'appear or claim to be old', while providing only a 'largely factitious' continuity with the actual historical past (Hobsbawm and Ranger 1983: 1, 2). In his book on nationalism, Anderson ([1983] 1991: 6) defines the nation as 'an imagined political community – and imagined as both inherently limited and sovereign'. He sees all communities larger than villages as imagined, and declares that '[c]ommunities are to be distinguished, not by their falsity/genuineness, but by the style in which they are imagined' (ibid.). However, Hobsbawm does not deny the existence of genuine traditions, and Anderson explicitly rejects any mapping of 'imagination' onto the 'falsity/genuineness' dichotomy. It is thus ironic that the introduction of the terms 'invention' and 'imagination' has had the effect of leading the debate on ethnicity in a direction whereby passing references to these titles serve as a misled claim that only narrowly constructed representations of difference, whether 'real or imagined', really matter.[3] Eriksen makes a similar observation that is worth quoting at length:

> In fact, many important studies of ethnicity ... seem to argue that culture and cultural variation are irrelevant in the study of ethnicity. What is usually the focus of enquiry is the way in which 'real or imagined' cultural differences assume social importance, and it has become a standard procedure for anthropologists to polemicise against the 'misplaced concreteness' involved in reifications of culture, whether they are undertaken by natives or by anthropologists. ... An extreme version of this argument would lead to pure constructivism. ... [O]ne seems forced to conclude that 'anything goes' – that *any* ethnic identity is imaginable, regardless of actual cultural variation or provable distinctive origins. ... This kind of argument has clearly been indispensable (and it pervades much of the anthropological literature on ethnicity), but it leaves important questions unanswered. Obviously, it would have been impossible to persuade Chamba that they were really Yoruba, or to convince English people that they belonged to the same ethnic category as Chinese. At the least, such categorisations seem very, very far off. It seems clear, therefore, that the construction of ethnic categories takes place within a defined space and that some new categorisations may be viable while others are not. The question is: can such a space be defined in terms of cultural variation at all? The answer is, probably, that this is sometimes possible, but not always. (Eriksen 2002: 91–92 – emphasis in the original)

Two points in this quotation are worth highlighting. The first is that theoretically discarding cultural variation as irrelevant indeed leads to pure constructivism in the narrow sense – i.e. viewing the essence of ethnicity as consisting solely in representational practices. Second, such a position is empirically implausible because not all representations of identity are equally viable for actors themselves, and cultural variation might help to explain how these more or less successful processes of identity formation are shaped. In other words, rather than theoretically prejudicing the importance of representational practices over represented practices of culture, what is needed is an analytical framework that allows for the empirical investigation of the interrelations between both of these facets.

So far, I have exclusively focused on narrowly defined constructivist approaches, which tend to disregard – theoretically if not empirically – the potential importance of cultural differences for the study of ethnicity. Of course, there have also been arguments within anthropology and beyond stressing that the 'cultural stuff' has to

---

3. In order to avoid this misleading connotation of complete arbitrariness, Schlee (2004: 148) suggests that we 'speak of "constructions" rather than "inventions"'.

be taken into consideration. Nevertheless, I agree with Eriksen (2002: 57) that 'very few studies of ethnicity have been undertaken within this tradition in anthropology'. In what follows, I will confine my discussion of approaches that reintroduce culture into the constructivist study of ethnicity to the works of Eriksen and Jenkins, because the analytical framework of the present study builds directly on these approaches.

In several publications, Eriksen (1991, 2000, 2002) emphasizes the need to complement the crucial insights of narrow constructivists – or 'formalists' as he calls them – with an analysis of actual cultural differences. Given that Eriksen most explicitly characterizes his own approach in an article entitled 'The Cultural Contexts of Ethnic Differences' (1991), I will confine myself to this text. Eriksen starts from the observation that the significance of cultural differences in otherwise comparable inter-ethnic situations varies and thus needs to be investigated within a comparative perspective. He provides three different criteria whereby cultural variations impact ethnic identity. First, the cultural significance of ethnicity itself varies according to context. Second, Eriksen writes:

[T]he cultural specificities or differences invoked in every justification of ethnic differentiation or dichotomization may (or may not) have a profound bearing on the experiential nature of ethnic relations themselves. This implies that the medium is not necessarily the message, and that *the differences themselves*, which represent a level of signification conventionally glossed over by the formalists, should be investigated, and not only the form of their articulation. (Eriksen 1991: 129 – emphasis in the original)

Third, general cultural differences in specific contexts may make a systematic difference in inter-ethnic encounters. It is on this third aspect that the remainder of his article focuses. Eriksen conceptualizes culture as a Wittgensteinian language-game – as 'a learned and internalized context of shared meaning bounded spatially, temporally and situationally, yet related to other such games through rules of translation and conversion, or through shared or continuous practices, personnel or other carriers of information' (Eriksen 1991: 142). Against the backdrop of comparatively discussing a number of inter-ethnic encounters in Trinidad and Mauritius, Eriksen ultimately proposes a threefold typology based on the degree of shared meaning or culture.

By combining the insights of narrow constructivists with an operationalized framework accounting for the varying significance of cultural differences in inter-ethnic contexts, Eriksen pushes the theoretical debate on ethnicity forward. His differentiation between three cultural contexts impacting ethnic identity is also helpful. First, he argues that the relevance of ethnicity itself can vary across contexts; in other words, contexts can be ethnicized by various actors to differing extents. Second, cultural differences marked in representational practices of ethnicity can vary in their actual significance. Third, ethnically unmarked cultural differences can vary in the degree to which they matter in specific contexts. Eriksen's examples as well as his proposed typology ultimately address only the third aspect. In contrast, the analytical framework of this book is more concerned with the second aspect, namely, the varying interrelations between representational and represented practices of ethnicity.

The second approach, which attends to 'the cultural stuff' of ethnicity and that I deploy herein, is advanced by Jenkins. Like Eriksen, Jenkins (1997: 165) wants to emphasize the virtues of 'the basic social anthropological model of ethnicity' based on narrow constructivism, while claiming that 'its potential has not been fully explored or appreciated'. Among his many insightful comments on ethnicity, one distinction is of particular import for my current discussion, namely, his proposed differentiation between 'nominal' and 'virtual identifications'. Jenkins develops his distinction between 'nominal' and 'virtual identifications' both regarding ethnicity (1997) and concerning social identity in general (2004). While he repeatedly comes back to this aspect of social identity throughout both his books on the subject, the basic idea is nicely encapsulated in the following quote:

> Barth's distinction (1969[b]) between 'boundary' and 'content' – the 'cultural stuff' which is supposed to characterise an ethnic group for example – allows a wider distinction to be drawn between *nominal identity* and *virtual identity*: between the *name* and the *experience* of an identity. It is possible for individuals to share the same nominal identity and for that to mean very different things to them in practice, to have different consequences for their lives, or for them to 'do' or 'be' it differently. (Jenkins 2004: 22 – emphasis in the original)

Jenkins goes on to insist that the nominal–virtual distinction is important because the nominal can stay the same while the virtual may change, and vice versa; alternatively, both may simultaneously change. Yet what exactly are nominal and virtual identifications? Jenkins contends that these two levels can be described in the following way: nominal identification refers to the 'name' of an identity; it is a matter of 'classification' (Jenkins 1997: 41) – 'the label with which the individual is identified' (Jenkins 2004: 76). As the 'description of an identification', nominal identification is 'always symbolised: in language, but also potentially in other forms, whether visual, musical or whatever' and may include 'heraldry, dress, ritual or other material and practical forms' (Jenkins 2004: 112, 116). Nominal identification thus refers to the level of *representational practices* in which individuals are ascribed an identity label and in which this identity is described in terms of its putative characteristics. In contrast, virtual identification refers to 'the experience of an identity', to those 'different things' that the nominal identity 'mean[s]' to actors 'in practice' and to its 'different consequences for their lives' (ibid.). The virtual 'encompasses the consequences of name and label (i.e. what the nominal *means*, in terms of experience)' (Jenkins 1997: 41 – emphasis in the original). It is 'a practical meaning' (Jenkins 1997: 56) and is 'in a sense, what the name *means*; this is primarily a matter of its *consequences* for those who bear it' (Jenkins 1997: 72 – emphasis in the original).

Considering his deployment of this distinction throughout the texts, it turns out that Jenkins' 'virtual identification' combines two aspects that, to my mind, should be kept apart. On the one hand, the virtual seems to refer to actors' experiences of those practices that are used as identity markers within nominal identifications – or, to use Jenkins' own words, the experience of 'the "cultural stuff" which is supposed to characterise an ethnic group'. On the other hand, the virtual is apparently concerned with actors' experiences of the practical consequences that follow from having a certain nominal identity. In my opinion, it is best to analytically distinguish these aspects because the practical consequences of a nominal identification (e.g. not getting a job), and thus the ultimate relevance of ethnicity, often refer to a different set of cultural experiences from those related to practices that are used as identity markers within that nominal identification (e.g. speaking a certain language).

Drawing on Eriksen's distinction, I argue that all three aspects – the relevance of ethnicity, the experience of ethnically marked cultural differences and the ways in which ethnically unmarked cultural differences 'may become relevant even when they are not consciously "made relevant"' (Eriksen 2000: 199) – need to be distinguished and analysed independently in order to show their various empirical interrelations. However, when addressing the interrelations between what Jenkins calls 'nominal' and 'virtual', to my mind only the second aspect seems important. Both the relevance of ethnicity and the role of ethnically unmarked cultural differences are independent of the relation between what is said and thought about an identity, on the one hand, and how the thereby proclaimed or referenced substance of that identity is practically experienced, on the other.

Analytical Dimension 1: The Relationship between Representations and Practices

Ethnic identity should thus be understood analytically to consist of two interrelated levels that have long been distinguished in anthropology, namely, the level of what people think and say they do, on the one hand, and what they actually do, on the other (Holy and Stuchlik 1983). This can be rephrased in more processual terms, which take 'practice' – i.e. the continuous flow of events of which an individual is the reflexively monitoring perpetrator (Giddens 1984: 3–9; see below the discussion of agency)[4] – as the generic term, incorporating as a subcategory 'representational practices', concerned with the production of meaning through language in the broadest sense (Hall 1997: 15–16).[5] Couched in such praxeological terms, the

---

4. Genealogies of sociological and anthropological approaches oriented towards 'practice' or 'action' – while being far too extensive to be described here – comprise Max Weber's early definition of social action as the subject matter of interpretive sociology (Weber 1978), Schütz's social phenomenology (Schütz 1967), works within the framework of symbolic interactionism (Blumer 1969), Garfinkel's ethnomethodology (Garfinkel 1967) as well as the structuration theories proposed by Bourdieu (1977) and Giddens (1984). For discussions of a theoretical shift within anthropology towards praxeological approaches since the 1960s, see Ortner (1984) as well as Holy and Stuchlik (1983).
5. This emphasis on representation as 'a form of practice' stands in a tradition building, among others, on Wittgenstein's usage theory of meaning (Wittgenstein 1953: §43) as well as other developments in the philosophy of language, notably speech act theory (Austin 1962; Searle 1969). Throughout the second half of the twentieth century, reflective approaches to representation have been increasingly challenged by social constructivist theories, leading among others to a crisis of representation within anthropology, as crystallized in the debate on *Writing Culture* (Clifford and Marcus 1986; for a critical discussion see Zenker and Kumoll

first level comprises the 'representational practices' through which individuals are categorized and labelled as members of an envisioned group, and through which certain practices are represented as metonymically referring to a distinctive 'culture' that is viewed as internally shared, while simultaneously making members different from non-members. The second level comprises the totality of actual practices to which the representational practices of the first level putatively refer. To be more precise, this second level – which makes up my concept of culture – consists of the totality of variously representable but actually realized practices of a defined plurality of actors during a defined period of time. These practices are not biologically or naturally determined; they are acquired or creatively invented by members of the group in social interaction.

By 'culture' (in quotation marks) I thus refer to what is represented by actors as constituting an allegedly distinctive way of life of an ethnic group and that is portrayed as internally shared, while simultaneously making members different from non-members; in contrast, by culture (*sans* quotation marks) I denote the totality of actually realized practices to which the representational practices of 'culture' putatively refer. I thereby assume neither a hierarchy of importance between these two levels nor that the objects of representation (i.e. cultural practices) are more 'real' than the acts of representing them (i.e. representational practices of 'culture'). Instead, the interplay between the realities of both representational practices and therein represented practices needs to be explored. Yet this distinction does allow for the possibility that people may also consciously produce counter-factual representations that do not sufficiently grasp their actual cultural practices (this is below called 'pretension') and that this – as we will see throughout the book – can then become the driving force behind ethnicist revivals.[6]

The notion of culture as suggested here has a number of implications that need to be further spelled out. First of all, culture includes a broad variety of representational and non-representational practices. Second, representational practices of 'culture' at the first level are themselves cultural; that is to say, they equally belong to the totality

---

2010). Yet as Latour (2005: 88–93) points out, such controversies on social constructivism have often been misleading in exclusively emphasizing either 'nature' (i.e. the represented domain) or 'society' (i.e. the representational domain) as the decisive factor within practices of representation. Without following Latour into his actor-network theory, this text equally argues for the necessity to focus instead on *the interrelations* between representational and therein represented practices.

6. This distinction between culture and 'culture' is akin to what Appadurai calls 'culture 1' and 'culture 2': 'Culture, unmarked, can continue to be used to refer to the plethora of differences that characterize the world today, differences at various levels, with various valences, and with greater and lesser degrees of social consequence. I propose, however, that we restrict the term *culture* as a marked term to the subset of these differences that has been mobilized to articulate the boundary of difference. ... [I]n this usage *culture* would not stress simply the possession of certain attributes (material, linguistic, or territorial) but the consciousness of these attributes and their naturalization as essential to group identity ... Culture 1, constituting a virtually open-ended archive of differences, is consciously shaped into Culture 2, that subset of these differences that constitutes the diacritics of group identity' (Appadurai 1996: 13–14 – emphasis in the original).

of variously representable but actually realized practices of a defined plurality of actors during a defined period of time. However, since these representational practices at the first level are concerned with the recursive representation of this very culture, thereby producing specific notions of an allegedly distinctive 'culture', it makes sense analytically to distinguish between the two. Third, the cultural practices of certain actors may or may not be shared with other actors within or beyond the predefined plurality of actors. In other words, sharedness is not a defining criterion for culture in my understanding of the concept. (In contrast, the notion of a distinctive 'culture' within representational practices is necessarily projected as being internally shared and externally differentiating an ethnic group.) In addition, the notion of sharedness is ambiguous in being a relative description depending on the level of abstraction. Imagine an ideal-type situation in which all actors are either practising Protestants or Catholics. In such a situation, all Protestants could be defined with reference to their internal shared attribute of 'Protestantism', while externally not sharing 'Catholicism'. Yet, they could also be described as internally not sharing 'the various brands of Protestantism' they practise, while externally being described as sharing with their Catholic neighbours a 'Christian' or 'monotheist' religious practice. For this reason, culture is conceptualized herein as referring to the totality of actually realized practices that are representable in a potentially great but finite number of ways. Fourth, cultural practices are neither assumed to be unchanging nor to be constantly changing. Both relative change and relative persistence are social productions to be observed and explained empirically. All in all, culture in the sense proposed here is thus a purely descriptive term referring to what a defined plurality of actors does over a defined period of time as a result of acquisition or creative invention. Culture is thus simply the inter-subjective point of reference for both my own representations and the representations of local actors.

In a way, we have come full circle to Barth's initial argument distinguishing between the culture of an ethnic group and their own selection of 'cultural' and hence 'ethnic' markers that serve to maintain their boundary vis-à-vis non-members. Yet the proposed framework departs from Barth in two important respects. First, representational practices with their 'cultural'/'ethnic' markers (Barth's ethnic boundaries) are not treated as more important than the culture (Barth's enclosed 'cultural stuff') to which these representations putatively refer. Second, the relationship between the two levels is not primarily conceptualized as unidirectional as it is in Barth's analysis, in which representational practices are seen to *select* existing cultural practices and turn them into ethnic markers of a proclaimed distinctive 'culture'. Instead, the conception I am proposing equally allows for the *pretension* of certain 'cultural' markers. By this I refer to representations of certain 'cultural' markers as emblematic that have little or no substance in the actual cultural practices of the defined plurality of actors. The relationship between representational practices of 'culture' and variously representable cultural practices can thus be described along a continuum ranging from ideal-typical selection to ideal-typical pretension.

At this point, it is crucial to emphasize that the distinction between representational practices and variously representable culture is not meant to correspond to the distinction between the 'subjective' emic perspective of actors and the 'objective' etic perspective of the observer. Instead, both levels are conceptualized as referring to the emic perspective of actors, which is something that must be reconstructed inter-subjectively. This has profound consequences for the interrelation between the two levels, because it makes the allocation of a particular representation within the continuum of 'selection' and 'pretension' solely dependent on the subjective perspectives of social actors. In other words, when trying to decide to what extent a particular representation 'selects' from the actual culture or fabricates something that is not actually present in cultural practice, all that counts is the actor's own reconstructed perspective. Given that the actually realized practices of culture are variously representable by actors themselves, it is thus possible that the same combination of representational practice (e.g. 'Irish people speak their own language') and actually realized practice (e.g. speaking Irish once a week in an Irish club) can be experienced by some actors as a 'good enough' selection, while others might see it as a form of pretension.

Analytical Dimension 2: The Relationship between Agency and Structural Contexts

So far, I have exclusively focused on the interrelation of representational practices of 'culture' and variously representable cultural practices – or between representations and practices, a couplet that I use interchangeably as shorthand throughout this study – as the first dimension of my analytical framework. I now turn to the second dimension, namely, the relationship between individual agency and respective structural contexts. In the field of ethnicity, this aspect has usually been discussed in terms of the interplay of self-ascriptions and ascriptions by others or internal and external definitions. It is in this dynamic that asymmetries of power and authority enter into the analysis.

While the interplay between internal and external definitions and accompanying power relations are crucial for the analysis of ethnicity, preceding from the first dimension of my model of ethnicity, I would argue that such an analysis is often too one-sided, primarily investigating the level of representational practices in terms of 'ascriptions' and 'definitions'. What is thus usually left out is the interaction between members and non-members at the level of representable cultural practices. Yet as I have tried to show, when investigating the formation of ethnic identity, it is not only the establishment of certain representational practices of 'culture' in interactions between members and non-members that are of importance but also the (re)production of certain representable cultural practices shaped by these interactions. It seems thus more appropriate to reframe this second dimension more broadly in terms of the relationship between individual agency and structural context, which then encompasses both the levels of representational and representable practices.

The relationship between structure and agency has been extensively discussed in the social sciences, most prominently by Bourdieu (1977) and Giddens (1984). Both authors attempt to synthesize subjectivist, actor-centred approaches, on the one hand, and objectivist, structure- or system-centred approaches, on the other. Giddens rejects a definition of 'action' as intentional behaviour and characterizes it instead – as mentioned above in the course of defining 'practice' – as the continuous flow of events of which the individual is a reflexively monitoring perpetrator possessing the capability – what Giddens calls 'agency' – to have acted differently (Giddens 1984: 9). Giddens contends that all actions are simultaneously made possible by and form the reproductive basis for rules and resources, which he subsumes under the notion of 'structure'. The subjective agency of actors and the objective structural properties of social systems thus come together in the 'duality of structure', in the sense that 'structural properties of social systems are both medium and outcome of the practices they recursively organize' (Giddens 1984: 25). Individuals as knowledgeable actors are thereby implicated in their practices at three stratified levels. First, they reflexively monitor their actions in their purposive, intentional dimensions. Second, they are capable of supplying reasons for their activities (rationalization). Third, their actions have motives that can be located to varying extents in individual discursive consciousness (what can be said), practical consciousness (what is known tacitly but hard to put into words) and/or unconsciousness (Giddens 1984: 1–16, 373–77).

Bourdieu makes a somewhat similar move in trying to bring together the objective and subjective structures of social practices. However, his attempt deviates from Giddens in at least three important respects. First, Bourdieu forcefully argues against what he calls the 'illusion' of 'individual finalism, which conceives action as determined by the conscious aiming at explicitly posed goals' (Bourdieu 1990: 142). In contrast to Giddens, for whom actors keep in touch with their actions through reflexive monitoring, ex post rationalizations and (occasional) discursive motivations, Bourdieu sees the mediation between practices and their surrounding objective structures as dominated by what he calls 'habitus'. According to Bourdieu, the habitus consists of

> systems of durable, transposable *dispositions*, structured structures predisposed to function as structuring structures, that is, as principles of the generation and structuring of practices and representations which can be objectively 'regulated' and 'regular' without in any way being the product of obedience to rules, objectively adapted to their goals without presupposing a conscious aiming at ends or an express mastery of the operations necessary to attain them and, being all this, collectively orchestrated without being the product of the orchestrating action of a conductor. (Bourdieu 1977: 72 – emphasis in the original)

In short, the habitus predisposes actors to certain practices, which only seem to be intentionally goal-oriented because they are so closely adjusted to the requirements of the very environment they thereby reproduce. Second, the objective structures of the environment that shape habitus are predominantly those of the objective class structure in which actors are embedded. This leads to the third way that Bourdieu deviates from Giddens' model: ultimately, all practices can be seen as taking part in power struggles over various forms of capital that are unevenly distributed in various social fields. Given that variations in class-induced habitus unevenly predispose actors to play field-specific games successfully, power struggles within particular social fields tend to reproduce the asymmetrical class structure that underlies their practical realizations (see Bourdieu in Wacquant 1989: 37–41).

For Giddens as well as Bourdieu, structure and action are hence mutually implicated in one another such that structural features are both a basis and outcome of individual actions. In other words, practices can be conceived as simultaneously being action-structures. However, Giddens' approach, encompassing not only unconscious and practically conscious but also discursively conscious motives, avoids a relapse into objectivist determinism that, as Jenkins (2002) cogently argues, ultimately characterizes Bourdieu's argument. If notions like 'strategies', 'interests' and 'improvisation' are used to fill the explanatory gap between objectively induced, subjective predispositions, on the one hand, and actually realized practices, on the other, while these notions are explicitly redefined as operating unbeknownst to social actors themselves, then the gap turns out to be closed deterministically. In other words, agency as the capability of actors to act differently disappears. While Giddens thus provides, to my mind, a more compelling account of motivation, Bourdieu focuses not only on the general duality of action and structure within any single practice but is also more explicitly attentive to the ways in which particular practices of actors are conditioned by and condition the action-structures of other actors. This leads to a certain methodological bias in this book, which needs to be characterized.

Generally, I subscribe to the preceding argument that any practice can be investigated with regard to its dual character as action and structure. However, when focusing on the agency and practices of a particular actor vis-à-vis the realized practices of his/her respective others, the latter practices can often (though not always) be methodologically treated only as structure. This is so because from the individual actor's point of view, the practices of others (rooted in the latter's own agency) appear primarily as enabling and constraining structures for the individual actor's own agency. This of course is not to say that individual actors cannot and do not attempt to modify or manipulate the actions of others – far from it. But in a crucial sense, the individual actor cannot act differently on behalf of others; ultimately, it is thus to a large extent the case that what counts as agency for other actors is relevant primarily as structure for the individual actor under consideration. It is in this sense of often but not always methodologically bracketing the motivations of respective other actors that I speak of the relationship between the agency of individual actors and their respective structural contexts.

Given that my focus in this study is not on an individual but on a set of actors – namely, Gaeilgeoirí in Catholic West Belfast – and given that the ultimate point of reference is Irishness, the notion of 'respective structural contexts' can be further specified. I distinguish between four general types of structural contexts vis-à-vis individual Irish learners/speakers who view themselves as Irish. First, internal structural contexts are composed of the practices of other actors with whom the actor shares a group notion of Irishness. Second, external structural contexts are composed of the practices of other actors who along with the actor agree that the actor is Irish and that they (the other actors) are not. Third, internalizing structural contexts consist of the practices of other actors with whom the individual actor is in disagreement regarding his or her identity; here, the individual actor insists that he or she is Irish and separate from these other actors, while these other actors maintain that the individual actor is in fact part of their own non-Irish identity. Fourth, externalizing structural contexts consist of the practices of other actors who do not view themselves as Irish, while the individual actor maintains that they are in fact also Irish.

Against this backdrop, I now want to formulate the theory of motivation that I will use to analyse why individual actors deploy their agentive capacity in particular ways. As I have already stated, I believe that Giddens' approach in this respect is more useful than Bourdieu's. However, Max Weber's well-known distinction between the four ideal-typical orientations of social action seems even more suitable, because it not only allows for a distinction between discursively conscious and practically conscious/habitus-like motives but also because it is more highly differentiated with regard to the realm of discursively conscious orientations. Weber (1978: 24–26) distinguishes between two types of rational (i.e. discursively conscious) motivations: instrumentally rational (*zweckrational*) actions are those in which the actor uses his or her conscious expectations as the means of achieving 'the actor's own rationally pursued and calculated ends'. In contrast, value-rational (*wertrational*) actions are based on the 'conscious belief in the value for its own sake of some … form of behaviour, independently of its prospects of success'. These two types of rational orientations are contrasted with affectual actions, which are 'determined by the actor's specific affects and feeling states' and traditional actions, which are "determined by ingrained habituation"' (Weber 1978: 24–25). Traditionally motivated actions thereby refer to those ideal-typical cases that Giddens conceptualizes in terms of practical consciousness and that Bourdieu understands as habitus-based.

Analytical Dimension 3: Biographical Time and the Presence of the Past

The third and final dimension of my analytical framework is concerned with the role of time and specifically biographical history in an understanding of ethnic identity in the ethnographic present. As mentioned before, the overall subject of this study consists in a reconstruction of the interplay between representations and practices in the interrelation of the Irish language and Irishness that existed among Gaeilgeoirí in Catholic West Belfast at the time of my fieldwork between 2003 and 2004. In other words, my main temporal point of reference is made up of a still rather recent 'ethnographic present'. While I thus engage in a degree of presentism in the treatment of my object of study, I strongly concur with Peel's (1989) objection to methodological presentism in searching for explanations of a particular present only in its respective contemporary setting. Against presentism, I argue along with Peel (1989: 198–99) for 'the need for a properly cultural and historical explanation of ethnicity'. I have already discussed the need to focus not only on 'culture' but also on its relation to culture. Turning to the role of history, the past is immediately relevant to any present ethnic formation in the sense that it helps us to understand how and why this ethnic formation came about. Yet history's impact, of course, goes much further. It is not only antecedent to whatever is the case in the present but also to a lesser or greater degree determines the present in the present itself. Translating this into the actual situation in Catholic West Belfast in 2003 and 2004, to understand what it then meant for various local actors to be Irish and to be engaged with the Irish language, it is heuristically necessary to assume that their positions then consisted of what they had individually become before in the course of divergent socialization biographies. In other words, it makes sense to conceptualize the ethnographic present of this study in terms of the simultaneous embodiments of potentially non-simultaneous trajectories of past individual identity formations. What this amounts to is an expansion of the temporal frame of reference throughout the study. Although the primary explanadum will remain the indicated ethnographic present of 2003–2004, the explanans will extend in relation to my oldest informants to include the period since the mid-twentieth century. I emphasize that this is not done as history for history's sake but in the attempt to develop a deeper understanding of the ethnographic present by coming to terms with the potentially powerful presence of its past.

In summary, in this section I have developed the analytical framework I will use in the subsequent study by suggesting three different dimensions of ethnicity. The first dimension is the relationship between representational practices of 'culture' and variously representable cultural practices, moving between the two ideal-typical poles of selection and pretension. The second dimension is the potentially asymmetrical relationship between the agency of actors under focus and their respective structural contexts, a relationship in which the actually realized practices of these actors can be investigated in terms of instrumentally rational, value-rational, affectual and/or traditional motivations. The third dimension is the potential significance of non-simultaneous trajectories of identity formation, which render the present into a co-presence of divergent individual pasts, and hence make biographical time a crucial focus for an understanding of the present.

While I have thus far developed this framework only in regards to ethnic identity, it can easily be applied to the study of the Irish language. In this case, the first dimension focuses on the relationship between representations and actual practices of the Irish language, the second dimension remains the same and the third dimension explores the simultaneity of potentially non-simultaneous trajectories of becoming a Gaeilgeoir. The analytical framework thus allows the overall topic of this study – the interplay between representations and practices in the interrelation of the Irish language and Irishness among Gaeilgeoirí in Catholic West Belfast at the beginning of the twenty-first century – to be translated into two related research questions. First, how had the Irish language been practically experienced and represented by and to Irish Gaeilgeoirí in their respective interactions with various structural contexts, creating the present configuration, and why had their experiences and representations taken on these particular forms? Second, how had Irishness been practically experienced and represented by and to Irish Gaeilgeoirí in their respective interactions with various structural contexts, creating the present configuration, and why had their experiences and representations taken on these particular forms? These two research questions will frame the subsequent empirical study after the following brief discussion of methodology.

On Methodology

Before my fieldwork in Belfast from July 2003 to September 2004, in 2001 I participated in the two-week 'Ireland: Northern Perspectives' international summer school at Queen's University Belfast. I returned to Belfast in April 2003 for a four-week preliminary research trip. During this time, the Irish language caught my attention as a phenomenon that was both related to questions of ethnicity and investigable at the representational as well as practical level. Hence, learning as much Irish as possible became my primary objective. At the beginning of my fieldwork, I thus attended full-time language courses both in Belfast and at a college in a *Gaeltacht* (i.e. an Irish-speaking area) of County Donegal. Subsequently, between September 2003 and June 2004, I participated in four weekly Irish classes taught in the Cultúrlann and the community centre *Ionad Uíbh Eachach* (Iveagh Centre).

I was also able to improve my language competence by informally conversing with and listening to Irish speakers. This was especially the case in the *Cumann Chluain Árd* (the Association of Clonard),[7] a somewhat maverick branch of the Gaelic League in Catholic West Belfast. Over the months, I spent many evenings at the bar of 'the Cluain Árd' (as the place is locally referred to), even bartending on a number of evenings between February and May 2004. Although my Irish progressed, I continued to be quite frustrated with my intermediate level of fluency, which allowed me to get the gist of most conversations without being able to make more than rather simple contributions. As an anthropologist doing research on the Irish language and with the objective of learning the 'natives'' language, I would have preferred to become much more fluent. Yet my somewhat slow progress also reflected the local dominance of English, with which learners and fluent speakers were equally confronted. My mode of communicating mainly in English and only occasionally in Irish *was* thus in an important sense the local natives' language, even though this situation left me and obviously many language activists strongly dissatisfied.

Irish language classes and places such as the Cultúrlann, Ionad Uíbh Eachach and the Cumann Chluain Árd not only helped me to learn the language; I simultaneously used these and other formal language settings for both systematic participant observation and as a way of building rapport with local Gaeilgeoirí. Most of my local contacts, acquaintances and friendships emerged from such settings and gradually expanded into more informal and private contexts. While playing an important role throughout my fieldwork, participant observation was also inherently limited as a method, given the scale and complexity of urban life (Jenkins 1993). I thus also became dependent on other sources and methods – even more so as I was particularly interested in the biographical developments of my informants. For this purpose, a life story approach based on extensive formal interviewing with selected key informants also proved necessary.

In order to maximize potential variation, I diversified my key local Catholic informants in terms of age, gender and degree of involvement with the Irish language. I ultimately ended up with twenty-eight key informants, conducting a complete

---

7. The community centre *Ionad Uíbh Eachach* (Iveagh Centre), the adjacent local *Gaelscoil na bhFál* (Falls Irish-medium Primary School) as well as the *Cumann Chluain Árd* (the Association of Clonard) are indicated by the encircled numbers (27), (28) and (29) respectively, on Map 1.1: 'My walk into Catholic West Belfast' in Chapter 1.

cycle of formal interviews with each one.[8] In order to ensure that my interview questions adequately covered locally relevant topics, I used the first three months as an exploratory phase before developing and modifying my interview guide for semi-structured interviews after discussions with one key informant and starting my first formal interview series. In the course of then using this topical list, some questions were dropped, modified or added to create the core themes of the ultimate interview guide. In the course of the interview series, which ranged between two and fifteen sessions per individual, I conducted a total of 145 recorded interviews with all twenty-eight key informants. Most of these individual interview cycles took between three and six sessions, with the interviews usually lasting between one and three hours. During all 145 formal interviews, I made MiniDisk (MD) recordings and took notes. This also allowed me subsequently to use my written notes to aid me in systematic analysis, since full transcriptions could only be made for about one-third of this material. Unless stated otherwise, all literal quotations cited in this book are taken from these interview transcriptions. I have refrained from providing further references for individual quotations, as this contributes to securing as much anonymity as possible for my informants, makes reading easier and does not impede critical evaluation of my data and analysis.

All data gathered during these formal interviews and in conversations and informal interviews during participant observation was, of course, the product of my own encounters with informants, and as such needed to be subjected to systematic source criticism. Having had long-term relationships with most of my informants thereby paid off by affording me a clearer picture of their personalities

---

8. In terms of age structure and gender, my ethnographic sample of twenty-eight key informants can be described as follows: seven (two female, five male) aged 11–20; two (one female, one male) aged 21–30; three (two female, one male) aged 31–40; seven (three female, four male) aged 41–50; six (two female, four male) aged 51–60; three (all male) aged 61 or older. In terms of relative involvement with the Irish language, I selected informants according to two categories – 'activists' and 'participants' – and there were an equal number of both within my sample set. The 'activists' category included two teachers of adult Irish classes (one female, one male), five teachers and support staff in Irish-medium nurseries, primary and secondary schools (two female, three male), two activists from the Cumann Chluain Árd (both male), one male activist from the Cultúrlann, two activists from other Irish language organizations (both male), one male producer of Irish-medium television programmes and one male founding member of the Shaw's Road Gaeltacht in Catholic West Belfast. The 'participants' category included two members of adult Irish classes (both female), four pupils from the local Irish-medium secondary school (two female, two male), one mother of children attending Irish-medium schools, one male regular at the Cluain Árd, two male frequenters of the Cultúrlann, two members of the Irish-medium choir in the Cultúrlann (one female, one male) and two Republican ex-prisoners who had learnt Irish while serving their sentence (one female, one male). Although my selection of activists and participants was thus symmetrical, it should be stated that these categories were not as neatly separated as it may seem. Several of my informants belonged to more than one context, being possibly considered, for instance, an 'activist' as an Irish teacher, but also a 'participant' in the choir. Furthermore, the respective internal differentiation by gender of the fourteen activists and fourteen participants was not as balanced as I would have liked. While the 'participants' group did in fact consist of seven men and seven women, the 'activists' group was made up of eleven men and only three women.

and positionality, and allowing me to compare their behaviour and accounts in informal settings with what they told me during interviews. When the need arose, I also confronted my informants with any contradictory accounts they had provided in earlier encounters. Using archival material and extant literature on relevant topics also allowed for another form of triangulation both during the actual data-gathering period and in subsequent analysis.

Although I am convinced that these strategies improved the quality of my data, one general difficulty remained, namely, the problem of how to interpret informants' present accounts of the past. This problem is, of course, not new. It has been discussed within the social sciences in relation to, amongst other things, life story research, on which I will concentrate here. According to Runyan (1996: 472–73), research on life histories, 'defined as the sequence of events and experiences in a life from birth until death in social, cultural and historical contexts', rapidly expanded from the 1970s onwards. An earlier preoccupation with the past has thereby increasingly given way to focusing on the present narrative itself:

> Life histories focused mostly on diachronic change within anthropology's traditional paradigm of naturalism or realism; research on life stories, on the other hand, focuses on the cultural scripts and narrative devices individuals use to make sense of experience. Life story research emphasizes the truth of the telling versus the telling of the truth. (Frank 1995: 145)

While life story research has thus recently focused on how present narratives about the past comment on the present, at the cost of focusing on the past itself as represented in narrative, various authors such as Peacock and Holland (1993: 371) have emphasized that life story accounts can be analysed with regard to both aspects. Following these authors, I would emphasize that such accounts not only can but must be analysed with regard to both aspects, given that they are mutually implicated. That plausible interpretations of probable pasts have to be reconstructed from a source-critical analysis of the narrative setting in the present has been long acknowledged (e.g. Siedler 1998: 167). However, the opposite also holds true, which is, to my mind, less often appreciated: when trying to provide an analysis of the present conditions that shape the actual process of narrating, an at least implicit reconstruction of a probable past is required if inconsistent or implausible conclusions are to be avoided.

Whether one prefers to investigate the presence of communicative acts or the pasts that are referred to in such accounts – a decision based on research interests with neither perspective inherently better than the other – each focus thus requires the other as its background. Both sides must be simultaneously reconstructed in a process of mutual interpretation that aims at both an internal analysis of the oral accounts and external triangulation. In a crucial sense, we have thus come full circle, as this discussion of source criticism regarding present accounts of past (and, in fact, present) events turns out to be actually but a variation of the overall theoretical problem of this book, namely, the question of how to address the relationship between representational practices and their alleged points of reference

– in other words, variously representable but actually realized practices. My own way of handling this problem directly derives from the argument just made, that both representational and represented practices are inevitably implicated in one another and hence always require simultaneous, mutual analysis and interpretation, whether the researcher's interests foreground the present or the invoked past. My own interest throughout this book moves between both, at times foregrounding the presence of communicative acts (chapters 6 and 10) and at times accentuating past developments (chapters 4, 5, 8 and 9).

Part I

The Irish Language in Catholic West Belfast

Chapter 3
Fáilte isteach – Welcome In

Imagine you were introduced to the Irish language scene in Catholic West Belfast at the place where I was first welcomed: the *Cultúrlann McAdam Ó Fiaich* ('Culture Place McAdam Ó Fiaich'). Approaching its premises on the Falls Road in the Iveagh/Beechmount area, you would see the compact, red-brick building of a former church, with its verdigris-roofed tower and its entrance facing the Falls Road. Passing these doors, you would reach a small entrance area with a lift to the left and a staircase to the right leading to the upper two floors, which were constructed during a restoration of the building before the Cultúrlann later moved in. Proceeding straight through another pair of glass doors, you would enter the main room on the ground floor that accommodates the cafeteria *An Caife Glas* ('The Green Café'), the book/gift shop *An Ceathrú Póilí* ('The Fourth Policeman'), as well as *Oifig Fáilte*, a small tourist information point. Standing at these doors, you would see a large room (about 20 x 15 metres) divided in half by a metre-high bookshelf-cum-wall that leads up to the counter of the cafeteria at the opposite end, leaving enough room at both ends to allow for movement between both sides of the room. You might perceive the dozen or so wooden tables and chairs to the right as forming a restaurant area, while the interior to the left would appear somewhat different with smaller wooden tables and chairs arranged alongside the tourist information desk and within the bookshop. The tables thus enclosed by storage racks along the walls and by freestanding bookshelves, this left side of the room has more the character of a café, even though customers would often have food or drinks on either side. With its walls painted light yellow, green and red, with the painting exhibitions in the restaurant area, the souvenirs for sale in the bookshop, the many small lamps that add warmth to the daylight coming through the windows and with the varied background music (from world music to Irish traditional and folk music), you would probably experience this place as being cosy and welcoming, like I did.

During hundreds of visits to the Cultúrlann, I developed some sense of the rhythm of the place. At the time of my fieldwork, the centre was open daily from 9:00 a.m. to 10:00 p.m. (or later in the case of special events) year round. During the week, a handful of customers usually showed up in the morning for coffee, tea or some kind of breakfast, often strolling around the bookshop, which had extensive offerings: learning materials for Irish and other Celtic languages; books in both Irish and English about the Irish language, 'Irish culture' in general and the political situation in the North of Ireland; an extensive CD collection emphasizing traditional and folk music; and greeting cards, T-shirts and craftwork exhibiting ornamental or language-related aspects of 'Irishness'. While some customers had a look at these products, other visitors chatted with acquaintances and friends or retreated to read the Irish News, *Andersonstown News*, the Irish-medium *Lá* ('Day') (the latter two of which were produced in West Belfast) or *Foinse* ('Source'), a national weekly in Irish. From noon onwards, the place normally filled up with numerous people lining up at the lunch counter of the cafeteria. Here, the daily offerings – typically salads, soup, different sorts of meat, chips, mashed potatoes, rice and vegetables – were indicated in Irish and English on a blackboard above the bar on which the food itself sat on a hotplate. Upon ordering in Irish or English, the dish was put together by the waitress, paid for and taken by the customer to their table of choice. As I repeatedly observed, typically around half of the nearly one hundred seats of the café/restaurant would be filled during lunchtime. The customers varied in terms of age and dress, amongst them men in suits and ties, apparently on break from their offices, and several uniformed individuals, who I assumed worked at the nearby Royal Victoria Hospitals.

Around 2:00 p.m., the lunch rush usually ended, and the calm atmosphere of the morning returned. The waitresses, dressed in dark trousers and green polo shirts, busied themselves bringing the dirty dishes back to the kitchen and cleaning the tables. Apart from serving the odd customer, during such slack periods they often sat around, chatting among themselves or with the employees at the tourist desk or bookshop. Occasionally, some of the people working in the upstairs offices of the Cultúrlann also came down for a break or an informal work meeting with other language activists. As the afternoon progressed, the Cultúrlann filled up again with a number of visitors arriving for the à-la-carte menu served between 4:00 and 9:00 p.m.

Depending on the night of the week, the participants for the various classes showed up a bit before 7:00 p.m., when the two-hour courses usually started. As the Cultúrlann announced in its quarterly booklet *Clár Ealaíon* ('Arts Programme'), from September 2003 onwards it had been offering an Irish drama club for young people on Mondays, the Irish-medium *Cór Loch Lao* (the 'Belfast Bay Choir') on Tuesdays and a watercolours class and Scots-Gaelic language course on Wednesdays, in addition to the Irish language classes offered weekly from Monday to Wednesday. Usually, some participants came down to the cafeteria during their short breaks or after their classes ended. The main room on the ground floor then typically quietened down after 9:00 p.m. before the centre finally closed its doors for the night at around 10:00 p.m.

Evenings with Irish-medium events – usually Fridays and Saturdays but occasionally other nights – were different. While the main room on the ground floor still closed at around the same time, the Cultúrlann building itself stayed open longer given the various plays, concerts and movie screenings that usually took place in the theatre space on the first floor. Offering seating for more than one hundred visitors, the theatre hosted Irish-medium drama performances (with simultaneous English translation) by the Cultúrlann-based company *Aisling Ghéar* ('Sharp Vision'), the local children's drama club *Ababú* and other visiting theatre groups. On other nights, it also hosted concerts featuring Irish traditional and folk music as well as Irish-medium reggae by the local band *Bréag* ('Lie'), blues, jazz and world-music varieties from Wales, Scotland, Corsica, South America, Africa and the

Basque country. Finally, the theatre screened art movies from various countries. The first floor also accommodated a workshop, some classrooms and the Gerard Dillon Gallery, named in honour of a well-known local artist, which hosted temporary exhibitions, lectures and occasional launches of new CDs, Irish-medium television programmes and the like produced by local Gaeilgeoirí.

Besides one-off events like Irish-medium day or weekend workshops on topics such as music and painting for children, flower arrangement, traditional Irish and *sean-nós* ('old style') singing and dancing, the Cultúrlann also provided a venue for a number of regular weekend activities, most of which took place in the main room on the ground floor. One such weekly event was the *Seisiún an tSathairn* (the 'Saturday Session') at which musicians were welcomed to join in a traditional music session between 1:00 and 3:00 p.m. in the Cultúrlann café. Typically, a rotating group of five or so musicians gathered, playing instruments like uilleann pipes, fiddles, boxes, tin whistles, flutes and bouzoukis. Occasionally, these Saturday sessions were delayed because of the odd Irish-medium book launch at 1:00 p.m. in the Cultúrlann café by the local *Club Leabhar Choiscéim Feirste* (the 'Belfast Book Club') of the Dublin-based Irish language publishing house Coiscéim, which also distributed books to its local membership. Saturday afternoons also saw the small table of *An Siopa Síol* ('The Bean Shop') run by an elderly lady and Gaeilgeoir who sold fair trade, organic goods like coffee, tea, chocolate and sugar. As this suggests, Saturdays were quite busy, with patrons beginning to arrive at the Cultúrlann café in the morning, and with the place packed by lunchtime and into the afternoon. Towards the evening it then slowly emptied out, with guests heading elsewhere or going upstairs for an event.

In contrast, Sundays were usually the quietest day of the week. Although the cafeteria offered three-course Sunday lunches from noon onwards, thus ensuring a steady stream of individual customers and families around midday and into the early afternoon, the room on the ground floor generally continued to emanate a drowsy air of calm as many locals retreated home to be with their families. This area remained equally calm on the last Sunday evening of the month when *Ciorcal Amhránaíochta* (the 'Singing Circle') met in an upstairs room to learn and sing traditional songs in Irish.

After several initial days of hanging around and observing various activities in the main room on the ground floor, I was introduced to several Gaeilgeoirí working in the building by an Irish-medium television producer with whom I had become acquainted during my stay in April 2003, and who became one of my key informants. From then on, I spent much of my time in the Cultúrlann with employees, chatting with them in the café and visiting them in their upstairs offices. I learnt that the second floor of the building accommodated several Irish language initiatives and companies. These included *Pobal* ('Community'), an umbrella organization for numerous Irish language groups in the North of Ireland and founded in 1998,[1] as well as the Irish-medium education agency *Gaeloiliúint* ('Irish language training'). Besides *Raidió Fáilte* ('Radio Welcome'),

---

1. For more details on this organization, see Pobal (2006).

which had operated on and off as a pirate station since the mid-1980s and which was still struggling to obtain a licence, the second floor also housed three private companies: the Irish-medium drama group *Aisling Ghéar* ('Sharp Vision'), which, although initially amateur-based, became the first professional Irish language theatre in Northern Ireland in 1996; the Irish-medium television production company *Scannáin Aisling Ghéar* ('Sharp Vision Films'), a spin-off of *Aisling Ghéar*, started in 2003; and the design company *Dúch Dúchais* ('Native Ink'), which produced Irish language cards and calendars.

These organizations and businesses as well as the bookshop on the ground floor were rent-paying tenants of the Cultúrlann. As I learnt in conversations and interviews with employees and tenants, the Cultúrlann itself was a recognized charity, committed in its mission statement to the promotion of the Irish language through the arts. Apart from employing the staff of the cafeteria and the tourist office, day-to-day business of the centre was managed by an events coordinator and an administrator, whose work and suggestions were discussed in the monthly meetings of the Cultúrlann committee. Given that members of the public could also purchase an annual membership in the Cultúrlann, this committee consisted of representatives from each tenant group and elected board members.

As several language activists involved in the establishment of the centre recalled, the Cultúrlann was first established in 1991 as the by-product of another local language initiative. In 1989, a number of language activists and groups had developed the idea of setting up the first Irish-medium secondary school in West Belfast (and in the whole of Northern Ireland) in order to ensure that pupils of the then two local all-Irish primary schools could continue their education in Irish. Given the amount of work that went into developing the concept of this secondary school, creating interest among parents, raising funds, negotiating with the Department of Education for Northern Ireland (DENI) and advertising for teachers, the initial goal of starting the school in September 1990 had to be postponed for one year. By early 1991, the group had found two teachers and nine pupils, but while DENI agreed to recognize the school, it did not opt to fund it because of the small number of pupils (a decision locally thought to be largely politically motivated by DENI's perceived opposition to the Irish language). While sufficient funds had been raised to pay the teachers, no suitable premises for the school had yet been found. In the process of looking for an appropriate space, these activists came across the former Broadway Church on the Falls Road.

The history of the Broadway Church was compiled by Réamann Ó Néill (n.d.) in his brief bilingual article 'Teampall Shlí Leathan/The Protestant Broadway Church', which was framed and publicly displayed in the Cultúrlann. According to Ó Néill, the Broadway Church was built and opened in 1896 by a local congregation of Presbyterians who at that time lived 'along the Falls Road as well as in the Broadway, Glenalina, Ballymurphy, Whiterock and Andersonstown districts'. However, the initially large congregation of more than three hundred local families decreased by half in the course of erupting violence in the 1920s and 1930s, and continued to diminish after the outbreak of the Troubles in 1969, with local Presbyterians leaving the area for other parts of Belfast. The intensification of the conflict throughout the

1970s made many members of the congregation fearful of attending services, which led to the closure of the church in June 1982.

In subsequent years, the church lay vacant with the exception of a period during which it was rented as a carpet warehouse. When local residents became aware of plans to use the building as a social drinking club, they asked the local parish priest of St Paul's, Reverend Montague, for help. He contacted the church-related Springfield Charitable Association and urged the association to purchase the building for its planned day centre for elderly people. In 1987, the association bought the building with some financial backing from the state, and restored it over the next few years, during which time the three floors were introduced. While the day care centre of the Springfield Charitable Association – named the Montague Centre in honour of the priest – has been in operation since 1990 in what was formerly the Church Hall and caretaker's house at the rear of the building, the church itself was initially rented to Beechmount Youth Training Programme (YTP), a government-funded youth training programme for trades. However, in the spring of 1991, the YTP decided to relocate, and it was at this point that a pressure group for the Irish-medium secondary school entered the scene.

When the language activists learnt that they could actually lease the entire building and not just the rooms they would immediately require, the idea emerged of establishing an Irish language, culture and arts centre, which could accommodate the new *Meánscoil Feirste* ('Belfast Secondary School'), a new Irish language café and various pre-existing language projects such as the bookshop, the theatre group and the Irish newspaper *Lá*, which did not have proper premises at the time. By arguing that such an Irish-medium arts centre would create jobs, provide 'an alternative to murder and mayhem' and project 'a positive image of West Belfast' – as one activist remembered – the group convinced the government development agency Belfast Action Team (BAT) to pay for the lease and insurance for the building.

It was also during these early days that the name of the centre, Cultúrlann McAdam Ó Fiaich ('Culture Place McAdam Ó Fiaich'), emerged. Activists created the neologism 'Cultúrlann', which uses the Irish suffix '-lann', indicating the 'place of something', to produce the meaning 'place of culture'. In addition, it was decided that the centre would be named after a Catholic and a Protestant Gaeilgeoir to demonstrate, as one founding member put it, that the Irish-speaking community 'is non-sectarian' and 'belongs to everybody – Protestant and Catholic'. As I was further told, the choice of name had been easy enough given that the Presbyterian businessman Roibeárd McAdam had 'without a doubt been the most active Irish language activist in nineteenth-century Belfast' and that Tomás Cardinal Ó Fiaich had been a stalwart of the Irish language in the twentieth century, supporting and putting pressure on the British government on behalf of various language projects in West Belfast until his death in 1990.

Thus in the summer of 1991, Cultúrlann McAdam Ó Fiaich opened its doors, housing, amongst other things, the new Meánscoil, an Irish-medium nursery, a new cafeteria, the bookshop, the newspaper *Lá*, Raidió Fáilte as well as the then-amateur theatre group. From the very beginning, each tenant group was entitled to have one representative on the committee of the Cultúrlann and was supposed to pay rent as soon as they could afford it. Due to a number of fundraising campaigns in the following years, the Cultúrlann managed to increase its financial support, allowing it to hire paid staff beginning in 1995. With various language projects coming and going – the Meánscoil, for instance, moved to a larger space up the Falls Road in the late 1990s as it had expanded beyond the capacities of the former church – the Cultúrlann had developed into an established language, culture and arts centre by the time of my stay in Belfast in 2003. By then, it not only housed various organizations but also received substantial funding from the Arts Council of Northern Ireland, *Foras na Gaeilge* (the 'Irish Language Agency') – a recently founded body run jointly by the United Kingdom and the Republic of Ireland, and responsible for the promotion of the Irish language throughout the whole of Ireland[2] – the Belfast City Council and the International Fund for Ireland.

Between April 2003 and March 2004, its wide range of Irish-medium events including drama, concerts, lectures, readings, launches, exhibitions, films, workshops and classes involved more than six hundred artists and workshop/class participants; and about nine thousand tickets were sold to these events, as is indicated in the Cultúrlann annual report for the Arts Council. This figure should be put in perspective: as both I and others observed, the audience at many events was composed of many of the 'usual suspects' of the local language scene of the Cultúrlann and beyond. Nevertheless, these numbers indicate the extent to which the Cultúrlann had firmly become part of the wider Irish-speaking community in West Belfast by pragmatically promoting the Irish language through bilingualism; or, as one of the leading figures behind the Cultúrlann once put it, by basically acting on two maxims: '*Gaeilge más féidir, Béarla más gá*' ('Irish if possible, English if necessary') and '*Is ábhar Gaeilgeora gach Béarlóir*' ('Every English speaker is a potential Irish speaker').

Figure 3.1 Photo collage from the webpage of the Cultúrlann McAdam Ó Fiaich (2006)

---

2. For more details on this organization, see Foras na Gaeilge (2007).

Departing from the Cultúrlann into the wider Irish language scene of Catholic West Belfast, the latter proved to consist of a plethora of language organizations, groups, projects and activities. This abundance of Irish language initiatives successfully resisted my attempts to develop a comprehensive list of all organized Irish-medium activities in Catholic West Belfast, given that many were informal, voluntary, highly bound to the activism and engagement of particular individuals (with whom they emerged and disappeared) and thus nowhere centrally registered. Therefore, the umbrella organization for Irish language groups in the North of Ireland, Pobal, did not have a comprehensive database. Other language groups – such as *Iontaobhas ULTACH* ('ULTACH Trust/The Trust for Ulster People'), a cross-community Irish language agency, promoting 'Ulster Language, Traditions and Cultural Heritage' (ULTACH) throughout Northern Ireland[3] – had earlier attempted to create such a list but had encountered similar problems and had finally given up.

Nevertheless, by compiling a list of all the groups that I had come across, talking to members of numerous projects and further incorporating pre-existing lists of knowledgeable Gaeilgeoirí, a sufficiently broad picture of the local language scene emerged that can be systematized as follows. The first subset of the scene consisted of 'places' (in a broad sense) in which there was a tangible presence of the Irish language. Besides Irish inscriptions on street signs, shops and offices, this type included first and foremost the *Gaeltacht Bóthar Seoighe* (the 'Shaw's Road Gaeltacht'), a small neighbourhood in Andersonstown where sixteen families lived and used Irish as their first language in daily life. This category also incorporated the office building *An Nasc* ('The Connection') on the Falls Road as well as Irish language meeting places such as the Cultúrlann and its café, the bar of the *Cumann Chluain Árd* (the 'Association of Clonard') and the local Irish language restaurant *Cúpla Focal* ('A Few Words').

The second subset was made up of Irish-medium events and activities such as the previously discussed art performances, workshops, choirs and book clubs housed in the Cultúrlann. Additional activities included several after-school and youth clubs like *Club Eachtra* ('Adventure Club') in the Whiterock area, the weekly Irish-medium mass at St Mary's Church in the city centre and a monthly Irish-medium Presbyterian service in South Belfast that was also frequented by some Catholic Gaeilgeoirí from West Belfast.

Companies and voluntary groups providing Irish language products and services formed a third subset of the language scene. In this class fell a variety of projects housed in the Cultúrlann such as the bookshop, the tourist office, the small desk of An Siopa Síol (selling fair trade, organic goods on Saturdays), Raidió Fáilte, the design company Dúch Dúchais, the drama group Aisling Ghéar and the television production company Scannáin Aisling Ghéar, as well as several film production firms that were loosely associated with the Cultúrlann such as *Tobar* (the 'Well') *Productions*. Additional television production companies existed beyond the Cultúrlann like *An Súil Aduaidh* ('The Northern Eye'), which had its office

---

3. For more details on this organization, see ULTACH Trust (2006).

at the local community centre in Conway Mill. Besides the Irish-medium daily *Lá*, which was headquartered in the Cultúrlann before becoming part of the local Andersonstown News Group in 1999 and moving to its facilities, *An Telelann* ('The Tele-Place'), an organization providing, amongst other things, Irish-medium IT courses in the An Nasc office building, also fell in this category.

The fourth subset of the language scene comprised a spectrum of organizations promoting and lobbying for the Irish language in one way or another. The umbrella organization Pobal and the cross-community ULTACH Trust have already been mentioned. Another group was the West Belfast division of *Glór na nGael* ('Voice of the Gael'), an all-Ireland organization furthering the Irish language through a nationwide competition in which the efforts and achievements of local branches of the organization are rewarded.[4] *Forbairt Feirste* ('Belfast Development') put a special emphasis on the development of Irish-medium enterprises and businesses.[5] In the field of party politics, *Roinn Cultuir* (the 'Cultural Department') of Sinn Féin lobbied for the Irish language from a Republican perspective.[6] As a consequence of the Good Friday Agreement of 1998, the North/South state(s) agency Foras na Gaeilge (the 'Irish Language Agency') had funded and advised administrations, public bodies and other groups in the private and voluntary sectors in all matters related to the Irish language since 1999. An equally recent organization was *Comhairle na Gaelscolaíochta* (the 'Council for Irish-medium Education'), which was set up in 2000 by the Department of Education to facilitate and organize Irish-medium education in the North of Ireland in an efficient way.[7] Its board was partly elected by the above-mentioned, Cultúrlann-based Gaeloiliúint ('Irish language training') and by *Altram* ('Fosterage') – both voluntary community groups promoting Irish-medium education in schools and pre-schools, respectively. Closely related to Comhairle na Gaelscolaíochta was *Iontaobhas na Gaelscolaíochta* (the 'Trust Fund for Irish-medium Education'), which financed all-Irish schools as a government-sponsored trust fund. Finally, *Taca* ('Support') raised funds for such schools throughout Northern Ireland through lottery sales, while *Cairde* ('Friends') consisted of people in Catholic West Belfast who directly supported the oldest local primary school, *Bunscoil Phobal Feirste* ('Belfast Community Primary School').

Two remaining subsets of the local language scene were more directly concerned with educational issues. The fifth category entailed various adult Irish language classes. These formally organized classes were run by diverse groups and bodies including the Belfast Institute of Further and Higher Education (BIFHE). They were taught – some free of charge – in numerous places: community centres like the *Ionad Uíbh Eachach* ('Iveagh Centre'), which was mentioned in Chapter 2; local branches of *Conradh na Gaeilge* (the 'Gaelic League') – an all-Ireland organization founded in 1893 with the aim of reviving the Irish language[8] – such as the Cumann

---

4. For more details on this organization, see Glór na nGael (2006).
5. For more details on this organization, see Forbairt Feirste (2006).
6. For an overview of past and current policy proposals for the Irish language, see Sinn Féin (2007).
7. For more details on this organization, see Comhairle na Gaelscolaíochta (2007).
8. For more details on this organization, see Conradh na Gaeilge (2005).

Chluain Árd or the one at Casement Park, the County Antrim home ground of the *Cumann Lúthchleas Gael* (the 'Gaelic Athletic Association, GAA'),[9] other local clubs of the GAA like the Patrick Sarsfield Gaelic Athletic Club in the Lenadoon area; the Cultúrlann as previously described; Irish-medium schools and nurseries catering specifically to parents with children in all-Irish education; some social clubs such as Roddy McCorley's; and informally in some pubs and private homes of language enthusiasts.

The last subset of the local language scene consisted of education in Irish. On the one hand, this entailed pupils learning Irish as a subject in local English-medium schools. On the other hand, this category also included the various local Irish-medium schools, besides third-level education through Irish for future teachers at the local *Coláiste Ollscoile Naomh Muire* ('St Mary's University College'). According to the above-mentioned Council for Irish-medium Education, at the time of my fieldwork in 2003–2004 there were thirteen Irish-medium nursery, primary and secondary schools with a total of 1,349 pupils in Catholic West Belfast alone, as compared to twenty such schools in the whole of Belfast and sixty-nine in all of Northern Ireland (Comhairle na Gaelscolaíochta 2004).[10]

These figures for local pupils at Irish-medium schools – thus notably excluding all pupils learning Irish at local English-medium schools – give some indication of the actual size of the language community in Catholic West Belfast. Generally speaking, however, it is quite difficult to estimate appropriately the number of actual Irish speakers in West Belfast and beyond 'due to the relative paucity of available data', as Mac Giolla Chríost (2005: 170) observes regarding the general dearth of figures for the Irish language in Northern Ireland. The only other source of systematic information for our period of interest is the 2001 Northern Ireland Census, which included a question concerning ability to 'understand, speak, read or write Irish' (Northern Ireland Statistics and Research Agency (NISRA) 2004: 6). According to the census, the whole of Northern Ireland was then inhabited by 1,617,957 people 'aged 3 and over' of which a total of 167,490 claimed to 'have some knowledge of Irish' (i.e. 10.35 per cent). In the local government district of Belfast, this category made up 13.57 per cent of the population (i.e. 36,317 out of the 267,716 city dwellers of the same age set). In Catholic West Belfast – consisting, as defined in Chapter 1, of ten electoral wards, in which more than 80 per cent of the respective ward populations were of a Catholic religious background –15,244 out of 55,008 local residents aged three and above indicated some knowledge of Irish. With more than 15,000 locals – i.e. 27.71 per cent of the population – claiming to know some Irish, Catholic West Belfast had one of the densest concentrations

---

9. For more details on this organization, see Gaelic Athletic Association (2008b).
10. These thirteen schools consisted of six nursery schools: *Naíscoil an Damba* (9 pupils), *Naíscoil an Lonnáin* (21 pupils), *Naíscoil an tSléibhe Dhuibh* (45 pupils), *Naíscoil Bhreandáin* (90 pupils), *Naíscoil na bhFál* (40 pupils) and *Naíscoil na Móna* (14 pupils); six primary schools: *Bunscoil an tSléibhe Dhuibh* (172 pupils), *Bunscoil Phobal Feirste* (301 pupils), *Gaelscoil an Lonnáin* (23 pupils), *Gaelscoil na bhFál* (192 pupils), *Gaelscoil na Móna* (19 pupils) and *Gaelscoil an Damba* (17 pupils); and one secondary school: *Meánscoil Feirste* (406 pupils). For further details, see Comhairle na Gaelscolaíochta (2004).

of Irish speakers in the whole of the North of Ireland (see also Mac Giolla Chríost 2005: 140).[11]

These figures must also be put in perspective. What Nic Craith observes with regard to the 1991 Northern Ireland Census (in which, after a vigorous campaign, a question regarding the Irish language reappeared after a eighty-year hiatus and for the first time since the foundation of the Northern Irish state (Mac Póilin 1997c: 183; Nic Craith 1999: 496–97) is also valid for the 2001 data: individual perceptions of personal language competence vary quite considerably, especially in response to questions involving vague categories like 'understanding, speaking, reading or writing', thus making it difficult to evaluate the overall response adequately. Furthermore, conscious or unconscious attitudes towards a language may 'interfere with the legitimacy of self-ascription', thereby potentially leading to a downplayed or exaggerated self-assessment (Nic Craith 1999: 496).

Similar reservations concerning the adequacy of the 2001 census figures were also made by local Gaeilgeoirí. Some of my interlocutors doubted that 15,000 locals actually had 'some knowledge of Irish' extending beyond the mere *cúpla focal* ('a few words'), and argued that this figure really indicated a positive attitude towards Irish and strong identification with the language regardless of the actual competence. Others strongly objected to such doubts and argued that questioning the census figures for Irish speakers was but another assault on the language. While I believe that the number of Irish speakers in Catholic West Belfast actually was lower than the proclaimed 15,000 locals, this does not change the fact that the Irish language had indeed experienced a considerable local revival from the near extinction and 'parlous condition of the language sometime around the middle of this (i.e. the twentieth) century' through 'its regeneration in the 1960s and subsequent growth', even though the Irish-speaking minority in Northern Ireland, while growing, will surely remain 'small in size and fragmented in its geographic distribution for the foreseeable future' (Mac Giolla Chríost 2005: 134, 170). It is one of the central aims of this book to explain this relative growth of the Irish language community through focusing exclusively on the involved Irish learners and speakers, and scrutinizing the significance that the language came to acquire for them, rather than to argue that the significance of the language for the identity of the Irish *as a whole* has depended on an increase in the number of its actual speakers. As mentioned in Chapter 1, an investigation of the meanings of the Irish language, or of Irishness in general, for Irish people who do *not* speak the language clearly lies beyond the scope of this study.

However, another important issue regarding the actual numbers of Irish speakers in Catholic West Belfast needs to be mentioned as well: grossly deviating estimates by local Gaeilgeoirí of the numbers of 'fluent', 'largely competent' and 'basic Irish speakers' in Catholic West Belfast, which mirrored their differences in evaluating the census figures, cannot be explained only by the discussed difficulties inherent in assessing the actual extent of local language practices. Instead, these discrepancies

---

11. These rates are based on the Northern Ireland Statistics and Research Agency (NISRA) 2006: Table KS24 ('Knowledge of Irish'), various levels.

also seemed to reflect crucial differences in local conceptions about what it meant to 'speak Irish' in the first place and hence about what type of communicative practice actually counted as 'speaking Irish'. In other words, locals not only disagreed about actual language practice but also about representations of the Irish language – an observation that highlights, again, the need to explore the various interrelations between local representations and practices of the Irish language.

Chapter 4
Becoming a Gaeilgeoir

The last chapter provided an initial picture of the Irish language scene in Catholic West Belfast at the beginning of the twenty-first century by characterizing the major domains of its organized and institutional presence, indicating its approximate size and describing the exemplary Cultúrlann McAdam Ó Fiaich as one of the central Irish language enclaves in a predominantly English-speaking environment. Yet who were the actors that moved within this scene? How and why did they become involved with the Irish language community? What were their experiences in the community? What did the language come to mean for them? How did their involvement in the community impact their lives?

This chapter provides some answers to these and other questions by reconstructing the range of ways in which some local Gaeilgeoirí became Irish learners and speakers. By following the trajectories of several individuals into the Irish language, this chapter aims to present a vivid image of the heterogeneous, divergent and changing circumstances under which the acquisition of Irish in Catholic West Belfast has transpired over the past few decades. The different intersecting conditions, processes and meanings that emerge from these biographies will subsequently be contextualized, systematized and refocused in the following two chapters.

The material for the biographies I reconstruct in this chapter stems from extensive formal interviews and informal conversations with my twenty-eight key informants. The process through which I developed rapport with and selected these particular local Gaeilgeoirí as key informants has already been described in Chapter 2. Here, it suffices to say that although my informants were not randomly selected, they were nevertheless chosen with a view of achieving a spectrum of ages, genders and degrees of involvement with the Irish language (either as 'activists' or as 'participants') in order to maximize diversity. Likewise, maximization of diversity in actual trajectories of becoming a Gaeilgeoir was the main reason I selected the ten biographies for this chapter.

The group of Gaeilgeoirí I deal with in this chapter was comprised equally of activists and participants in language activities. I present the stories of six men (three activists and three participants) and four women (two activists and two participants). In terms of age, this group covered a broad range, with the oldest informant being over sixty and the youngest seventeen at the time of my fieldwork. The following stories are retold in the order of informant age, with the oldest informant presented first.

As space limitations have forced me to exclude much of my material, I have deliberately left out details both on informants' lives and the contexts of our encounters. This exclusion is regrettable from a methodological perspective since it reduces the potential for the reader to evaluate the process of source criticism that was realized during the production and analysis of the data leading to what I believe to be sufficiently plausible reconstructions of 'actually lived lives'. Yet this omission is necessary and desirable in order to ensure as much anonymity as possible for my informants, to whom I have also assigned pseudonyms.

When constructing the respective ten narrative accounts of how my informants became Gaeilgeoirí, I have used many direct quotes in order to maintain as much as possible of the original tone, retaining the vernacular phrasings and ambiguities of my informants. Correspondingly, quotations are only slightly edited in the case of interrupted statements. Within quotations, noticeable breaks in speech are indicated with dashes ('–'); words that were clearly emphasized by interviewees are underlined and my own clarifications within quotations are put in square brackets ('[ ]').

Roibeárd, age 63

I met Roibeárd at the *Cumann Chluain Árd* ('Association of Clonard'), a local branch of the Gaelic League in Catholic West Belfast, where he was and had been for several decades one of the dominant figures. During numerous informal conversations and over the course of nine semi-structured interviews, I developed the following image of his trajectory into the Irish language.

Born in the early 1940s in Belfast, Roibeárd seemed to have always had some Irish around him. As he put it:

> I cannot remember not having been in contact with the Irish language. Since I was small, people who could speak Irish were pointed out to you and revered. And most people around me had gone to an Irish language class. My elder sisters were studying Irish as well. And my mother had been to Irish language classes. And I knew from an early age that my great-grandmother couldn't speak English. So there wasn't any period in time when I wasn't aware of the Irish language. And again – as a boy, we were interested in [Gaelic] football, and we were interested in the football results, and quite a lot of the time on Radio Éireann [the public radio service of the Irish state in the South], you would hear greetings in Irish before and a farewell in Irish afterwards. … We would learn these up; I would have known these up by heart.

Roibeárd thus grew up in a family that itself illustrated that Irish as the historical language of the people had only recently been supplanted with English. He thereby recalled growing up in an environment in which the 'two national goals of the unification and the restoration of the Irish language' were things that 'just everybody all around' and surely his mother wanted and that he came to want as well, even if he never consciously gave it a thought.

While Roibeárd was not exposed to Irish in primary school, he studied Irish at the Catholic grammar school in North Belfast he attended in the early 1950s.

As Roibeárd recollected, however, his Irish classes at the grammar school did not cover spoken Irish, the curriculum being comprised only of what Roibeárd derisively called 'comparative philology', by which he meant the comparison of Irish with English through Latin. When Roibeárd left this grammar school for a technical college run by the Christian Brothers, his opportunities to learn Irish significantly improved. He began to study with an Irish teacher who 'said he was teaching us Irish not to pass exams, but as a language of the people'. After only one year of the class, much to the delight of the pupils, the teacher was communicating with his students exclusively in Irish. Roibeárd realized that language teaching centred on spoken Irish made all the difference. He was impressed by his teacher, who depicted speaking Irish as an act of patriotism:

> He said that the greatest thing we could do for our country was to learn its language and speak it. He thought that was a great act of patriotism. And you've got to remember that in those times the IRA had just started another campaign … . And we were young people who could be very impressed by these things. … He certainly wanted us to think about it: do we live for Ireland or die for it?

During the first summer holidays at the technical college, Roibeárd travelled for the first time to a *Gaeltacht* (i.e. an Irish-speaking area) in Donegal where he attended an Irish-language college in *Mín an Chladaigh* (Meenaclady) for four weeks. The trip was organized by his school in Belfast, which covered half of the costs, and many of his classmates joined in as well. Because the primary purpose of the trip was to allow students to learn Irish in a natural environment, class instruction was only of minor significance:

> You went to the little school in the morning, but most of time you were left to your own devices, which meant that you got to know the local people very much, you know. And you helped them in works, sort of like bringing in turf and things like that. And <u>they</u> believed, as <u>we</u> believed, that we were there to learn Irish. And they taught us. You know, it wasn't like a holiday camp that you have nowadays.

Upon coming back to Belfast from the Gaeltacht college to which he would return during two subsequent summer holidays in the mid-1950s, he and his classmates began to attend extracurricular Irish language classes. These classes took place at the *Árdscoil* ('High school') – the Gaelic League headquarters in Belfast – which offered additional events such as *céilí* dancing (a particular type of Irish dancing). Since Roibeárd and his friends had learned such dances at the Gaeltacht college, they started to attend céilí nights at the Árdscoil and other places like St Paul's Hall in West Belfast.

At this point, another aspect in Roibeárd's life became important in shaping his path to becoming a Gaeilgeoir, namely, his involvement with Gaelic games. One of his uncles had been a founding member of a local club of the Gaelic

Athletic Association (GAA) in Belfast, where Roibeárd started playing Gaelic football at the age of thirteen or fourteen. As he remembered, a lot of people in the club spoke Irish, and the language was present in other ways as well:

> The correspondence to you would have been in Irish, telling you about a game. It was in Irish, but the time and the place where the game was to be, and the date would have been in English. So that you knew what it was all about. And they had Irish classes in the club. My mother went to those. I suppose I did as well. They used to teach Irish twice a week.

Roibeárd also began to frequent the *Rann na Feirste* (Rannafast) Gaeltacht in western Donegal, accompanying a football friend from this GAA club whose father was a native Irish speaker from that area. Yet when he went to Rannafast, he never attended an Irish college again. Instead, he enjoyed playing Gaelic football with locals of his age who would gather and play each evening. By then, Roibeárd already played football for his county's (Antrim) under-18 team and would later play for its senior team, the highest level one can reach as a player of Gaelic games in Ireland. Locals in Rannafast were thus quite keen to get Roibeárd playing for their local GAA club under an assumed name – a necessity, given that he officially played for a Belfast club already. Roibeárd agreed to do so, and for about the next five years, he played for both clubs. Even after the local team in Rannafast fell apart, for years Roibeárd continued to commute from Belfast to this Gaeltacht during holidays and on weekends, as the locals had come to regard him almost like one of their own:

> He [i.e. Roibeárd's friend] was with me most of the time. Now his father is from Rannafast. Which meant that he was accepted as being a local, okay? I was accepted as a local because I played for the local team. Now that opened all the doors! You know, that meant that there wasn't a <u>house</u> in Rannafast that I couldn't go into and wouldn't be welcomed. Okay? Now my friend's father, I would ask him: 'Where's the best stories? Where's the best music? Where's the best of the tradition?' And he would tell where to go. Now, and I went to these houses and I was welcomed.

Roibeárd developed an interest in stories, music and tradition in Irish, which he started tape-recording from old people in Rannafast. Bringing his tapes home to Belfast, he would then listen 'to Irish as spoken <u>correctly</u>; and listen to songs that were sung <u>correctly</u>'. As Roibeárd insisted during our interviews, both playing for the local GAA club and his recordings of songs and stories in Rannafast were motivated by his wish to learn Irish properly, as it was spoken by native speakers in the Gaeltacht, rather than by an interest in Irish sports or folklore as such. As he put it: 'Well, I realized that Irish is a living language, was living there; wasn't living anywhere <u>else</u>. And, you know, to try and become part of that. To improve, that's why I went there in the first place.'

During his late teenage years, Roibeárd also began to visit the Gaelic League branch Cumann Chluain Árd ('Association of Clonard') in Catholic West Belfast, when a large group of his friends started to frequent the place:

> And we all went and meet. And we discovered then that they had these great recordings, old stories and recording music. And that, what they were at in Cumann Chluain Árd, was <u>exactly</u> what we were trying to do. We felt that we had come across a stepping stone, if you might call it that, or a bridge to the Irish-speaking areas. He [i.e. his friend's father, the Rannafast man] was there. We used to go to his class. And Cluain Árd to us in those days was like a <u>satellite</u>, if I can put it that way, a <u>Sputnik</u> of Donegal, to the Irish-speaking areas of Donegal.

Although already quite fluent, Roibeárd began attending language and literature classes, especially those taught by native speakers. Whilst participating in classes for most of the next ten years, Roibeárd began to teach language classes from 1960 onwards, and continuously did so for the next four decades. Nevertheless, Roibeárd repeatedly emphasized to me that it had been the exclusive use of Irish in all communications in the Cluain Árd rather than the classes themselves (also taught through the 'direct method', i.e. through Irish) that had mattered and still mattered for any successful transmission of Irish from one generation to the next:

> Well, you see, there'd be <u>no</u> <u>English</u>. You see, you weren't learning English. All the discussion, question and answer [in classes and elsewhere], was all done in Irish. That's why Cumann Chluain Árd is successful or has been successful teaching people Irish. Not the classes! The fact that people are there, speaking Irish around you! You never learn Irish in a class. I mean, you have discovered that yourself. You pick it up if you are working in the bar. All those young people, some of them were there [in the Cluain Árd] last night: this time last year, they couldn't speak Irish. Why are they speaking it today? 'Cause there was Irish all around them. People say: Why aren't there thousands in Cluain Árd? There aren't thousands in Cluain Árd because people know that the Irish language is supreme. And that it isn't a drinking club. People go there simply to use their language and hear it spoken. And then <u>because</u> they are there, if anyone wants to learn Irish.

What is interesting in this quote is not only Roibeárd's insistence on the irrelevance of formal teaching and the paramount importance of an all-Irish context, but also his shifting temporal references. From a description of how he experienced the Cluain Árd in the 1960s, he refocused on the current situation with which I was familiar, thereby indicating the club's continuity in putting Irish and Irish only 'all around you'. As he came to be ever more involved in the all-Irish spirit of the Cluain Árd of the late 1950s, Roibeárd and his friends shifted from the Sunday céilí in the Árdscoil to the one in the Cluain Árd because there was very little Irish in the former, whilst the latter was 'all Irish'.

Apart from céilís,[1] classes and informal meetings, Roibeárd and his friends also got involved in language-related political activism at the Cluain Árd, for instance, resisting the *Caighdeán Oifigiúil* ('Official Standard/ization') of Irish introduced in the 1950s by the Irish State in the South of Ireland. The official standard entailed a substitution of the old Irish with Roman script, orthographic changes and modifications to spoken Irish. According to Roibeárd, this last aspect was heavily resisted by Cluain Árd people because it was viewed as 'an attempt to take the Irish language from the people and to impose this other, civil-service-type language'. By contrast, the Cluain Árd wanted to maintain the superiority of Irish as it was spoken in its natural Gaeltacht environment. Language standardization including the new script was rejected in the club and still was when I was in Belfast in 2003–2004.

From the mid-1960s onwards, Roibeárd's life as a Gaeilgeoir began to deepen when he started playing the guitar and composing his own arrangements of the old songs he had recorded and learned in Rannafast. A friend suggested that he should enter the John Player Irish Ballad Competition, one of the prizes for which was an appearance on local television in Northern Ireland. Roibeárd won the competition:

But this was about 1966, '67. And troubles were on the horizon. And the appearance on television, the organizers told me, that couldn't happen. I'd have to sing in English. And I said: 'No'. But one of the adjudicators was from RTÉ [Radio Telefís Éireann, the public television broadcaster in the South]. And they had programmes then on traditional music and songs, and of course I was invited to one or two of those. And I did those on television. … And then I was approached by Gael Linn, the Irish record company, to do an EP, which I did.

Other singles and LPs with songs in Irish followed. Meanwhile, in 1970,

RTÉ asked, would I do a series of thirteen [television] programmes. And I said, 'Alright'. So I did that. And then they asked me, would I like to extend it to twenty-six, the whole winter. And I said, 'Okay'. And I did that for three years. … The programme was in Irish, but the producer and generally all the people working behind the cameras, that was English. But I used Irish only. And I came under great strain to use English. And I refused to do so. I said, no, I wouldn't. But it was very successful. Well, I presented the programme as well as sing. But you also had groups in Ireland then like Clannad who were just about to come starting. You had the Chieftains, who were virtually the one group. They weren't known, but they were becoming fairly big. And you know all these different groups that were coming, they were all on this programme. And that helped to make it a very, very successful programme.

---

1. The word 'céilí' has several meanings, referring to a certain type of Irish dancing, social dance events at which these are performed, as well as to social visits generally (see Chapter 9). The proper plural for the word 'céilí', according to Irish reformed spelling, is 'céilithe'. Yet since the anglicized plural 'céilís' is common in English everyday usage, I use this form herein.

Roibeárd eventually 'got fed up' – as he put it – and then only rarely performed publicly. As he repeatedly told me and as his refusal to sing or speak in anything but Irish on both Northern and Southern television illustrates, his main interest had always been the language rather than the singing. As he said, he was annoyed that people were interested only in melodies and guitar lines, without understanding 'the sophistication' of the language, 'the poetry and how it was phrased': 'I just wasn't prepared to just be a – musician.' Instead, Roibeárd increasingly concentrated on his engagement in the Cumann Chluain Árd. He estimated that he had spent on average five nights each week at the Cumann Chluain Árd since the mid-1970s, speaking and thereby teaching Irish to one and all – and even his dog.

Rónán, age 61

I got to know Rónán at the Cultúrlann, which he regularly frequented. Apart from various informal chats, it was primarily our nine formal interviews that provided me with extensive material concerning Rónán's involvement with the Irish language.

Like Roibeárd, Rónán was born in the early 1940s in Belfast. Yet unlike Roibeárd, Rónán grew up in a family in which the Irish language played no important role. Although some of his older siblings studied Irish in school, they did not speak the language at home. Rónán first was exposed to Irish in the late 1940s at the local parish school he attended. When the pupils were called by their names in the morning roll-call, they were supposed to answer '*anseo*', meaning 'here' in the Irish language. However, Rónán and his friends did not realize that this was actually Irish and mistook it for English because it sounded similar to the two words 'hand' and 'chalk'. Likewise, Rónán remembered how the prayers 'Hail Mary' and 'Our Father' would be said in Irish at the end of the mass, even though the latter was delivered in Latin at the time. Rónán claimed that most children from his generation would have known these prayers in Irish, but 'exactly knowing what you were saying was another thing'. 'You learned it like a rote, you know?'

Thus, while he could, in effect, perform minimal Irish in such contexts, Rónán emphasized that he still did not really become aware of the Irish language at that time. This situation changed when Rónán was fourteen and consciously realized for the first time that there was actually such a thing as the Irish language. This discovery came about when he joined his sister and her husband on a trip to an Irish-speaking area in Donegal, something Rónán did not even know existed beforehand. One brother then suggested that he start learning Irish at the Cumann Chluain Árd, and Rónán ended up going there one night. But he did not see any value in it at all:

> And I went for one night. And never went back again. I guess it sort of struck me then that I was as Irish as anybody. Whether it was very deep or not, I couldn't tell you. But I was about fourteen. You know? Didn't have to know the Irish language to be Irish, you know?

Thereafter, Rónán's teenage years continued without any further Irish, and his whole life might have done so had it not been pure chance that brought him back to the Cluain Árd in the early 1960s. At that point, a close friend of Rónán, who came from a very Irish-minded Republican family, had decided to learn Irish at the Cumann Chluain Árd. However, since he had a bad stutter, he asked Rónán to come along for support, and Rónán agreed. As neither of them had any prior knowledge of Irish, their participation in the evening classes at the Cluain Árd turned out to be quite an experience:

> Well, first of all, they spoke a wee bit of English. Told you, maybe, a wee snippet of English, alright? And then, after that, it was all Irish. So we didn't know what they were talking about – literally. … When they were learning Irish in the Cluain Árd, they always had a storyline. They had this storyline that you got up in the morning, and you pull on your trousers, or whatever it might be. You go to the bathroom. Now, you didn't do your functions. You didn't say, 'I had a whiddle in the pot', or anything. But you washed your face, you washed your ears, and you washed your neck. And then you went out. If you were going to work, you went out and you stood at the bus stop – to get the bus down to work. And that was – there was a thing to introduce you into the story. That was all done through Irish. And a lot of occasions, you were just guessing what they were saying. Just didn't know. So you felt like a – well, we would say you felt like a prune.

It is no wonder that Rónán's friend thus decided not to come back again after the summer break. Rónán, however, did return in September, and within a short period of time became 'part of the furniture'. Initially, he only went twice a week to the Monday and Thursday night sessions. Yet soon he was to join in other activities as well such as the céilí dance class on Tuesday nights and the céilí itself on Sundays. Other nights were rather quiet, with only a few people chatting in Irish and cleaning the place. As Rónán recalled, these were people who were really serious about the language and 'had got the bug'. While they spoke amongst themselves in Irish, Rónán like others did not say much but rather learned by listening. Eventually, Rónán went to the Cluain Árd every night of the week, being 'sucked into this thing':

> I mean, I didn't go out and say, 'Here, I'm going to become a red-hot Irish language speaker', you know? [Rónán chuckles] It's something you sort of drift into, you know? And that's why I'm saying that people you meet, that's so important, you know? And that community aspect, and the, sort of, work ethic among the people who were teaching Irish in those days was unbelievable. … The amount that they put in, and the amount of time they were willing to spend with you, and trying to teach you bits and pieces of Irish, you know? I mean, you could never pay for it. It was an education. Like, they educated me. So I mean, that's bound to have an effect on you. You're bound to see substance in that. They're bound to get a lot of credibility from you, you know? … Now, these were good people. … Their main ambition was to try and revive Irish … Those were very exciting years. You know, I mean, for a young person, even though I

was about nineteen or something. I mean to be with men who were a lot older than I was; you know, the amount of knowledge they had and the sense of humour they had, as well. It wasn't all doom and gloom, like. ... 'Cause you'd céilís, you had classes, you had dances, you went out walking, swimming.

Learning from these people not only to speak Irish but also about their views on the history and relevance of the Irish language for Ireland and his own Irish identity, Rónán experienced an 'awakening, educationally' and a 'real revelation'. Ultimately, Rónán did in fact become a 'red-hot Irish speaker':

It's like a, sort of a – a big bolt of light hitting you. That you've learned about this thing that's been part of your country for thousands of years, but you really didn't know much about it. But when you start to learn, particularly the language itself, you know that there's a history to it. You go back and go back in the history of the persecution, trying to really subvert the language. And then you really become like a real convert. And you're very enthusiastic, maybe that you're near fanatical about it, you know?

During these years in the 1960s when he was heavily involved in the Cluain Árd and began teaching Irish, Rónán believed with others in the club that 'everybody should know Irish' and that Ireland should ultimately become monolingual Irish-speaking. Conversing in the language gave him a 'sense of really being Irish' and a feeling that 'you've went, possibly, the whole way of identifying yourself as Irish'. For a couple of years until the outbreak of the Troubles, this experience made him 'fairly dogmatic', believing that 'to be Irish, you had to have Irish – the Irish language'.

As Rónán recalled, the Irish speaker, writer and leading Republican in the Easter Rising of 1916, Patrick Pearse (Irish: Pádraig Mac Piarais) 'would've been our sort of hero' at that time. However, and contrary to my own expectations, Patrick Pearse was apparently only revered for his radical statements concerning the Irish language, not for his Republicanism. In fact, Rónán repeatedly emphasized that the Cluain Árd was not at all politically Nationalist or Republican in aspiring to a united Ireland because the latter would only be English-speaking anyway. Correspondingly, it was the government in the South rather than the Northern Irish parliament in Stormont that was the target of agitation in the Cluain Árd because 'the twenty-six county government had turned their back on Irish', whereas 'Stormont didn't really figure', as 'Irish didn't come into their reckoning at all'.

Apart from this language activism, there were other, more practical ways in which Rónán started to put his convictions about the Irish language into practice. In 1967, he followed the example of a few Gaeilgeoirí from around the Cluain Árd in officially changing his name. Within Irish-language circles it has long been common informally to use the Irish version of names. For example, one might refer to 'Patrick Pearse' as 'Pádraig Mac Piarais'. However, very few Gaeilgeoirí in West Belfast took the further step of officially adopting the Irish form of their name through the legal act of a deed poll. Rónán emphasized that he thought 'long and hard' about this decision and 'wasn't going to be stupid about it'. At the time, he worked as a joiner alongside predominantly Protestant co-workers in a mixed environment, and he was well aware that changing his name might invite trouble. On the other hand, Rónán was about to get married to a Gaeilgeoir he had met at the Cluain Árd, and 'if you did the change before you got married – well, it meant that when you had family that they were going to be known by that name'. Eventually, Rónán decided in favour of the change, given that living his life through the medium of Irish had become a priority, rather than just speaking it now and again.

Establishing a position in which Irish would be the language of his family became the next step in 1967 when Rónán and his newly-wed wife, Ailís, got involved with an attempt to found a small Irish-speaking community in West Belfast. As Rónán recalled, this project 'was well under way by the time we'd come in'. A number of married couples who were slightly older than Rónán and Ailís had been developing an idea from the early 1960s to have an urban Gaeltacht in which the common language would be Irish. Despite some broader interest within Belfast's Irish-language circles, only five couples – including Rónán and an older brother and sister with their respective spouses – went ahead with the plan. Using a company to facilitate the necessary legal procedures, they took out a loan to buy a parcel of former farmland located at Shaw's Road. With the support of the wider Irish-speaking community, the five couples got approval for the project and started building their row of five terraced houses in early 1968. Rónán recalled, 'I went up and marked out the foundations'. The first family moved in around Easter of 1969, and the other four families followed during the same year. Another row of three terraced houses was added in the next two to three years. However, Rónán and other Gaeilgeoirí from the community did not really help in this round of construction because they were by then involved with rebuilding Bombay Street.

In the summer of 1969, the Troubles started. In the Clonard district of West Belfast, a mob burned down large sections of Bombay Street, which is near the Cluain Árd in a Catholic area adjoining a Protestant area. As Rónán remembered, after this and several other incidents, Irish speakers began thinking about how to respond. They came up with the idea of renovating Bombay Street because by this point they had experience in building construction, and they thus thought 'it was a practical thing to do' and a way of giving 'confidence back to our community'. After the decision was made, the former residents and owners had to be located, which was not easy given that there were 'thousands' of refugees living in halls, schools – 'everywhere'. Once the group had secured the consent of the neighbourhood's former residents, it began construction. Rónán abruptly left his job in order to head up the rebuilding process, which ultimately lasted from 1969 to 1972.

As Rónán repeatedly told me, the events surrounding the outbreak of the Troubles in 1969 deeply affected his attitudes towards the Irish language in general and its decisive role in drawing a line between 'us' and 'them' in particular:

We might've been separated from our own community by then, the fact that we're Irish speakers, right? That was very – our – like a tunnel vision. That's the way we were going. People who hadn't got Irish might've been – we might've thought, maybe, they weren't Irish. When '69 happened, that went out the window.

Rónán realized:

that you were part of a wider community. You were very insular, within the community. We were living in the Cluain Árd, and then, when the terrible things of '69 happened, we found we were really – that at the end of the day, we're part of a wider community; and had cut ourselves off, slightly.

According to Rónán, this recognition was a good thing because 'if you thought that you were something special because you knew Irish', it became quite evident that there were 'more things important in life', and that 'it's just not all black and white'. While continuing to live and expand his life through Irish, Rónán departed from his earlier uncompromising views and consciously reopened himself to his wider Catholic community.

At the time of the restoration of Bombay Street, the Shaw's Road community was making progress in expanding the use of Irish into the realm of education. From late 1970 onwards, all of the families regularly got together to plan the 1971 opening of their own all-Irish *Bunscoil Phobal Feirste* ('Belfast Community Primary School'). This urban Gaeltacht had long planned to set up an Irish-medium school, and although Rónán had not been involved in the early stages, apparently exploratory talks with the Department of Education (DENI) had already taken place, in the course of which such a step was depicted as illegal. However, when it actually came to the establishment of the bunscoil, there was little threat of prosecution by DENI 'because of the Troubles all around us; we were a minor factor'.

In 1971, the first nine pupils began to attend the then still unrecognized and unfunded school, which was housed in a prefabricated building. From the very beginning, the entire community was involved in one way or another. People sold homemade products and organized benefit céilís to raise funds for the school. In addition, the building had to be looked after and cleaned. After two years, external teachers were reluctant to work at the school because of the political situation, and education had to be taken over by community members. Three women from the community had been trained as teachers and ended up teaching voluntarily in the school for years after. Rónán emphasized, 'the women were the backbone' of the whole school. In 1978, another female member of the community – which had grown to encompass a total of eleven families by the mid-1970s – opened an affiliated Irish-medium nursery as a language immersion setting for future bunscoil pupils from the wider English-speaking environment. Gaeltacht members continued to negotiate with and lobby the Department of Education for official recognition and state funding, which they eventually obtained in 1984.

Mairéad, age 58

I met Mairéad recurrently at both the Cultúrlann and the Cumann Chluain Árd. The following reconstruction of the process through which Mairéad became a Gaeilgeoir is largely based on our series of five semi-structured interviews.

Born in the mid-1940s in Belfast, Mairéad only learnt basic Irish phrases in her family, even though her father was actually fluent in the language:

> Initially, I was introduced to the Irish language by my father who was a fluent Gaelic speaker. But we weren't brought up speaking Gaelic because my mother wasn't a Gaelic speaker, although she did have a 'cúpla focal', which is 'a few words'. So we were familiar around basic Irish in the house. And then when we went to school at primary level, we had a little Gaelic. We learnt how to say prayers, and a few songs, a few words. But that was all because, as I said to you before, it wasn't on the curriculum. So you were just lucky to get a teacher who had an interest in the Gaelic language, and she would have maybe taught you a few little words.

As Mairéad recalled from primary school, there was a very small minority of teachers who were 'kind of Republican' and had an interest in the Irish language – or 'Gaelic' as Mairéad (and some others) referred to it. Although the language was thereby represented as 'our own native language', Mairéad could not actually remember any concrete words 'ever being said, any form of really, indoctrination. I have never ever kind of felt that I was totally indoctrinated in anything other than Catholicism'.

Coming from a strongly Republican family herself, Mairéad explained that from a very young age she would have been aware of Gaelic, politics, 'and the close association of the language and politics'. So when Mairéad entered secondary education at the age of eleven and had the choice to take either French or Irish, she chose Irish because, she claimed, even by that age she already regarded Irish as 'my own native language and I wanted to speak it and be aware of it'. Throughout her secondary education, Mairéad continued studying Irish and sat her junior and senior exams (equivalent to the current GCSE and A-Level respectively) for Irish.

When she was in secondary school in the late 1950s and early 1960s, Mairéad attended the Donegal Gaeltacht twice to learn Irish. The first time, around Easter, she spent a week at the *Rann na Feirste* (Rannafast) Gaeltacht in western Donegal, where her group was hosted by a local family. Mairéad remembered how being in Donegal for the first time 'was a whole new experience for me staying in this cottage' as she partook in a daily routine that was 'so very different from the city life'. The second trip took Mairéad as part of the same group to the *Gort an Choirce* (Gortahork) Gaeltacht in northern Donegal for one month in the summer. There she was hosted by a local Irish-speaking family and attended a Gaeltacht College:

> We attended the college every day and had classes in Gaelic. And then we had lunch break, and then we came back to the college in the afternoon. And you had classes again. And you may have had, you know, some

singing classes or you know. And then in the evening, you had evening events. … There would have been some form, some kind of entertainment – where you got together for concerts or céilís or talks by people.

Although being away from home and mixing with other people was 'a lovely experience', Mairéad did not attend any further summer schools, as she had become heavily involved with playing tennis. As she put it, whether or not one attended a Gaeltacht college 'just depended on your circumstances'.

In a way, it seems to have been contingent circumstances as well that first prevented Mairéad from continuing with Irish after leaving school and later brought her back to the language in the early 1970s. When Mairéad was training to be a teacher in the mid-1960s, her Gaelic went on hold because 'there was no Gaelic ethos whatsoever' at the college of physical education she attended. In her experience, it was not a place where 'Catholics were really accepted or your heritage or your culture'. Mairéad came back to the Irish language in the early 1970s through attending an evening class run by a local GAA club:

> It was only circumstances. It was just that, you know, you got married and then we had the baby. And also there was probably, more Gaelic classes were beginning to open up then as well, you know, in the seventies. And that may have been related to the struggle that was going on, the struggle for our own identity and our own land, our own language, our own self-determination. You know, it was. But I'd always had that interest anyway. So I can't genuinely say that that was the reason why I went back. The time was right for me to go to class.

After attending the GAA class for two years, Mairéad switched to another night class offered at a local Christian Brothers' grammar school. This time, she was joined by her husband, who only knew a 'cúpla focal', but who was determined to learn and speak Irish:

> My husband was also encouraged by my father. This is why my father enabled us to go, and he came and babysat. But that class didn't last for very long. I think it may just have lasted for six months. And it stopped running, because at that particular time, that was of course after the Troubles started, at the early days of the Troubles, and it was so dangerous, you know, to travel, and people were afraid of going out at night. And there were raids and riots and things. So they cancelled the class. And that is why that stopped.

Again, some years passed by before Mairéad and her husband came back to the language in the late 1970s. This time they went to the Cumann Chluain Árd, which was 'a very vibrant place to learn Gaelic', offering 'about three or maybe four classes' at different levels throughout the week. While Mairéad enjoyed these classes, she stopped attending after two years, as she was expecting her third baby and was quite ill: 'so you can see the learning of the language was very piecemeal'. Another bit of learning Irish consisted of a class that Mairéad attended for one year in the mid-1980s. Initially, the class was held at a local parish hall but later had to move to a private house. The relocation was necessitated when the teacher – a Sinn Féin activist – encouraged participants to assist in an ongoing campaign of illegally erecting bilingual street signs in Catholic West Belfast and the priest subsequently cancelled all Irish classes at the hall.

In the mid-1990s, when Mairéad returned to the language, it was once more 'nearly like starting over again'. Yet this time things were different: Mairéad had retired and hence persisted in her study for the better part of the next decade. By the time I met her in 2003, Mairéad had attended day classes, night classes and intensive courses in a number of venues: the Cultúrlann; community centres like the Ionad Uíbh Eachach; social clubs like the Republican 'Felons'; and Gaelic League branches like the Cumann Chluain Árd and another at the GAA County Antrim headquarters and home ground, Casement Park. It was at Casement Park that Mairéad was first asked and consented to teach an Irish night class in 2000.

Personally, Mairéad felt that Irish was a very 'poetic' and 'gentle' language, which had enhanced her life and added 'an extra dimension to your person; it gives you a better understanding of who you are and where you've come from'. Because of the political situation in the North of Ireland, for Mairéad the language was 'almost like an act of defiance':

> Gaelic is just part of the struggle for your own identity, I would probably say. … I think it's all intertwined, the language, the music, the poetry; everything, the armed struggle. I really can't differentiate between it, as in a fight for your own identity.

Micheál, age 55

The following characterization of Micheál is based on a series of five extensive interviews. Micheál worked as a full-time activist for a local Irish-language organization, and we first met at a function at the Cultúrlann, which he frequented from time to time.

A Belfast man born in the late 1940s, Micheál was in contact with the Irish language from an early age, as his mother was a fluent Irish speaker and 'very keen on it', and his father was what is locally called a 'hardy annual', that is to say 'an enthusiastic Irish learner, who never learnt it' because – a little bit like a hardy-annual plant – he returned annually at the beginning of the class cycle in September but then always dropped out after a couple of weeks. Within his family, Irish was thus not really the language of the house. Nevertheless, 'there were a number of phrases that we only ever used in Irish':

> '*Oíche mhaith*' ['good night'] and '*codladh sámh*', which is 'a sound sleep'. And at the table, there was a rule that you couldn't ask for anything at the table, except in Irish: '*Cuir chugam an siúcra*', 'Pass me the sugar'. 'Pass me

the milk'. But the rest of the conversation was in English. … '*Cuir chugam na prátaí*' ['pass me the potatoes'] or '*tabhair dom*' ['pass me', in Ulster Irish]. '*Cuir chugam*' – my mother was from the South, you see, so she used '*cuir chugam*' as the southern version of 'pass me'. And 'hurry up' in Ulster Irish is '*déan deifir*', but we always said '*brostaigh ort*', which is the Munster version of it. Because that was what she had, and my father didn't know any different. And when we said the rosary at night, we would always say one decade in Irish. It was a symbolic thing, you know.

Micheál's parents also taught him and his siblings the words of the Irish national anthem, '*Amhrán na bhFiann*' ('A Soldier's Song'). They evidently held the language in high regard and actively encouraged him and his siblings to learn Irish at school. The language thereby seems to have been explicitly linked to questions of identity:

What my parents would have said was, 'We are Irish; this is our language.' They would have subscribed, agreed with the ideals of the language revival [of the Gaelic League] that the survival of the language was necessary for Ireland to survive as a nation.

This subscription also manifested itself in his parents' choice of primary school for Micheál:

I mean, I lived three miles away from the school. And one of the reasons I was sent to that school was because it was a Christian Brothers' school, and at the Christian Brothers' school I would be exposed to Irish, whereas at some of the other schools, I wouldn't. … I think I was the only boy on the street who went to that school.

However, although this primary school had 'a strong Irish tradition' Micheál actually learnt very little Irish there, most of his study being focused on instructional language like 'close the door'. The morning roll-call was also meant to incorporate some Irish, yet Micheál and his friends did not realize for years that they were supposed to answer with the Irish word '*anseo*' ('here'), but – as was the case with Rónán – said 'hand chalk' instead.

During the summer of 1960, before entering a local grammar school also run by the Christian Brothers, Micheál was sent to his first Irish-language summer school. During two further summer holidays in the mid-1960s, Micheál went to another Irish-language college in the Donegal Gaeltacht of *Gaoth Dobhair* (Gweedore), which pupils from Micheál's grammar school could attend at a reduced fee, when regularly attending a weekly Irish-language club at his grammar school in Belfast. At grammar school, Micheál had Irish as a regular subject from his first to fifth year. Afterwards, pupils like Micheál who chose to specialize in science could no longer study Irish in school. However, as Micheál emphasized, he would not have taken it anyway, partly because the Irish language increasingly came to be associated with very old-fashioned, turn of the century ideas about Irishness:

> This was the Sixties. Now, the school was still the Christian Brothers' school. There were more than seventy teachers in the school, and of those, twenty-two were Christian Brothers. And all the Christian Brothers, with one or two exceptions, were very, very keen on Irish. So it was part of the school atmosphere. But the atmosphere was changing among the students because this was the Sixties, and Irish was beginning to look like something that was very old-fashioned, that belonged to your parents' generation and to authority. It wasn't fashionable among the students. But most of the students would have approved of it. … In that it was, you know, 'our native language'.

As the last sentence indicates and as Micheál further elaborated, there seems to have been a strange ambivalence within Catholic West Belfast throughout the 1960s: while in theory people were in favour of the language and respected people who had taken the trouble to learn it, Irish speakers were nevertheless viewed 'as being a bit odd'. Thus when Micheál regained his interest in the language and started seriously studying it in 1968, he was considered to be fairly unusual.

Micheál had discovered Anglo-Irish literature, which he began to read extensively. He was fascinated and really impressed by it, because in contrast to English literature it reflected both his experience and the linguistic atmosphere that he had come from:

> Frank O'Connor and James Joyce, for example, wrote about, sort of, crisis of faith of Irish Catholics. And I was doing my crisis of faith at that time. They wrote about petty bourgeois and working class, urban society, which is what my experience was. … Just, the language spoke to me in a way that no other reading had. … There was a Gaelic substratum that was running through their writing style that made it different and was actually closer to my own voice. That they were writing in a way that I would like to be able to speak or in a way that echoed my own experiences. They would use phrases, they would use turns of phrase, rhythms and sometimes vocabulary that were different from anything else I'd read in the English language. … I wouldn't have used the word 'substratum' at the time, but I knew that the flavour of the way that they wrote had come from Irish.

Thus deciding to learn Irish in order to better understand this literature, Micheál started frequenting the Cumann Chluain Árd. He had already been in contact with the Cluain Árd through its Sunday céilís, but in 1968 he began to attend night classes on Mondays and Thursdays as well as 'the musical night' on Fridays: 'The language was quite natural around you'. Yet although he frequented Cluain Árd for more than two years, Micheál was not getting very far:

I hadn't made the breakthrough to fluency. I wasn't studying very hard either. I was going to classes, but I wasn't sort of taking homework home with me. And my father told me the secret of learning Irish – which is that, he said, you need to drop everything for a year. The reason he had not learned Irish was that he had been too busy with other things. And to learn Irish, and this is how he put it, 'You drop everything for a year or so, until you get over the hump.'

In principle, this is what Micheál did. He left his job in Belfast in 1971 and went to live in a Donegal Gaeltacht for three months. There, he worked hard and spent a lot of time talking to people until he made the breakthrough and got to a point where he could speak 'fluent bad Irish'. He subsequently passed his A-Level in Irish before attending the new Irish Studies course at the University of Ulster in Coleraine.

Micheál claimed that his decision to live in the Gaeltacht in order to become fluent in Irish was motivated by his ultimate interest in Anglo-Irish literature. However, once he got over the hump, his perspective began to change:

Once I'd sort of gotten inside the skin of the language, it began to mean more to me than Anglo-Irish literature because it was speaking to me louder than Anglo-Irish literature. That discovery of a voice that meant something to me through Anglo-Irish literature was even stronger through Irish literature; that in some way that I can't understand, my second language was closer to some part of my emotional life than my first language. And I – I still can't explain it. But – the language got a grip on me, of itself. And the value – some inherent value in the language began to assume more and more importance.

Micheál felt confronted by the fact that the language was going to live or die in his generation, so he had a choice of either becoming an activist or merely becoming accomplished in the language, only to watch it die in his own lifetime: 'It was not a particularly pleasant dilemma'. During this time, the Troubles broke out. According to Micheál, the eruption of violence raised local awareness of questions of identity and what it meant to be Irish. All of a sudden, 'the questions that I've been struggling with, or working, engaging with for different reasons actually became central to the society'. As Micheál told me, the Irish language provided a 'very simple answer' to such questions: 'On a personal level, and that's just speaking about myself, it solves some problems to be involved in activities that are very clearly identifiable markers. So that one solution to a dilemma, "What does it mean to be Irish?" – one possible solution to that dilemma is to learn the language and speak the language.'

The Troubles sent Micheál even more towards the cultural as opposed to the political end of Irishness. As Micheál recalled, the early Seventies was a 'truly ghastly period' in which his society 'was collapsing into barbarism'. During this horrible time, there was no political activity that had anything to offer for him, but he would have felt uncomfortable not doing anything at all. Micheál thus became deeply involved in cultural issues. He decided to become a language activist, resisting the forces of Anglicization so that the language would continue for another generation. After officially changing his name to its Irish form (as Rónán and others also did), Micheál and his family moved to the Shaw's Road Gaeltacht. He became heavily involved with running and campaigning for the Irish-medium primary school located in this urban Gaeltacht, while his wife was the driving force behind setting up the affiliated language-immersion preschool. At the same time, Micheál worked for years as an Irish teacher in a local English-medium grammar school before shifting his professional life towards full-time activism, working for a local Irish-language organization.

Looking back over his personal development as an Irish speaker, Micheál conjectured that although his identity had historically developed out of 'a Nationalist cultural revival', for him it had 'transcended that' and had 'gotten much, much bigger' because – as he said – 'at this stage in my life, I rejected most of the arguments of the cultural revival':

> There were three, if you like, main tropes [in Nationalist ideology]. One was the cultural continuity and the shame of allowing something of value to die. I find that still valid. The other one was that the Irish nation, it was connected to the fight for Irish independence and the need for a distinctive culture in order to maintain a distinctive polity. And the third one was the notion that the language was deeply implicated in a specifically Catholic worldview. I rejected the specifically Catholic worldview because I can do the Irish language without having it. I haven't rejected the Nationalist one, but I see it as something entirely different to the cultural argument. Because that particular argument was based on a notion of nation-statism. That has now become irrelevant [in the context of the European Union with its diminished importance of nation-states].

While thus insisting that of all those arguments, only the position supporting cultural continuity is still highly relevant today, Micheál's language activism was characterized by an explicit attempt to put the language above everything else:

> One of the things that I have been trying to do, one that I really believe in, is this idea of bringing the Irish language to Unionists in their terms. Not my terms, in their terms. Where I could come to Unionists, and I would sort of say: 'You don't have to take on my baggage. You don't have to take on my ideology. You don't have to take on anything. But this language, this is an <u>important</u> thing. There's a culture here that you're denying yourself because you think it is tied in with a political agenda. And I'm coming to you, and I'm saying it doesn't have to be. Historically, it has been. But it doesn't have to be. Because there's nothing essentially Unionist or Nationalist or anything about this language. This is a cultural artefact. History. Tradition. Whatever it is. And you can engage with it, and I want

you to engage with it in your own terms. Not under me. You don't have to buy my values. And I went to these people and said, 'I am a Nationalist, but the language is bigger than that.'

Dónal, age 49

I first met Dónal just after my arrival in 2003 at a one-week Irish-language course in Belfast. Afterwards, in various informal conversations at the Cultúrlann and especially during our five extensive formal interviews, I obtained the material basis for the following reconstructions.

Born in the mid-1950s in Belfast, Dónal grew up in a home in which both the Irish language and pronounced esteem for 'Irish culture' were markedly absent:

> I wouldn't have been brought up with the kind of romanticism a lot of people might have been brought up with of Irishness. You know, of the Irish language, of the Irish culture and so on. We had very little of that in the house, at home. ... We would never have had any Irish at all, any singing or any speaking, in the house. Nothing, nothing particularly Irish in our house.

It was only when Dónal started attending a Catholic grammar school in the mid-1960s, where Irish was a compulsory subject, that he was introduced to the language. The grammar school also provided Dónal with an opportunity to attend a Gaeltacht college in *Teileann* (Teelin), Donegal, after his first year. Through the school system, as Dónal recalled:

> The Irish government used to offer a grant to pupils who wanted to study Irish in the Gaeltacht. So I went for the grant and I succeeded. And, you know, it was then only eleven pounds in those days to send you off for nearly a month, everything paid for a month. From my father's point of view, you know, cost-effectively [Dónal laughs], it was cheaper to send me off for a month's holiday than to keep me at home and feed me. ... And I was getting a holiday. And I was getting the Irish language as well. And that's when I fell in love with the language. ... I loved the language, the dancing, the singing, the camaraderie. There's a small group of people, and you got to know everybody quite quickly. And the programmes were very packed with both entertainment, sports and language, and that made it much more interesting. ... It was such a wonderfully pleasant experience, and coming out of, you know, West Belfast, I really hadn't had that much experience of the country or Donegal, you know. And to be introduced to all the beauty! And so there was a kind of romantic feeling instilled in me. Or stirred in me, if you like, for that whole experience.

While his thereby instilled 'great love of the language and the music particularly' made Dónal return the following summers in the late 1960s, the emerging political situation back in Belfast eventually put an untimely end to these formative Gaeltacht trips:

> I went three summers in a row when I was twelve, thirteen, fourteen. It was a fantastic time; each of those times was absolutely wonderful. And I really only stopped going because the Troubles started. It was not a good time to be going away. And you wouldn't know what you were coming back to face, you know. I was afraid then. So I didn't go after that. But I continued with my Irish in school.

Dónal also continued with Irish outside school at the then-still-flourishing Gaelic League headquarters in Belfast, the Árdscoil. Yet again, the Troubles literally got in the way:

> I used to go down to the Árdscoil, which no longer exists, but it was down the Falls Road. ... And they would have céilí dances and so on, and I would have done a little bit of Irish there. But I didn't make enough effort to keep the language up. The Troubles really got in the way, 'cause we're talking 1969, 1970 now. ... Around that period, '69, '70, '71, '72. But that was an awkward time 'cause the road sometimes was littered with vehicles and burnt-out buses and, you know, you couldn't get any transport; you had to walk. And I lived up in Andersonstown at that time. It was a three- or four-mile walk into town. I mean, I did it, you know, quite often, but it certainly wouldn't have been the commonest thing. So I think we went through this discussion in an early part of our interviews. That people tended to then associate with their own local areas rather than have to take the risk of walking into town or not getting home or maybe a bomb going off. So, and that's really what happened with me as well. You had to; you really ended up with local entertainment. And there was a huge growth in local entertainment then because this suddenly was the only choice, the only sensible choice to make. And I suppose there was also this safety thing. You didn't want to leave your area. You knew your own area, so you didn't want to leave it.

While the political context thus played an important role in decreasing Dónal's engagement with the language, it was other, more idiosyncratic factors that further contributed to this development. As Dónal put it: 'and then the rest of my life intervened, you know, it got in the way; all sorts of things happened'.

For a long period in Dónal's life, the Irish language basically fell by the wayside. However, in the early 2000s, Dónal was confronted with illness that forced him to leave his job. Suddenly having more free time, 'I started to think about my Irish language and music because it was always something, a good memory for me, from many, many years ago'. He recalled, 'while I was young, I went to the Gaeltacht, learnt Irish at school; very strongly had those – strong affiliations with the language and music. And <u>still</u> would have that!' Hence realizing how much he actually missed them, Dónal decided to return to his Irish language and music 'because it's for me!' He could thereby draw on memories from his youth in the Gaeltacht and on related feelings that were 'strong enough for making me want to go back and renew them [i.e. the Irish language and music], you know, after forty years, you know. And it is that long. Something that I've always wanted to return to and I didn't want to lose completely. And I've never lost them; they're inside me somewhere.'

Fíona, age 47

Fíona and I got to know each other when attending the same Irish language classes from September 2003 until June 2004. While we had countless informal conversations, it was primarily our four semi-structured interviews from which my understanding of Fíona's path into the Irish language emerged.

Like Dónal, Fíona was also born in the mid-1950s in Belfast, and like Dónal, Fíona did not encounter the Irish language in her own family. However, she had always been aware of the language but simply lacked the opportunity to learn it in her youth:

> I didn't have the opportunity to doing it at school. But yet, I know there was Irish classes in the [secondary] school as part of the curriculum. But I never done it, and I don't know what I would have felt like if I had to do it. If I had to, like, 'Right, this is one of your subjects, you have to do that', I don't know how I would have felt then. It wasn't till the Troubles sort of way started out; and I thought, 'I might have a wee bit of my identity.' That I thought – that the Irish [language] made – made me who I am! So I think, it's only been influenced from the Troubles, that I said, 'Right, this is about time that I started thinking seriously about this.'

For Fíona – who was in her early teenage years in 1969 – the Troubles brought the issue of her own Irishness to the fore, and, in the process, made her realize that it was (at least in part) the Irish language that 'made me who I am':

> And it wasn't till sort of way that when the Troubles broke out and I says, 'Right, well, I've an identity here, and I'm getting denied this identity. It's about time I done something about it.' … You realized then, how much we were being denied, so you have to sort of way turn around and say, 'Right, I have a right to speak my language in my country. This is, to me, this is my country. I have a right to speak what I want to.' As then, before the Troubles set off, anything Irish wasn't acceptable. And it comes down to a personal level too: right, if you're feeling that strong, do something about it. Don't turn around and say, 'Right, I've been denied this', and getting upset about it if you're not planning on doing anything about it.

Fíona came to feel 'embarrassed to say I was Irish and I didn't know my own language', reasoning that 'to class myself as an Irish person and not know my language, I thought was very wrong!' This was so even though Fíona reckoned that if the Troubles never had happened, the absence of the language 'probably wouldn't have annoyed me; it wasn't till sort of way that the Troubles came on that the Irish identity sort of way came out'.

While the Troubles thus turned the Irish language into something that – as Fíona put it – 'I've always wanted to do', it nevertheless took two further decades before she finally overcame her laziness and actually started learning Irish in the early 1990s. Fíona attended a night class at a local GAA club. However, 'it wasn't really good enough because it was only a one-night-a-week thing, and what you were learning you were sort of way forgetting'. After a while, Fíona discontinued her studies.

Not long after this, Fíona's first child was born. 'And then when I had my children, I decided, "Right, I <u>have</u> to start; I <u>have</u> to take it seriously!"' Fíona had always wanted to send her future children to a local Irish-medium school – an intention for which she gave the following reasons:

> I think it's a very good opportunity for them for to be able to speak more than one language. Plus I class myself as an Irish person, so I want my children to be classed the same way; and I don't think it's right for to call yourself an Irish person if you can't speak your own language! And I think it's a beautiful language.

Against this backdrop, it is not surprising that Fíona started attending adult language classes again in the late 1990s when her children entered school. Initially, she participated in a class for parents in the Bunscoil Phobal Feirste. After two years, she moved on to the *Ionad Uíbh Eachach* ('Iveagh Centre'), where I would eventually meet her. At that time, she described the communicative skills that she had by then acquired in Irish in the following way:

> Well, I know I am not fluent enough to sit down and have a conversation with someone, but maybe if I see something written up on the wall or whatever, I sort of way can tell you what it says. Or if I overhear someone speaking, I might be able to pick up a few words of it. Which I think is good. And I do wish to God I had a wee bit more of it! I do find it very hard! It's not getting too bad with the children now. They are able to speak quite a bit of it now. And I would, when we're at home, tell them, 'Try and speak a wee bit more of your Irish'; and sometimes they sit and have a conversation; I would go, 'Oh God almighty, what are they talking about?' [Fíona laughs] You know? But I just love listening to them, conversing together. … For instance, when we're sitting down at the dinner table or whatever and they start talking, I'd say, 'Now come on, where's your Irish?' And they would sit and talk away. In fact, we've got, especially now that it's Lent, there's a wee Trócaire [an Irish charity agency] box sitting on the table. And we say anybody that talks English has to put money into the Trócaire box. And it's so funny because, right, if you say one word, even if I said, 'God, I don't know what that word

is in Irish?' 'Oh mummy, you said it', you know, 'Put your money in the box!' [Fíona laughs] And it's good for them because then they are using it, you know. And I feel good that they are able to beat me at it [Fíona laughs].

Fíona further contemplated how, 'in an ideal world, I think it'd be lovely to speak Irish all the time, but it's just, that's not the way it works'. Hence – as she realistically put it – 'to be honest with you, all that I really want to do is be able to converse with my children and help them with their homeworks, 'cause that was another reason why I did start it'.

Pól, age 47

Pól was one of a handful of key informants with whom my contact was largely restricted to the formal interview cycle. As a Republican ex-prisoner, who had been imprisoned in the H-Blocks of Long Kesh from the mid-1970s until the early 1990s, Pól had been 'on the blanket' as well as on the 'no-wash protest' and had survived the subsequent hunger strike in 1981. During that time, he became a fluent Irish speaker and was hence an invaluable source of information about the role of the Irish language in prison. Pól kindly agreed to be interviewed on three occasions, facilitated by the fact that he was then working at the West Belfast office of the Republican ex-prisoners support group *Coiste na nIarchimí* ('Committee of ex-prisoners').

Like Dónal and Fíona, Pól was born in the mid-1950s and did not encounter any Irish at home. He had been exposed to the Irish language in secondary school, where he had studied it as a compulsory subject, even though he had 'absolutely no interest in it whatsoever'. After leaving school, Pól joined the IRA in the early 1970s and was soon on the run before being caught and sentenced in the mid-1970s:

I didn't come from a Republican family! My parents weren't political in any way. But then like most people who ended up becoming involved, didn't come from families that previously were involved! And that was because of the situation that was happening on the ground. I just became more conscious of it, more politicized. And made a decision that I would join the IRA, which I did when I was seventeen. And, well, as a result of my involvement, I ended up being arrested. I was charged with attempted murder of an RUC [i.e. police] man and causing explosions. I was sentenced to life imprisonment. And that was 1976. And that was the year that the protest began in the jails. Up until 1976, if you were a prisoner as the result of the conflict, you were given political status. You were recognized as political prisoners. Then 1976, the First of March, the British government removed that regulation and said, 'From now on, you're just ordinary criminals.' Even though you were still arrested on the special legislation, special interrogation, special courts with no juries only one judge; despite all this special process, but that was then worth at the end of the day, you'd just be treated as an ordinary criminal! And we refused to go along with that! We refused to wear the uniform and were on protest for five years, where we just lived in our cells naked.

After the withdrawal of so-called 'Special Category Status' in 1976, convicted prisoners were housed in the eight new 'H-Blocks' – each with four wings off a central administration area – that had been recently constructed at Long Kesh, a former Royal Air Force station outside Lisburn. When the first Republican prisoner after status withdrawal arrived in Long Kesh in September 1976 and refused to wear a prison uniform, he was locked up naked in a cell, covering himself with only a blanket. The 'blanket protest' demanding the reintroduction of 'political status' had thus begun, as many other sentenced Republican prisoners replicated the protest. In response to their insubordination, the prisoners were kept locked up in their cells with nothing except cell furniture, a bible and the prison uniform. By 1978, about 250 men had joined the protest, but as there was no sign that progress was being made in getting their demands met, the prisoners decided to intensify their struggle. They embarked on a 'no-wash protest' and, being denied access to the toilet, smeared their excrement on the cell walls. When several years of such intensified protest had not produced the desired effect, a hunger strike was finally begun in 1981, which ultimately saw the deaths of ten men and only one out of the five demands met, namely, the right to wear their own clothes (McKeown 2001: 27–80; Coogan 2002).

It is within such a context of intensified struggle and inhuman living conditions that Pól's experiences with the Irish language need to be understood. Within the adverse conditions in 'the blanket blocks' in which prisoners were locked up one or two to a cell with no access to books, pens or paper (except for toilet paper), let alone a proper language teacher, learning Irish was an enormous challenge. Yet the prisoners found ways to master the situation. Certain prisoners knew some Irish, and these people became teachers in improvised classes that the prisoners started to organize on several levels within each wing:

Even though we were locked up all the time, the prison guards left the wings during lunchtime and teatime in the evening, 12:30 to 2:00 and 4:30 to 5:30. And we would do the classes during that period of time. What it meant was: the teacher would get up to the door and would have put his face straight up onto the side of the door. And we would do likewise to hear him. And the rest of the wing would be quiet because there was a class on. And he would literally be saying, 'This is a verb', like the verb 'to run'. So he would give you the tenses of it, the present tense, the past tense. And we had then to write down. So you were able to score it onto the wall. ... He would spell it out. And you would write it onto your wall. And there'd be a number, an amount given out. ... You know, we'd get bits of pencils smuggled in. Or even sometimes, you were allowed religious medals. And then you could use that to write on the paint. ... At other times, we smuggled in cigarette papers; sometimes, we had access to toilet paper, which was very stiff, not this tissue paper, which we used to write on.

… In the early days, we were out, allowed to the toilet. But from '78 until '81, erm, we had a 'no-wash protest'. We went to the toilet in the cell, erm; it was smeared on the walls. … The prison guards would come in to do a search, and just left anything that had nothing written on, you know. So it became sort of impossible, after a while, to keep a large amount of written stuff. Whereas, when it was on the walls, they couldn't really; okay, they came in at times and tried to scrub it off, but – too much hassle for them, you know! … We would write it down, a new bit of vocabulary, around about ten words. People would ask for particular words. Like, 'How would you say, you know, "good morning"'. And the classes were going generally between half an hour and an hour, depending on the teacher.

As Pól remembered, 'in any one day, there could be maybe four classes, different levels' and 'of the people on the protest, which would have been 450, I would say, at least two-thirds of them would have gained a fairly good proficiency at that time'. Apart from attending the classes:

You would use the time between then and the next day to learn your Irish. You'd try to speak it to maybe the person who was in the cell with you. Maybe somebody next door. But other times, it was just in your own head. You would go over it, you know. And because you had nothing else, maybe you had a big interest in learning it.

In the early stages of the protest, there was confusion about what actually constituted correct Irish, until the whole situation became much more coherent and streamlined over time. Yet this was the reason why Pól initially did not want to learn Irish: 'I decided in a very naive way at that time that once we got political status, once the protest was over, I would then learn the Irish because I would be clear about what I was learning!' However, things turned out differently:

I was moved from that wing I was in, into another wing. And there was a guy who had Irish from when he was in school, had been to the Gaeltacht in Donegal. He had been in the prison earlier, already spent several years in prison. And he had a brilliant recall of Irish, was a fluent speaker in it. … And he was doing classes. And it was very apparent that he knew the stuff, you know. Unlike the other, the previous wing that I'd been in. So, I just joined the class to learn it. And that was the first exposure to it. I continued. I was lucky enough that I remained in the wings with him for probably the next two years almost. By which time I had gone through all of his classes. And I ended up then teaching it myself.

According to Pól, a number of factors were responsible for this 'massive boost' for the Irish language during the prison protests, some of them political, others more practical. First of all, within Republicanism historically, 'there was always a culture of learning Irish in the jails', given 'the fact that it was your national language'.

Furthermore, practical considerations became relevant once the protest confined the prisoners to their cells: 'When the protest began, it was crucial to have a language that you could speak to one another [between cells] without the prison guards understanding what you're saying! So there was immediately a need for a language! And obviously what you wanted to learn was Irish'. In addition, 'there was a rule that you weren't supposed to be speaking Irish', 'so it was like a revolutionary act to actually learn it!' Alongside such political motivations, there was also the simple fact that being on protest, locked up and thus without distractions, learning Irish constituted just 'something to pass the time'. Finally, there was increasingly 'the curiosity factor: if you're hearing people speaking the language ... you're wondering, are you missing something? You know, is there something being said, some news?' Hence, 'there's nearly a need to start to learn it'.

Against this backdrop, it is perhaps not surprising that interest in the Irish language waned to some degree within the prison after the protests ended in 1981:

> When the protest ended, the Irish language was set back. Because people now left their cells! They weren't able to get books immediately, but shortly after that: education, TV, radios. There was a whole pile of distractions if you want. ... Now, people still knew how to speak Irish and they did. But it became nearly that it was just used when you needed it. ... Now, as we're outside [the cells], if I could talk to you without the screws [derogatory term for prison guards] hearing, then it was nearly like; well just, 'Why do you speak Irish? Why do you not just speak English?' So I think it was that element that came into it, you know. There's now a massive change in our social set-up in the jail; when I could get out of our cells, go out in the yard walking. ... We were allowed to wear our clothes, to get out of the cells, get in the canteen for food, get in the yard for exercise, go out in the night for association; well, it's the whole life cycle that would change then. We continued the struggle and battled with the authorities over the next number of years till we got far better conditions even than had existed prior to '76. But I think initially the Irish language took a knock, because of the way it had been given a big impetus because of the protest. Now that that element was gone – well, okay, people still did converse with it. But it wasn't the same crucial need to converse. Classes still continued on in various ways. But now, there was a pile of other things happening: other classes; university courses; there was football. Well, so Irish was now competing with a whole lot of other things.

While the Irish language to some degree faded away during the years after the hunger strike, this was to change once more in the early 1990s. This was so, as Pól suggested, because the upsurge of the Irish language in the North of Ireland had to be seen as the outcome of the interplay of developments inside and outside of the prison: initially, it was the peculiar conditions and practical necessities during the prison protests that produced a massive boost for the Irish language within the prison, while simultaneously also being the very reason behind the subsequent decline of Irish in the post-protest '*Jailtacht*'. However, in the 1980s the initial boom in the prison sparked off a massive upsurge of Irish on the outside, over the course of which the Irish language, the 'revival of cultural identity, national identity' and the political struggle became much more intertwined. As a result, in the 1990s, many young Republicans came into prison not only 'with Irish' but also with an attitude that highlighted the intrinsic nationalist value of the language rather than its immediate practical use-value. This, in turn, had an impact on older Republican prisoners like Pól – 'so it was also changing with people who had been in the jail from the mid-70s' – in that they increasingly identified with the Irish language in terms of their own Irishness and the political struggle itself. Hence, the whole language situation transformed both inside and outside the prison.

Seen in this light, Pól did not doubt that during the protest years the fact that Irish 'was your national language' had not been at the forefront of his own thoughts:

> Not at that time! I look on it differently now and think that it is important! My own daughters go to an Irish-language school now. Because there are language schools! I mean, at that time, you got to remember like, the Irish language was spoken by very, very few people in the North. The South was probably different. But it was generally a dying language, whereas now it's reviving. And it's reviving because a whole new generation of people took it on. In fact, the prison struggle and the use of language in the prisons actually inspired probably most of the major developments in the North here! Like here in Belfast! 'Cause people had an attitude, 'If prisoners can learn it under those circumstances, then we should be learning it!' And at the same time, the Irish-language community which, in general terms, was fairly elitist, very small groups and very much amongst themselves, you know, probably changed as well; became a bit more integrated with the wider community. So a whole new generation of people started to learn it, who had never been reared in Irish-speaking families. And the prison was a big impetus to them.

Pádraigín, age 40

The following description of Pádraigín is largely based on our four semi-structured interviews. Apart from these encounters, however, we had numerous informal chats and conversations in the context of Pádraigín's Irish-language class, which I attended for ten months.

Pádraigín was born and raised in a Catholic family in a mixed neighbourhood of North Belfast. Her father was a solicitor, and Pádraigín's family could be described as somewhat middle class, although her *clann* turned out to be noticeably different from other local middle-class Catholic families. Born in the mid-1960s, Pádraigín claimed that she had been aware of the Irish language 'from, what I think, always':

> When I was a child, my father would have used Irish with us as much as he had and encouraged its use in the house. Simple things like, '*Tabhair*

dom an siúcra, le do thoil' ['Pass me the sugar, please']. *'Cá bfhuil do mhála scoile'* ['Where is your satchel?'], and, you know, very simple bits. And we always heard, *'sláinte'* ['cheers'], and *'dia duit'* ['hello'] and, you know, vocabulary like that. So, I had an awareness of Irish from quite a young age. But my mother wouldn't have been an Irish speaker. And daddy's confidence wouldn't have been great! … But he put the seed into us that we had another language.

During her last year at primary school, Pádraigín (like all pupils in Northern Ireland) had to sit a transfer test called the 'Eleven Plus', which would determine whether she was entitled to free education at a grammar school or merely at a secondary school. Pádraigín failed her Eleven Plus. However, at the time there was still 'a system then where you could be paid into that school; where they accepted fee-paying students', and, as Pádraigín told me, 'my parents paid for me to go to the grammar school rather than the secondary school'. As it then turned out, Pádraigín:

> went to a brilliant school for Irish. The grammar school was really, really good, and the teachers were excellent and really interested in that and did everything to cultivate an interest in that. Now I failed the Eleven Plus. And if my parents didn't have the money to pay me into the grammar school, I would have gone to the local secondary school next door. And at that time, they didn't have an Irish teacher. So my life could be completely different. You know, and that's a Catholic secondary school.

At her grammar school, Irish was a compulsory subject up to third year, 'but most students in my school would have taken Irish on to O-Level' (i.e. up to fifth year). In fact, Pádraigín continued with Irish throughout her seven years of grammar school, also doing her A-Level in Irish. This was so, Pádraigín recollected, because:

> I loved Irish. And I loved it for lots of reasons. And probably more, well, – I wouldn't have thought consciously of Irish as my national language and I have to learn it! Because that was in me without thinking about it. I mightn't have defined that necessarily, although, maybe a bit. … But then there was another factor in my interest in Irish in that I had some before I went to school! And I had probably very low self-esteem in that I'd failed the Eleven Plus. And I went to that school because my sister was there, and my parents paid for me to go to the grammar school rather than the secondary school. So in Irish class when they were saying, 'Does anybody know the word for "sugar"?' I remembered it, you know! And the teacher was very good on positive phrase! She was probably ahead of her time. You know, she was very good with me, you know, and she, with everybody, she was dramatic. I kind of looked at her and watched her move around the classroom and she gave us commands, *'Téigh go dtí an doras'* ['Go to the door']; it was fun! And I understood what she said! And when I did my homeworks, it was always eight out of ten, nine out of ten: *'maith thú'*

['well done'], '*girseach mhaith*', '*bulaí girsí*' [both meaning 'good girl']. That really – I needed that at the time, and I was making good progress with that in a way that I wouldn't have stood out in a French class, and I wouldn't have stood out in hardly any other classes. But I did stand out in Irish! And I think that for a youngster who'd just been failed in life, you know, failed the Eleven Plus, I think, my motivation had a lot to do with that as well as – with Irish identity, you know.

Being highly motivated to pursue the Irish language, Pádraigín started going to summer colleges in the Donegal Gaeltacht. For years, she had spent many weekends and the whole summer with her family at their summer cottage in Donegal. Yet, after her second year at grammar school, she attended her first Gaeltacht college in *Loch an Iúir* (Loughanure) in the western Donegal region of *Na Rosa* (The Rosses) because 'our school always sends people to Loch an Iúir':

> The teachers in our school were very highly connected to that college. So they'd've sent their students to Loch an Iúir. But my brother got a scholarship to Rannafast, and daddy had connections with Rannafast. And Rannafast had a better name as a college and as an Irish-speaking area in general; a lot of the writers came from there, and it was a quite famous Gaeltacht area in Donegal. So I really, really wanted to go to Rannafast, and my teacher said, 'You haven't enough Irish to go to Rannafast. You will not be able to cope'. Because they were very, very strict [at the college]. You were sent home if you spoke English! … So, when I was in Rannafast, I was terrified to speak English. And so I spoke Irish, and that was another, probably, you know, a life-changing experience! In terms of, that I survived speaking Irish! … So I was in a house [staying with a local family] and I knew nobody. … So I spoke Irish all the time. And my teacher from Belfast met me on the last week. And I spoke Irish to her and she was like, 'Wow!' you know, '*Tá feabhas iontach ar do chuid Gaeilge! Bulaí girsí! Maith thú! Sin iontach maith, tá Gaeilge*', you know, '*Tá tú ag labhairt Gaeilge anois!*' ['Wow, your knowledge of Irish is great! Good girl! Well done! This is really good, now, you're speaking Irish!']. And I was just like, 'Ah!' [Pádraigín performs, how she was beaming with pride]. You know and I went to Rannafast ever after that! I really did think, eat, sleep in Irish then, you know.

Over the years, Pádraigín became engaged with the Irish language to an extent that went far beyond the typical commitment of her peers at the grammar school in North Belfast. In fact, as Pádraigín remembered with regard to 'Irish culture' generally, her family was 'very strongly into that and I think we were clearly identified like that at school; we weren't a typical family'.

About a year before leaving grammar school, Pádraigín had an experience that strongly influenced her subsequent decision to continue with Irish Studies at university:

In the early '80s my teacher took us to – we went on an expedition, two buses – up to West Belfast and we went to the nursery, the [Irish-medium] nursery school [affiliated to Bunscoil Phobal Feirste]. And that clearly affected my entire career because that's when I realized I would *love* to do this! I could use my Irish <u>and</u> work with children! And I really wanted to work with children, and so I knew then, you have to speak Irish; up here it is the all-Irish, Irish-medium school. ... You know, that was very motivating for me!

After school, Pádraigín went on to do a Bachelor of Arts in Irish Studies with Education at the University of Ulster in Coleraine, and eventually worked at Irish-medium nursery and primary schools in West Belfast. By the time I met her in 2003, Pádraigín had been teaching full time in continuing education Irish classes for years.

When I asked her what the language meant to her personally, Pádraigín characterized her all-encompassing relationship to the Irish language in the following way:

The Irish language is a whole life for me. How do you describe what it means? It means just everything for me! I even think when I'm speaking Irish a sort of different part of my brain's working [Pádraigín laughs]. You know, it's very important to me. I am very proud to be an Irish speaker. And to be involved and, you know, teaching Irish to adults, and to have been involved in the Bunscoil in Shaw's Road, you know. And – Irish is me! ... It's been who I am; it's what made me; maybe it's what made me different through my school life. It's part of my unique, idiosyncratic identity!

Sinéad, age 33

I met Sinéad when doing participant observation in an Irish-medium primary school in West Belfast. Sinéad, whose child attended the school, volunteered in the after-school club, which first brought us into contact and facilitated our two semi-structured interviews.

Sinéad was born in the early 1970s into a family with no Irish, as her parents 'were not Irish-minded'. She was exposed to the language mainly through secondary school, where she had it as a subject from first to fifth year. During fourth year, Sinéad started to attend an additional Irish class that was taught for free at the Springhill Community House in West Belfast, run by the dissident priest and social worker, Father Des Wilson. The class itself was taught by a local artist and Gaeilgeoir: 'He was old then, but he was <u>very</u> strict! Just, "You <u>have</u> to pronounce every word properly!" And see, if you said something wrong, he shouted at you. He did, I mean, <u>embarrass</u> you! He would embarrass you; really <u>cut</u> you to the bone, so he would!' Sinéad did not feel comfortable in the class and stopped going after a couple of weeks. She continued with Irish at school, but subsequently dropped it completely: 'I just wasn't interested anymore; I just didn't speak another word of Irish for eleven years.'

Sinéad finally returned to the Irish language at the turn of the millennium because of her children. Her son was about to begin nursery school, and Sinéad decided in favour of an Irish-medium crèche. Her decision was thereby not motivated by a desire to push Irish as her 'own native language':

> They were setting the nursery up. She [Sinéad's friend] kept torturing me [to send her son to the crèche]. Now, it <u>always</u> <u>was</u> in the back of my mind to send my kids into an Irish school. But I just never got round to it. I was just actually being lazy! But then, since it was a school being opened here [in Sinéad's local area], my friend kept, 'Come on, put him in, put him in!' … Once this nursery was set up, I jumped at the chance.

Yet Sinéad and her husband also had additional reasons for deciding in favour of all-Irish education: 'I think you get educated better in the Irish-language school because it's not as many in your class, and they have more time for you'. Furthermore, 'You got to take part more in your child's education here than what you would in an English school'.

Once she had decided to send her child to the Irish-medium nursery, Sinéad also decided to refresh her own Irish in order 'to be able to speak to thems, to push thems a wee bit further because if you don't speak it in the house, then they'll lose it'. Sinéad recalled how the Irish-medium nursery made her:

> more determined to go and learn the language! At the start it was, 'ach'; couldn't be annoyed. 'There's no point in wanting to know the language!' But now, the two kids are in the school. I mean, I <u>don't</u> <u>have</u> to go and learn it! But, now that they are here, I wanna learn it! So then I know how to speak to them and what they are saying to me! I mean, I could be glad. Most of the other parents are just sitting back and go, 'Ah, let the school learn them!' and, 'I don't need to know it!'

Sinéad attended night classes offered at the nursery as well as, again, at the Springhill Community House. When I met her, she was awaiting the results of her GCSE exam and planned to go on with further classes in the future.

Sinéad was somewhat atypical in comparison to other parents at the nursery and primary school in that she belonged to a rather small minority of people who had themselves learnt Irish. She was further set apart by her volunteer work in the after-school club, where she spoke Irish with the children, and was happy with the results: 'It works out 'cause, I mean, if I don't know how to say something in Irish, I would ask the kids! And they would tell me! [Sinéad laughs] And even if I say something wrong, the kids would then correct me and tell me how to say it properly. Which is good!'

Although Sinéad was much more engaged with the Irish language than many of her immediate peers, she nevertheless displayed some ambivalence in her attitudes towards Irish. On the one hand, she seemed to ascribe little if any symbolic value to the language as a marker of Irishness, instead emphasizing pragmatic reasons for sending her children to all-Irish schools. On the other hand, she also said, 'It makes you Irish, as, you have to know your language and be interested in the Irish', even if she did not seem to really identify with this position herself. This ambivalence is nicely encapsulated in Sinéad's reply after I asked her, 'Would you see Irish as your own language?'

> Not necessarily. I mean, it's something I do want to learn because I've been told, 'It is our <u>native</u> language!' But – ... [I was told so by] Irish people [Sinéad laughs], not my family! Just – the likes of my Irish-language teacher and all. He would say it, like, 'It's your native language! It's nice to learn it!' And that's coming from someone who is really Irish-minded and would <u>know</u> everything about the Irish history and all. ... [He would say] just, that it <u>is</u> good to learn it because, as I say, it is your language and – that's about it.

Caoimhín, age 17

I became acquainted with Caoimhín through the Cumann Chluain Árd, where he typically hung out with friends in the bar on Monday and Thursday nights. My account herein is based on three semi-structured interviews as well as on our numerous informal conversations.

Caoimhín was born in Belfast in the mid-1980s and at the time of my fieldwork was attending a Catholic grammar school where he was working towards his A-Levels (including in Irish). He was first exposed to the Irish language at home:

> It would've always been a wee bit [of Irish] about in the house. Just, I don't remember anything – big, you see. Just '*gabh i leith*' ['come here'], '*druid an doras*' ['close the door'], just such phrases, you would get. So I always knew a wee tiny bit. But then it <u>really</u> started when I went to grammar school, first year. I picked Irish as a language, and then went to the Gaeltacht and stuff, and then, just since then, just.

Caoimhín's decision to learn Irish (besides French) out of a choice of five languages had apparently been motivated by two factors: 'It's the language of the country; and the social aspect of it, like the Gaeltacht'. Through his grammar school, Caoimhín went to the Gaeltacht college in *Machaire Rabhartaigh* (Magheroarty) in north-west Donegal, where he spent three weeks with his friends every summer from his first year to his fifth year. In fourth and fifth year, he additionally attended a one-week Easter college in *Loch an Iúir* (Loughanure) in western Donegal. However, the latter was:

> more of an intense course. To get you ready for doing your school exams. So instead of, in the afternoon, having games, you would have more

classes. Then before the céilí, or the night activity, there was a class before that, as well. So basically you had classes all day. It was six hours of classes.

In contrast, in the summer colleges it was Irish classes in the morning, then an afternoon class, which usually involved activities such as singing or dancing, to be followed by sports or games.

> Then you'd go home, get something to eat, and have an hour or so of free time, just to go around to the different houses and talk to your friends. And go to the shop or whatever, and phone. Then you had a céilí. Half seven. It was half seven to ten, half ten. Would be a céilí. Then you went home.

When talking about these summer trips, it became quite clear that Caoimhín had really enjoyed these annual 'three weeks, just with all your friends in Donegal; it was brilliant'. For him, these stays had been 'probably one of the best holidays you ever had'.

Caoimhín's father had studied Irish for years and ended up attending the Cumann Chluain Árd. He recommended it to his son, but Caoimhín did not like the prospect of attending classes on Monday and Thursday nights. However, having passed his GCSE in Irish, he knew he would have to improve his Irish for his A-Levels, so he started coming down to the Cluain Árd in September 2003. However, he was only to attend a single class there:

> And then I found out after one class that I'd be better off just sitting at the bar and listening to the *comhrá* ['conversation']. ... One of the fellows, he was sitting down there, says to me, 'You're better off sitting in the bar.' And then I was sitting in the bar later on that night, and, like, was talking to Roibeárd [i.e. the first key informant in this chapter] and all thems. And he knew my dad and all. ... He says, 'If you come down every Monday and Thursday and sit at the bar for a couple hours, you'll be fluent in no time!'

Thus like me, Caoimhín ended up following the dominant doctrine of the Cluain Árd: one does not learn a language by attending a class but by being surrounded by people who just speak it all the time. As was the case with my own experience, Caoimhín and some of his friends soon started bartending because – as Caoimhín recalled – 'that was another thing that Roibeárd said to me: "If you work behind the bar as well, people are coming up and talking to you in Irish. It'll accelerate your learning".' This approach to learning Irish in the Cluain Árd was also recommended by Caoimhín's Irish teacher at grammar school. This was so because the teacher had actually learnt his Irish in the Cluain Árd as well, also working behind the bar.

Thinking about his year of study at the time of our interviews, Caoimhín emphasized that he had started coming to the Cluain Árd just to learn Irish; 'but now, I enjoy going down; it's good *craic* [fun, a good time]. It's just part of my routine now. I look forward to going down Mondays and Thursdays; a few games of pool, a pint, a lot of craic'. Caoimhín's Irish improved too. As he put it, 'I've learnt more in this one year from going to the Cluain Árd than I have sitting in classrooms the last five years'. Yet to me, it was also evident that having frequented the Cluain Árd for a year had not only changed Caoimhín's linguistic skills, but also his attitudes to the language itself, as evidenced in the following quote in which Caoimhín summed up his personal development as a Gaeilgeoir:

> When I was younger, I wasn't, like, very serious about the Irish language. It was just something I did in school, and I'd go down to the Gaeltacht for a laugh and all that. But now, I just see it, take it a lot more serious. But you know how when you hear people down the Cluain Árd speaking away in English, or else if you're in the Gaeltacht, and you hear the local people speaking English, it's just – it can be annoying! … It's not right!

Preliminary Observations

In this chapter, I have aimed at maximizing diversity in presenting the idiosyncratic trajectories into the Irish language of ten contemporary West Belfast Gaeilgeoirí. Spanning a period of more than five decades, these Irish speakers have been described with regard to the specific conditions that shaped their respective developments as Gaeilgeoirí at the intersections of different stages in their lives and different events of the second half of the twentieth century. These reconstructed biographies thereby generated ethnographic information that is relevant for all three analytical dimensions of this study as discussed in Chapter 2, namely, the role of time, the interplay between structural contexts and individual agency, and the relationship between representations and practices of the Irish language.

With regard to the dimension of time, a preliminary synopsis suggests certain commonalities that seem to be related to specific stages within individual life cycles. In particular, these features seem to be the relative absence or presence of Irish during childhood; the extent to which interviewees had been exposed to the language in primary, secondary and tertiary education; what types of careers were being pursued afterwards; and, finally, to what extent these individuals instituted the Irish language in their own families by speaking Irish with their children or sending them to Irish classes or Irish-medium schools. Simultaneously, broader trends and developments within a more inter-subjective time equally left their mark on and interfered with these more personalized developments – most notably the outbreak of the Troubles in 1969, the subsequent ups and downs of political conflict as well as the eventual emergence of the peace process in the 1990s.

Turning towards the dimension of structure and agency, it is equally clear that various forms of structural contexts – such as the family, schools, Gaeltacht colleges as well as more informal relationships with friends – heavily influenced pathways into the Irish language, as did – again – the wider political context of the Troubles. The latter evidently modulated the acquisition of Irish in complex ways, among which the situation of the '*Jailtacht*' in prisons was but one obvious example. However, such structural contexts only set the initial parameters in which these (and other) Gaeilgeoirí were then left to use their own agency. All of my key informants had obviously decided at some point in their lives to learn the Irish language, but there was also considerable variation concerning the specifics of this decision and the degree to which each individual identified with the language and committed him or herself to its revival; some even chose to live the rest of their lives through the Irish language and rearranged their social environments accordingly.

Finally, this chapter aimed at describing in as detailed a manner as possible how and through what types of phrases and expressions these future Gaeilgeoirí came into contact with the language and how, where and in what ways their language practices subsequently developed. I repeatedly referred to different ways in which the Irish language was represented by and to these individuals. I also alluded to changes in their perception of Irish that occurred in the course of their being drawn into the language. All in all, the representation of Irish as 'our own native language' turned out to be rather widespread, even though this notion seemed to mean different things to different people.

In the following two chapters, this empirical 'raw' material will be systematized, contextualized and explicitly refocused with regard to the three analytical dimensions. It is important to note, however, that within this procedure, the relationship between individual life stories and analytical chapters is not meant to be one of unilineal analysis. Instead, this interrelation is construed as one of mutual substantiation: on the one hand, the analytical chapters substantiate the individual life stories by embedding them in explanatory frameworks, which offer deeper understandings of their, thus far, rather idiosyncratic evolution. On the other hand, these quite specific reconstructions of 'lived experiences' also substantiate the analytical chapters, which – in their necessarily generalizing and somewhat homogenizing narratives – are in danger of oversimplifying the complexities of local life that they purport to represent. In this sense, the present life stories chapter and the subsequent analyses do not square up neatly but only loosely, thereby producing and maintaining what I hope is a productive tension.

Having a final look at these ten biographical sketches, it is worth noting that the oldest and the youngest Gaeilgeoir were both linked to the Cumann Chluain Árd. This underlines the continuing centrality of the Cluain Árd in the local Irish language scene over the past fifty years. In a sense, this fact also foreshadows a main thesis of the next chapter, namely, that in order to understand the current Irish language scene in Catholic West Belfast, one has to both begin and end with the Cumann Chluain Árd. It is to the development of this argument that I now turn.

Chapter 5

On Prophets, Godfathers, Rebels and Prostitutes

A Contemporary History of the Irish Language in Catholic West Belfast

On a Thursday night in June 2004, I went to the *Cumann Chluain Árd* (the 'Association of Clonard'), a local branch of the Gaelic League on Hawthorn Street in the Clonard area of Catholic West Belfast. Early on during my stay in 2003, I had succeeded in finding the large grey building with its permanently closed green blinds, hidden away on a backstreet near the Falls Road, but in the absence of any further information on the building, I had found myself in the position of the 'uninitiated', not knowing when, for whom and for what purpose the club actually opened its doors. Once I had been welcomed in, however, I knew that there were language classes on Mondays, Wednesdays and Thursdays from about eight to ten in the evening as well as traditional music classes for children on Saturday evenings, with the bar opening daily around eight or nine in the evening, except for Tuesdays when the Cluain Árd stayed closed. As I eventually learnt, one just had to knock on the door at the right time, and upon entering the building to follow the strict monolingual policy of speaking only Irish. While the Cluain Árd had thus initially been less easily accessible for me than, for instance, the Cultúrlann, it proved to be by no means less welcoming or supportive. On the contrary, Roibeárd, one of the leading figures in the club and around almost every night of the week, kept his promise that he would teach me Irish for free through endless informal conversations at the bar of the club, which had been run for decades voluntarily and virtually without any external funding.

It was against such a backdrop that, when I arrived at the Cluain Árd on this particular Thursday evening, I was immediately incorporated into a scene that I had encountered many times before: five male teenage friends (including Caoimhín) were hanging about the bar, as was a middle-aged regular and – of course – Roibeárd. Sitting on high stools in a semicircle around the counter of the bar, these Gaeilgeoirí were chatting away in Irish, with Roibeárd doing most of the talking, as usual. I joined the group and, ordering my drink, sat down and listened to the conversation, which went on in Irish except for a few clarifying translations into English provided upon my request. From time to time, Roibeárd corrected others, when they used expressions or pronunciations that he regarded as wrong. People seemed quite willing to be corrected and often specifically asked Roibeárd for certain phrases in Irish, given that the Cluain Árd had a reputation within the local language scene for housing some of the best Irish in Belfast.

In terms of conversational topics, this Thursday night was somewhat typical in that our ongoing chat shifted easily and quickly between various subjects that were often also related to the Irish language. At some point, for instance, the conversation focused on a book – Séamus Ó Grianna's (1986) autobiography *Nuair a bhí mé óg* ('When I Was Young') – which was being taught in the *Rang Litridheachta* ('Literature Class') at the Cluain Árd. Roibeárd informed us that the literature teacher was the nephew of the two famous Irish writers Séamus Ó Grianna and Seosamh Mac Grianna, both of whom came from *Rann na Feirste* (Rannafast) in Donegal. Roibeárd told us about the teacher's family and how he had spent a lot of time in his youth with them. I asked Roibeárd whether the teacher's family and his own had been friends. Roibeárd explained that they had shared a relationship of *dáimh*, the meaning of which he went on to explain in a manner that was, in my experience, typical for conversations in the Cluain Árd.

As Roibeárd explained, there was no simple direct translation for '*dáimh*' in English. Instead, he related how he had learnt the word himself. Many years ago, Roibeárd and some friends had spent the night in a local pub in a Gaeltacht area, and it was closing time. A policeman came in, and they all chatted for a while. The policeman asked Roibeárd whether they did not want another drink. Roibeárd responded that it was already closing time, but the policeman only laughed and left the pub, thereby de facto allowing them to have another pint. After he had left, an old man said that the policeman obviously had '*dáimh*' for Roibeárd. Roibeárd did not know the word; thus, the old man explained that it basically meant something like 'sympathy' or 'affection' for somebody. After Roibeárd had finished this story, he tried to find an appropriate English translation for '*dáimh*'. Eventually, he looked up the word in one of the club's revered objects, a copy of Dinneen's old-scripted Irish-English dictionary ꝼoclóıꞃ Ꞡaeóılꞡe aꞡuꞃ óéaꞃla (Dinneen 1927), and together we all settled for 'sympathy' as a sufficiently appropriate translation.

Roibeárd then used his story about *dáimh* as a kind of prelude for one of his recurrent topics, namely, that the only way to learn Irish (like any language) properly was through being among the people who speak it – like there at the bar in the Cluain Árd – and that Irish language classes, even the Irish-medium ones in the Cluain Árd, did not really matter. Roibeárd subsequently spent quite some time criticizing other, bilingual Irish language initiatives in Catholic West Belfast such as the Cultúrlann, arguing that bilingualism resulted in poor Irish and limited progress among learners. In fact, as Roibeárd argued, bilingualism and indifference towards the bad Irish it produced showed that many self-declared language activists did not actually care for the language itself and were not really committed to its revival. Instead, they were evidently only after the money and state funding that had recently been poured into what Roibeárd dismissively called 'Irish language industries'. After this quite extensive excursion into one of Roibeárd's most preferred subjects, the usual topical meandering began again, taking many further twists and turns before we all eventually hit the road shortly before midnight. On my way home (like on many other occasions) I could not help but smile and think that while my own language competence was surely benefiting enormously from hanging around in the bar of the Cluain Árd, it was equally clear that I was acquiring a disproportionately elaborate vocabulary in Irish for the quite specific, normative domain of how one should be learning and speaking the Irish language properly.

In this chapter I will argue that in order to understand the internal dynamics and tensions within the local Irish language scene as exemplified in this vignette from the Cumann Chluain Árd, it is insufficient to only take into account present relationships, practices and representations of the Irish language. Indeed, it is also necessary to explore the recent past of the Irish language scene, not only because this past has brought about the current present but also because this past itself has its own presence, namely, in the form of then-contemporary experiences and attitudes that Gaeilgeoirí had formed throughout their lives, and which they embodied and made relevant in current situations. Drawing on the historiographical and ethnographical literature, and cross-referencing my own material such as the life stories in Chapter 4, I will thus reconstruct a contemporary history of the local language scene by analysing the evolving interplay between individuals and their various structural contexts (dimension 2) within the frame of biographical time (dimension 3), in other words from the mid-twentieth century onwards.

For this purpose, I will first briefly sketch a 'prehistory' of the language leading to the structural contexts that set the scene for subsequent language developments since the 1950s. I will then characterize the local language revival that began in the 1950s largely as the outcome of what I see as four dominant types of agency, which both responded to and thereby changed their respective structural contexts. As I will show, a dominant value-rational motivation for wanting to learn and speak one's 'own native language' can be discerned as a main thread running through much of this language activism, thereby ultimately bringing about a present language setting in which habitual and instrumentally rational engagements with Irish have become more widespread. In the course of this overall development, the four types of agency that I metaphorically identify with the roles of 'prophets', 'godfathers', 'rebels' and 'prostitutes' each strongly influenced the language scene in more or less consecutive order, even though representatives of each ideal-type persisted into and thereby configured the ethnographic present of this study. It is with regard to this latter observation that I will argue that recurrent criticism by Cluain Árd-type 'prophets' of a contemporary 'prostitution' of the Irish language (as briefly sketched in the opening scene) is somewhat misled because this current situation was indirectly one of the prophets' own making. In other words, far from being a contemporary 'prostitution' or sell-out of the original 'prophecy', to my mind, the present Irish language revival should instead be seen as this prophecy's realization.

Emerging Structural Contexts for the Irish Language in the 1950s: A Prehistory

The general history of the Irish language has been told from various angles and at different temporal, spatial and social scales (see, for example, Hindley 1990; Mac Póilin 1997b; Purdon 1999; O'Reilly 1999). Here, it suffices to concentrate on some of the well-established steps in the overall demise of the language and on a few specificities that relate to the Irish North after Partition.

One such well-established step and a crucial one for the subsequent development of the language is the fact that Irish experienced a pronounced decline throughout Ireland in the nineteenth century. Besides enforced Anglicization, growing urbanization, the Great Famine – which killed around a million people in predominantly Irish-speaking areas between 1845 and 1852 – and subsequent mass emigration further contributed to the decline in the number of Irish speakers (Purdon 1999: 33–35), whose proportion of the total population dropped from 23.3 per cent (about 1.5 million) in the first census collecting language data in 1851, to 14.4 per cent (about 680,000) in 1891 (Hindley 1990: 19).

While Irish was thus rapidly diminishing, the late nineteenth century also saw the emergence of a language revival movement situated within a general upsurge of Irish cultural and political nationalism (Hutchinson 1987). *Conradh na Gaeilge* (the 'Gaelic League'), founded in 1893 in Dublin, proved to be the organization with the biggest impact on language revival. It set out with two primary goals, namely, the restoration of Irish as a vernacular for the whole of the Irish people and the creation of new literature in Irish (Purdon 1999: 37). While the Gaelic League – like other cultural organizations at that time – explicitly aimed at de-Anglicization and a restoration of Irish culture, it initially propagated what Hutchinson (1987: 1–47) calls 'cultural nationalism': the restoration of the Irish nation through a return to Irish culture in a strictly non-political and non-sectarian manner. This vision, which was strongly publicized by the Protestant Douglas Hyde, a founding member and first president of the Gaelic League, emphasized the necessity of including people from all religious and political persuasions in the revival movement. In the initial stage of the movement, this ethos prevailed and the Gaelic League also attracted some Protestant language enthusiasts. Yet, the league would soon shift towards 'political nationalism' (Hutchinson 1987: 1–19), which saw the restoration of the Irish cultural nation as inextricably linked to the project of political self-determination within an independent Irish nation-state. This trend culminated in 1915 in the resignation of Hyde as president and the takeover of the Gaelic League by Republicans. At that time, the two conflicting representations of the Irish language as either an issue of cultural or political nationalism had thus emerged, and they continued to pervade the Irish language movement in 2003–2004 (O'Reilly 1997: 98–103). As one might have expected, the strong association between the Irish language, political nationalism in general and Republicanism in particular 'fuelled Unionist hostility to the language' (Mac Póilin 2006: 121). This hostility was seemingly enforced by two other developments that took place at the same time: Protestants were increasingly moving from Irish Unionism towards a Unionism discarding any form of Irish cultural identity, and the Gaelic League was intensifying its contact with the Catholic Church (Mac Póilin 1997a: 39).

This increasing association with the Catholic Church was due to the fact that the Gaelic League – apart from providing Irish language classes and functions with traditional music and Irish dancing in its various local branches – was engaged in a campaign pushing for Irish in the public education system. As part of this endeavour, the league founded its own teacher training colleges such as the *Coláiste Chomhghaill* and the *Ardsgoil Ultach* in Belfast (Andrews 1997: 57) and was involved in the establishment of *Coláistí Samhraidh* ('Summer Schools'), which were set up in *Gaeltachtaí* ('Irish-speaking areas') of the three dialectal areas of Irish – Munster, Connacht and Ulster – from 1904 onwards (Purdon 1999: 44). The Gaelic League was quite successful in its educational campaign:

> By 1921, due largely to pressure from the Gaelic League, the British Government had given the language a more privileged position than other optional and extra subjects on the fringes of the national school curriculum. Irish was available as an optional subject in all standards during the normal school day and as an extra fee-paying subject outside normal school hours from Standard III upwards. ... Irish was taught as a subject for examination in secondary schools and for degree courses at universities. It was also available as an option in teacher-training colleges for prospective national teachers who sought teaching qualifications in Irish. Apart from that, the government supported the language by paying teacher training grants to independent Irish language colleges run by the Gaelic League and by validating their teacher training certificates. ... Additional curriculum support was provided by the employment of a number of Irish Language Organisers who, with the inspectorate, helped to improve standards in the teaching of Irish in national schools. (Andrews 1997: 54–55)

While this momentum was taken up in the new independent state in the South – Irish was recognized as the first official language and was made a compulsory subject in all primary and secondary schools, and all aspects of administration were handled bilingually (Maguire 1991: 41; Purdon 1999: 50) – the fate of the language was to take quite a different direction in the new 'Northern Ireland'.

From the very outset of Partition, which resulted from the Anglo-Irish War (1919–1921), the Northern Irish state was established as a polity in which the overall Protestant Unionist minority within the whole of Ireland would be the locally dominating majority (Fraser 2000: 2–3). Legally based on the Government of Ireland Act (1920), the first government of Northern Ireland, installed in June 1921, ensured from an early stage the political and cultural predominance of Unionism, while attempting to diminish the destabilizing forces of Irish Nationalism and Republicanism prevalent among the local Catholic minority (Andrews 1997: 57). The Special Powers Act (1922) endowed the state with wide-reaching powers such as internment without trial and the banning of organizations, literature, meetings and processions. The 1920s saw further enactments of legal measures that undermined the political power of the Catholic minority: proportional representation was abolished in favour of single member constituencies; various forms of gerrymandering ensured Unionist majorities within redrawn constituency boundaries; and extra votes were granted to local business owners, who were mainly Protestant Unionists (Coohill 2000: 150). These and other policies established a political atmosphere that was aptly described by the first Prime Minister of Northern Ireland, James Craig, when he characterized the local assembly as 'a Protestant parliament for a Protestant people' (Mac Póilin 2006: 122).

Against this background, the attitude within the state apparatus towards the Irish language oscillated between neglect, suspicion and hostility. Confronted with the status that Irish had gained within the school system in pre-Partition times, any regulations which were introduced by the new Northern Irish Ministry of Education 'were restrictive rather than encouraging' (O'Reilly 1999: 21). An uneasy equilibrium was reached between the language lobby and the government in that although Irish had been restricted it had still survived in the education system. According to Mac Póilin (2006: 123):

> Its survival may have been partly due to a decision taken by pragmatic unionists not to ban Irish outright from the education system, but to marginalize it, and to make whatever teaching was undertaken as ineffective as possible. Lord Charlemont, Londonderry's successor [as Minister of Education], provided the most quotable rationale for this policy in 1933, one which demonstrates the centrality of west Belfast to the language movement: 'forbidding [Irish] under pressure will stimulate it to such an extent that the very dogs in Belfast – at any rate the Falls Road dogs – will bark in Irish'.

Beyond education, other state policies also reflected the attitude that Irish was a foreign language with little place in Northern Ireland. Irish street names were prohibited in the course of the Public Health and Local Government Act (1949) – a policy that was reversed only in 1995 (Maguire 1991: 11; O'Reilly 1999: 139). The fact that Irish was rarely heard or seen on BBC Northern Ireland before 1981, while the BBC had broadcast programmes in Scots Gaelic and Welsh since the 1920s (Mac Póilin 2006: 129; McDermott 2007: 114–16), provides another example.

So far, I have exclusively concentrated on the Northern Irish state as one emerging structural context. However, the future development of the language in Catholic West Belfast was also to be conditioned by a number of other important contexts. One of these was provided by the Catholic Church. Although the liturgy continued to be conducted in Latin until Vatican II (1963–1965) when English was locally instituted as the language of the mass (Maguire 1991: 11–12), the Catholic Church still tended to be somewhat favourable towards the Irish language. In some parish churches, it was customary during the 1950s to have a closing prayer in Irish (ibid.: 57), and as Rónán, Mairéad and Micheál recalled, prayers such as 'Our Father' or the 'Hail Mary' were occasionally taught in Irish as well. Generally, the Catholic Church seems to have advanced a pro-Irish ethos, not only with regard to social functions like traditional Irish céilí dances in local parish halls, but also within a third structural context with important consequences for the fate of the Irish language: the Catholic educational system. The National School System had largely developed along denominational lines towards the end of the nineteenth century. McGrath (2000) shows that when the Northern Irish state came into being, the Department of Education aimed at transferring existing schools into the state-controlled system. A scheme was implemented in 1923 that divided the existing schools into three categories – state-controlled schools, so-called 'four-and-two schools' (run by four representatives of the former managers and two of the local government authorities) and entirely independent, voluntary schools – and allocated government aid in direct proportion to its control over the respective institution. While this policy laid the foundation for an increasing transfer of Protestants into state-controlled schools, it was fiercely opposed by Catholic schools, which overwhelmingly opted for voluntary status. In 1947, a radical educational reform was introduced that was largely modelled on the Butler Education Reform Act in Great Britain (1944). Apart from increasing capital grants to voluntary (mainly Catholic) schools, the reform established a new tripartite system for secondary education, which became free of charge. When leaving primary school at the age of eleven, pupils would now sit a transfer test called 'the Eleven Plus'. The most able 20 per cent would be entitled to attend grammar schools, whilst the remaining 80 per cent would go to intermediate or technical secondary schools (McGrath 2000), except for the tiny minority of pupils such as Pádraigín, whose parents could afford to pay for their children to attend grammar school.

While state-controlled (de facto Protestant) schools rarely if at all made use of the legal possibility to offer Irish as a school subject, firmly established educational segregation allowed the situation to be rather different in Catholic schools. From the 1950s onwards, following secondary education reforms, Irish seems to have been taught as an optional subject (among other officially 'foreign languages') in many Catholic secondary and grammar schools in Belfast, whereas the extent to which it could be encountered in Catholic primary schools varied greatly depending on the interest and ability of individual teachers. The pro-Irish ethos behind the teaching of the language, to some extent a general feature of the Catholic educational system (Coulter 1999: 25), was even more pronounced in Catholic schools, which were run by the Christian Brothers. Founded in 1802 by Edmund Rice as a Catholic lay order dedicated to education, the Christian Brothers had a longstanding scholarly interest in Irish and a high reputation for teaching the language. As we saw in Chapter 4, it was explicitly for this reason that Micheál's parents sent him during the 1950s to a distant Christian Brothers' primary and then grammar school, where the 'optional' subject Irish was actually a compulsory 'choice' from first to third year.

Within the general parameters set by the state, the Catholic Church and the Catholic educational system, the extent to which local Catholics experienced the Irish language in the familial context throughout the 1950s seems to have been quite variable. The number of families attempting to bring up their children through the medium of Irish must have been extremely small. A 1965 article from the *Irish Press* is indicative, referring to thirty-six Irish-speaking families scattered throughout Belfast at the time, an increase over the seven such families it counted in 1961 (Maguire 1991: 72). The number of families in which at least one parent had some fluency in Irish must have been considerably higher in the 1950s and 1960s, ensuring a certain exposure to the language through simple phrases and prayers (as was the case with Mairéad, Micheál and Pádraigín). But apart from those families with the odd *cúpla focal* ('a few words'), there were also numerous families such as Rónán's, Dónal's, Fíona's and Pól's in which Irish was literally unheard of. While several of my older informants recalled that throughout the 1950s the general attitude within the Catholic community was largely favourable towards Irish, actually learning and practising the language to a degree worth mentioning nevertheless seems to have been fairly unusual. But the actual distribution of the Irish language is hard to establish for this time since questions regarding the language only began to be included in official statistics with the 1991 Northern Ireland Census (O'Reilly 1999: 13).

Beyond the narrow confines of family life, the Irish language occasionally appeared in daily life, for instance in the form of the Irish national anthem, '*Amhrán na bhFiann*' ('A Soldier's Song'). As Micheál recalled from his childhood in the 1950s:

> In all the GAA [Gaelic Athletic Association] pitches, the Tricolour flew. And all the major matches all started with the Irish national anthem. And we all stood for that. And, if you went to a céilí, the céilí would finish with the Irish national anthem. So there was a parallel universe; it was sort of Catholic Northern Ireland. All the communal events that were organised within the Catholic area had the Irish national anthem.

This quotation is interesting in also pointing to the special role of the Irish language within the context of the Gaelic Athletic Association (GAA). Founded in 1884 amidst a general upsurge of cultural nationalism, the GAA's primary aim was to strengthen Irish identity (and to de-Anglicize Ireland) by preserving and promoting Gaelic games and pastimes such as Gaelic football and hurling (Cronin 1999; De Búrca 1999). Yet from an early stage, the GAA also actively supported 'the Irish language, traditional Irish dancing, music, song, and other aspects of Irish culture', as the organization's contemporary 'additional aims' are still described in its 'Official Guide' (Gaelic Athletic Association 2003: 4). Beginning in the early twentieth century, the GAA increasingly spread throughout Ireland, with local clubs generally organized on a parish basis (Sweeney 2004). By the 1950s the GAA was firmly established in Belfast, and several local clubs encouraged the use of Irish not only through the national anthem but also – as described by Roibeárd in Chapter 4 – by providing written communications in Irish. Some clubs offered Irish language classes and thereby contributed to the last structural context of interest for subsequent local developments, namely, the work of local Irish language organizations.

Partition had constituted a serious blow for the Gaelic League in the North of Ireland (Andrews 2000: 143). With its agenda explicitly taken up by the new state in the South, its members in Northern Ireland suddenly found themselves in an all but encouraging political situation. In this general atmosphere in which the language revival was locally losing momentum, the idea emerged among northern activists to form their own organization. This move was partly motivated by a perception that the particular problems of the northern situation were poorly understood elsewhere in the country. It partly also emerged out of controversies about dialects, with an underlying concern that local Ulster Irish was not adequately promoted by the Gaelic League (Maguire 1991: 29). This led to the establishment of *Comhaltas Uladh* (the 'Ulster Fellowship') in 1926, which was technically part of the Gaelic League while effectively remaining independent. Comhaltas Uladh more or less successfully lobbied for the preservation of Irish in the school curriculum, got involved in the organization and funding of Gaeltacht summer colleges and ensured that the number of Gaelic League branches in the North would rise again from a mere handful at its outset to about 150 in the 1950s (Mac Póilin 2006: 124). In 1928, Comhaltas Uladh built the *Árdscoil* ('High school') on Divis Street, which as the league's city headquarters became the venue for various language classes, céilí dances and lectures as well as other functions such as story-telling evenings for the next several decades. Throughout the 1950s and 1960s, the Árdscoil thus constituted one of the focal points of the local language movement (Maguire 1991: 29–30; Mac Póilin 2006: 128–29). Yet, as several of my informants recalled, the location of the Árdscoil on Divis Street, situated on the fringes of Catholic West Belfast and the city centre, and dangerously close to the Protestant Shankill area, proved to be one of the main reasons for its subsequent demise during the Troubles, long before it accidentally burnt down in 1985 (Kachuk 1993: 285): it had simply become too dangerous to go there.

Apart from language activities within Comhaltas Uladh and various GAA clubs, the 1940s and 1950s saw several other Irish language societies, campaigns and enterprises come and go. Yet it was the establishment of a particular branch of the Gaelic League in Catholic West Belfast that created the space for a peculiar form of agency that proved to trigger and inspire local developments of the language throughout the second half of the twentieth century.

Prophets on the Moral 'High Meadow': The *Cumann Cluain Árd*

According to Mac Póilin (2006: 130–32), in 1936 the O'Neill Crowley GAA club set up a branch of the Gaelic League in the Clonard district of West Belfast. When the club moved into new premises in 1938, it renamed itself *Cumann Chluain Árd* (the 'Association of Clonard') – 'Cluain Árd' being the original Irish place name, literally meaning 'high meadow', which had been Anglicized into 'Clonard'. Operating from its new, much larger premises in a former garage on Hawthorn Street, from 1944 onwards the Cluain Árd ran language classes, céilí dances and concerts as well as more general leisure activities such as cycling, boxing, painting and drama groups. Apart from 'Irish-only' nights on Tuesdays, English was the dominant language. In terms of its clientele, the club exhibited a somewhat distinct flavour up to the early 1950s. As Mac Póilin (ibid.: 130–31) notes:

> Cumann Chluain Ard was rather more radical than other branches of Comhaltas Uladh at the time. Its membership was mostly working-class,

republican and left-leaning. Because the club had no links with the church, it attracted the militant, the disaffected and the mildly disreputable – artists, actors, Protestant nationalists, Esperanto enthusiasts, free-thinkers and communists as well as republicans and a sprinkling of ordinary decent citizens.

During the early 1950s, the club further radicalized in terms of its language activism. It got engaged in *Sábháil an Ghaeltacht* ('Save the *Gaeltacht*'), a campaign by language activists in the South who were promoting a proper state support structure for the traditional Gaeltacht areas in the west of Ireland. During this campaign, members of Cluain Árd refused to speak anything but Irish to local reporters, an act that exemplified their understanding of commitment even if it did not necessarily advance the actual cause. In the course of this campaign – which actually led to the establishment of a Ministry for the Gaeltacht in the South – the Cluain Árd underwent a significant ideological transition, which resulted in what is locally known as 'the purge of 1953'. During a committee meeting that year, the decision was made to introduce an 'Irish-only policy' for all operations within the club because the perception prevailed that the club was going nowhere in terms of promoting Irish, with English being the main language. A number of members left the organization in reaction to what was to become the effective transformation of the club into an 'English-free zone' (Mac Póilin 2006: 131).

However, as Mac Póilin (2006: 131–32) highlights, the transformation did not stop there. The emerging ethos of the new Cluain Árd also promoted a strong form of cultural nationalism, with the language as its primary objective in relation to which everything else had to be subordinated. In a sense, this marked a return to the early ideals of the Gaelic League. However, it was based on more than fifty years of experience that – from the point of view of the Cluain Árd – had taught the lesson that the language always lost from being associated with politics. Leading figures of the Cluain Árd argued that in such circumstances political ideologies tended to prevail over the interests of the language and that political parties, once in power, always betrayed the language. The situation in the South – against which the Gaeltacht campaign had been directed – was a case in point: the ideals of the Gaelic League had been taken up by the government but were decreasingly followed through in practice. Against the baseline of uncompromising idealism and language purism that came to pervade the Cluain Árd, this was a clear betrayal of the cause of restoring the Irish cultural nation, envisioned in the words of Patrick Pearse as '*chan amháin saor ach Gaelach chomh maith; chan amháin Gaelach ach saor chomh maith*' ('not free merely but Gaelic as well; not Gaelic merely but free as well') (quoted in Ó Muilleoir 1986: 20).

In Chapter 4, Rónán explained how Patrick Pearse had been looked up to as one of the heroes within the club. This is somewhat astonishing because as one of the leaders in the 1916 Rebellion, he clearly represented a language activism linked to the same sort of political nationalism to which the Cluain Árd became so strongly opposed. Yet it is the first half of the previously cited quote – 'not free merely but Gaelic as well' – that to my mind captured (and still captures) the imagination within the club: what use was it to be politically free from Britain if Ireland was not truly Irish – that is to say, entirely Irish-speaking and, ideally, monoglot? Did not the situation in the South illustrate that mere political independence did not ensure true Irishness but, on the contrary, threatened to corrupt it? It is important to note, however, that the club's suspicions towards politics did not necessarily imply that its members were not Nationalist or even Republican in their own political outlook. The club's point was simply that language activism and politics should be clearly separated and the cause of the language should always be treated as supreme. It was in fitting with this programme that the opposition to politics within the Cluain Árd throughout the 1950s and 1960s was mainly directed against the twenty-six-county government in the South, which – according to Rónán in Chapter 4 – 'had turned their back on Irish', whereas the Northern Irish government in 'Stormont did not really figure'.

While the Cluain Árd's new ethos rejected any association with politics, the same also applied to religion. A non-sectarian outlook had already become characteristic of the club before the purge in 1953. This was further enhanced by the non-sectarian tradition within the increasingly dominant philosophy of cultural nationalism, as well as by the growing perception within the club that the Catholic Church was retreating from the language, proving that no church could be trusted (Mac Póilin 2006: 132). However, ensuring a non-sectarian outlook was somewhat difficult. As Óisín, who was secretary of the Cluain Árd before the Troubles, observed:

> It was not easy to follow that policy, you know, where Cumann Chluain Ard was located – right in the heart of the Catholic ghetto in Belfast, but at the same time, people understood that it was a sort of Freedom Hall. Anyone who was interested in Irish, it did not matter where he was from, it did not matter if he was well-to-do, or poor, or black, or white, or yellow, it did not matter. People understood they were welcome in Cumann Chluain Ard, and Cumann Chluain Ard followed that non-sectarian policy when organizations such as the GAA did not care if their events had a Catholic tinge to them. ... I must admit that there were Catholics who thought Irish belonged to them and I was always fearful that they would insult the Protestants, perhaps by accident or on purpose through conversation – that they would say something irrational or stupid that would hurt them. (quoted after McCoy 2006: 160–61)

Given its suspicions towards politics, religious institutions and the establishment in general, the Cluain Árd was to develop a fraught relationship with (and a sort of maverick position towards) its own umbrella organizations, Comhaltas Uladh and the Gaelic League, which it would leave and re-enter at irregular intervals over the next decades (Mac Póilin 2006: 131).

Besides weekly céilí classes and dance nights as well as informal music sessions and sing-songs, the Cluain Árd also provided Irish language classes from the early 1950s onwards. On Monday and Thursday nights, classes at various levels were taught using the 'direct method', exclusively in Irish. In Chapter 4, Rónán provided a vivid description of such Irish-medium teaching, while Roibeárd was also quoted insisting on the necessity of being surrounded by people who 'speak Irish around you'. Spending time at the Cluain Árd, listening to and eventually informally chatting with other members or participating in various events was thus depicted from early on as a (if not the) crucial part of the learning experience.

This emphasis on being among people who speak the language was not restricted to the Cluain Árd itself. On the contrary, the 'holy land' and true homeland of 'authentic' Irish was thought to lie in the traditional Donegal Gaeltacht in the west, of which the Cluain Árd was but a 'sputnik' (Roibeárd's phrase). The club particularly revered the *Rann na Feirste* (Rannafast) area in western Donegal, not least – as mentioned at the beginning of this chapter – because some of its influential members originated from there and still maintained contacts with relatives, among them the two famous local writers, Seosamh Mac Grianna and Séamus Ó Grianna. According to Seosamh Mac Grianna, Belfast Gaeilgeoirí treated his native region almost like a shrine:

> To give Belfast people their dues, it would do the Gaels of Rannafast no harm if they [Belfast people] were to keep coming to them until the world ended. For they were people who never sullied anything Gaelic that they came across. ... I have to say that they were as respectful in Rannafast as a pious person is at a church altar. ... They criticized neither person nor place and they did valiant work for the [Irish] language. (quoted after De Brún 2006: 11)

Given its reverence for the 'original' Ulster Irish dialect as spoken by the native speakers in Rannafast and beyond, it is no surprise that the Cluain Árd strongly objected to the *Caighdeán Oifigiúil* (the 'Official Standard[ization]') of Irish by the Southern state in the 1950s, seeing it as an attempt – as Roibeárd explained in Chapter 4 – 'to take the Irish language from the people and to impose this other, civil-service-type language'. Consequently, the substitution of the Roman script for old Irish as well as modifications in orthography and spoken Irish were rejected within the club (and still were in 2003–2004 when I was there), hence my symbolic use of the old Irish script in this section's headline. As I personally experienced, the club's isolated insistence on non-standardized Irish did not make language acquisition easier; yet this has been but one of the many facets contributing to the overall ethos of the place, fascinating many Irish learners and speakers in West Belfast for decades and ensuring that – as Mairéad observed about the late 1970s – the Cluain Árd was 'a very vibrant place to learn Gaelic'. The following statement by Stiofán, a local language activist describing his motivations as a teenager for going to the Cluain Árd during the 1970s, nicely encapsulates this attraction:

> I wanted to go to where people spoke Irish and that was the Cluain Árd. And also there were intellectual people down there who had very positive attitudes, who had, you know, a philosophy about Irish and all that that I liked to hear. And, you know, Roibeárd, of course, and other people who

were strong Irish language speakers, but also who had a philosophy about it all. Who got a reason to do it! And it was just a desire to mix with them.

The club was magnetic. It was the only place in Belfast where nothing but Irish was spoken, and it was run by some impressive, passionate and charismatic personalities (so nicely described by Rónán in Chapter 4) with a great knowledge of and a strong philosophy about the language – which was purist, uncompromising and constructing the restoration of Irish as the ultimate crusade transcending all minor political and religious considerations. These people were driven by a zeal to hand down their knowledge and convictions to subsequent generations; combine that with an atmosphere full of activities, and it is not too hard to see why the Cluain Árd became the place to be for generations of Gaeilgeoirí up until at least the early 1990s.

This is not to say that there were not phases at the Cluain Árd during which its overall ethos was threatened. As I was told, the club was bombed in the early 1970s. The incident happened at night and nobody was hurt. Within the organization this incident was ascribed to either the Official or Provisional IRA, both of which had been effectively denied access to the premises because of the club's Irish-only policy. In the late 1970s and again in the mid-1980s, there were further attempts by various Republican groups to establish some dominance within this four-walled Gaeltacht. Yet the people running the club successfully resisted the temptation to leave the right path of cultural nationalism, by excluding people who did not attend classes and by ensuring that no one active in a political party could become a committee member.

By and large, however, the Cluain Árd has shown remarkable continuity in its ethos from the early 1950s into the (ethnographic) present. To my mind, this is largely due to a remarkable continuity in its personnel, particularly with regard to the undisputed succession of its two leading figures. From the 1953 purge in which he played a leading role up to the early 1970s, the above-quoted Óisín seemingly dominated the club as its secretary. Being a very strong personality who inspired many with his clear vision and strong commitment to the language, he became involved in the foundation of the urban Gaeltacht and its all-Irish primary school in the 1960s and early 1970s (see below). However, when the school was unable to attract a native Irish teacher during the early days of the Troubles, Óisín was not willing to compromise on this issue. He and his family left Belfast for good and have lived in the Donegal Gaeltacht since that time. The resulting gap in the Cluain Árd was filled by Roibeárd, who – having been in the club since the late 1950s – became the new chairman and has been the 'prophet' of the Cluain Árd ever since. The following exchange I had with Stiofán, who frequented the club in the 1970s and 1980s, illustrates how the Cluain Árd came to operate:

Stiofán: Roibeárd used to always have sort of assistants around him. A group of young people who would be, you know, the sort of the next generation. I wasn't with them. But I moved down to the Cluain Árd just because that's where you heard the best Irish and speak Irish and be spoken back to.

OZ: My impression is, from having been to the Cluain Árd many times and
              having talked to people who all went to the Cluain Árd, that it was
              always kind of – almost like Roibeárd being a 'prophet' [as many of these
              people had described him – OZ] and having a circle of young acolytes or
              disciples around him.

Stiofán: It is still like that, yeah.

OZ: Was it a bit like that?

Stiofán: Oh, it was completely like that! And, you know, they would sit with
              Roibeárd and – but it didn't last very long. After a while the boys grown
              up and moved away. Or there be a split or a camp or something like
              that. … Roibeárd is the sort of person who can make an impression
              on you. And there was always something sort of charismatic about
              Roibeárd. And for some people, he just made it easier to gather them
              around, and you know, they go to places with him, and he always
              speaks Irish to them, and he always gets them to speak Irish back. So
              a lot of people actually learnt Irish through speaking to Roibeárd and
              being in Roibeárd's company.

Generations of local Gaeilgeoirí thus came to the Cluain Árd, learnt Irish, became
involved in running the place for a couple of years and then moved on, whilst
Roibeárd – virtually married to the language – stayed on. In a sense embodying
the Cluain Árd, he and others around him had claimed the moral high ground of
the Irish language, from which the uncompromising gospel of language purism
and cultural nationalism was being preached. From this idealistic stance, many of
the subsequent developments in the local language scene may not have lived up to
the propagated standards. While this caused a degree of friction within the scene,
during my time in Belfast, few denied that the Cluain Árd had integrity and offered
a level of language perfection rarely met elsewhere. Roibeárd once told me that
'radicals go nowhere, but without radicals, you also go nowhere'. This was certainly
true in the case of local language development. Nevertheless it was a group of Irish
speakers from the Cluain Árd that was able to effect concrete advances by taking
a pragmatic approach to the language in the 1960s, thereby turning the prophets
'going nowhere' into a 'going somewhere'.

From a Hedge(d) School to Irish Language Industries: Godfathers of the Irish Language

The place to which Irish was literally moving in the late 1960s was a two and a half
acre site: the former farm land, Horner's Fields, at Shaw's Road on the then outskirts
of West Belfast. The idea to form 'Ireland's first urban Gaeltacht' in Belfast (De
Brún 2006: 12) had emerged in the early 1960s within a group of young couples
who met and were learning Irish at the Cumann Chluain Árd. Inspired by its
ideals and by the ideas of Máirtín Ó Cadhain – a radical language activist from
the South who emphasized the primacy of urban centres for the survival of the
language (e.g. Ó Cadhain 1964) – they were determined to extend the use of the
language as far as possible in their lives, and planned to raise their children in an

Irish language environment. Yet having made contact with the handful of isolated Irish-speaking families within Belfast that were trying to raise their own children in a predominantly Irish environment revealed the difficulties of such an endeavour in a context in which English was ubiquitous. The solution to this dilemma consisted in forming a cohesive community nucleus with its own Irish-medium school, thereby creating a 'natural' language environment in which the children would not have to resort to English every time they went out to play or attended school (De Brún 2006: 12; Nig Uidhir 2006: 136–37).

Building on the work of Maguire (1991 and 2006),[1] who did extensive educational research among the Shaw's Road community and its Irish-medium school, and using my own fieldwork material, the foundation of the Shaw's Road Gaeltacht and its affiliated Irish-medium school can be described as follows. To begin with, the obstacles to implement the plan for an urban Gaeltacht were many, as the founders of the Shaw's Road community were mainly young working-class people with limited resources. They had no experience in purchasing land, urban planning or extensive fund-raising, nor could they fall back on the know-how of others. Furthermore, Irish-medium education had never been an issue in Northern Ireland; hence resources for Irish-medium teaching were not available. In addition, as Rónán recalled, the Ministry of Education made it clear from early negotiations in the mid-1960s onwards that it would not only refuse to officially recognize and fund the proposed Irish-medium primary school, but it would actually regard it as illegal.

The five remaining families out of the original nineteen couples met these and other problems with a form of agency that can be described as 'idealistic pragmatism', which is nicely summarized by Maguire (1991: 73): '"Potential" problems were not dwelt upon. Despite long-term aspirations the scheme was tackled on a day to day basis. Having admitted that, logically speaking, a particular task was impossible, the group got on with the business of finding a means of carrying it out.' As was already described in Rónán's section in Chapter 4, the participating families established a company in order to meet legal requirements and facilitate credits from building companies. With the help of the wider Irish-speaking community, especially regarding legal and architectural matters, they got planning approval and started to build their houses in 1968 on the site, which they bought from the Christian Brothers with a loan from Comhaltas Uladh. Given their scarce resources, the houses were largely built consecutively. As Rónán recalled, 'Whatever money was left helped another house to progress until they got their mortgage, and then their money helped another house to go so far'. The first in the row of five terraced houses was completed and moved into in 1969; the other four families followed suit over the following months. Yet much of the energy from the construction work on Shaw's Road came to be diverted during that year due to wider political developments.

Since the mid-1960s, two opposing forces had emerged in the political climate of Northern Ireland. While the extremist Reverend Ian Paisley represented the

---

1. Maguire's 2006 text was actually published under her Irish-version name, 'Nig Uidhir' (see Bibliography). In order to avoid confusion, I refer here to both works with the English version of her name, 'Maguire', used for the first text.

interests of many hard-line Unionists, the Northern Ireland Civil Rights Association (NICRA), founded in 1967, pressed for equality in housing, employment and voting. While NICRA did not actually question the political existence of the Northern state and intended to encompass all religions and traditions in the North, it largely appealed to a critical mass of well-educated Catholics who had emerged since the educational reforms in 1947 and who became politically mobilized in an era of civil rights and student movements in the United States, France and elsewhere. Protest marches of this and other organizations throughout 1968 and 1969 led to attacks and the violent suppression by Protestant mobs, often in collusion with local police. Within this atmosphere of growing sectarian violence, the situation deteriorated in mid-August 1969 with violent encounters in Derry and in North and West Belfast marking the outbreak of the subsequent Troubles. Sectarian rioting was particularly intense in the Clonard district of West Belfast, where three-fifths of the houses on Bombay Street were burned down by a Protestant mob (Fraser 2000: 36–47).

This political context of mayhem, violent attacks, British soldiers patrolling the streets and numerous families displaced (1,505 Catholic and 315 Protestant families were forced to move in Belfast alone [Fraser 2000: 47]) could not leave Irish-speaking circles unaffected. After a number of controversial debates about whether or not the Cluain Árd should be opened for non-Irish speakers in need, this 'sanctuary or shrine' of the Irish language, as the then committee member Rónán put it, was turned into a temporary refugee camp. Members of the Shaw's Road community decided to use their by-now acquired building expertise to rebuild Bombay Street, which was just a couple of streets away from the Cluain Árd. Until 1972, Irish speakers from the urban Gaeltacht and beyond rebuilt a total of thirty-one houses on Bombay Street. These events marked a degree of change in the attitudes of many of the Irish speakers involved. For instance, Rónán was already quoted in Chapter 4 explaining how he personally experienced this profound transformation:

> We might've been separated from our own community by then, the fact that we're Irish speakers, right? That was very – our – like a tunnel vision. That's the way we were going. People who hadn't got Irish might've been – we might've thought, maybe, they weren't Irish. When '69 happened, that went out the window.

Instead, Rónán and others became aware:

> that you were part of a wider community. You were very insular, within the community. We were living in the Cluain Árd, and then, when the terrible things of '69 happened, we found we were really – that at the end of the day, we're part of a wider community. And had cut ourselves off, slightly.

This realization was to engender a conscious reopening towards the wider Catholic community, leading to the subsequent engagement of the Shaw's Road company in various local community projects such as setting up an industrial estate, a knitting factory, an investment company and a petrol station, not all of which were Irish-language based. Back on Shaw's Road, three other families became involved in construction work in 1970. These plus an additional three families that had moved into the community by 1976 brought the total number of families in the urban Gaeltacht to eleven.

While the foundation of this small Gaeltacht community in itself constituted an important step forward for the Irish language, giving it a tangible presence and a point of reference, it was the establishment in 1971 of the all-Irish *Bunscoil Phobal Feirste* ('Belfast Community Primary School'), the first of its kind in the North of Ireland, which was to heavily influence local language developments (Maguire 1991: 67–83; and 2006). Accommodated in a mobile hut and hedged in by a row of terraced houses along Shaw's Road, the bunscoil was to display, in a way, many similarities with the 'hedge schools' of the eighteenth century. Like those small, informal schools which secretly emerged in reaction to the Penal Laws restricting Catholic education (McManus 2002), the bunscoil catered to the needs of those that the state rejected, operated illegally and was totally dependent on its own community for funding and the provision of teachers and teaching materials. What made the case of the bunscoil different was that the contentious issue was ethnic rather than religious, and the Shaw's Road Gaeilgeoirí would continue to be in negotiations with the Department of Education. The protracted and unproductive nature of these negotiations, which would stretch on for many years, was caused by 'implicit Government policy and ill-concealed cultural hostilities on part of the authorities' (Maguire 1991: 79). The school eventually succeeded in gaining official recognition as a registered 'Independent School' in 1979, yet it took five further years of campaigning before the bunscoil finally received state funding as a grant-aided school.

As described by Rónán, the initial impetus for founding the bunscoil was the determination of Shaw's Road parents to provide Irish-medium education for their children. So when school opened in 1971, all nine pupils came from Irish-speaking families and mainly from Shaw's Road itself. In subsequent years, other children from the community entered the school, as did pupils from English-speaking backgrounds eventually. For this latter development to become possible, an affiliated Irish-medium nursery was established in 1978 in order to provide the language immersion necessary for entering the bunscoil. This step proved to be crucial because it opened Irish-medium education to the wider English-speaking community and thus ensured the continuous growth of the bunscoil (Maguire 1991: 67–83; Mac Corraidh 2006: 177–80).

This slowly expanding supply of Irish-medium education thereby met a demand within the wider West Belfast community that was increasing for various reasons: the quality of teaching measured in terms of passage rate for the transfer test (Eleven Plus) was high (Mac Corraidh 2006: 179); during the Troubles, local Catholics were becoming increasingly disillusioned with the Church, which was perceived as selling out its own constituency, and hence local Catholics found schooling independent of the Church attractive; interest in Irish was generally growing for reasons that will be dealt with in the next section; and last but not least, the slowly growing supply of Irish-medium education itself produced an increase in demand because it modified the structural context of education in a way that reduced the time and effort needed to become involved with the language. In other words, while the layout of the educational system in Northern Ireland had hitherto not broadly promoted extensive contact with Irish, the emerging Irish-medium sector provided an opportunity for parents without Irish (such as Fíona and Sinéad) to let their children live their dreams and become Gaeilgeoirí in a relatively easy way.

Against this background it is not surprising that Irish-medium education has been growing ever since. When it obtained state funding in 1984, the bunscoil catered to 162 pupils. In 1987, a second bunscoil – *Gaelscoil na bhFál* (the 'Falls Irish-medium school') – was opened in West Belfast, and one year later, nine Irish-medium nurseries were feeding into the all-Irish primary education system (Maguire 1991: 77; Mac Corraidh 2006: 179–80). In 1991 on the twentieth anniversary of Bunscoil Phobal Feirste, *Meánscoil Feirste* ('Belfast Secondary School') opened its doors in the Cultúrlann to cater for the growing number of children who had received their primary education through Irish. After a period of effective campaigning, the meánscoil eventually received government funding and recognition in 1996 (O'Reilly 1999: 123–37). All in all, it was evident at the time of my fieldwork that Irish-medium education was surely *the* success story of the local Irish language revival, with six nurseries, six primary schools and one secondary school in operation, and with a total of 1,349 pupils in Catholic West Belfast alone in 2003–2004 (Comhairle na Gaelscolaíochta 2004).

While triggering this development was perhaps the single most important contribution of the Shaw's Road community, members of this circle furthered the cause of Irish in various other forms as well. A number of community projects throughout the 1970s have already been mentioned. Another opportunity for promoting the language opened up in the mid-1970s when some of the Shaw's Road people were asked to take over and manage the local *Andersonstown News*. By then they already had a reputation within the wider West Belfast community for being idealistic pragmatists who had founded their own all-Irish community, rebuilt Bombay Street and were fighting for recognition of and funding for their school. Over the next few decades, these Gaeilgeoirí would transform what had started as a small community newspaper informing locals about events and campaigns related to internment (imprisonment without trial between 1971 and 1975) into a viable news group with local papers in West, North and South Belfast. From early on, they regularly featured articles in Irish and promoted the cause of the language in numerous English texts.

From the 1980s onwards, additional Irish language initiatives emerged, ultimately producing the present plethora of Irish language organizations, groups, projects and activities described and systematized in Chapter 3. What is important to note, however, is that many of these projects – and most notably the Cultúrlann McAdam Ó Fiaich – would probably not have been the successes they proved to be if it had not been for the involvement and/or advice of a few of the leading figures from the Shaw's Road community. Within the local language scene it is not uncommon to refer to these people and to one outstanding individual in particular as the 'godfathers of the Irish language', and this is meant mostly in an affectionate way. Stiofán, who was the main driving force behind the Irish-medium newspaper *Lá*, provided me with the following interpretation, which I think nicely captures the essence of people's usage of this 'godfather' phrase:

> I think they mean someone who's been there for a long time. Have you ever seen *The Godfather* [the movie], the opening scene? It's the first *Godfather*, where people come to him with their problems, you know, and they assume he has the best way to get it sorted out. If he can do anything to sort things out, he'll do it! So, I think, that's the way, like – even, I didn't know him when we wanted to publish our first magazine. We went down to the *Andersonstown News*, and he was there. He was prepared to use whatever he could because it was in Irish, you know! So if the 'godfather' phrase means anything, it means that sort of counsellory person to go to when you don't know how to go about with something related to the language.

By combining a strong idealism regarding the Irish language with an equally strong pragmatism, the Shaw's Road community in general and 'the godfathers of Irish' in particular have thus achieved a remarkable transformation within West Belfast towards an ever-greater presence of the Irish language. Seeing in every English speaker a potential Irish speaker, they have often enough compromised on the purist's ideal of 'Irish only' in order to get people speaking '*Gaeilge más féidir, Béarla más gá*' ('Irish if possible, English if necessary'), as one of the 'godfathers' in the Cultúrlann put it. By doing so, over the years they have contributed to an extending infrastructure for Irish in various domains of daily life. As mentioned before, the very fact of expanding the supply of Irish to some degree produced its own demand by improving the structural contexts for Irish within education, (thereby) families, state policies as well as language organizations and initiatives generally, which increasingly made it easier for the less committed to get involved with the language. Nevertheless, this cannot fully explain the extent to which local demand for Irish has grown. For this purpose, changes accompanying political developments in the North of Ireland must also be taken into account.

Rebels with/out a Political Cause: The *Jailtacht* and Beyond

The 1960s was an important period for the Irish language in West Belfast, with committed Gaeilgeoirí laying the foundations for later developments by moving from the Cluain Árd to Shaw's Road. However, this should not make us lose sight of the fact that, generally speaking, the Irish language did not really matter in local daily life, especially for the younger generations. Against the backdrop of an emerging 'modern' pop culture with Elvis, the Beatles, rock 'n' roll records and ballroom dancing in big dance halls throughout Belfast, the ideal of a good Irish person going to céilís, wearing a Pioneer Pin (communicating a life commitment to alcohol abstinence) and speaking Irish seemed increasingly old-fashioned and like something from the previous generation. This is not to say that learning Irish was generally not respected. But, as Micheál succinctly explained in Chapter 4, there was an 'odd kind of ambivalence' during the 1960s that was present, and although people were in theory in favour of the language, seriously engaging with it was actually regarded as a bit odd and fairly unusual.

While the Irish language scene in West Belfast, centred mainly in the Cluain Árd and the Árdscoil, was thus in fact rather small and somewhat detached from the wider community, it was also in an important sense separated from the local Republican movement, which, in turn, was equally rather limited throughout the 1960s. This is neither to say that Republicans did not participate in Irish language activities nor that Gaeilgeoirí were not involved in Republican politics. But in terms of the respective agendas of the two circles, they pursued clearly distinct interests. As we have seen, the local language circle tended to be cultural nationalist, non-political and, when concerned with politics, largely oppositional towards the Irish Republic in the South. By contrast, the Republican movement found itself in a process of political transformation in which everything except language issues played a prominent role.

The IRA had been engaged in a militant border campaign since 1956, which had been largely ineffective because it could not get real support from Catholics in the North and because both the Republic and Northern Ireland governments interned suspected volunteers without trial. After the IRA terminated its campaign in 1962, the Republican movement became largely militarily inactive and increasingly embraced a Marxist-socialist point of view in its now broadened analysis of the national question. This shift towards political agitation for a socialist republic was ultimately to provide the main reason for the split of the IRA in 1970: while the northern IRA, which came to be known as the Provisional IRA, was to argue that a militant protection of local Catholics and an enforced settlement of the national question had to come first, the remaining Official IRA in the South stuck to its socialist priorities. The Officials would cease to be a significant force in the following years, leaving the term 'IRA' to refer to the Provisional movement (which is how I use the term throughout this book) (Patterson 1997: 96–139; Coohill 2000: 161, 177–78; Fraser 2000: 34).

Despite these later controversies, the drift of the Republican movement throughout the 1960s towards an anti-Imperialist reading of the local situation was in tune with broader political developments. Increasingly politicized and radicalized youth in the North of Ireland, largely composed of Catholic students, began to gather around the civil rights movement of NICRA, the more radical People's Democracy and various other leftist organizations. Within this general atmosphere of left-wing politicization, an internationalist and often anti-nationalist spirit emerged that left little room for the distractions of cultural nationalism concerned with the Irish language. It is thus not surprising that – as Stiofán emphasized – within the civil rights movement at the time, 'There was never any demand for Irish; the use of Irish in road signs or the use of the language in anything, in civil service or anything'.

While the Irish language thus had a rather low profile towards the end of the 1960s, the outbreak of the Troubles brought about quite fundamental changes. Stiofán, who was twelve in 1969, described these changes:

Before the Troubles, to be Irish was just, you know, it was really an innocent sort of – even though violence was part of it from time to time. But the Troubles back then became a huge factor in all our lives. All our lives were different from then on. … The fact that we were now in a conflict situation and that we were on one side of it and there was another side that we weren't on. And even people who had no intention of getting involved in the conflict were beginning to find out why there were two sides. … And then, as the Troubles progressed, you were forced to take sides, you know, even on an intellectual basis, even within your own community. As the [Provisional] IRA campaign started, well, your choice was, either to be for it or to be against it or to be neither for it nor against it, trying to ignore it. It was very difficult to be sort of neutral. So, that's why there's a division within Nationalism for some people who were Nationalist but who were against violence and some people who were Nationalist but who could accept violence. And, you know, this was the atmosphere as I was growing up as a very teenager. But these were the years after '68; this was following the hippie generation, following the peace movements and against the [Vietnam] war in America, when the young intellectual position was to be against war. So it was difficult to rationalise that with what was happening here on the doorstep, where it seemed that the young intellectual position was to be in favour of war. So, it was, you know, it was quite difficult to work that out, and in fact it was probably incidents on the ground that forced people to take sides.

As shown in Chapter 4 with regard to Rónán, Mairéad, Micheál, Dónal, Fíona and Pól, many people I talked to also recalled how the Troubles constituted a major break in their lives. While not all people reacted in the same way, for many in the deeply affected area of Catholic West Belfast this process led to an upsurge in Nationalist and Republican attitudes, the baseline of which was to read the situation in terms of Irish people being ethnically oppressed for centuries by an external agent, the British state. Since this brought people's sense of identity to the fore, this heightened awareness of individual feelings of Irishness made many people think about what it actually meant to be Irish (as extensively exemplified in chapters 4 and 8). Fíona, a young teenager in 1969, characterized this process in the following words:

When the Troubles came about, it hit me then! I started to question and being able to say, 'Right, I'm Irish here; hold on a moment!' – I wouldn't say it was a slow process. I think it was something that was hitting me very quick! … And it was only when I started to see things happening that I stopped and said, 'Right, hold on'; gettin' my own identity for myself; findin' out who I was or what I was!

For a growing number of locals, identifying with and learning their 'own language' became one way of dealing with these questions that emerged from an intensifying sense of identity. Repossessing the Irish language as a lost part of personal identity thereby almost inevitably turned into a rebellious act – not necessarily out of intention (although for some of course it was) but surely within the logic of the overall political context, which was becoming ever more suspicious and hostile towards issues related to Irish culture and identity. To put it differently: while learning Irish as a way of embracing one's own culture as well as of reappropriating one's own Irish identity could not help but be viewed as a political act in the context of an unfolding ethnic conflict, it was not necessarily intended to reach political ends through the use of the language. Like before, the motivations for the slowly spreading acquisition and practice of the language in West Belfast since the early 1970s oscillated between a self-declared non-political 'cultural' and an explicitly 'political' nationalism. Yet the altered structural context of the Troubles ensured that both the ideal-typical 'political' and 'cultural' Gaeilgeoir would increasingly be ascribed the uniform image of 'rebel' by the powerful state apparatus (O'Reilly 1999: 122) as well as within the wider Protestant Unionist community (McCoy 1997 and 2006: 152; McDermott 2011: 28). Ironically, this external ascription played into the hands of truly political 'rebels with a cause' while making it increasingly difficult for cultural 'rebels without a political cause' to fight that very image both within the language scene and vis-à-vis the wider Northern Irish audience (see Chapter 6). This development further accelerated as growing numbers of Republicans turned towards the Irish language in a very special structural context that would achieve a high level of publicity in the late 1970s and early 1980s, namely, in prison.

In 1971 the Northern Irish government introduced internment without trial in order to deal with escalating levels of violence, especially after the IRA campaign had started. When direct rule from London was introduced in 1972, internees numbered 924. The vast majority of these suspects were accommodated in long, half-cylindrical, prefabricated huts – the 'Cages' in local jargon – at a disused airfield in Long Kesh, south of Belfast. In reaction to a hunger strike by sentenced Republican prisoners demanding political status as well as a concession in secret negotiations with the IRA, the first Northern Ireland Secretary under direct rule, William Whitelaw, introduced 'Special Category Status' in 1972 for those sentenced for crimes related to civil violence. This meant that prisoners at Long Kesh were freed from prison work and allowed free association, extra visits, food parcels and could wear their own clothes. Under Special Category Status, Republican prisoners also established their own command structure, played Gaelic football and organized their own educational programmes, including Irish language classes (Kachuk 1993: 196–201; BBC 2000; McKeown 2001: 27–48).

Learning Irish in prison already had a long tradition among Republicans before the Troubles. Several of my informants had relatives or knew people who had acquired some Irish while imprisoned in the 1920s, 1940s and late 1950s. The situation was not different during the years of this internment when individual Cages were even set up by prisoners as Gaeltacht huts (Kachuk 1993: 198; McKeown 2001: 248). Yet learning and speaking Irish proved to have a more significant impact on convicted prisoners with longer sentences than internees, who were imprisoned on a short-term basis.

As described in Pól's section in Chapter 4, Special Category Status was withdrawn in 1976, leading first to the 'blanket protest' and then to the 'no-wash protest' in 1978, before culminating in the Republican hunger strike in 1981 that saw ten men die, while the Thatcher government remained steadfast (Coogan 1996: 264–84). Throughout these protests, which lasted for more than four years, the Irish language came to play an important role for the prisoners. A new form of teaching had to be devised, as the prisoners were usually kept in pairs in cells they could not leave. Shouting the lesson out through the locked door thus provided a means of teaching the language in these adverse circumstances (Feldman 1991: 212). Yet learning Irish still met with other problems. For instance, few of the prisoners were fluent Irish speakers, and they lacked teaching experience and learning materials such as grammar books and dictionaries (Kachuk 1993: 196–205). This produced a distinct form of spoken Irish that is locally referred to as '*Jailtacht* Irish', occasionally deviating from 'normal' Irish in terms of pronunciation, grammatical structure and certain expressions.

In Chapter 4, Pól provided five main reasons for this massive upsurge of Irish during the prison protests: first, the Republican tradition of learning 'one's own native language' when imprisoned; second, the need to communicate without being understood; third, the strategy of wearing the guards down by breaking their rules (e.g. the prohibition of speaking Irish); fourth, the mere distraction of learning Irish; and fifth, 'the curiosity factor' of not wanting to miss out on Irish conversations between other inmates (see also McKeown 2001: 67–69).

While increasing numbers of Republicans, coming from the political end of nationalism hitherto somewhat disinterested in the language were thus getting involved with Irish in the '*Jailtacht*' throughout the 1970s, this development did not leave the outer Catholic community unaffected (Kachuk 1993: 206–8). This was so because the protests were widely publicized throughout Ireland, the U.K. and beyond, not least through the work of the National H-Block/Armagh Committee, which began operating in 1979. These campaigns not only publicized the general conditions and political demands in the prisons but also highlighted the use of Irish within these four-walled *Jailtachts*. Bobby Sands, the first of the hunger strikers to die in 1981, used the Irish language in much of his writing from the jail. His funeral in West Belfast was attended by an estimated one hundred thousand people. Sinn Féin, the political wing of the IRA, emerged as a political party after gaining influence by abandoning its abstention policy when Bobby Sands and two other hunger strikers were elected as their MPs for London and Dublin while starving themselves to death (Coogan 1996: 264–84). In 1982, Sinn Féin established its own *Roinn Cultuir* ('Cultural Department'), which promoted Irish through the provision of language classes and lobbying for Irish street signs. The Sinn Féin Cultural Department thereby advanced an explicitly political-nationalist rationale with its language activism, which was perhaps most aptly expressed by one of its leading members in the mid-1980s when characterizing the use of Irish as 'another bullet in the freedom struggle' (Ó hAdhmaill 1985: 37; O'Reilly 1999: 34). This was a considerable change in attitude, since Sinn Féin had before largely 'paid lip service to the Irish language but was not closely identified with the cultural movement' (Ó hAdhmaill 1985: 7).

This all contributed to an upsurge in interest in the Irish language in West Belfast, which was recorded in a survey conducted in 1984–85 in fourteen centres offering thirty-six classes with a total of 233 interviewed adult learners (Ó hAdhmaill 1985). As Ó hAdhmaill noted, the number of local language classes increased from eighteen in 1980 (as advertised in the Andersonstown News, 1 November 1980) to about sixty in 1985 (Ó hAdhmaill 1985: 3–4). When asked without prompting what had encouraged them to learn Irish, 18 per cent of the Irish learners indicated 'Sinn Féin/Republican Movement' as their first choice, followed by 'Irish identity' (17 per cent), 'British Army/RUC presence or oppression' (13 per cent), 'Hunger Strike/Bobby Sands' (10 per cent), 'The Troubles' (10 per cent), 'Own language/ culture' (6 per cent) and 'Bunscoil' (5 per cent) (Ó hAdhmaill 1985: 35). These figures indicate that the move of the purely political rebels towards the language had encouraged many beyond the prisons to follow suit, thereby ensuring that by the 1990s – as Pól put it – 'Irish had become much more identified, as a result of the hunger strikes and all the rest of it … with the struggle itself'. Yet the fact that several of the members of Sinn Féin's Cultural Department had been Irish language activists *before* being drawn into politics in the course of the H-Block campaigns also illustrates that cultural rebels were increasingly going political (O'Reilly 1999: 52, 87): what had started as two largely independent circles at the outset of the Troubles had evidently grown into a broader movement with considerable overlap in the mid- and late 1980s. Nevertheless, this overlap was not complete. While not all Republicans, of course, developed an interest in the language, many cultural rebels also continued to fight what they saw as the growing instrumentalization of the language for purely political purposes by Sinn Féin. The issue of the politicization of Irish, and in particular the question (to be discussed in Chapter 6) as to whether Sinn Féin and Republicans in general had 'hijacked' the language, are to be seen in this context (Kachuk 1993: 237–57; O'Reilly 1999).

Despite controversies, differing positions and conflicting interpretations within the language scene and beyond, the fact remains that at the time of my fieldwork, Catholic West Belfast had experienced a remarkable revival of the Irish language throughout the Troubles. To my mind it is evident that while other reasons for engaging with Irish existed as well – most notably, initially more instrumentally rational reasons during the prison protest – re-appropriating their 'own native language' as part of their Irish identity developed into the main motivation for many if not most local Gaeilgeoirí. However, as we will see in Chapter 6, interpretations with regard to what that actually meant varied greatly, with political and cultural nationalism as explicit positions only marking the extreme points of a usually much more fuzzy continuum. While this motivational field for becoming a Gaeilgeoir had existed before, it is obvious that it was the structural context of political conflict in the late 1960s and beyond that generally heightened people's sense of ethnic and/or political identity, and in that way induced ever more locals to translate this potential motivation into an actually changed language practice. The growing demand among language 'rebels with(out) a political cause' for various contexts in which Irish could be experienced and used was thereby being matched by the simultaneously expanding supply of a language infrastructure through the work of committed activists; or, to be more precise, both developments mutually reinforced one another over the years. At the time I was conducting fieldwork in West Belfast in 2003–2004, the Irish language had moved into a new stage, exhibiting a much greater degree of normalization than before. However, not everyone within the language scene was content with the accompanying side-effects.

Prostitutes of the Irish Language?

In the 1990s, the conditions for the Irish language began to improve to a degree unheard of before. Due to extensive campaigning by language activists and as a spin-off of the emerging Peace Process, which started to make its presence felt after the first IRA ceasefire in 1994, the British government slowly began to revise its official attitude towards the language. The state had begun to fund some language projects in the 1980s, mainly – it seemed – in an attempt to loosen the ties between Irish and the Republican movement (Kachuk 1993: 310–15). It thereby established a policy of 'political vetting' under which funding was withdrawn from organizations suspected of having paramilitary contacts (such as the West Belfast branch of *Glór na nGael*), while financial support was granted to more moderate initiatives (Kachuk 1993: 333–62; O'Reilly 1999: 114–23).

Although in the early 1990s the relationship between the language scene and the state was quite fraught, with conflicts and mutual suspicion abounding, it slowly began to improve from the mid-1990s onwards. After years of campaigning, Irish street signs were legalized in 1995 and 'political vetting' for state funding became less and less of an issue (O'Reilly 1999: 137–46, 122). The changes in state attitudes towards the language found their clearest expression in the Good Friday Agreement of 1998. For the first time in history, the British government committed itself, to 'take resolute action to promote the language', to 'facilitate and encourage the use of the language … in public and private life', to 'encourage and facilitate Irish medium education in line with current provision for integrated education' and to 'seek more effective ways to encourage and provide financial support for Irish language film and television production in Northern Ireland' (Northern Ireland Office 1998: Section 6-VII-§3-4). For that purpose, *Foras na Gaeilge* (the 'Irish Language Agency'), the North/South implementation body responsible for the promotion of Irish throughout Ireland by both states, was established in 1999. Two years later, the British government also ratified the European Charter for Regional or Minority Languages, thereby extending its commitment to the promotion of Irish and other minority languages within the U.K.

Some language activists complained to me that hostile attitudes towards Irish remained in certain quarters of the state apparatus, and rightly pointed out that the government had to be constantly pressured to actually implement its commitments (like, for instance, with the Irish Language Broadcast Fund, which only came into being six years after its announcement in the Good Friday Agreement). However, there were also other voices in the scene, stressing – as one activist put it – that 'things have changed so much; it's really a matter of choice now; if people want to create an Irish-speaking community, what's to stop them?'

Apart from generally facilitating the ongoing expansion of the movement and somewhat depoliticizing the whole issue of the language, these fundamental changes in official attitudes over the past ten years have also, in an important sense, engendered an increasing transformation of the local language scene from what could be described as a community-driven enterprise to an enterprise-driven community. Although many language classes were still taught free of charge and many projects continued to depend on the voluntary work of committed activists, a growing number of language activists were able to make a living through the Irish language. Several projects that first emerged as initiatives of often unemployed language enthusiasts had thereby turned into heavily subsidized Irish language businesses. In addition, the language movement was becoming increasingly diversified, incorporating everyone from infants in local *Naíscoileanna* ('Irish-medium nursery schools') to elderly Gaeilgeoirí, and was thus exhibiting an ever broader range of attitudes to and usages of the language.

However, these recent developments did not meet with the approval of all within the language scene. On the contrary, several language purists aired to me their discontent about what they saw as the aberrations of the present language movement. Roibeárd's criticism of the 'Irish language industries' in the opening scene of this chapter is but one case in point. These purists often complained that despite the widely celebrated 'revival' of Irish in Catholic West Belfast, the language was not actually being used by competent speakers in as many contexts as it could be; in addition, professional language activists were criticized for not even sending their own children to Irish-medium schools. The dissatisfaction of these purists also centred on the quality of Irish, both as taught in schools and adult classes and as used in various events and services provided by local language initiatives. This Irish, they complained, was often a form of '*Géarla*', a 'broken Irish' in the sense of a mixture of *Gaeilge* ('Irish') and *Béarla* ('English'). These observations often led the purists to question the actual commitment of those involved in this 'degeneration' and fuelled suspicion: since these Gaeilgeoirí were obviously not involved in the language as an end in itself or out of pure commitment (otherwise, they would of course enact the same ideals as the purists), these Gaeilgeoirí must have been involved for other reasons, namely, for financial or for political (i.e. Republican) gain. In the course of such reasoning, one purist expressed her aversion to such behaviour by claiming that such activists did not have 'a single Irish bone in their bodies'. When talking to another language activist and close friend of mine about this perceived type of actor, this friend proposed I call them the alleged 'prostitutes of the Irish language'. To me that nicely captures the purists' perception of these people as selling their 'Irish souls' by being involved in the language revival, not out of inner commitment but only out of a base desire for money or political gain.

While there may have been a grain of truth in such suspicions among purists, to my eye this was ultimately a misrepresentation of the scene, basically resulting from the application of a one-sided, very idealistic and uncompromising standard. To my knowledge, it seemed indeed to be the case that most Gaeilgeoirí in West Belfast lacked the fanaticism and purism propagated by the prophets of the movement, but this was largely due to practicalities rather than to a lack of commitment. For instance, a Gaeilgeoir and mother of three children attending Irish-medium schools told me that, being involved in a stressful family life, her first priority had always been to learn in Irish what she really needed to help her children with homework and get along in daily life. For her it was simply of more practical importance to know words occurring in everyday life in Belfast than to focus on specialized Gaeltacht vocabulary – 'fifty different Irish terms for turf' – or to bother too much about the ultimate grammatical truth. A teacher in a local bunscoil rhetorically asked, 'What is wrong with earning money through the Irish language?', thereby emphasizing that turning your language activism into a livelihood did not necessarily make you less committed.

In a crucial sense, however, I did observe a certain lack of 'conscious commitment' among the younger generation of local Gaeilgeoirí. During a period of participant observation in the local meánscoil, I could observe (and hear) that pupils – while following the 'Irish-only' policy of the school in their communications with teachers – tended to speak English among themselves or, when older, often used a form of 'broken Irish', as they themselves referred to it. Neither the pupils nor the teachers were particularly secretive about this language practice, and although teachers strongly encouraged the wider use of correct Irish, most pupils did not seem to have a problem with bilingualism or use of 'broken Irish'. When talking to older pupils and ex-pupils of the school it was equally clear that most would move between different English, Irish or 'broken Irish' contexts according to their personal interests rather than due to any conscious decision to enter as many Irish contexts as possible. As a sixteen-year-old pupil of the meánscoil put it when talking about various Irish language activities, functions and events in the Cultúrlann: 'I wouldn't go there just because it is Irish'. This attitude was actually quite different from the one among older Gaeilgeoirí, who often described their motivation for supporting concrete language initiatives less in terms of personal interests but more in terms of *ar son na cúise* – doing it 'for the cause' of the Irish language.

Far from indicating a lack of identification, however, I would argue that this behaviour among younger Gaeilgeoirí did in fact indicate an identification with the Irish language, yet in a profoundly transformed sense in comparison with the ideals of the purists. By living a bilingual life without being too consciously committed to speaking Irish, these youngsters and perhaps most local Irish speakers increasingly embodied a shift through which a formerly mainly value-rational commitment to a hitherto rather arbitrary language usage was increasingly being transformed into a habitualized, 'normal' practice. Instead of signifying the abandonment of an idealistic commitment to the language, the usage of Irish in Catholic West Belfast at that time seemed to represent the enactment of this very commitment, albeit adjusted to the realities of an overwhelmingly English-speaking environment. This development thus exemplified a move of the Irish language towards the field of *doxa* (Bourdieu 1977: 163–71), in which speaking Irish increasingly went without saying, because decades of conscious and outspoken language activism had produced such a local 'normality' for the language both in representations and practices as to increasingly naturalize the initial arbitrariness of the endeavour.

Conclusions

In this chapter, I have described and analysed the local revival of the Irish language in Catholic West Belfast stretching from the 1950s to the early years of the new millennium. At the outset of this period, Irish could be encountered only to a limited extent in local families, although it was on the curriculum for quite a few Catholic schools and promoted by a small cluster of Irish language organizations with some support from local GAA clubs and the Catholic Church. Yet the language scene had to operate within the highly powerful but unfavourable structural context of the Northern Irish state, which treated Catholics as second-class citizens and handled the language with a mixture of neglect, suspicion and hostility. Given such conditions, the number of actual Irish speakers constituted an almost negligible minority. At the time of my fieldwork in 2003–2004, the situation had changed in a fundamental way. A local infrastructure in Irish had emerged, which catered to the various domains of daily life and included an independent all-Irish educational sector as an alternative to the provision of Irish in Catholic schools. Irish language organizations and initiatives had greatly expanded, and some were operating as Irish-medium businesses with paid employees. Although still a minority phenomenon, the number of Irish speakers had dramatically increased as had the number of families in which Irish was spoken (not least because children were attending Irish-medium schools). This all took place in the context of a Northern Irish state that had officially committed itself to actively promoting the Irish language according to demand.

In order to explain this historical development from a structure-agency perspective, I have attempted to reconstruct the diachronic and synchronic interactions between four distinct types of agency and respective structural contexts. In keeping with local parlance, these forms of agency were metaphorically identified with the roles of 'prophet', 'godfather', 'rebel' and 'prostitute'. I have thereby repeatedly highlighted how a dominant value-rational motivation to speak one's 'own native language' has run through much of the local language revival, as was clearly the case for the 'prophets', 'godfathers' and 'cultural rebels' but also – over time – for those 'political rebels' who only became engaged with Irish because of the prison protests. This is not to say, of course, that other motivations did not also play their part. As described in Chapter 4, some of my informants – such as Roibeárd, Mairéad, Micheál, Pádraigín and Caoimhín – had already become accustomed to a few Irish phrases in early childhood and hence used them out of habituation (or traditional motivation in Weber's terminology). Others clearly exhibited strong affectual motives for a continued engagement with Irish, as with Rónán, who accompanied a friend to the Cluain Árd and then initially stayed on because of the community aspect or Dónal, who through the experience of being at a Gaeltacht college strongly fell in love with the language. Instrumentally rational motivations, of course, also existed: Micheál initially learnt Irish in order to better understand the Gaelic substratum within Anglo-Irish literature; political rebels such as Pól learnt Irish during the early protest years mainly in order not to be understood by prison guards, to annoy the guards, to relieve boredom and in order not to miss out on other prisoners' conversations; Fíona and Sinéad needed Irish in order to help their children attending Irish-medium schools; and finally, Caoimhín chose Irish in order to be able to go to Gaeltacht colleges with his classmates.

However, such additional motivations notwithstanding, many if not most of my informants at some point also were exposed to the idea that learning one's 'own native language' was an important value in itself, worthy of being pursued in practice, and the individual life stories in Chapter 4 provide fascinating variations on this topic. I thus maintain my interpretation that for much of the recent language activism, this value-rational motivation has been a dominant driving force, ultimately bringing about a more normalized present in which more and more people have made speaking Irish a habit (or Weberian traditional motivation) and in which the growing Irish-medium employment sector also has provided an instrumentally rational incentive for learning the language.

While I insist on the crucial motivational capacity of the representation of Irish as 'our own native language' throughout much of the local Irish language revival, I hasten to add that this phrase has clearly meant different and at times opposing things within the dynamics of representations and practices in Catholic West Belfast. Building on the life stories in the preceding chapter as well as on the reconstructed contemporary history of the language scene developed in this chapter, I will address this last analytical dimension in the next chapter, namely, the relationship between representations and practices of the Irish language.

Chapter 6

'Our own native language'

Local Representations and Practices of the Irish Language

Towards the end of March 2004, I participated in another *Dianchúrsa Aonlae* ('One-Day Irish Language Crash Course') that took place on a Saturday from 10:00 a.m. to 4:00 p.m. at the local *Ionad Uíbh Eachach* ('Iveagh Centre'). For months, I had been attending several weekly morning classes in this community centre, which was conveniently located in my immediate neighbourhood of Iveagh/Broadway, which also housed the Cultúrlann and the *Gaelscoil na bhFál* ('Falls Irish-medium Primary School'). Having learnt about the intensive course through a leaflet, I arrived on that day shortly before 10:00 a.m., and the place was already crowded. Irish language classes were being offered at four different levels, ranging from 'Beginners' to 'Level 2/3' to 'Level 3/4 – GCSE' and '*Comhrá*' ('Conversation'). In addition to coffee breaks between sessions, there was a one-hour lunch break during which some finger food was delivered from the nearby Cultúrlann. I decided to join the 'Level 3/4 – GCSE' as usual, which meant that I met a few acquaintances from my weekly classes at the centre. However, there were also many new faces, with all in all about twenty people attending this class that – like everywhere except for the Cluain Árd – was conducted in English.

While this one-day Irish language course provided a context in which the Irish language could be *practised* at different levels and to differing extents, it also provided an arena in which the Irish language turned out to be *represented*. One such incident of representing the Irish language occurred during a coffee break as I ended up chatting with an elderly gentleman, Seán, who I had met that day in my class. Our conversation began when Seán half-jokingly mentioned that the Irish language could teach you humour. As he went on to explain, you have to be able to laugh about yourself when making mistakes since these mistakes expose that – as he put it – 'you can't even speak your own native language', 'the language of your country'.

As Seán told me, he learnt Irish in his youth both at grammar school and in the Árdscoil but had not then spoken it until about three years ago when he returned to the language after retiring. We started talking about the local Irish language revival in West Belfast, and Seán agreed that interest in Irish had increased in the course of the Troubles, when – as he put it – learning and speaking Irish came to be perceived as 'repossessing', 're-establishing' and 'reinforcing' individual Irish identity. Seán emphasized that his personal interest in Irish was motivated by such a desire to learn more about his own culture and identity. But he stressed that he was strictly against the idea of using or representing the Irish language as a political weapon against the British. He claimed that it was only for a short period in the late 1970s during the prison protests that the Irish language was used by Irish people as a weapon against British colonialism. However, Seán claimed that in public perception, the Irish language subsequently came to be viewed as a political weapon and as linked to Republicanism, and this was precisely the reason why he then stopped speaking Irish himself, as he completely disagreed with this image of the Irish language.

Seán told me that although many Republicans learnt Irish in prison as a secretive means of communication, this upsurge in the *Jailtacht* had not really increased outside interest in Irish; instead, the local language revival was to be seen as a consequence of the growing Irish-medium educational sector over the past fifteen years. According to Seán, the involvement of Republicans with the Irish language had been purely political anyway. In recent years, Seán claimed, learning and speaking Irish had become increasingly dissociated from Republicanism and had turned into something about 'your culture and identity only'. As Seán had had such an apolitical stance all along, this recent development had thus again made it possible for him, he concluded, to re-engage with his 'own native language'.

In this chapter, I will deal with the complex dynamics between representations and practices of the Irish language (dimension 1) as I encountered them in numerous situations during my stay in Catholic West Belfast in 2003–2004, such as the one outlined above. I will begin by analysing the relationship between representations and practices regarding the micro-dynamics of concrete Irish language usage. Variable practices of 'code-switching' can hereby be interpreted as situational and conversational forms of mediating between purist and pragmatist norms of appropriate language usage, in which notions about what actually constitutes 'the Irish language' are implicated in complex ways.

In a second step, I will address the meso-level of the local Irish language revival, conceiving the latter as a label for a set of increasingly expanding Irish language practices, which were locally represented in conflicting ways. Most importantly, this issue links up to the locally contentious question of whether or not Sinn Féin and Republicans generally 'hijacked' the Irish language in the 1980s and 1990s for their own political purposes.

Finally, I will analyse the relationship between representations and practices at the macro-level of the Irish language itself. It is at this scale that ideas about Irish as 'our own language' – equally noticed in its ubiquity for the 1990s by O'Reilly (1999: ix–x) and, as such, eponymous for Maguire's (1991) study of the all-Irish educational sector – need to be situated and unpacked.

Between Purism and Pragmatism:
The Micro-Dynamics of Irish Language Usage

As soon as some capacity emerges to express oneself in more than one language, the question arises as to when, where, with whom and why a certain language or language variety (also called a 'code') is used at the expense of another – be it that such shifts occur between communicative turns, within such turns or between constituents of single sentences. Within linguistics, this issue has been discussed under the label of 'code-switching', defined as 'an individual's use of two or more language varieties in the same speech event or exchange' (Woolard 2006: 73–74). Generally speaking, linguistic approaches to code-switching have been threefold: first, psycholinguistic studies have mainly framed the issue in terms of the varying degrees to which different languages are mentally activated; second, grammatical approaches have prominently addressed grammatical constraints that configure the potential for code-switching between specific languages; and third, sociolinguistic research has interpreted such language usage primarily in terms of the social meanings that emanate from the motivations for and functions of code-switching (Gardner-Chloros 2003; Woolard 2006: 74).

Restricting myself to the sociolinguistic approach herein, it can be observed that many taxonomies of code-switching build on an early distinction by Blom and Gumperz (1972) between 'situational' and 'metaphorical switching', the latter being later renamed 'conversational switching' (Gumperz 1982: 61). According to Bailey (2001: 239), situational switching is characterized by 'conventionalised associations between codes and context/activity/participants', ensuring that 'codes are switched when observable changes in the context occur'; code-switching thus reflects its communicative context. In contrast, within conversational switching, 'changes in language effect changes in context and social roles, without tangible changes in the outward context' (Bailey 2001: 239); code-switching thus creates its own communicative context.

Before drawing on this distinction for the subsequent analysis, it needs to be emphasized that a comprehensive sociolinguistic study on the communicative functions of code-switching between English and Irish is, of course, neither envisioned for this section nor for the whole chapter. While all three levels of the dynamics between representations and practices of the Irish language that are covered in this chapter do indeed have an impact on the actual use of Irish, this list is obviously far from exhaustive. Instead of aiming for comprehensiveness, I will thus concentrate on only one issue, namely, on what Gumperz (1982: 68) calls 'norms of appropriateness'. By this, he means those explicit norms that specify, from the actor's point of view, which forms of code-switching are deemed legitimate and hence shape specific configurations of language practices. As I will show with regard to three such configurations within the Irish language scene in West Belfast, local norms of appropriate code-switching were characterized by a profound tension between language purism, insisting on the necessity to speak only Irish as much as possible in order to prevent it from dying in an overwhelmingly English environment, and communicative pragmatism, dominated by an ideal of politeness that opposed excluding or offending non-Irish speakers and hence encouraged code-switching.

The first local configuration of Irish language usage to be analysed herein consists of two exemplary places with a tangible presence of the Irish language that were already depicted in great detail in earlier chapters, namely, the Cumann Chluain Árd and the Cultúrlann McAdam Ó Fiaich. At the time of my fieldwork, the Cluain Árd had been following an explicit monolingual Irish-only policy on its premises for five decades. The club accommodated a rather small, close-knit community of committed Gaeilgeoirí who admired 'pure' Donegal Irish and aimed for its acquisition and maintenance. On the surface, the club was neither easily accessible nor inviting; yet once inside, anyone with a genuine interest in the language was integrated and actively supported on his or her path to becoming a Gaeilgeoir (see Chapter 5).

In contrast, and as described in Chapter 3, the Cultúrlann only had an implicit language policy of bilingualism that could be reconstructed from observable language practices, namely, from the coexistence of Irish and English signage, the frequent use of both languages in Irish-medium events and the general absence of any sanctions for using English. Given its location on Falls Road, its extensive hours of operation, its bilingualism, the wide range of activities offered and its deliberate publicizing (especially in the quarterly *Clár Ealaíon* – 'Arts Programme'), the Cultúrlann was easily accessible and inviting. In my experience, many people working at the Cultúrlann were friendly and welcoming, yet given that the Cultúrlann provided a space for a large and rather loose network of Irish speakers, there neither were nor could be any systematic attempts to proactively integrate new guests at the centre.

Viewing these two local Irish language venues in light of the sociolinguistic analysis of code-switching, they can be interpreted as different attempts to mediate between language purism and communicative pragmatism through the institutionalization of specific norms of language usage. In other words, both places represented attempts to define language usage in terms of situational switching in which both actors' agency and responsibility for code-switching were treated as largely transferred to institutionalized contexts, which then merely had to be reflected in specific language usage.

In the case of the Cluain Árd, this was achieved through an institutionalization of an Irish-only policy, a rule that had to be made explicit given the overwhelming presence of English and hence the constant temptation to switch to the dominant language. By instituting an Irish-only policy within its premises and creating a conventionalized association between a specific code and a certain context/activity/ participation, the club could thus ensure that it did not have to compromise on its highly valued norm of language purism, while simultaneously absolving its frequenters from the norm of communicative pragmatism: their Irish-only usage simply reflected the rules of the club. This produced a context in which only a small number of people actually went to the Cluain Árd – mainly those who were not annoyed by the fact that only Irish was spoken there.

By contrast, the Cultúrlann mediated between purism and pragmatism by offering an implicit institutionalization of bilingualism. However, one needs to be precise here: the Cultúrlann was, of course, first and foremost an Irish language, culture and arts centre – in other words, a place intended for the use of Irish. By not explicitly barring English from also being spoken, given the predominance of English, the Cultúrlann implicitly made itself into a bilingual venue. The Cultúrlann thus instituted the whole spectrum of possible compromises between language purism and communicative pragmatism through first and foremost providing room for Irish speakers who wanted to follow the norm of language purism without excluding those who were not (yet) Gaeilgeoirí or who did not want to exclude or offend but rather interest non-Irish speakers by including them in conversations. In sum, both the Cluain Árd and the Cultúrlann constituted alternative institutionalizations of situational switching, mediating between purist and pragmatist norms of appropriate code-switching through externalizing the actors' agency and responsibility and thereby providing institutional legitimacy for quite different forms of language usage.

Apart from such institutionalized forms of situational switching, I also encountered many local configurations of Irish language usage in which conversational switching prevailed. In other words, during such interactions, both the actors' agency and responsibility for code switches were treated as lying with the actors themselves, whose language usage actively created specific communicative contexts. For instance, during my stay in West Belfast I befriended a group of mainly middle-aged Catholics with whom I went for regular walks around Belfast. Many of these people were Irish speakers, although their levels of fluency varied considerably: some were Irish teachers while others (including myself) were beginners. Usually, this circle of friends would go on Sunday morning walks, after which some members of the group would attend the Irish-medium Catholic mass, which took place at noon at St Mary's Church in the centre of Belfast. During these walks, I repeatedly observed that code-switching was dependent on who was talking to whom. One determining factor was, of course, proficiency in Irish, with fluent Irish speakers tending to speak Irish with other Gaeilgeoirí, while switching to English when addressing those who were much less skilled in the language. However, there was also considerable variation, as some Gaeilgeoirí almost exclusively spoke Irish with other competent speakers, whereas several Irish speakers also used a lot of English among themselves.

Within this setting, conversational switching built on the skilful capacity of Irish speakers to use code switches in order to split up the group and creatively produce different situational audiences: when engaging in a situational exchange that was exclusively directed towards people equally capable of speaking Irish, these Gaeilgeoirí would often switch into Irish, thereby creating an aside communication that was unintelligible for non-Irish speakers, yet inoffensively so, since it was not addressed to them anyway. Switching back to English abandoned this communicative 'bubble' since this language usage reopened the audience to potentially include everybody present, as English was the communicative code shared by all. Another form of conversational switching consisted in the strategy of addressing the same group as a bilingual audience. The group as a whole would be addressed first in Irish *as if* they were an Irish-speaking audience, although the message could actually not be understood by all. Subsequently the group would be addressed in English, thereby providing the relevant information for non-Irish speakers.

When talking to one of my key informants – Micheál – about the peculiarities of his personal usage of English and Irish, he provided me with the following summary of his 'basic principle' according to which he tried to mediate between his conflicting interests through conversational switching:

I have made a conscious decision <u>never</u> to make anyone feel excluded by speaking Irish. But I will also manipulate a situation where – when I'm in the company of an Irish speaker and we are surrounded by English speakers, I will create a bubble in which we will speak Irish. ... I will generally not speak Irish in the company of people who will be offended by me speaking Irish. Or be threatened or excluded by me speaking Irish. But I will also make sure that when I am with someone who does speak Irish, I will speak Irish to that person. And that person will do the same. There's a very interesting kind of dynamic where you don't want to exclude people, but you also want to ensure that you don't speak English by default because there are English speakers present. ... Occasionally, there are people who are ideologically hostile to Irish. And in that case, I don't give a shit. And I will speak Irish to spite them.

So far, I have exclusively conceptualized the problem of how local Gaeilgeoirí handled tensions within norms of appropriateness as an issue of code-switching, while taking the codes themselves for granted. However, local mediations between purism and pragmatism within code-switching also concerned the very question as to what actually counted as a code (such as 'Irish') in the first place. Take, for instance, language usage among pupils at the local meánscoil (see also Chapter 5). Based on my participant observation at this school and descriptions by both teachers and pupils, it was quite clear that the use of Irish among pupils varied systematically depending on the context; that is to say, according to situational switching. While pupils' communications with teachers in and beyond classes almost exclusively adhered to the 'Irish-only' policy of the school, younger pupils in particular seemed to speak English amongst themselves in the playground. Liam, one of four older pupils I formally interviewed at the meánscoil, described the youngsters' logic behind this switching in the following way: 'They think it's a school thing, that's the way they see it. That's the way I used to see it as well: "It's a school thing! And it's only for school! And you don't need it outside!"'. However, as Liam explained, older pupils would identify more with the language so that now 'it would be "broken Irish" for us'. As Liam explained, this 'broken Irish' (*Gaeilge bhriste*) was 'like half and half'; 'it's English and Irish mixed in'. When I asked him to characterize this 'broken Irish' in more detail, he gave me the following example:

> '*Amharc* at that paper,' like, 'Look at that paper.' Just like '*amharc*'. Just different words mixed within different sentences. And like a, there's some phrases we would learn in Irish, that would explain something. And then it would be easier to explain things in English. And we would use that there.

As Liam put it, 'we would all speak "broken Irish". And it's all just "broken Irish" because as soon as you walk outside school, English is all around us!' He thus seemed to argue that this 'broken Irish' emerged in practice as a compromise between the desire to speak Irish and the overwhelming power of an English-speaking environment.

During my stay in Belfast it was evident that 'broken Irish' was regarded by language purists as an unacceptable switch between English and Irish within single sentences. The above-quoted descriptions by Liam suggest that, while not sharing this negative evaluation, he equally regarded this language usage as a form of intrasentential code-switching, also called 'code-mixing' within the sociolinguistic literature (Mahootian 2006: 512). However, such a code-mixing interpretation is far from the only possible one. Given that this particular form of speaking clearly prevailed throughout much of Liam's daily communication, it is equally possible to take a more 'monolectal view' that interprets such language usage as an emerging single code of mixed origins rather than as a switching between two distinct varieties (Meeuwis and Blommaert 1998). The point I am trying to make is not that 'broken Irish' should be seen as a single code rather than a mix of two codes; instead, what I am highlighting is that whatever position one assumes, such a position invariably entails a certain stand on language purism and pragmatism. The issue then becomes primarily one of classification: how does one cluster certain language practices together and represent them as 'a pure code' from which any pragmatic transgression constitutes a switching or mixing of codes?

This point is more easily demonstrated with regard to a third variety of local Irish language usage above and beyond pre-Standardization Donegal-Gaeltacht Irish and 'broken Irish', since the status of this third variety was contested locally. This way of speaking was sometimes labelled '*Gaeilge Bhéal Feirste*' ('Belfast Irish') and comprised a middle ground of sorts between these two poles. Apart from orienting itself towards standardized Ulster Irish, 'Belfast Irish' typically deviated from 'pure' Donegal Irish through differences in pronunciation that reflected the fact that, for the most part, Irish in Belfast was 'spoken without contact with native speakers' (Kabel 2000b: 650) and hence showed traces of English as the first language of virtually all local Gaeilgeoirí (Kabel 2000a: 136). According to Roibeárd, this influence of English on 'Belfast Irish' could also be detected with regard to additional features: 'Belfast Irish' often directly echoed English syntax; it sometimes imported hitherto non-existent grammatical rules from English into Irish (e.g. the use of nouns as verbs); and it occasionally used expressions based on literal word-for-word translations from English into Irish, rather than drawing on established ways of imparting the same ideas in the Irish language itself.

Roibeárd and others clearly despised such English corruptions of 'pure Irish' as degradation and hence regarded 'Belfast Irish' as an inappropriate mixing of two languages. Other Gaeilgeoirí, however, propagated a different notion of 'code purity', emancipating themselves from the Gaeltacht by insisting that 'Belfast Irish' was in fact 'a dialect in its own right' (see also Kabel 2000b: 650). In other words, instead of representing 'Belfast Irish' as an illegitimate mixture of English and Irish, they effectively treated it as an appropriate single code of mixed origins, which – like 'Hiberno-English' being a form of English profoundly shaped by an Irish substratum – constituted a new form of Irish profoundly shaped by an English substratum. 'Belfast Irish', which could thus also legitimately be called 'Anglo-Irish', illustrates that the very definition of what counts as a code can be quite variable. Such variability in what counts as a code can have profound consequences for how norms of appropriate code-switching are mediated and enacted in language practices. To put it bluntly, if you see your own language practices, which happen to be intelligible to most people around you, as one single code, the conflict between language purism and communicative pragmatism ceases to exist because your language usage complies with both norms. Such might possibly be the future of 'broken Irish' in Catholic West Belfast.

The Political Hijacking of the Irish Language Revival: The Meso-Dynamics of Supply and Demand

In the course of reconstructing a contemporary history of the local Irish language revival in Chapter 5, I argued that the strong purism among 'prophets' within the Cluain Árd contributed to their suspicions that more pragmatic Gaeilgeoirí were less than committed to the language itself, pursuing it for ulterior motives. Within this historical reconstruction, I specifically focused on recent accusations that pragmatic activists were merely interested in obtaining state funding. In this section, I will address another facet of the dynamics between representations and practices of the Irish language, one equally situated at the meso-level of interpreting trends of practices within the broader Irish language revival. However, this time I will analyse a political issue that I only mentioned in passing in Chapter 5, namely, the locally contentious issue of whether or not Sinn Féin and Republicans 'hijacked' – to use the local phrase – the Irish language in the 1980s and 1990s for their own political purposes.

The following quote by Pádraigín provides an initial overview on the contentious subthemes that were implicated in this highly contested accusation of political 'hijacking'. When I asked Pádraigín what local people meant by 'hijacking', she responded:

> They think Sinn Féin jumped on the bandwagon – do you know what that means? ... If you're jumping on the bandwagon, you didn't think of it yourself, but everybody else is going, so you just jump on the wagon yourself. You know, maybe people may mean that, you know, because there's a strong interest in the Irish language, say for example in West Belfast. So it's a Sinn Féin lobby for the Irish language because there's a whole section of voters for them. ... And if you're a Unionist, you might think, 'They are getting money for the Irish language; and really a lot of money is going to arms or something!' ... And therefore some people might think Sinn Féin really don't bother about the Irish language. Also because some of those people may have been at some time associated with the armed struggle, people are assuming, 'Oh, they are promoting the Irish language, and they promote "the ballot box in one hand and the armelite in the other",[1] then all people into the Irish language are getting equated with that as well.' And people don't all want that.

---

1. This memorable phrase marking the beginning of a new dual strategy for Republicans, consisting of the continued armed struggle using armelite rifles and the political process of elections, was coined by Danny Morrison at the Sinn Féin party conference in 1981. It developed into the new party line throughout the 1980s after three hunger strikers were elected as Sinn Féin MPs (Fraser 2000: 66).

Pádraigín's lengthy description alludes to three different aspects of the overall 'hijacking' representation on which I want to elaborate. The first aspect is concerned with impression management and is related to a criticism that publicly combining the Irish language with Republicanism created a situation in which 'all people into the Irish language are getting equated with that as well'. Furthermore, the bandwagon-charge linked up with questions of historical legitimacy within the revival since it often implied an allegation that Sinn Féin was reaping the fruits of someone else's work. Finally, accusing Republicans of hijacking the language also implied questioning their inner motives and true intentions. In other words, it was claimed that 'Sinn Féin really don't bother about the Irish language', but had only been into language activism 'because there's a whole section of voters for them'.

Within West Belfast, I came across the first subtheme of impression management in two guises. In its strong version, people argued that Sinn Féin or at least certain Republicans within Sinn Féin had consciously and strategically taken over certain Irish-language organizations in and beyond West Belfast in order to politically dominate the field of 'culture'. According to such allegations, as one of my informants put it, Sinn Féin used 'a kind of classic broad front politics in that an ostensibly non-political institution in effect could be used to promote Republican politics'. This was achieved by getting Republicans into prominent positions within such Irish-language initiatives, thereby 'assuming leadership of the language movement or giving the impression of leading the language movement through making statements that tied the language movement to their politics'. Another non-Republican language activist recalled how a cross-community Irish-language initiative he had co-founded was 'taken over by Sinn Féin' when a Sinn Féin councillor was elected to the committee, then made chairman and subsequently changed the whole orientation of the project.

In the weaker version of this allegation, other Gaeilgeoirí accused Republicans in and beyond Sinn Féin of deliberately creating the impression of an inextricable link between the language and Republicanism, even if they did not actively take over Irish-language organizations. This was the position suggested by Seán in the opening scene when he explained to me that he ceased speaking Irish in the 1980s when the language came to be publicly represented as a political weapon linked to Republicanism. Another Irish speaker aptly summarized the reasoning behind the weak allegation in the following way:

> You can <u>say</u> and everybody does say that the Irish language and Republicanism are not connected. You can also say, as everybody does, that Republicans have every right to be involved in the Irish language. Because they have! But if you deliberately choose to give a high profile to prominent Sinn Féin people involved in it, you're giving out a message, and you <u>know</u> you're giving out a message! And you're very stupid if you don't know you're giving out a message! And if you do that, then you are polluting the message as far as I'm concerned. And to my mind, that was what Sinn Féin did!

Such allegations concerning deliberate impression management by Republicans were locally countered by other Gaeilgeoirí who rejected the idea that a language could be hijacked in the first place, insisting on the right of anyone to speak Irish, for instance, in statements like 'How can you hijack a language? It's anybody's language, anybody can speak it'. Others explicitly dismissed the notion that the Irish language and Republicanism were linked, most prominently perhaps the leader of Sinn Féin, Gerry Adams himself, who wrote in 1986: 'Culture is not a party political question or the monopoly of any one section of the people' (Adams 1986: 146). Furthermore, responding to such 'hijacking' allegations in an interview with *An Phoblacht/Republican News* in 1990, the then head of Sinn Féin's Cultural Department emphasized that Republicans were involved with language projects as individuals rather than as party members: 'It is true that republicans are prominent and numerous in many language initiatives but this is due to individual commitment and an understanding among republicans of the need to be active on the issue' (quoted in Kachuk 1993: 248).

Finally, several critics of the impression management allegation strongly maintained that while Sinn Féin had definitely not taken over any Irish-language initiatives, the accusation itself had in fact been purposefully devised and propagated by the state in order to undermine the whole Irish language movement. This line of argumentation is strongly supported by Kachuk (1993: 256), who concludes her discussion of the 'hijacking' allegation in the following way:

> Individual Irish-speaking Sinn Féin members are encouraged to pursue their cultural interests by joining and working within Irish language groups and associations, but Sinn Féin as an organization shies away from taking a direct controlling, leadership role in any of these groups. By distancing itself from community action groups in general, including Irish language activist groups, Sinn Féin assumes a supportive role, encouraging the nationalist population, either individually or collectively in groups, to speak up for themselves and make their demands heard by the State. Sinn Féin's stance of supporting and encouraging individual activists and single issue community groups to act on their own behalf, becomes a powerful weapon against the State. Far more powerful than 'taking over' the leadership of a group directly, as the State has accused them of doing, or in the State's terminology 'hijacking the Irish language'.

Kachuk's conclusion is problematic because her development of her argument seems to be somewhat naive in methodological terms. She provides a number of quotes by Sinn Féin activists who proclaim that they did not take over language groups and then uses these statements to prove that Republicans did not in fact hijack the language. But this is precisely what one would expect Sinn Féin members to say, regardless. I am aware of at least two cases of Irish-language initiatives in and beyond West Belfast that started off without any party affiliation and ended up having Sinn Féin members on their committees without the approval of all the pre-existing members. However, instead of insisting that such cases either were or were not cases of 'hijacking' by Republicans, my point is rather to show that such incidents could be – and more importantly, were – locally read in both directions! In other words, rather than settling the debate about hijacking myself, it is my intention to show how and why this debate actually took place in the way that it did.

It is in this spirit that I turn now to the second subtheme concerned with the question of to what extent Sinn Féin actually secured historical legitimacy for its emerging prominence within the local Irish language revival throughout the 1980s. This links up with an issue I have already dealt with in my reconstruction of the contemporary history of local language developments, namely, the interplay or 'meso-dynamics' between an ever-expanding supply of Irish-language infrastructure brought about by committed language enthusiasts and growing demand for Irish-medium activities fuelled by Republicans in and beyond the prisons. In my account in Chapter 5, I gave equal weight to both developments. But locally, there was some dissent as to whether the Irish language revival was 'supply-' or 'demand-driven', and this argument had immediate consequences for Sinn Féin's legitimacy within the scene.

On the one hand, some people claimed that Sinn Féin had only recently 'jumped on the bandwagon' of the Irish language revival and had thereby established a dominant presence within the local scene, without actually having historical legitimacy. By this they meant that Sinn Féin was illegitimately reaping the fruits of a remarkable language revival, which actually was and had been primarily 'supply-driven'. These people viewed the language revival as the product of the work of non-political language enthusiasts from the Cluain Árd, the Shaw's Road Gaeltacht and beyond, who had established, most importantly, an Irish-medium educational sector. This was evidently Seán's point of view as described in the vignette at the beginning of this chapter. Seán suggested that the revival was primarily the result of the heightened presence of Irish-medium education rather than a product of the *Jailtacht*. This line was also taken by other local Gaeilgeoirí who equally emphasized that 'developments in the Cluain Árd, Shaw's Road and the schools have been more important than ex-prisoners bringing the Irish language into the community'. In a more radical tone, another of my interlocutors went so far as to insist that it was exclusively because of the schools and 'not because of the Troubles' that the use of Irish had expanded locally.

On the other hand, other Irish speakers insisted that the Republican presence within the language scene was indeed historically legitimate since these people saw the local revival as mainly 'demand-driven'. In other words, seen from this point of view, Republicans in and beyond Sinn Féin were rightly prominent within the language revival because it had been primarily Republicans who – first through their use of Irish in prison and then mainly through the work of Sinn Féin's Cultural Department – had taken the language out of small, elitist places such as the Cluain Árd and had popularized it to a hitherto unheard of extent. A local Gaeilgeoir adhering to this position told me that 'the revival of the Irish language was mainly due to the ex-prisoners and internees', who having left prison, 'started a lot of Irish-language classes in community centres, private houses and GAA clubs'. Another Irish speaker who equally subscribed to this position was Pól, who suggested that 'the Irish language in the sixties and probably into the seventies, I think, would have been regarded as very elitist'. It was then only 'as a result of the jail' – as Pól put it – that the Irish language became more popular outside in the 1980s. Pól thereby explicitly argued (as quoted in Chapter 4) that 'the use of language in the prisons actually inspired probably most of the major developments in the North here'.

The last subtheme that was locally implicated in the sweeping accusation that Sinn Féin had hijacked the Irish language consisted in questioning the inner motives and true intentions behind Republican engagement with the language. Local Gaeilgeoirí who accused Republicans and Sinn Féin of pursuing a hidden agenda suggested that the latter only feigned commitment to the Irish language as an end/value in itself. These critics claimed that Sinn Féin simply instrumentalized the language as a means of achieving purely political ends, believing that Sinn Féin would push for the Irish language only as long as this did not conflict with their own Republican agenda.

During my stay in Belfast, I came across two variants of this instrumentalization thesis. One consisted of a suspicion referred to by Pádraigín in the opening quote that Sinn Féin lobbied for Irish only to secure votes. Another variant of the instrumentalization thesis claimed that Sinn Féin used the Irish language only as a political weapon against the British. The Irish language, these critics argued, thus merely served as a means for Republicans to express their own 'cultural distinctiveness' against the British in a primarily outward-oriented fashion. Within such an outward and oppositional orientation, it became more important to substantiate that one was not British or English (and the means for achieving this were not really meaningful in themselves) than it was to substantiate in a primarily inward orientation that one was Irish. This was clearly the way in which Seán interpreted Republican engagement with the Irish language, while he himself preferred a language activism that was not directed against British colonialism or a British or English identity, but rather was about one's own culture and identity in comparison and contrast to, not in opposition to, others. Other local Gaeilgeoirí were equally suspicious that 'some members of Sinn Féin would only use the Irish language for their own political ends, instead of for the Irish language in it's own right', and 'therefore they would only see it as a weapon, amongst other weapons, and not for the greatness of itself'. However, as the same informant expressed on another occasion, echoing Seán, Irish should be used 'positively' rather than 'in a negative way':

> Irish could be used to deny yourself being English, but it's more important that it's expressed more positively as a thing, as being Irish, not as being not English. … It shouldn't be looked on in a negative way. It should be looked on positively, that you speak Irish first and if something threatens the Irish language, then it becomes an enemy. But you don't speak Irish to be anti-English or to be negative, do you understand?

In my experience, Republicans typically countered such allegations of merely instrumentalizing the Irish language without being truly interested in it as a value in itself by insisting that, for them, the Irish language and political struggle were two inseparable sides of the same coin; hence, any accusations of secretly prioritizing the political struggle at the expense of the language were misplaced. This was apparently the position of Pól, who depicted the language revival as a process through which Irish 'had become much more identified, as a result of the hunger strikes and all the rest of it, much more identified with the struggle itself'. Mairéad was another person who explicitly emphasized the inseparability of all the different aspects in the following, quite forceful way (see Chapter 4):

> Gaelic is just part of the struggle for your own identity, I would probably say. ... I think it's all intertwined, the language, the music, the poetry; everything, the armed struggle. I really can't differentiate between it, as in a fight for your own identity.

This last contentious subtheme concerning the inner motives and true intentions within the overall debate on the political hijacking of the Irish language revival in Catholic West Belfast shows a close affinity to controversies between positions on the third and most general level, to which I now turn.

'Our own native language?':
The Macro-Dynamics of Rights Activism, Ethnicism and Nationalism

In this third and final section, I will be concerned with representations related to the generalized practice of 'speaking Irish' that specified certain positions for the Irish language within the wider sociocultural and political universe and thereby provided the most general reasons for actually engaging in this practice. In a way, this focus is close to Kachuk's (1993) project, even though her endeavour is based on a different analytical framework and speaks to another body of literature. Based on fieldwork in Belfast between 1990 and 1991, Kachuk interprets 'Irish language activism in West Belfast' as 'resistance to British cultural hegemony', as the title of her thesis reads. Evidently meant as a contribution to the anthropology of resistance (e.g. Comaroff 1985; Scott 1985, 1990; Ong 1987), Kachuk operates within a cultural-Marxist framework that builds primarily on Williams' (1977, 1980) model of cultural hegemony and counter-hegemony. Elaborating on Gramsci's (1971) notion of 'hegemony', this approach contrasts the 'cultural hegemony' of an effective dominant culture with forms of resistance, which gain their subversive power through counter-hegemonically activating cultural meanings and practices that are neglected in or excluded from the dominant culture. Applied to the Northern Irish context, Kachuk interprets language activism in Catholic West Belfast as resistance to British cultural hegemony, which had marginalized and silenced the Irish language for centuries. Kachuk then analyses her material about the local language scene in terms of two ideal-types of counter-hegemonic resistance: its 'alternative' and 'oppositional' variants. She concludes:

> I have argued that the two forms of resistance do differ in their adherents' visions of a future for Northern Ireland. Alternative Irish language activists

are seeking a permanent space for the Irish language and culture in Northern Ireland regardless of its future political status. Oppositional Irish language activists, on the other hand, have incorporated the Irish language into the revolutionary struggle for a 'free and Gaelic' thirty-two county Republic of Ireland. (Kachuk 1993: 364)

While Kachuk's argument rightly draws attention to the inevitable situatedness of local language practices within the wider context of power asymmetries and the hegemonic use of 'culture', and while her distinction between alternative and oppositional activism equally points towards important differences within the language scene, I find her approach problematic for three reasons. First, the analytical distinction between 'alternative' and 'oppositional' resistance is too general to grasp the dynamics she is actually describing. Kachuk again draws directly on Williams, who characterizes the alternative resistor as 'someone who simply finds a different way to live and wishes to be left alone with it', whereas the oppositional resistor is rather 'someone who finds a different way to live and wants to change the society in its light' (Williams 1980: 42; quoted after Kachuk 1993: 14–15). However, these two definitions do not really spell out what types of behaviour fall into which category, since both types of activists do in the end want to change society at some level. Hence the specificities of such envisioned changes need to be clarified. To my mind, the alternative ideal-type should be specified as wanting to reintroduce a lost cultural element into recognized daily practice but does not use this new element to substantiate demands for further political changes (such as national independence) *beyond* the confines of policies directly related to this very cultural element (such as language policies); the oppositional ideal-type does precisely this. However, such a specification, or any other, is missing in Kachuk's work. Although she ultimately realizes that a crucial *differentia specifica* in the local language scene consists in the question of whether or not language activism should be used for nationalist politics (see Kachuk's quote above), her analytical model cannot capture precisely this difference, since – based on her own too unspecific conceptual distinction – linguistic nationalism could actually fall into both categories.

A second problem consists in Kachuk's lack of attention to the conceptual relationship between her two types of resistance and different forms of collective identification. She simply proclaims that 'in the Irish language activist community of West Belfast, language and ethnic identity are synonymous' (Kachuk 1993: 23) without clarifying whether this is her empirical observation or whether this is a crucial assumption of her own theoretical approach. Certain formulations tend towards the latter position, for example, when Kachuk equates 'ethnicity' with 'a symbolic expression of differentness from the "effective dominant culture"' (Kachuk 1993: 19), but in the end, this theoretical issue is not sufficiently addressed.

This leads to a third difficulty built into Kachuk's overall approach of cultural Marxism, which has been generally noted for the anthropology of resistance (e.g. Spencer 1996: 489), namely, the danger of reading resistance into practices that actors themselves actually describe in quite different terms. It remains unclear to what extent Kachuk's informants themselves understood their behaviour only and exclusively in terms of 'resistance'. To put it differently, based on Kachuk's writings, it is impossible to say whether or not her depiction of the early 1990s language scene as exclusively concerned with counter-hegemonic, identity-related, alternative or oppositional resistance appropriately reflects the spectrum of emic points of views at that time, or whether this depiction is rather the product of Kachuk's own cultural-Marxist approach.

Be that as it may, when turning to my own characterization of different macro-positions in the dynamics between representations and practices of the Irish language in West Belfast, I begin with a macro-position that was not covered by Kachuk at all, possibly because this position did not conceive the Irish language in terms of 'our own native language' and hence also not as an issue of Irish identity. Instead, this first macro-position – which I call 'rights activism' – represented Irish as an issue of human, civil or minority rights above narrow political concerns such as the constitutional status of the North of Ireland. From this perspective, the language was viewed as a precious cultural object in danger of being lost. It is important to note, however, that in this context the culture-term was used not to refer to a distinctive ethnic 'culture', one typically associated with Irishness (as in the following two macro-positions) but to an overarching 'human culture', the diversity of which needed to be protected as a value in its own right through a kind of cultural environmentalism.

Such rights activism clearly prevailed, for instance, during a conversation with a local language activist, who – as she emphasized – wanted the language to be treated 'as a civil rights issue' and who compared her language activism with biodiversity: 'when it's gone, it's gone and you never get it back'; hence biodiversity needed to be protected. Yet, as she argued, 'if it is worth to protect plants and animals, why should it not be important to protect endangered languages such as Irish and thereby protect cultural diversity?' As she went on to argue, people in Ireland had a special responsibility because 'if Irish is not protected here, where will it be protected?' Thus, she concluded, 'we have to preserve the language as a living language, which cannot be done anywhere other than in the country where it is spoken. You need the Irish-speaking community in Ireland'.

Arguing from a similar point of view, another Irish speaker and language lobbyist strongly objected to my suggestion that his language activism had anything to do with his Irish identity, explaining that – as he put it – 'I don't like that formulation, "It's my language"', firstly because 'it's not my language, except I repossessed it', and secondly because he saw this formulation as being 'nearly always misused'. Instead, he provided me with what he called his 'ideological position' of 'a cultural ecologist':

> My ideological position is that of a cultural ecologist. That there is a language in the world, dying every fortnight. And that the narrowing of cultural options, the loss of – wisdom is maybe the wrong word, but the loss of all these civilizations. The loss of whatever inherent wisdom is in the – the historical richness, linguistic richness of this world. It's not a good thing for the world. That's, I feel, is the kind of global perspective. And – that anybody who's interested in culture, in a broad sense – anybody who

knows more than one culture, knows that each culture is incomplete. And they're all incomplete in different ways. That the survival of the cultural diversity in this world is, in terms of culture and civilization, is extremely important, in terms of the intellectual, aesthetic and moral resources that – linguistic resources that is in the diversity. And – in particular – you know, it's dead <u>easy</u> to be an ecologist, if you're talking about the Amazonian rainforest. If it's far enough away. It's very easy to be worried about that stuff. But this particular piece of cultural disaster is happening on our own front doorstep. This is <u>our</u> <u>responsibility!</u> The Irish language will not live or die, except in Ireland. So, somebody in Ireland has to take measures to maintain it. That's how I see my role.

This Gaeilgeoir thus cherished 'cultural diversity', and linguistic diversity in particular, as values in their own right in need of protection. While he thus argued that the protection of *any* endangered language was of equal importance (and precisely *not* only Irish as part of one's 'own distinctive Irish culture' as others argued), he still saw his own responsibility as a 'cultural ecologist' to lie with the Irish language, since 'this particular piece of cultural disaster is happening on our own front doorstep' and 'the Irish language will not live or die, except in Ireland'. His decision to engage with Irish had little to do with any notion of it being his 'own native language' but merely with the pragmatic decision that 'if you appeal to the general principle [of cultural environmentalism], you then look to what's close to you'.

A third example of rights activism consisted of the mural 'Irish is all around us' that was described at the end of Chapter 1. This bilingual mural explicitly proclaimed that 'language rights are human rights' and demanded that 'the bill of human rights must reflect the unique circumstances of the Irish language' (see Figure 1.1). This mural was part of the lobby work by the local Irish language umbrella organization *Pobal* ('Community'), which agitated for the inclusion of specific rights concerning the Irish language in the Bill of Rights for Northern Ireland, which was then being developed in accordance with the Good Friday Agreement of 1998. Apart from providing another example of rights activism, this framing of the Irish language in terms of human rights in the course of an explicit lobbying campaign by *Pobal* also highlights another aspect that was rather typical for this macro-position: to my knowledge, rights-activist representations of the Irish language were particularly prominent among Gaeilgeoirí within the fourth domain of the Irish language scene as characterized in Chapter 3, namely, within organizations promoting and lobbying for the Irish language.

This observation also draws attention to the fact that the framing of the language in terms of human, civil or minority rights protecting cultural diversity had obvious strategic advantages. This was so because, by tapping into international rights discourses and distancing themselves from the local Northern Irish conflict, local language activists clearly increased their chances of getting through with their political demands for the Irish language (including funding) vis-à-vis the state and international organizations. While rights activism could thus be used as a strategic smokescreen, covering up different stances on the Irish language, I did indeed meet a number of Gaeilgeoirí who – I am convinced – truly identified with and stood behind this macro-position. Rights activism hence also made up one authentic configuration of representing and motivating the practice of 'speaking Irish'.

In contrast to rights activists, who did not subscribe to the representation of Irish as 'our own native language', the vast majority of local Gaeilgeoirí, or at least the ones I talked to, did in fact adhere to this notion, ensuring – as O'Reilly puts it – that 'the phrase "our own language" has come to symbolize the importance of the Irish language to Irish identity for *Gaeilgeoirí* in the North' (1999: 175 – emphasis in the original). In the following, I will unpack this phrase by showing how this representation provided the common ground for two macro-positions, which, while both conceiving the language in terms of Irish identity, had distinct political implications.

The first of these two macro-positions – which I call 'language ethnicism' – represented the Irish language as a fundamental yet largely lost element of one's 'own Irish culture and identity' in need of repossession through individual practice. However, language ethnicists explicitly argued for a strict separation between the Irish language and nationalist politics, and demanded that the interests of the Irish language should be put above any other concerns. This did not imply that language ethnicists necessarily regarded the language as apolitical. On the contrary, many saw their language activism as political in being directly concerned with state policies related to the Irish language such as regulations for Irish-medium education, official funding and the availability of public services in Irish. Beyond this, however, speaking Irish was clearly not intended to be political. But language ethnicists often recognized that, against their will, the use of Irish had been made into a political issue because the structural context of the state had effectively denied them the right to use their 'own language' and thereby to express their 'own identity', which externally politicized the act of speaking Irish. Against this background, many language ethnicists told me that the Irish language was to some extent political, but political only with a small 'p': it was not political in any nationalist sense. Instead, such language ethnicists saw their activism primarily as an inward-oriented, *ex positivo* attempt to internally substantiate with regard to other group members what it meant to be Irish. At this point, an analytical distinction suggested by Eriksen is helpful:

> [W]e can distinguish between two modalities of group solidarity, which we may, following Sartre (1943), call *we-hood* and *us-hood*, respectively. Being *us*, people are loyal and socially integrated chiefly in relation to *the other*; through competition, enmity, symbiosis or the contrastive use of stereotypes and boundary symbols. Being *we*, on the other hand, entails being integrated because of shared activities within the collectivity. (Eriksen 2002: 67 – emphasis in the original)

Following this distinction, it is possible to characterize language ethnicists as exclusively focusing on the 'we-hood' of their Irishness.

Against the backdrop of this overall characterization it is evident that the way in which Seán represented the Irish language constituted an almost prototypical example of this macro-position of language ethnicism. First, Seán emphasized that he regarded his engagement with Irish as an attempt to reinforce his 'own culture and identity' through learning his 'own native language'. Second, Seán made it clear that he was strongly against conflating language activism with nationalist politics through using or representing the language as a weapon against British colonialism. Third, Seán insisted on reading his involvement with the Irish language strictly in terms of 'we-hood' by characterizing it as an inward thing concerned with 'your culture and identity only'.

Other local Gaeilgeoirí also highlighted these aspects of language ethnicism when discussing their attitudes towards Irish. For instance, one local language activist emphasized the first characteristic when explaining why he had chosen Irish for his A-Levels in grammar school. He had apparently done so because he had come to see learning and speaking Irish 'as part of a process of – sort of re-establishing your identity. … You know, I wanted to learn it not just as a school subject but as a way of repossessing the idea of an Irish cultural identity'. Another Irish speaker made the same point about her engagement with the language when stating that 'you might just want to be Irish and speak the language of the country that, you know, that you were born in'. The second aspect of language ethnicism, namely, its stance on the politics of the language, was nicely summarized in the following quote: 'The Irish language is not political for me. The only political thing about it is, in terms of, it might have been denied to you before, so it becomes a political issue if you haven't got rights, but it's the lack of rights that makes it political not the language itself.'

Finally, insistence on the 'we-hood' approach towards the practice of speaking Irish was also strongly supported by Gaeilgeoirí such as the one I have already quoted above when discussing the political hijacking of Irish. I characterized this informant as wanting the language to be used 'positively' rather than 'in a negative way' and as insisting that while he acknowledged that 'Irish could be used to deny yourself being English', he found it 'more important that it's expressed more positively as a thing, as being Irish, not as being not English'.

As with rights activism, the macro-position of language ethnicism had clear strategic advantages, namely, in representing the language as an issue of Irish identity, while strictly isolating it from any concern with nationalist politics. This could be advantageous when trying to convince external actors such as the state or international institutions to acknowledge and support the cause of the Irish language. This was so because such language ethnicism created a platform for such external agents to engage with local identity politics, while simultaneously depoliticizing the language. Language ethnicism could hence be used strategically as an apparently harmless approach to Irish as an issue of 'culture' and not of nationalist politics by actors who actually saw Irish as inseparably both a 'cultural' and 'nationalist-political' issue and hence adhered to the third and last macro-position (see below). Having said that, it was again more than clear to me that many local Gaeilgeoirí very strongly identified with language ethnicism and truly objected to mixing the re-establishment of their Irishness through speaking the language with any nationalist politics.

Before moving towards the third and last macro-position, it is necessary to explain why I use the term 'ethnicism'. In the literature, it is common to differentiate between 'cultural nationalism' and 'political nationalism', and for the Irish context (e.g. O'Reilly 1997, 1999) this might particularly be the case because of Hutchinson's seminal text *The Dynamics of Cultural Nationalism in Ireland* (Hutchinson 1987) in which he elaborates on precisely this analytical distinction. In fact, I used this terminological couplet myself in Chapter 5 when briefly differentiating between two representational strands of the Irish language that brought about 'cultural rebels without a political cause' and 'political rebels with a cause' in Catholic West Belfast throughout the Troubles. (These two strands are, of course, identical to the two macro-positions I am currently describing, namely, 'language ethnicism' and, as we will see below, 'language nationalism'.)

However, in this chapter I have started using another terminological couplet – the distinction between 'ethnicism' and 'nationalism' – because this terminology seems much less ambiguous. One way of characterizing the current ambiguity with regard to 'cultural' versus 'political nationalism' consists in emphasizing that within studies of ethnicity and nationalism, there are two main conceptions about the relationship between these key concepts. In one version, nationalism is conceptualized as a generic phenomenon that exists in either an 'ethnic' variant (based on shared culture and/or descent) or a 'civic' variant (based on shared territoriality and/or a common political project). The distinction between 'cultural' and 'political nationalism' is in fact but one of many variations on this basic opposition, and as I have argued elsewhere, this 'civic/ethnic divide' should analytically and terminologically be replaced by several more precise dimensions like 'autochthony' and 'activism' (Zenker 2009; see also Chapter 10). The second conception concerning the relationship between ethnicity and nationalism – which is endorsed here – inverts this first conception by treating the ethnic group as the generic phenomenon, of which the nation is only a specific variant: a nation is here seen as an ethnic group that, as an ethnic group, politically demands or maintains its own state. Eriksen nicely captures this second understanding:

> The distinguishing mark of nationalism is by definition its relationship to the state. A nationalist holds that political boundaries should be coterminous with cultural [read: 'cultural' – OZ] boundaries, whereas many ethnic groups do not demand command over a state. When the political leaders of an ethnic movement make demands to this effect, the ethnic movement therefore by definition becomes a nationalist movement. (Eriksen 2002: 7)

As Eriksen suggests, an ethnic movement can thus be defined as only turning into a nationalist movement when it also demands political control over a state. Building on this understanding, I suggest treating 'ethnicism' as a generic term that refers to a position that intentionally engages in maintaining and/or reviving certain elements of a distinctive ethnic 'culture' that is viewed as being shared within a particular ethnic group, while simultaneously making members different from non-members. In other words, ethnicists are driven by the desire to protect and/or reinvigorate precisely that distinctive 'culture' that defines their own ethnic group. Ethnicism thus aims for defending or renewing the very existence of a particular ethnie. Such ethnicism then only turns into 'nationalism' when such aims are linked to political demands for political autonomy within a state coterminous with the group itself. By definition, both ethnicism and nationalism are hence 'cultural', yet only nationalism is political in a very specific, state-centred sense.

Against this backdrop, it needs to be added that when talking about the second macro-position, I use the compound 'language ethnicism' in order to highlight that adherents to this position were actually ethnicists only with regard to the Irish language. In other words, to be a language ethnicist (or, for that matter, a rights activist) did by no means preclude local Gaeilgeoirí from also being a Nationalist or Republican in terms of Irish constitutional politics; in fact, most of my language-ethnicist informants *were* Nationalists or Republicans but still insisted on handling the Irish language independently from nationalist politics – that is, from any political activism working towards a united Ireland. A good example of this dynamic, which is unfortunately quite often overlooked within the language scene itself, consists in a quote by Micheál in Chapter 4 where he described how he tried to bring the Irish language to Unionists in their own terms, not in his. Micheál claimed that he 'went to these people, and said, "I am a Nationalist, <u>but</u> the language is bigger than that"', thereby clearly indicating that while he saw himself politically as a Nationalist, he wanted the language not to be treated in terms of nationalist politics, but actually as a rights-activist issue.

After this detour into conceptual clarifications, it should be evident what I mean when referring to the third and last macro-position of the Irish language in terms of 'language nationalism'. This macro-position shared with language ethnicists the conviction that the Irish language was a fundamental yet largely lost element of one's 'own Irish culture and identity' in need of repossession through individual practice. Language nationalists also agreed with language ethnicists that it had been the British state that, through denying Irish people the right to use their 'own language' and express their 'own identity', had politicized the language. Yet language nationalists drew quite different political conclusions from this observation. In contrast to language ethnicists, they argued that – given the fundamental context of ongoing British colonialism – it was inevitable that by speaking Irish, one already was and, more importantly, should be engaged in the political struggle for decolonizing the island of Ireland and, thus, liberating it from its external British oppressor. In other words, adherents of this macro-position saw Irish as political with a capital 'P': they represented the language and the political struggle for a united Irish nation-state as two inseparable sides of the same coin. Speaking Irish was hence not only an ethnicist but also a nationalist activity in the sense outlined above. Such a position implied that language nationalists conceived their engagements with Irish not only as inward-oriented, *ex positivo* attempts to substantiate internally with regard to other group members what it meant to be

Irish; engagement with Irish was also intended as an outward-oriented, *ex negativo* statement that one was not British or English. Drawing on Eriksen's terminological suggestion, language nationalists were not only concerned with the 'we-hood' but also with the 'us-hood' of their Irishness.

Having provided an overview of the general characteristics of language nationalism, the following quote by a local Gaeilgeoir nicely encapsulates and exemplifies the basic features of this macro-position. This Irish speaker claimed that, especially throughout the Troubles, 'Irish was looked at here as another weapon to use against the Brits: "They're trying to not let us be Irish, so what do we do? We learn Irish. Fuck 'em!!"' This quote is revealing in that it combines in compressed form all core elements that made up language nationalism: First, learning Irish is characterized as a means of countering 'the Brits' who were 'trying to not let us be Irish', which implies that Irish is understood as an element of one's 'own Irish culture and identity'. Second, the depiction of Irish as 'another weapon to use against the Brits' clearly shows that the reappropriation of 'Irish culture' is not separated from nationalist politics at all but is used instead as a crucial element within nationalist agitation. Third, following from this observation, speaking Irish is evidently directed not only towards 'we-hood' but also towards the 'us-hood' of Irishness, since the main addressees in this symbolic act of language acquisition are 'the Brits' rather than other Irish people.

In a similar vein, several statements by Mairéad already quoted in Chapter 4 also showed that she subscribed to language nationalism. This could be seen when Mairéad explained that she had regarded Irish from early on as 'my own native language and I wanted to speak it and be aware of it'; when she insisted on the inseparability of 'the language, the music, the poetry; everything, the armed struggle'; and when she finally interpreted the practice of speaking Irish within the Northern Irish context as being 'almost like an act of defiance', which also implies a notion of 'us-hood' through defying 'the Brits'.

Like rights activism and language ethnicism, language nationalism also had obvious strategic advantages. In fact, my whole discussion of the alleged political hijacking of the Irish language at the meso-level of the local revival addressed nothing but the question of whether or not this existing instrumental potential of language nationalism had actually been used by local Republicans in and beyond Sinn Féin. Language nationalism could thereby be instrumentalized in the two ways that I have already described above under the heading of 'inner motives and true intentions'. First, vis-à-vis the internal structural context of Irish people in West Belfast, language nationalism could be used as a means of feigning support for the language in order simply to expand local support for Republicanism (and for Sinn Féin in particular). Second, vis-à-vis the external structural context of the state, language nationalism could function as a means of challenging the state by using the language as a political weapon; as a means of underlining Irish 'us-hood' even if the language was not really regarded as important in itself. Against the backdrop of the local debate on the political hijacking of Irish, I am convinced that some strategic use of language nationalism did occur in Catholic West Belfast. Yet it would be quite inappropriate to mistake language nationalism as a whole for a sham.

Many Nationalists and Republicans such as Mairéad spoke Irish in order to revive their ethnic 'culture' and, simultaneously, to substantiate their political demand for a united Ireland. The co-occurrence of such intentions should be taken seriously.

I began this section on macro-positions – which I have so far presented in their ideal-typical form, even though individual actors combined or even switched between these positions in actual practice – by critically discussing Kachuk's approach. Her forms of 'alternative resistance' and 'oppositional resistance' can now be seen as basically referring to the same empirical configurations that I hope I have conceptualized more precisely in terms of 'language ethnicism' and 'language nationalism'. Having my own tripartite classification of macro-positions in place, I now turn to a critical reflection of O'Reilly's work (1997 and 1999), which – largely based on research in West Belfast between 1993 and 1995 – exclusively focuses on the level of representations and thereby exhibits the same one-sided preoccupation with discourses that was already criticized in Chapter 2 regarding the prevailing constructivist approach to ethnicity. O'Reilly isolates three different positions and declares that '[t]he fundamental difference in each of the three discourses lies in the way in which the relationship between the Irish language and politics is conceptualized' (O'Reilly 1997: 100). Based on this criterion, she first describes a 'decolonizing discourse' that treated the language as inherently political in general and Republican in particular, especially by identifying Irish as a part of the decolonization process (O'Reilly 1999: 49–63). She then identifies a 'cultural discourse' that emphasized the inherent beauty and cultural worth of the language and insisted on keeping Irish separate from politics (ibid.: 64–84). Finally, she speaks about a 'rights discourse' that sidestepped the political/apolitical dichotomy of the first two discourses, argued for 'multipoliticization' instead, and reframed the Irish language primarily in terms of civil, human and minority rights (ibid.: 85–104).

As this short synopsis indicates, there is more than a superficial resemblance between my own distinction of three macro-positions and O'Reilly's three discourses on the Irish language, and I am obviously indebted to her work. Nevertheless, I have two profound criticisms that led me to develop my own classification. My first criticism relates to O'Reilly's use of the culture-term, which is best illustrated through correlating my representational types with her own. By and large, my 'rights activism' refers to phenomena very similar to the ones covered by O'Reilly's 'rights discourse', and my 'language nationalism' is basically identical to her 'decolonizing discourse'. However, her 'cultural discourse' cannot be so easily correlated since it treats as unitary phenomena that I separate under the headings of 'language ethnicism' and 'rights activism'. This is so because O'Reilly does not distinguish between the two different meanings of the culture-term that I proposed in Chapter 2, namely, an ethnically marked notion of an allegedly distinctive 'culture' that defines a certain ethnic group and is hence identity-related, versus an ethnically unmarked notion of culture that is not identity-related but merely consists of any learnt or invented practices within a predefined spatial, temporal and social context. As I have argued above, 'language ethnicism' crucially relied on a notion of distinctive ethnic 'culture', while 'rights activism' instead evoked 'cultural diversity' within an ethnically unmarked notion of human culture. Since O'Reilly does not distinguish between these two aspects, her 'cultural discourse' remains ambiguous with regard to the question of whether or not this discourse is ultimately defined in terms of identity.

This leads to my second criticism, namely, O'Reilly's claim that the root difference between her three discourses is to be seen in their divergent positions on the relationship between the Irish language and politics, namely, as 'political' (decolonizing discourse), 'apolitical' (cultural discourse) and 'multipoliticizing' (rights discourse). To my mind, this use of 'politics' is too broad and hence misleading since the question at hand in West Belfast was actually much more specific: should the Irish language be connected to nationalist politics? In my understanding, language nationalists answered this question in the affirmative, language ethnicists in the negative, and rights activists proclaimed it to be a misguided question and instead conceived the problem as one of rights within a modern state-system. In other words, and as I have already made clear above, all three macro-positions viewed themselves as political, yet language ethnicists and rights activists did not want the Irish language to be connected to 'nationalist' politics.

Bringing both lines of criticism together, rather than following O'Reilly in distinguishing between three different macro-positions on the Irish language in terms of a single (and overly broad) *differentia specifica* – 'politics' – and instead of using an ambiguous culture-term, I suggest discriminating between these macro-positions according to two criteria: first, whether or not the language was represented in terms of identity, which separated identity-unrelated 'rights activism', on the one hand, from identity-related 'language ethnicism' and 'language nationalism', on the other; and second, whether or not the language was represented as part of nationalist politics, which was explicitly the case within 'language nationalism', explicitly rejected by 'language ethnicism', and sidestepped within 'rights activism' through the evocation of an altogether different political vocabulary.

In my own conception, language ethnicism and language nationalism are thus united under the identity-related core representation of Irish as 'our own native language', whereas rights activism did not subscribe to this notion and rather celebrated the Irish language as a valued element of cultural diversity that was not marked in terms of identity. Nevertheless, all three macro-positions concerning the dynamics between representations and practices of the Irish language were also united in the common perception that Irish was still not sufficiently practised and hence needed a sustained revival in order to survive. Seen in this light, rights activism, ethnicism and nationalism ultimately only provided different reasons for exactly the same generalized practice – (increasingly) speaking Irish.

Conclusions

This last observation that the three macro-positions of rights activism, language ethnicism and language nationalism constituted divergent rationales in what ultimately amounts to the same generalized practice (speaking Irish) sounds a note of caution against treating as homologous the dynamics between representations and practices of the Irish language at the three different levels that have been covered in this chapter. To my mind, there was no inherent correlation between a certain stance within the purism-pragmatism continuum and, for instance, one of the ideal-typical macro-positions. What could be observed, however, was a tendency among certain purist Irish speakers to accuse more pragmatic Gaeilgeoirí of only strategically using the Irish language as a means of ultimately achieving rather different ends. In Catholic West Belfast, such accusations mainly targeted language nationalists, who were criticized for allegedly having 'hijacked' the Irish language revival at the meso-level of aggregate language practices. As I have made clear, however, all three macro-positions had instrumental potentials and could thus at least potentially be accused of being insincere. Finally, treating more pragmatic language usage as an indicator of a lack of commitment was itself of course heavily contested within Catholic West Belfast.

That all three macro-positions only provided different reasons for the very same practice can also be reformulated in motivational terms, leading to the recognition that rights activism, language ethnicism and language nationalism all provided rational motivations in the Weberian sense (see Chapter 2) for engaging with the Irish language. Rights activism suggested a value-rational motivation for learning and speaking Irish through conceiving the language as a valuable element within the cultural diversity of humankind that had to be preserved through some form of cultural environmentalism. This position, which to my knowledge was supported by only a minority within Catholic West Belfast, offered a value-rational orientation that was unrelated to questions of identity.

In contrast, the vast majority of local Gaeilgeoirí identified with the representation of Irish as 'our own native language'. For language ethnicists, this constituted a purely value-rational motivation since learning and speaking Irish were only concerned with the 'we-hood' of Irishness as an end in itself. For language nationalists, however, engagement with Irish was based on both a value-rational motivation addressing this 'we-hood' and an instrumentally rational motivation additionally using the language as a means for communicating the 'us-hood' of Irishness towards the British state in order to further nationalist politics. It is against this backdrop that my interpretation in Chapter 5 needs to be refined. I stated that wanting to learn and speak one's 'own native language' locally constituted a dominant value-rational motivation. It is clear by now that while this representation of 'our own native language' was seen by all its adherents as value-rational, it was additionally interpreted by language nationalists as part of an instrumentally rational motivation. The question of whether or not Irish should also – or, as some suspected, only – be used as an instrumental means was precisely at the heart of the whole debate on the alleged 'hijacking' of the Irish language.

Against the backdrop of this analysis of the multifaceted dynamic between representations and practices of the Irish language, my findings can now be fully interpreted in terms of the first analytical dimension of this study, by also situating this dynamic within the continuum between 'selection' and 'pretension' (see Chapter 2). As I have argued, all three macro-positions on the Irish language shared the same perception that Irish was only insufficiently practised and thus in continuous need of revival and active maintenance. The locally prevalent macro-positions of language ethnicism and language nationalism, while reading different political implications into their joint representation of Irish as 'our own native language', hence started from the shared assumption that this representation still largely feigned something that was only insufficiently there in actual practice. In other words, these actors (whether language ethnicists or language nationalists) treated the notion of 'our own native language' as an obvious case of *pretension*, which was only slowly shifting towards the pole of *selection* because of their own revivalist engagements. It was thus precisely this emic interpretation as pretension that turned the representation of Irish as 'our own native language' into such a powerful value-rational (and partly instrumentally rational) motivation and thereby encapsulated the very *raison d'être* of the Irish language *revival* in Catholic West Belfast: in order for there to be a 'revival' in the first place, there had to be a relationship between representations and practices viewed by the actors themselves as a case of pretension.

So far so good: in a sense, the Irish language scene in Catholic West Belfast in 2003–2004 could be seen as being ultimately built on the central idea that Irish was 'our own native language' and hence should be revived in practice. Yet upon further consideration, this identity-related construction is, in fact, quite strange: why, how and under which circumstances could it actually be plausible that in order to *be* what you already *are* (i.e. Irish), you have to *become* what you yourself agree you *are not* (i.e. an Irish speaker)? The second part of this book is designed to complementarily dissect Irishness in general along the same three analytical dimensions in order ultimately to answer this question. It is my hope that this will not only help us to explain why people such as Seán actually bothered to learn Irish, but that it will also allow us to understand more profoundly the general mechanisms at work in the overall social construction of ethnic identities.

Part II

Irish Identity in Catholic West Belfast

Chapter 7
'It's part of what we are'
Identifying Identity

It was a rainy Sunday, 22 August 2004, a little after three in the afternoon. Two Gaelic football teams, County Mayo (green/red) and County Fermanagh (green/white), came onto the pitch at Croke Park, Dublin. They followed the band and the colour party, carrying the Irish tricolour as well as the flags of the four Irish provinces and Mayo and Fermanagh counties around the field before the start of the game. More than 64,500 spectators – including myself and two friends, who had come down from Belfast to watch the match – filled the stands and rose for the Irish national anthem before the semi-final match of the Bank of Ireland All-Ireland Senior Football Championship 2004 began.

This championship is the premier knockout competition in Gaelic football played in Ireland between senior county teams, comprising the best players aged twenty-one and older. It is organized by the Gaelic Athletic Association (GAA) and the games are played throughout the summer months, with the Final taking place on the third or fourth Sunday of September at Croke Park. The prize for the

Figure 7.1 The county teams of Mayo and Fermanagh enter Croke Park for the semi-final match of the 2004 Bank of Ireland All-Ireland Senior Football Championship (photo: Olaf Zenker)

winning team is the Sam Maguire Cup, named in honour of an influential GAA footballer (Sweeney 2004: 21). In 2004, the competition was sponsored by the Bank of Ireland.

Within Ireland, it would be difficult to find anyone who has not heard of Gaelic football. But for those readers, who – like me when I first came to Ireland – do not know much about the sport, here is a brief account by the GAA, characterizing some of the basic rules of the sport, which is called *peil, peil ghaelach* or *caid* in Irish:

> Gaelic Football can be described as a mixture of soccer and rugby, although it predates both of those games. It is a field game which has developed as a distinct game similar to the progression of Australian Rules. Indeed it is thought that Australian Rules evolved from Gaelic Football through the many thousands who were either deported or emigrated to Australia from the middle of the nineteenth century. Gaelic Football is played on a pitch approximately 137m long and 82m wide. The goalposts are the same shape as on a rugby pitch, with the crossbar lower than a rugby one and slightly higher than a soccer one. The ball used in Gaelic Football is round, slightly smaller than a soccer ball. It can be carried in the hand for a distance of four steps and can be kicked or 'hand-passed', a striking motion with the hand or fist. After every four steps the ball must be either bounced or 'solo-ed', an action of dropping the ball onto the foot and kicking it back into the hand. You may not bounce the ball twice in a row. To score, you put the ball over the crossbar by foot or hand/fist for one point or under the crossbar and into the net by foot or hand/fist in certain circumstances for a goal, the latter being the equivalent of three points. Each team consists of fifteen players …. A game is played over two halves of 30 minutes (at club level) or 35 minutes (at inter-county level). (Gaelic Athletic Association 2008a)

As already indicated, Gaelic football is organized by the *Cumann Lúthchleas Gael* (CLG) (the GAA), which was founded in 1884 in a general climate of Irish ethnicism and nationalism. To this day, the GAA sees itself as 'a National organization which has as its basic aim the strengthening of the National Identity in a 32 County Ireland through the preservation and promotion of Gaelic Games and pastimes', focusing particularly on 'the National games of Hurling, Gaelic Football, Handball and Rounders' (Gaelic Athletic Association 2003: 4). Besides the bat-and-ball game of rounders, and Gaelic handball (in which two players use their hands to hit a ball against a wall), the second most popular GAA game apart from Gaelic football is hurling. Hurling (*iománaíocht* or *iomáint* in Irish) is comparable to Gaelic football in that it is played on the same pitch by two teams of fifteen players and the game consists of two halves of thirty minutes (at the club level) or thirty-five minutes (at the inter-county level). Apart from that, hurling is often said to be the fastest field game in the world (Sweeney 2004: 68) and is characterized by the GAA in the following way:

Hurling is a game similar to hockey, in that it is played with a small ball and a curved wooden stick. It is Europe's oldest field game. When the Celts came to Ireland as the last ice age was receding, they brought with them a unique culture, their own language, music, script and unique pastimes. One of these pastimes was a game now called hurling. It features in Irish folklore to illustrate the deeds of heroic mystical figures and it is chronicled as a distinct Irish pastime for at least 2,000 years. The stick, or 'hurley' (called *camán* in Irish) is curved outwards at the end, to provide the striking surface. The ball or 'sliotar' is similar in size to a hockey ball but has raised ridges. ... You may strike the ball on the ground, or in the air. Unlike hockey, you may pick up the ball with your hurley and carry it for not more than four steps in the hand. After those steps you may bounce the ball on the hurley and back to the hand, but you are forbidden to catch the ball more than twice. To get around this, one of the skills is running with the ball balanced on the hurley. To score, you put the ball over the crossbar with the hurley or under the crossbar and into the net by the hurley for a goal, the latter being the equivalent of three points. (Gaelic Athletic Association 2008c)

Paralleling the All-Ireland Football Championship, the GAA also runs its annual All-Ireland Senior Hurling Championship, which is the prime knockout competition between senior county hurling teams. These hurling matches take place throughout the summer, with the All-Ireland Hurling Final being played on the first or second Sunday in September at Croke Park. The winning team gets the Liam McCarthy Cup, which commemorates an official who was involved in the GAA for many years (Sweeney 2004: 21). Like in previous years, the sponsor of the All-Ireland Senior Hurling Championship in 2004 was Guinness, which referred to the competition as the Guinness Hurling Championship.

There are female versions of both Gaelic football and hurling, respectively known as 'ladies Gaelic football' and 'camogie', which are very similar to the corresponding men's games with only a few minor rule changes. Although ladies football and camogie are organized by their own distinct associations, they are often represented as belonging to the same 'G.A.A. family' (Gaelic Athletic Association 2005: 15) and also share facilities and playing fields with local GAA clubs.

For quite some time, the GAA understood its basic aim of strengthening 'the National Identity in a 32 County Ireland' as not only *ex positivo* comprising 'the preservation and promotion of Gaelic Games and pastimes' (see above); the GAA also protected these 'Irish sports' through *ex negativo* discouraging so-called 'foreign games' like soccer, rugby, hockey and cricket by means of 'the Ban':

For many people, The Ban is the great black mark against the Association's name. The Ban, or Rule 27, which was introduced in 1902, forbade GAA members to play, attend, or promote rugby, hockey, soccer, or cricket, ie, 'foreign games', under pain of suspension from the Association. ...

In 1938, the GAA removed Dr Douglas Hyde, President of Ireland, as patron because in his capacity as President he had attended a soccer match. (Sweeney 2004: 14–15)

This Ban, which even led to the establishment of vigilante committees whose members attended rugby and soccer matches in order to check and report if any other GAA members were present, was finally abolished in 1971 (Sweeney 2004: 15).

Leaving aside the politics of the Gaelic Athletic Association for now and describing this organization instead in more general terms, it is characterized by its strong community basis, volunteer ethos and amateur status (Delaney and Fahey 2005: 13; Gaelic Athletic Association 2003: 7). This core value of amateurism in particular has meant that except for certain expenses and a few fringe benefits, there is still not a single player who gets any financial rewards for participating in the games (Sweeney 2004: 20–21). This is particularly remarkable considering how popular Gaelic games are in Ireland, both in terms of active play and support for the games. In 2004, the GAA reported that there were more than 2,500 clubs in Ireland alone (almost 2,900 clubs worldwide) and over 20,000 active teams, of which 12,686 were football teams and 7,516 hurling (Gaelic Athletic Association 2005: 90, 24). According to Delaney and Fahey, who analyse the social and economic value of sport in Ireland, there is no precise membership data available, but the GAA estimates there are around seven hundred thousand members and active supporters, which is some 15 per cent of the population (Delaney and Fahey 2005: 12). Taking into account solely attendance at matches for the All-Ireland Football and Hurling Championships in 2004 (i.e. excluding all club competitions), the GAA recorded more than 1.9 million attendees at the main GAA stadiums (Gaelic Athletic Association 2005: 93). Putting this in the context of the relatively small population in the whole of Ireland – around 5.6 million[1] – this means that, at least statistically speaking, one out of three people in Ireland personally attended an All-Ireland match at the end of the 2004 season. And this total attendance of 1.9 million did not even include all those who watched the All-Ireland Championships 2004 on television.

A part of this 1.9 million attendees was comprised of myself and the 64,518[2] spectators who watched the semi-final on that rainy Sunday afternoon in August 2004. After the Irish national anthem was played, the match began under slippery

---

1. This estimate of the total population of the whole island of Ireland is based on the last censuses in Northern Ireland (2001) and in the Republic of Ireland (2002). Combining the rate for the resident population in the North (1,685,267) (Northern Ireland Statistics and Research Agency (NISRA) 2006: Table KS01 ('Usually Resident Population')) and the figure for people living in the Republic of Ireland (3,917,203) (Central Statistics Office – An Phríomh-Oifig Staidrimh (CSO) 2003: Table 1 ('Persons, males and females in the State at each census since 1841')), this adds up to a total of 5,602,470 people living in Ireland during the early years of the new millennium.

2. See the statistics for 'Championship Attendance 2004' in Gaelic Athletic Association (2005: 93).

conditions, soon developing into a neck-and-neck game. In the beginning, Fermanagh gained the lead in its first ever All-Ireland football semi-final, but lost it to Mayo before the break. Early in the second half, Fermanagh levelled the game, and in the forty-third minute, Mayo went down to fourteen men as a half-forward was sent off the field after a second yellow card. Fermanagh then came to the fore, only to let Mayo retake the lead. Shortly before the end of the match, Fermanagh succeeded in tying the game, and the semi-final thus ended in a draw with no goals, but nine points on either side (0-09 vs. 0-09). Instead of deciding the winner of this match through extra time or a penalty shoot-out (like in soccer), we had to wait for a replay on the next Saturday. Being only a novice follower of Gaelic games, I was somewhat disappointed by the lack of a definite result, but I still thought that it had been 'a very good match', as I wrote down in my notes at the end of the day. It was only the next morning when reading the news coverage of the match in the *Andersonstown News* back in West Belfast that I learnt that '[i]n a dreadful match, the Ernemen [from Fermanagh] had plenty of chances to book their place in the final for the very first time, but wayward shooting and sloppy loss of possession allowed 14 man Mayo to stay in and force replay next Saturday' (*Andersonstown News*, Monday 23 August 2004, page 57).

The semi-final, its replay the following Saturday (which saw Mayo win against Fermanagh, 0-13 to 1-08) as well as the All-Ireland football final in late September (in which Mayo eventually lost to the then new champion Kerry, 2-09 to 1-20) were all held at the stadium Croke Park. Situated in north Dublin, Croke Park – or *Páirc an Chrócaigh* in Irish – is the headquarters of the GAA. It is the largest sports stadium in Ireland and is amongst the five largest in Europe. According to the history and development section on the stadium's webpage, the site was known as the 'City and Suburban Racecourse' in the late nineteenth century (Croke Park Stadium – Páirc an Chrócaigh 2008a; see also Carey 2004). It was bought by the GAA in 1913 and renamed in honour of one of the association's first patrons, Archbishop Croke of Cashel. While having occasionally hosted the All-Ireland finals since 1896, it was through its formal acquisition by the GAA that the new Croke Park came to host virtually all subsequent All-Ireland finals. In the decades after 1913, different stands and terraces in Croke Park were built and (re)developed, including the famous terrace Hill 16, which was constructed in 1917 from the rubble left behind after the 1916 Easter Rising (Sweeney 2004: 29). In the course of a massive redevelopment programme that began in the mid-1990s, Croke Park was still being modernized and expanded in 2004, having entered the last phase of replacing the old Hill 16 with modernized terraces. This was also the reason why that particular stand was empty at the semi-final match – as can be seen in Figure 7.1. As of 2004, building regulations hence only allowed for an overall capacity of 78,300 visitors at Croke Park, while the stadium would eventually have a capacity of 82,300 (Gaelic Athletic Association 2005: 90; Croke Park Stadium – Páirc an Chrócaigh 2008b).

Thus, the semi-final's attendance of 'only' 64,519 spectators did not make use of Croke Park's full capacity – as would also be the case a couple of weeks later for the hurling and football finals (Gaelic Athletic Association 2005: 93).

Nevertheless, when correlating the semi-final's attendance figure with the relatively small overall number of inhabitants in the whole of Ireland (around 5.6 million, as mentioned before), it is evident that more than every hundredth person living on the entire island of Ireland was physically present at the match in Croke Park.[3] This observation points towards recognizing – as Delaney and Fahey do in their above-mentioned study on the social and economic value of sport in Ireland – that the GAA 'is by far the largest sports body in the country [i.e. in the Republic of Ireland] and is the strongest representative of the voluntarist, community-based model of sports organization' (Delaney and Fahey 2005: 11). As these authors show, the GAA is the dominant organization when it comes to volunteering, as it attracts the highest percentage (42 per cent) of all sports volunteers (ibid.: 31). The GAA also has the largest proportion of sport club members (29 per cent), which is exceptionally balanced in terms of age and social class, and, 'while weighted towards men, is the second most common sport (after aerobics/fitness) joined by women' (ibid.: 39). Finally (and my above calculations underline this), the GAA also takes the lead in terms of event attendance. According to Delaney and Fahey (ibid.: 42), 'GAA sports account for almost 60 per cent of sport attendances in Ireland (34 per cent for football, 23 per cent for hurling). Soccer and rugby come a long way after the GAA with 16 per cent and 8 per cent of sport attendances respectively'. Against this backdrop, Sweeney is thus probably right, when proclaiming: 'it's obvious that the GAA is intertwined with Irish communities in a way unmatched by any other sporting organisation in Europe. No part of Ireland is untouched by the Championship Summer. In the end, you don't really know Ireland, if you don't know the GAA' (Sweeney 2004: 13).

I have gone a long way to show that Gaelic games and their organizing body, the Gaelic Athletic Association, contribute considerably to those practices that, while being variously representable, are actually realized on the island of Ireland, and can hence legitimately be described as part of culture in Ireland as defined in Chapter 2. But are these specific sporting practices therefore also relevant for people's sense of 'Irish identity'?

When travelling to Croke Park on that particular Sunday, I noticed that a certain advertisement poster had been put up all over the place, forming part of the promotional campaign for 'the Guinness Hurling Championship'. I secured a smaller version of this same advertisement some weeks later when hanging around in a local GAA club in West Belfast, where it was also displayed. A good friend of mine, himself a local football and hurling player for many years, was with me, and he managed to get a copy of the poster for me from the club manager. The advertisement displayed a human skull in the style of an X-ray photograph, overlaid with a picture of the lower, convex striking surface of a hurling stick (see Figure 7.2).

---

3. When using the overall population figure for Ireland as calculated before on the basis of the Northern Ireland Census 2001 and the Republic of Ireland Census 2002, it seems that 1.15 per cent of the island's entire population (i.e. 65,519 out of 5,602,470) attended the All-Ireland football semi-final on Sunday 22 August 2004.

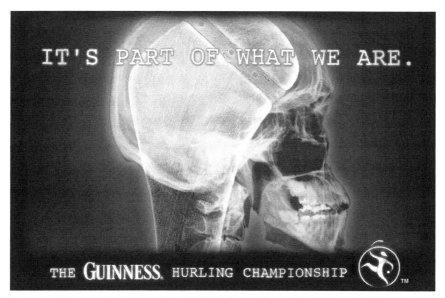

Figure 7.2 Guinness advertisement for the 2004 Guinness Hurling Championship – 'It's part of what we are' (photo: Olaf Zenker)

This representational fusion of human being and sports gear was framed in a specific way, namely, with the slogan 'It's part of what we are'. This slogan was evidently meant to suggest that 'hurling' – and, by metonymic extension, Gaelic games generally – formed part of the collective 'Irish identity' of all those self-ascribed Irish people (the 'we' of the slogan) who would read this advertisement during the 2004 All-Ireland Hurling Championship.[4] This advertisement hence represented Gaelic games as part of an allegedly distinctive 'Irish culture' that was internally shared, while simultaneously making members different from non-members. In other words, this representation transformed these sports from being merely a dominant part of culture in Ireland into a prominent element of an ethnic 'Irish culture'. It is only through such representational practices that Gaelic games effectively became an issue of 'Irish identity'.

In this chapter, I have used the example of a Gaelic football semi-final, which Guinness 'wrapped' in public representations of Gaelic games as forming part of people's Irishness, in order to highlight a methodological problem that is crucial for the entire second part of this book, namely, the problem of how to identify identity. As I argued in Chapter 2, it is one of my overall intentions to investigate Irish identity with regard to the relationship between both representational practices of

---

4.   There was actually also another version of this Guinness advertisement that used the same stylistic principle and evoked the same message. This second advertisement poster showed an X-ray photograph of a human chest, which was overlaid with a picture of a hurling ball – a *sliotar* – precisely at the place of the heart. The slogan read again 'It's part of what we are'. Taken together, both posters can be interpreted as suggesting that hurling/Gaelic games equally occupy 'the hearts and minds' of Irish people.

'culture' and variously representable cultural practices, without privileging either representations or practices at a theoretical level. Nevertheless, I do acknowledge that, methodologically speaking, one still has to begin with representations. This is so since it is only by focusing on identity-related representations that it seems possible to identify those cultural practices that, precisely because they are portrayed as 'cultural' practices, form part of the ethnic identity at issue.

It is thus necessary to figure out first how relevant actors ethnically identify themselves. Second, their identity-related representations need to be considered in relation to the question of which cultural practices are proclaimed as forming part of their distinctive ethnic 'culture'. Based on this identification of both identity-related representations and therein represented domains of cultural practices, it is then possible ultimately to investigate the complex relationship between these representations and practices as they unfold within the dynamics of structure and agency over the course of divergent biographies.

Turning to Catholic West Belfast, it can be observed, first, that almost all local Catholics with whom I conversed about matters of identity self-ascribed as 'Irish'. In Chapter 1, I referred to statistical data available for the whole of Northern Ireland, which shows that despite some variation and cross-cutting affiliations, '[t]he majority of the population clearly identify themselves as either Irish Catholics or British Protestants' (Trew 1998: 66). Given that the Northern Ireland Census in 2001 did not ask about 'ethnic identity' as defined herein, there is no systematic data on religious background or ethnicity for the area of Catholic West Belfast. However, my personal experience in this part of the city echoed the overall trend within the North, in that most Catholics evidently regarded themselves as Irish.

Having established that many if not most locals identified themselves in terms of Irishness, it is now possible to identify the main domains of cultural practices that were represented by these actors as forming part of their own distinctive 'Irish culture'. Let us look, for instance, at the following description by seventeen-year-old Caoimhín. When I asked him what made somebody Irish, Caoimhín began talking about typical elements of 'Irish culture'. He first mentioned the Irish language and then went on to enumerate a number of other practices:

> I'd say Irish would be a very rich culture. There's Gaelic games, hurling, Gaelic football. The music, traditional music and the singing – old Irish singing. And there's, like, loads of traditional things and traditional meals, stew – ... Like, – *seanchaí*, you call them – people, like – the Irish storytellers. You'd get them in Donegal, people who'd be really good at telling stories and would sit and talk all night. ... I'd say storytelling would be still one of the big things. If you walked into any bar along the Falls Road there, there'd be old men, or whatever, just sitting there – telling you stories about everything. If you ask them about, like, Belfast fifty years ago, they'll be sitting and tell you about it all night. Even a total stranger. ... Irish dancing, as well, that's another thing I could imagine [as part of 'Irish culture']. That would be very big!

That Caoimhín thereby regarded these elements as clearly belonging to a distinctive 'Irish culture' that was projected as being internally shared while externally differentiating 'the Irish' from other people became clear when I asked him how he actually knew these things were 'Irish'. Caoimhín replied: "'Cause you wouldn't find this stuff anywhere else in the world; 'cause you're not going to go to China and find people playing hurling; unless Irish people have come over there and played it.' Caoimhín thus saw 'Irish culture' as comprising things that only existed in Ireland – or, to be more precise, that were seen as originating from or rightfully belonging to the Irish people, hence making the Irish people distinctive *as* Irish people.

Against the backdrop of this initial overview of the breadth of 'Irish culture' as provided by Caoimhín, consider how sixty-one-year-old Rónán referred to different elements of 'Irish culture' when asked about how he knew another person was also 'Irish':

> Well, see – people might look on themselves as being Irish, even though they mightn't know the Irish language. For example, someone might love hurling, he might love Gaelic football. There's a big world out there – in GAA circles, for example, that's their Irishness, you know? ... They feel that the fact that they play hurling, play Gaelic football, that that's showing they're Irish, you know? Or, it's people who play diddle-de-dee music [i.e. traditional instrumental music], you know? And play céilí music. Or dance set dancing or céilí dancing, you know? It's a very complex thing, you know? That's their showing. That's their Irishness, you know? In fact, you might get elements with them saying, 'If everybody played Gaelic football or played hurling, that'd be the real Irish,' you know? Whereas, there's other elements that would say, 'Well, you know, if you knew the Irish language that really is being Irish,' you know?

This quotation is interesting in that Rónán also mentioned (like Caoimhín above) those four aspects of 'Irish culture' that were most commonly invoked by my Gaeilgeoirí interlocutors in Catholic West Belfast when specifying their sense of Irishness, namely, the Irish language, Gaelic games, Irish music and Irish dancing. Given how strongly these four domains of cultural practice were represented to me as forming part of local 'Irishness', I will from this point forward exclusively focus on them as both crucial and exemplary aspects of 'Irish culture'. As the Irish language was already covered in great detail in the first part of this book, I will hence concentrate in this second part solely on Gaelic games, Irish music and Irish dancing.

Rónán's quote is interesting for another reason, namely, for his observation that Irish people obviously differed with regard to the relative importance they assigned to each of these four domains. As he put it, 'in GAA circles' people 'feel that the fact that they play hurling, play Gaelic football, that that's showing they're Irish', whereas for others playing 'diddle-de-dee music' or doing 'set dancing or céilí dancing' showed their Irishness. Others thought that 'if you knew the Irish language that really is being Irish'. This observation by Rónán sounds a note of caution against assuming that the subsequent analysis of Irish identity in Catholic West Belfast is in any way representative of the whole area. On the contrary, my reference group is clearly selective, exclusively consisting of a specific subset of local actors, namely, Irish learners and speakers. Even for this subset, my descriptions cannot be taken as representative in any statistical sense. Finally, my decision to henceforth exclusively focus on the above-mentioned three exemplary domains of 'Irish culture' (besides the already covered language) defies any pretence towards phenomenal comprehensiveness within the overall analysis of local Irishness. Yet this study has all along aimed neither for comprehensiveness nor for representativeness, but rather for reconstructing typical patterns in local dynamics between representations and practices, and for this, neither comprehensiveness nor representativeness is needed.

Bearing this in mind, I turn towards the third and last quotation to be cited in this chapter in order to substantiate and legitimate my decision to concentrate solely on Gaelic games, Irish music and Irish dancing as typical elements (besides the language) of 'Irish culture' and 'Irishness'. In this excerpt, fifty-five-year-old Micheál provided me with the following quite spontaneous answer when I asked him about what made somebody Irish:

> I was going to say that anybody who wants to be is Irish, but that isn't true [Micheál laughs]. You need to have some connection with the island. You need to identify with the island or with the culture or the people in some way. So the paradigm, the caricature paradigm [for an Irish person] would be – an Irish-speaking, hurling player, céilí dancing, singing and – drunk, right? … That would be part of it, of the caricature – I do all of those things! [Micheál laughs]

This quote makes three points that are worth spelling out. At first, Micheál emphasized that while Irishness was to some extent a matter of choice, it still required some form of self-identification 'with the island or with the culture or the people in some way'. This insistence on self-identification and, in a certain sense, territoriality ('you need to have some connection with the island') will be explicitly addressed in Chapter 10 when I analyse local representations and practices of Irishness. Subsequently, Micheál depicted 'the caricature paradigm' of an Irish person in terms of 'Irish culture', which evoked the above-mentioned four domains of the Irish language ('Irish-speaking'), Gaelic games ('hurling player'), Irish dancing ('céilí dancing'), Irish music ('singing') – plus alcohol drinking ('drunk'). By characterizing these aspects of 'Irish culture' as forming 'the caricature paradigm', Micheál ironically distanced himself from this widespread representation of 'Irishness' and simultaneously marked it as 'stereotypical'. This implied that Micheál saw this 'caricature' as by and large misrepresenting the actual cultural practices of Irish people. Yet in another self-ironic move, Micheál repudiated his own representation of 'the paradigm' as a misrepresenting 'caricature' by laughingly revealing that he, in actual fact, did do 'all of those things'. In other words, while questioning the truth of such stereotypical representations of 'Irishness', Micheál simultaneously (and ambiguously) asserted their very truth, at least for his personal case. This final ambiguity in Micheál's account points to the variable relationship between local representations and actual practices of 'Irishness' that need to be addressed in the following chapters in order to grasp more deeply the nature of Irish identity in Catholic West Belfast.

Chapter 8

Becoming (Aware of) Who You Are

Irish

The previous chapter addressed the methodological problem of how empirically to identify identity. I argued that even though one should not theoretically privilege representations of 'culture' over cultural practices (focusing instead on their diverse interrelations), for methodological reasons one still has to begin with representations in order to know which variously representable but actually realized cultural practices should be investigated in the first place. Besides the Irish language, three further cultural domains turned out to be often represented as forming part of a distinctive 'Irish culture', namely, Gaelic games, Irish music and Irish dancing. In the second part of this study, I hence decided to focus only on these three cultural domains in their interrelations with concomitant representations of Irishness.

Yet, thus far, this entire endeavour has been fairly abstract and hence needs to be brought down to the level of tangible everyday life. To what extent and in what ways, one may ask, did the cultural domains of Gaelic games, Irish music and Irish dancing actually make themselves felt in Catholic West Belfast? Or, rephrasing the question from the perspective of concrete actors, how and why had real individuals become involved with these activities, practising them to varying extents? What kinds of experiences had they had being involved in these activities, and what had these cultural practices come to mean for them? What consequences, if any, did this process have in their lives?

This chapter addresses these and other issues by reconstructing a range of ways in which certain local Gaeilgeoirí came to experience and think of themselves as being (mostly) 'Irish'. By again following the ten Gaeilgeoirí already encountered in Chapter 4 on their paths to becoming Irish, this chapter presents a graphic image of the diverse and variable circumstances under which the transformation of individuals into 'Irishmen' and 'Irishwomen' has taken place in Catholic West Belfast over the past few decades. The different intersecting conditions, processes and meanings that emerge from these biographies will be contextualized, systematized and refocused in my analysis in the following two chapters.

I begin each section by briefly sketching the respective actor's overall development as an Irish person before addressing his or her individual engagements with Gaelic games, Irish music and Irish dancing, respectively. In many cases I also include the cultural practice of soccer into my reconstructions because this game turned out to have a close and ambiguous relationship to Gaelic games: on the one hand, until 1971 'the Ban' or Rule 27 of the Gaelic Athletic Association (GAA) strongly barred its members from playing, attending or promoting so-called 'foreign games' including soccer (see Chapter 7); on the other hand, soccer has been quite popular among segments of the population of Catholic West Belfast for some time and has itself been used as a means of expressing Irishness, especially – as we will see – through the support of Glasgow Celtic in Scotland.

Roibeárd, age 63

As Roibeárd recalled of his childhood in the 1940s, his sense of identity – 'the Irishness in me, Irish language, music, Gaelic football' – was present from a very early age, given that 'everything Irish would be laid out in front of me'. Roibeárd remembered how he was told about Irish history and its consequences for his own family. Places in rural Ireland were pointed out where relatives had hidden during the Anglo-Irish War (1919–1921), only to be arrested by the infamous Royal Irish Constabulary Reserve Force, the so-called 'Black'n Tans'. While Belfast-born himself, Roibeárd's matrilateral kin came from an area in County Down that was still Irish-speaking at the turn of the twentieth century, and he often visited his relatives there. He recalled a big portrait of the late-eighteenth-century Irish rebel Robert Emmet above his grandparents' fireplace:

> So it was all around you. It was expected of you, you know? ... You were to follow in, you know – if you were playing Gaelic football, you would be reminded that your Uncle Jimmy played for [the team of County] Down. The family would like to think that you would be like Uncle Jimmy and play for [County] Antrim.

With these different aspects of 'Irishness' all around, Roibeárd claimed that he 'never ever considered' being Irish 'as something to think about. I'm Irish, that's it'. He could neither recall his Irishness ever having been questioned nor having been told that he actually was Irish, because 'What else can you be but Irish?' When I expressed my surprise that his sense of Irishness had never been a conscious issue despite the ongoing context of conflict in the North of Ireland, Roibeárd declared: 'It may have been a political issue, but for the two sides it was no issue. It's the same today. One side's Irish, the other side believes themselves to be British. But the Irish have never questioned themselves as to what they are. Never.'

Roibeárd was exposed to Gaelic games when he was still very young. His mother took him to Gaelic football games, and with a long tradition of relatives playing Gaelic games – some even for their county team during the All-Ireland Championship – it was almost natural for him to do the same: 'My grandfather played Gaelic football, great-grandfather played Gaelic football and my great-uncles played for County Down. You know, it was the thing to do. I've a second cousin playing for Down at the minute. And his grandfather played for County Down. So, you know, it's <u>tradition</u>.'

One of Roibeárd's uncles was a founding member of a local club of the GAA in Belfast, and Roibeárd remembered hanging out in the club since its formation in the early 1950s. All of his cousins started playing Gaelic football there, as did Roibeárd when he was aged thirteen or fourteen. Before this point, he and his classmates played Gaelic games such as Gaelic football and hurling during physical education (PE) at his Catholic school. While on the under-18 team, Roibeárd was selected to play for his County (Antrim), which he continued to do at the senior level for seven additional years. He thus indeed turned out to 'be like Uncle Jimmy and play for Antrim' during the annual all-Ireland competition between all counties of the island. At the same time – as was described in Chapter 4 – Roibeárd also played under an assumed name for the GAA club in Rannafast, which allowed him to enter and become part of the local Irish-speaking community in Donegal. When I met Roibeárd, he would still listen to radio commentaries and watch Gaelic games on television or live at the County Antrim home ground Casement Park in Catholic West Belfast.

Concerning Irish dancing, Roibeárd emphasized that while many if not most types of 'traditional' dance actually originated elsewhere or were invented in the 1900s, they had still become somewhat 'traditional' in his youth in the sense of being part of everyday life. As Roibeárd recalled, solo dancing was extremely popular among girls:

> I would say you'd <u>hardly</u> meet <u>a</u> girl on the Falls Road that wasn't sent to some school of Irish dancing when she was small. My sisters, they <u>all</u> were sent to it. The girls of a good friend went to it as well. They didn't stay; some of them didn't stay very long because they weren't terribly good at it. And it's a similar thing with all these things that if a wee girl isn't very good at dancing and doesn't get a lot of medals, the teachers aren't interested in them. I mean, they are interested in getting medals so that they can get their school of dancing a higher reputation. Because it's a costly business. They all take money off the children for it.

In contrast, boys seemed not to have been too keen to go to Irish dancing given that they 'had to wear a kilt, and boys didn't like wearing kilts'. As Roibeárd remembered laconically, 'I was told as a boy I either go to boxing or go to Irish dancing; I went to boxing'.

Apart from such solo 'young children's dancing', group dances – so-called céilís – were even more common. Roibeárd claimed that in his age set, virtually everybody knew his 'sevens' – the basic steps – and that 'you'd been frowned upon if you didn't do your sevens right':

> <u>Even most children</u>; you know, this 'one, two three, four, five, six, seven, one, two three, one, two, three.' You know, we were <u>all</u> <u>taught</u> to do that, you know [Roibeárd gets up and performs the steps in front of me, counting in Irish]. '*Aon, dó, trí, ceathair, cúig, sé, seacht, aon, dó, trí, aon, dó, trí*', and then you went back and forward. And that was the initial, the original step. ... I mean, my age group ... we <u>all</u> knew how to do <u>our sevens</u>.

Roibeárd thought that 'probably either my sisters or my mother or somebody taught me my first steps, when I was going to the céilí. And then you picked up the steps, and then you practised in the toilet'. Roibeárd must have been 'about ten or eleven or twelve or so' when he started going to his first céilí nights. At that time in the 1950s, céilís could be found in all Nationalist parts of the city, and Roibeárd usually went to parish halls such as St Paul's Hall in West Belfast or to Irish-language places like the Árdscoil or – later on – the Cumann Cluain Árd. According to Roibeárd, the main attraction and motivation among teenagers for going to céilís was quite clear: at a time when the moral teachings of the Catholic Church still exercised an almost catholic influence and when virtually all schools were gender segregated (as was still largely the case in 2003–2004, one of the few exceptions being Irish-medium education), such céilí dances constituted one of the few contexts in which boys and girls could meet in a morally acceptable way.

Roibeárd claimed that there were still about four or five céilís per week in the 1960s right up until the Troubles started. The Cluain Árd also continued to organize its céilís throughout and beyond the 1970s, as did some other places. However, in the 1980s, céilí dancing 'was dying except you had certain groups formed like a céilí club', specifically promoting just céilí dancing. Although Roibeárd continued to do some céilí dancing in the context of the Cluain Árd, he decreasingly did so as the céilís were to some degree fading away, and he had never been excessively interested in Irish dancing anyway: 'Dancing to me was something you did if you were asked to do it. It wasn't something you <u>wanted</u> to do. Or you went out of <u>your way</u> to do, you know? It was part of your upbringing to dance. And you could dance.'

As with Irish dancing, Irish music was also part of Roibeárd's environment. He grew up with music – as he said – 'all around' him, as did 'everybody in Ireland'. In his family, his father played accordion, Roibeárd and all his sisters were taught the piano and it was a common thing to sing. As he observed:

> A lot of the songs would have been attached to the GAA, in a sense. You know, the GAA, the Gaelic Athletic Association, each county in Ireland has its own song, in English. And you would be used to singing these county songs at matches at half time, you know? And the band would play them, and everybody would sing. Just [County] Kerry were playing in the All-Ireland, as a boy you'd be in Croke Park, and they were playing 'The Rose of Tralee' or [County] Galway with the dreadful 'Galway Bay'. And, you know different songs. I mean, when [County] Antrim were playing in Croke Park, there'd be 'The Green Glens of Antrim'. So that's the sort of songs that we were used to. … And then you would have the martial tunes like being played by bands at one of the football games. And we'd know all those tunes as well.

Roibeárd also remembered how as a child he listened to music on the radio from the South. There was a lot of this sort of music about in Roibeárd's youth – 'the type of music that the Clancy Brothers made popular' when this Irish folk group became famous in the 1960s, especially in the USA. Many people including Roibeárd himself at that time would have thought that theirs was 'Irish music'. However, as Roibeárd explained, while such songs in English had been common in Ireland for one hundred and fifty years, they were still not 'traditional' for Ireland:

> Well, if 'tradition' is a hundred fifty years old, you could say the work 'God Save the Queen' then is the most traditional song in Ireland, being in the country since that arrived. You know what I mean? It's <u>not</u>, it didn't come from the tradition within the country. It came from the Big House and the piano and somebody writing music, which was not a feature of Irish life at all.

As Roibeárd recalled, it was only when he started to travel to the Rannafast Gaeltacht in his late teenage years that he realized that what he had hitherto regarded as Irish music actually belonged to the Anglo-Irish ascendancy of the Victorian era with big country houses and sheet music. In contrast, the actual 'music of Ireland' that he was to encounter in the Gaeltacht was in the Irish language and 'difficult to write down in the European mode of writing music' and 'very much different, entirely different'.

The processes by which Roibeárd got deeper and deeper into this 'traditional' music in the course of recording storytelling and singing from Rannafast Gaeilgeoirí have already been described in Chapter 4. The same applies for Roibeárd's development into a successful traditional Irish musician with several records and his own television show. What shall be repeated as a concluding remark, however, is Roibeárd's claim that he had always been more interested in the Irish language than in singing:

> I'm not really involved in Irish music, in songs in Irish. Erm, and really that came about simply because of an understanding that in the poetic language is the <u>best</u> language. This is why people study poetry. And the best Irish was in the poetry of Ireland, which was generally set to music. And it was as a means to an end, in that I was more interested in the poetry of it rather than the music. <u>But</u> I got very attached to the old methods of singing and how it was done.

Rónán, age 61

Talking about his sense of identity and how it had changed throughout his life, Rónán emphasized that 'I think you would have always looked upon yourself as being Irish, you know?' Music seemed to have played an important role in instilling this sense of collective identity. As Rónán recalled of his Belfast childhood in the 1940s, getting together and having 'what you call a sing-song' created an 'incredible atmosphere' and 'a real sense of belonging'. These sing-songs often happened spontaneously in the context of parties or when people just came around for an informal visit or social evening, 'what they called a céilí': "'Cause there's a lot of céilí-ings going on. I don't know if you know what céilí-ing is? It's just – you sit down, and people would sing and tell stories, you know? … That was still very prevalent, going up into the sixties, you know?' During this type of 'céilí' (to be distinguished from the group dances by the same name), people took turns singing. Some would be quite willing to sing, while others had to be coaxed, even though 'deep down, they wanted to sing'. At times, when a song was popular, other people would also join in:

> We all know a wee bit of a song. And the bits that you pick up are, most probably, the bits that everybody's picked up. So, you feel great, you know? The fact that – [Rónán sings] 'We're sailing along' – and then, oh – 'on moonlight bay'. Everybody knows those wee bits, you know? And they can do it all. But then comes the, sort of, chorus. Everybody got involved in the chorus, you know?

Over time, certain songs came to be identified with particular individuals. So people would say 'that's Harry's song. "Harry, give us that song!" you know?' Looking back, Rónán remembered that sing-songs often evolved within a certain sequence, moving from 'the modern songs of the day' to an 'Irish type of song':

> You would've started off with modern type of songs, you know? They'd've been whatever the songs would've been, at that particular time – so, the ballads, I suppose. You had a period that ballads – crooners and that type of thing. More like the Bing Crosby and Frank Sinatra. Those are the big – Vic Ramone and all that type of thing was a whole rage. And at the sing-songs, you'd've started off with that. You'd've had the latest song, and then, you'd maybe had the songs going back maybe thirty years before that. And then, you broke down eventually, it all would come into Irish sentiment songs.

When it came to these songs of Irish sentiment, their meanings were 'completely different'. According to Rónán, there was 'something put into them', and they were sung 'with feeling' without people 'trying to copy anybody' because 'you could identify with that' and 'knew the meaning of them'. Such songs were in English but 'seemed to be identified with' and were 'about Ireland'. They covered a broad range of topics such as humorous events, sad love stories, incidents related to a particular area, acts of armed rebellion against British rule in so-called 'rebel songs' or in the genre of the 'Come-All-Ye' characterized by the eponymous opening line 'Come all ye [young rebels/lads and lassies/etc.]'. Echoing Roibeárd, Rónán emphasized that not yet knowing the Irish language and songs in Irish in his youth, 'that would have been Irish traditional music to us'. His perception seems to have been reinforced by the way in which such songs were represented on the radio:

> And then, I suppose the thing that brought us closer to looking at ourselves as being Irish too was Radio Éireann. That was the radio from Dublin. We'd've listened to that a lot. In Catholic areas, that was widely listened to. … You'd've had 'The Walton's Programme', for example. A big record

company in Dublin. And they produced this programme called 'The Walton's Programme', and they had all these records of Irish sentiment. ... The way he [the broadcaster Leo Maguire] finished the programme off was: 'If you feel like singing, do sing an Irish song.'

Apart from music on the radio, local cinemas were also places where Irishness had some practical relevance. Rónán often used to go with a group of friends to the local cinemas, one of which was situated in a 'Loyalist' or 'Protestant area' even though 'you didn't think in terms like that' and 'everybody went to that one'. As Rónán recalled:

> They played 'God Save the Queen', at the end of the performance. Now, normally, we got out before that. Normally. You know, you never stood for 'The Queen'. It was never any problem, like. Because you could discreetly get out before they played it. Why was that? I don't know. Do you understand what I mean?

While symbolically protesting against British rule certainly had something to do with being Irish, the crucial point about this incident seems to be that 'it just was done, and that was it'. In fact, Rónán's whole point in recounting this episode was precisely to underline that although he had always looked upon himself as being Irish, this was not a consciously relevant category in his life: 'I don't think you ever thought in terms of that. Do you understand? Like, there was nobody telling you in my house that you were Irish'.

So generally speaking, Rónán did not grow up in a family in which Irishness or 'Irish culture' (other than Irish music) played a very important role. As he put it, there always have been 'GAA families' where 'Irish culture ... goes down generations', but 'that wasn't our situation'. He said that he might have played Gaelic games at school, but generally he neither played nor followed Gaelic games in any form. As he said, 'I can't remember; maybe I was hopeless', but in any case he had 'just no interest in that type of sport'.

In his social environment, other sports were much more prominent. 'We played soccer day and night in our area. We built three pitches on our own, levelled 'em out and all. Where the M1 Motorway is now, that was the bog meadows.' Apart from building these pitches and playing soccer there 'day and night', Rónán also played on a local team for a couple of years when he was a teenager. His father was a fan of the local Belfast Celtic team until the club decided to leave the league after serious sectarian attacks in the late 1940s, and also fervently supported Glasgow Celtic. Rónán, however, did not really get into Glasgow Celtic, remembering that he always thought of it as 'a bit staged Irish'.

As with Gaelic games, Irish dancing did not figure in Rónán's family. To Rónán's knowledge, nobody in his family had been into 'Irish dancing' in the form of solo dancing, and Rónán could remember only a few people from his area who danced competitively. Rónán did not participate in céilí dancing until he eventually ended up in the Cumann Cluain Árd. Instead, he became 'mad' about rock 'n' roll, listening to Bill Haley and others on Radio Luxembourg in the 'late fifties, sixties' and getting involved with ballroom dancing and especially 'jiving' – 'like, rock 'n' roll type of stuff' – in big dancehalls such as the Plaza in the city centre or the Jig in West Belfast. Rónán continued doing ballroom dancing for another couple of years after starting to attend the Cluain Árd at the age of nineteen, even though this step was to lead him away from this former life.

As described in Chapter 4, for Rónán, entering the Irish-speaking world of the Cluain Árd increasingly meant entering a whole new life in which speaking the Irish language and being Irish became very important. 'Before I went to learn Irish, I mean, I felt I was as Irish as anybody. It didn't even figure in my life, you know, that I was Irish and that was it.' 'You just sort of took it for granted you were Irish, in a way, you know? It just didn't come into your life, at all.' However, in the course of learning the language in the Cluain Árd, Rónán began to identify strongly with the idea that 'to be Irish, you had to have Irish – the Irish language'.

In this process, Rónán also first came across songs in Irish, given that with the system they had then in the Cluain Árd, after the classes everybody came together and 'you learnt a song'. Thus learning Irish songs – many of which had just recently been compiled by young Gaeilgeoirí from the Cluain Árd and beyond in the small songbook *Abair Amhrán* ('Sing a Song') – Rónán ended up singing in the group *Cluainfhondúirí* ('People from the Cluain Árd').

Upon entering the Cluain Árd, Rónán also got involved with céilí dancing, but 'only because of the association with the Irish language, really' since learning céilí dances through the medium of Irish was also part of acquiring the language. As Rónán recalled, these Tuesday night classes were taught by a dancing master who also travelled and taught in Gaeltacht areas and beyond. In comparison with others who had been into Irish dancing and 'knew the steps, "do the sevens", and all that', Rónán was 'a greenhorn'. However:

> It was a fun thing, in fact, you know? It was a way of getting to know people, you know? And, I suppose that's what brought you to the céilí [on Sundays] eventually. Because you'd known these people, it meant you were not going to be sitting there like a walrus, you know?

The actual céilís started around nine in the evening and usually lasted until about half past eleven on Sunday nights except for special occasions such as Easter, Christmas or New Year's Eve, when 'you'd had, maybe, a céilí 'til two o'clock in the morning, you know?' The local McPeake Family, which achieved considerable international fame in the 1950s and 1960s, used to perform as the céilí band. Like most céilís in the 1960s, these were alcohol-free events, and the boys and girls sat separately, which all contributed, as Rónán put it, to the then current image of a céilí-goer as a morally good, 'very possibly religious' person. For years, Rónán attended weekly céilís in the Cluain Árd until the birth of his first child in 1969 made it more difficult for him and his wife to go out at night. But he and other members of the Shaw's Road Gaeltacht continued to be involved throughout the 1970s with organizing numerous céilís as fundraising events for their all-Irish primary school.

In Chapter 4, I described the processes surrounding the outbreak of the Troubles in 1969 and the rebuilding of Bombay Street, which led Rónán to depart from his earlier uncompromising views concerning the necessary link between the Irish language and being 'really Irish'. Looking back, Rónán thought, 'I was being fairly silly, you know?' While he obviously still saw the Irish language as an important aspect of his own Irishness when I met him, Rónán had opened up to other conceptions as well:

> There's people who spend their whole lives and their big thing would be Irish competition dancing. That's their Irishness, they might never come across anything else. That's the way they show their Irishness, you know? … The same with music as well. There's people spend their whole lives playing Irish traditional music. That's their Irishness, you know? And speak English; a lot of them don't speak any Irish at all. But still, they'll have the so-called trappings of being Irish, you know? … So you can't be too much carried away with your own importance [only because you are an Irish speaker], you know? [Rónán chuckles].

Mairéad, age 58

Thinking back to her childhood in Belfast during the late 1940s and 1950s, Mairéad could not really remember any particular event that 'could've overly influenced me or identified the fact that I was Irish. I just knew who I was. I just, you know, always knew what I was'. However, as she reasoned, her family background possibly shaped her development as an Irish person:

> Well perhaps because my father, you know, he had a very strong sense of identity as being Irish, being Republican, a Socialist. And my mother, my mother was a Nationalist rather than a Republican. She came from a more Nationalist background. So, we just had the ethos. I can't remember ever been indoctrinated as such. I mean, we were just brought up.

In this environment, as Mairéad recalled:

> Singing would have been part of our family life when we were children. And when I think of it now, you know, I was aware of historical facts through our songs. And my brother and I, we would have washed the dishes after the meal and the two of us would have been singing while we were doing it. And singing in harmony about certain things that had happened and certain people in the songs. … Well, there would have been songs like 'Kelly, the Boy from Killane', 'The Lonely Woods of Upton'; struggles that would have gone back to 1798, you know, to the United Irishmen and the rising. Then the different struggles, you know, like up to [the Easter Rising of] 1916, like of James Connolly, the song about 'James Connolly, the Irish rebel'; and Sir Roger Casement, the name of the song

is 'Banna Strand'. Because that's where he was captured by the English. He had gone over to Germany and came back with arms and ammunition for another rising. That's before 1916.

Mairéad could not remember actually learning these and similar songs but assumed that she had come across them 'just in the house probably', at sing-songs or other social events. As she recalled, 'there was always music of every variety, but there would have been a lot of Irish music in our home' as well. Her music class in primary school was 'very much kind of Irish kind of music', although not 'overly political. Just songs about Ireland and people in Ireland and activities in Ireland: folklore'.

> And then of course, as I got older, then I would buy my own records, which of course was very much influenced by the time because being a child in the sixties was brilliant, you know? And in the fifties and sixties we had Elvis. So that is music that was known at the time as music from the top ten, the top ten records. My daddy didn't really approve of this kind of music, you know, he absolutely did not. 'Pop music', 'English music', 'American music' as we would've called it. So, we would have listened at night, very quietly, to Radio Luxembourg, which was a great station because they did all the modern music.

While Mairéad thus came to very much enjoy 'modern music' as a teenager in the 1950s and 1960s to the disapproval of her father, she claimed that 'Irish music' still maintained a somewhat special status for her:

> Because you knew when Elvis sang, it was about his 'Blue Suede Shoes', and it really got nothing to do with you and your culture. You know, because we didn't have blue suede shoes in those days, we didn't even know what blue suede shoes were, you know? But you knew some of the Irish songs, you know? It was about you, about your family, about your race, about your neighbours. So it gave you that sense of identity. … I think maybe it [Irish music] did have a little bit of status with us because, again, we were always fighting for our own identity. So this gave our own identity a degree of importance. So the music took on a degree of importance; anything that identified you as a nation was very important to us. … So, yes, it was very important. And we kind of knew that. But it didn't prevent us from enjoying all the other kinds of music.

Another cultural domain that Mairéad grew into from an early age was Gaelic games:
'My daddy would have taken us, you know, to the parks and things like that. There would have always been hurling sticks. I mean, you know, we just kind of knew how to hit a ball with a hurling stick. So we would have always had that ability, you know, from young children.' Although Mairéad was the oldest of her siblings, her brothers actually started competitively playing Gaelic games before her.

This was so, Mairéad said, because 'boys always had more sports in our schools than girls, probably because of the hurling and [Gaelic] football. And they wouldn't have been playing soccer or anything like that. That wouldn't have been popular as a game.' In fact, nobody in her family ever played soccer or even took an interest in this 'incredibly boring' sport: 'That would have been totally alien. Yes, totally.' Instead, her family frowned upon soccer as – following GAA parlance – a 'foreign game':

> Maybe we were kind of purists, Olaf, I really don't know. Just because it was soccer, there was never a place for it in our lives. And even today I can't understand the mentality [among Catholics to support Glasgow Celtic in particular]. I know it exists very strongly and people have very strong feelings about it.

Thus focusing on Gaelic games, Mairéad started playing camogie (the women's variant of hurling) from around age eleven for her secondary school and for a local GAA club that was 'just handy' because it was 'near where I lived' and 'my friends were going' there as well. Yet while her brothers continued to play, and one even followed his father in also playing for the county team in the All-Ireland Championship, Mairéad only played for a few years, when after a bad injury she switched to tennis.

Around the age of seven, Mairéad was sent to a school of Irish dancing:

> What I was dancing, it was basically the legs were used and the upper body is kept very upright and very stiff and mostly with hands, you know, solo dancing, the hands would always be at your side. So there's no upper movement from the waist up. Except when you're doing dancing in groups. You know, well, then you would obviously have to lift your arms to form arches, to let people underneath and to hold people's hands. That's the only time the hands ever went up. So that was the kind of traditional dancing.

According to Mairéad, the purpose of the dancing schools was 'to promote the Irish dancing and put you in for competitions and to see which school gets the most cups and trophies and things'. While the whole activity was hence very competitive, Mairéad was glad that competitions were not very frequent, as she did not particularly like them and 'never had the makings of a champion'.

After five years of practising competitive Irish dancing, Mairéad stopped when she was about twelve years old. By then, she was so involved in other things like camogie, netball, tennis and the school choir that 'the Irish dancing went by the wayside'. As Mairéad recalled of her active period, a lot of girls went to one of the many local schools of Irish dancing. Her own daughters eventually learnt dancing, as did the daughters (and granddaughters) of her friends; as Mairéad put it, 'I suppose it's nearly like a tradition, you know?'

A year or so after she stopped doing this 'high kicking style' at the dancing school, Mairéad got involved with the much more informal céilí dancing 'because it was a great social outlet'. As Mairéad told me, people came into contact with céilí dancing 'very much in your parish where you lived', where céilís used to take place in parish halls or schools under the control of the clergy as well as, occasionally, in GAA clubs. While Mairéad thought that she might have learnt 'the odd dance' in physical education at school, she basically became acquainted with these group dances:

> Just at the céilí. You kind of just went and you kind of picked it up, you know? And sometimes just before the dance would take place, maybe someone would say, 'This is how you do this.' And you just did it. And also you would have had someone who would have called out the dances as you were doing it, you know, until you learnt how to do them.

During the late 1950s, when Mairéad first went to local céilís, modern dances were not yet accessible to her given that 'we were very much outside of the town where dances would have been held'.

> As I grew older, I was allowed to go to, as my father called it, 'English dancing'. And I had to really fight. And that was what we used to call 'hops'. And it was like rock 'n' roll and dancing to modern music and you were able to do those in the parish centre. They were again organized by the church in the church halls. And that was a thing then going to hops and dances where you could meet people.

After having been allowed reluctantly by her parents to go to such 'English dancing' as well, both céilís and 'hops' existed side by side for a number of years. As Mairéad recalled, 'there was some people who would have never gone to céilí dancing, wouldn't have been interested. But I would have been interested in both':

> You know, as a matter of fact, céilí dancing was more fun than when you went to the hops and the dances. Because you only got to dance with one boy at the time. And of course it was all boys in those days, that's what you were interested in. You only got to dance with one boy. Whereas if you went to a céilí, you got a chance to dance in the course of one dance with eight different boys. [Mairéad laughs] So, it was fun.

When Mairéad started going to college in the mid-1960s, she still enjoyed the odd céilí – 'and that's the way I have continued to this day' – although she generally just 'went dancing at the centre of town' when 'the twist came in; oh, jiving, we did jiving big time'.

Before 1969, 'there would have been some massive céilís, but gradually the numbers began to decline' after the outbreak of the Troubles:

> But things changed because, don't forget, there was new entertainments as well. I'm saying this tongue in cheek because there was rioting. It was

much more fun than céilí dancing. And people were out on the streets. You know, you have no idea of what it was like. I mean people would have been out on the streets on a nightly basis. And even when events were run, there would have been, you know, maybe a patrol of British soldiers driving past and people were on their way home. That was confrontation, confrontation constantly. There was never such a thing as just going out and having a nice drink and whatever you were going to do and not being confronted. I mean, I would have gone out for a drink. And, you know, the British soldiers would have gone in with their guns all around each table. And they were just there with their rifles.

From the mid-1980s onwards, Mairéad was involved with yet another form of 'Irish dancing', namely, set dancing. Together with a female friend, she attended a number of local classes for this type of group dance from which céilí dancing was to be distinguished at the beginning of the twentieth century (see Chapter 9).

Recollecting the overall development of her Irishness, Mairéad emphasized the taken-for-grantedness of her identity's evolution:

It wasn't like an apparition on the road to Damascus. It was just part of me and part of my family, and it was something really that perhaps I didn't even investigate. I mean, I was just comfortable in my life. I had no need to really ever question; just accepted, this is who I am, and to be happy in that. And I think obviously with 1968–69, the beginning of the war, it heightens your awareness, and you begin to question things and question institutions and organizations and perhaps even question your identity or the strength of your identity or your perceived identity.

While the Troubles had 'a big impact' on Mairéad's life – raising her awareness and endorsing 'what I always believed: that I was Irish, that I had a strong sense of identity and was going to maintain that through my life' – the 'war' obviously also had much more practical consequences in forcing people to take sides:

When the war was declared here, it was very important to know which side you were on. Again, to have a sense of identity. You were prepared to stand up and be counted. And really your life was on the line then. And that sounds rather dramatic, but I mean that was just the way it was. It was a war in a very small area, which meant that you could be identified and taken away at any time and interned. I mean, you didn't have to actually be doing anything. You could have been interned and imprisoned as so many people were. You could have been assassinated, disappeared, whatever. So that was important to know, who you were and where you were at. … For me it was important to be able to identify the fact that I was Irish and opposed to what was happening and to stand up and be counted.

Micheál, age 55

When discussing being Irish, Micheál emphasized the continuity and 'givenness' of his sense of identity: 'I can't remember not thinking of myself as Irish'. Questions of identity were thereby made an issue both by his family and the surrounding society, 'which sort of kept on bringing it forward':

> I was brought up in Belfast in the fifties and sixties, which was in my formative years. And at that time, we were sort of constantly reminded that we were British. And politicians on the television would tell us that we were British, and some people – if you said you were Irish, they would ask you, 'Why don't you go back to Ireland?' … I never saw the end of the film [in cinemas], for years and years, because at the end of every film, by law, they had to play 'God Save the Queen'. So you had a choice of sitting down through 'God Save the Queen' to assert your difference from the dominant ideology and possibly get beaten up, or … unless I was in a cinema in a Nationalist area, I would leave before the film was over, rather than risk a confrontation. … If we were in a Nationalist area, there were two cinemas on the Falls Road, when I was young. And, at the end of the film, by law they had to play the [British] national anthem. And they would play it, and everybody would sit through the national anthem. Some people would stay after the film was over in order to sit down through the national anthem. … And I didn't go to the graduation at University because it was compulsory then to play 'God Save the Queen.' And I basically didn't want to offend people by sitting down, but I also did not want to stand up for the British anthem. Because I'm Irish. [Micheál chuckles]. So it was a constant issue, all those times, that your definition of your self was in conflict with the official definition of the society you lived in.

Local Irish people thereby maintained 'a constant counter-narrative to the dominant narrative of the society' through establishing a 'parallel universe' in which the Irish tricolour flew and 'all the communal events' had the Irish national anthem:

> In all the GAA pitches, the tricolour flew. And all the major matches all started with the Irish national anthem. And we all stood for that. And, if you went to a céilí, the céilí would finish with the Irish national anthem. So there was a parallel universe; it was sort of <u>Catholic</u> <u>Northern</u> <u>Ireland</u>. All the communal events that were organized within the Catholic area had the Irish national anthem.

Apart from these more general conditions of Micheál's upbringing, it was seemingly also the narrower confines of his family that proved to be influential in shaping his development as an Irish person. As Micheál put it, 'my family was a GAA family' and 'unusually strong' in its 'commitment to Gaelic Ireland'. Both his father and his mother had played Gaelic games for the county in the All-Ireland Championship – 'a difficult heritage', as Micheál laughingly said – and 'their whole social life revolved around the GAA'. Unsurprisingly, Micheál was thus exposed to Gaelic games from a very early age.

When attending a Christian Brothers' primary school and later grammar school, Micheál competitively played Gaelic football and hurling both for his respective school teams and in physical education. As he laconically observed, 'That was PE. We didn't have any other kind of PE', given that 'the only games played in the Christian Brothers' schools were Gaelic football and hurling'. For two years in his mid-teens in the early 1960s, Micheál also played in a local GAA club, as did his sisters.

Micheál thought that on his street 'there were three GAA families, and all the rest of the people, the children, would have been followers of soccer'. With children from these families and other friends, Micheál used to play soccer in the schoolyard and 'in the streets with gardens'. However, as Micheál recalled, handball, which is a Gaelic game that is 'a bit like squash, except you use the hand', was 'the more common game in the streets where there were no gardens': 'you needed a gable wall and some very patient people living inside it'.

While Micheál thus did play soccer (besides handball) as a street game, he personally found it a 'terribly boring game' to watch and thought that 'there's no beauty in soccer'. Apart from personally disliking it, Micheál further claimed that he would have never played for a soccer club in his youth because 'the Ban was still going at the time'. As mentioned before, until 1971 'the Ban' or Rule 27 of the GAA forbade members from playing so-called 'foreign games' like soccer under pain of suspension from the GAA. At the time, Micheál supported the principle of the Ban in 'that if you're going to play a silly game, you might as well play a silly game that's Irish as opposed to playing a silly game that's English'. Besides not getting into playing soccer, Micheál also never supported any soccer team, and – as he derisively emphasized – 'especially not Glasgow Celtic':

> Partly because the Celtic/Rangers thing is much more overtly and rigorously sectarian than any other division that I know of. And I am against sectarianism in principle – in anything. Secondly, why should you bother to express either your sectarianism or your Irishness through a Scottish team playing an English game?

Apart from obviously influencing his attitudes to and practical engagements with sports, Micheál's family sent him to a school of Irish dancing from the age of seven: 'my family was a GAA family, and they thought that I should learn how to dance'. Dancing thereby meant 'Irish dancing': 'there was no one in our area who did ballet dancing or modern dancing or any of that. If you did dancing, you did Irish dancing. But I think I was the only boy in the street who did it.'

After doing Irish dancing for three years, Micheál switched to 'elocution':

> Elocution was one hour a week, and dancing three hours a week. So I took elocution. ... The worst part of the dancing was the competition. You had to go to a *feis* ['competition'] two or three times a year, in a dress, wearing

a kilt. And in elocution, you would wear your own clothes. And there were fewer 'feises' … You just walked up on stage, and you recited your poem, went off. In the dancing, you had to go up with a kilt, jump around stage, and then go off. So [Micheál laughs].

Although Micheál's career as an Irish competition dancer hence met an untimely end when he was ten years old, having attended a school of Irish dancing nevertheless came in handy later on:

When I was in my late teens, I developed a great love of céilí dancing. And because I had been to these [Irish dancing] classes, I couldn't do the steps, but I knew the rhythm. I knew how to get 'round the floor. I could recognize when to move on the music. And I found out that I was quite a good céilí dancer. Different style of dancing. And the advantage of céilí dancing is that it wasn't, in those days anyway, quite as – what's the word? – overtly sexual as modern kinds, as other kinds of dancing were. And there was sort of a rule, an unwritten rule, that you were never refused a dance. So the purpose was dancing as opposed to getting off with each other. That was the ethos. And you could also talk. In the other dances, in the discos and showbands – showbands were going in my youth – the music was extremely loud, and communication was extremely difficult. So in the céilí dancing, the music tends to be much less loud. So you could have a conversation. And because there were steps that you did, and once you knew what the steps were, you could get through the dance okay. I couldn't do the modern dancing at all. I couldn't – I could do the head, I could do the legs, I could do the arms, but I couldn't do them all together.

Being in contact with céilí dancing from 1960 onwards, through his stays at Irish-language summer colleges where 'we had céilís every second night' and attending the Irish-language club of his grammar school, which had céilís every month, Micheál thus developed a great love of céilí dancing from the mid-1960s onwards. He attended a series of weekly dances that the GAA began to run in the Fiesta Ballroom in the centre of Belfast from 'about 1966'. After this GAA céilí stopped around a year later, Micheál switched to the céilís in the Cumann Cluain Árd, which – as we saw in Chapter 4 – was to facilitate his subsequent re-entry into the Irish language. As Micheál recalled, he went to the Cluain Árd céilís for years but decreasingly did so from the early 1970s onwards, partly because 'I wasn't as fanatical as I had been' and partly because, as a consequence of 'probably the Troubles', 'during the 1970s, there were not so many céilís'. While continuing to attend the odd céilí, Micheál also 'got interested in the set dancing for a while' in the mid-1980s.

In the late 1960s and early 1970s, at the same time that Micheál was extensively involved with céilí dancing, Anglo-Irish literature and learning Irish, he also began to get interested in traditional music:

I had been interested in traditional music anyway, partly through exposure at home, partly through records. And the Clancy Brothers and the Dubliners were coming up at that time, and then Seán Ó Riada was emerging. So I was at the edges of that [Irish music revival]. And when I went to [the University in North Antrim at] Coleraine, I discovered there was a very, very strong singing tradition up in North Antrim. And actually through a Protestant friend of mine, I got to know some of the traditional singers. And began to learn more about the songs. The – how do you put it? – the genuine traditional songs. What I had been exposed to had been a mixture of rebel songs, traditional songs, music hall songs and parlour ballads. ... In the seventies, I began to explore the more – folk, rural traditional songs. And partly through these people I met in Coleraine and partly through my wife, whose father was a traditional singer.

According to Micheál, at sing-songs at his home 'the songs tended to be either Irish or thought to be Irish'. This was apparently also the case with songs that Micheál – like Rónán – heard on Saturday afternoons on 'The Walton's Programme' on 'the radio from the South'. Like it did for Rónán, the programme's motto, 'If you feel like singing, do sing an Irish song', suggested to Micheál that its songs were 'Irish' and that 'they belonged to me, belonged to my culture': 'I've actually found out since that a lot of them are actually local versions of traditional English folk songs, but we thought of them as being Irish because that was the context that we heard them in.'

Against this family background, Micheál started going to a number of folk clubs in Belfast in the late 1960s such as the Pike Folk Club and Friday night musical sessions in the Cluain Árd up until the mid-1970s. Micheál insisted that he began to get interested in traditional music, Anglo-Irish literature and the Irish language 'all before the Troubles', and of these, only 'traditional music was fashionable at the time'. However, the outbreak of the Troubles in 1969 brought questions of identity and 'Irish culture' to the fore and forced people like Micheál to think about the relationship between violence and identity. Chapter 4 characterized how this new situation in which Micheál was not attracted to any available political activity and in which doing nothing at all was also not an option intensified for him the 'urge to investigate the cultural actually more'. Micheál became more and more active in all those areas of 'Irish culture'. And this was so – as he was already quoted saying regarding the Irish language in Chapter 4 – partly because being 'involved in activities that are very clearly identifiable markers' also worked as a personal solution to the by then pressing question: 'What does it mean to be Irish?'

Dónal, age 49

From early on it became clear that Dónal lacked a sense of self-evident, stable and continual Irishness when compared to that expressed by many of my other informants. Instead, our interviews often leaned towards presently making sense of past experiences in terms of his ethnic identity. Eventually, this resulted in an overall shift between two positions, which Dónal came to see as alternatives, while I conceive(d) them rather as complementary sides of the same configuration.

Before addressing this disagreement, I will first refer to some of Dónal's more straightforward experiences that formed the backdrop for his personal troubles with Irishness.

Dónal grew up in Belfast in the 1950s and 1960s in a family in which Irishness was given a rather low profile:

> My father was a trade unionist. He wasn't particularly a classic Irish Nationalist as such .... So even though I was brought up in a Catholic home, I wasn't brought up in an Irish Nationalist home. You know, the home environment wasn't particularly – Nationalistic or Irish-ish [Dónal laughs]. I don't know how to describe it, but can you get the point I am saying? That my home wasn't decorated with tricolours; we didn't have like pictures of James Connolly [the Irish Socialist and a leader in the 1916 Easter Rising]; or we didn't discuss, you know, 'the British has been really bad' or 'the police has been really bad'; it was none of that. 'Cause my father recognized that even though the police were anti-Catholic in many cases, he recognized that you needed police in any state. ... I wouldn't have been brought up with the kind of romanticism a lot of people might have been brought up with, of Irishness. You know, of the Irish language, of the Irish culture and so on. We had very little of that in the house, at home. ... Nothing, nothing particularly Irish in our house. I knew there were other houses where the people would have had, you know, [pictures of then incumbent Irish] President de Valera. You know, they would have something. Or maybe a flag or they would've an emblem, you know – a harp. Something which, for them, you know, described their Irishness. We didn't have anything like that. Nothing!

Against this pronounced absence of Irishness at home, Dónal was really only introduced to some of that after entering primary school. For instance, one Republican teacher:

> would have provided us with the history about the Easter Rebellion and so on in a very one-sided perspective. Very much about, you know, 'British oppressors', 'they deserved all they've got. The Black and Tans were just bastards', and that kind of thing. I was only a child, and I was hearing this kind of language, which I'd never have heard at home. Nothing like that would have come across in my house. And I certainly never discussed anything like that that I picked up at school, in my house. 'Cause I had a feeling that it wouldn't have been acceptable to talk that way. So I had a kind of a divided view very early on about it [i.e. Irishness].

It was also in the context of schooling that Dónal became variously engaged with some of the more concrete elements of 'Irish culture'. For instance, while attending his Catholic grammar school, 'you had to play sports, so you had to play Gaelic football, sometimes hurling'. In addition:

I played soccer a bit, and I suppose I played [Gaelic] handball, which is an Irish game. In secondary school, I played handball the whole of my seven years I was there. I really liked it. I was quite good at that. I didn't play Gaelic [football] 'cause I wasn't very good at it. But I enjoyed it. I would enjoy a match. I would enjoy watching Gaelic sports, and I love watching hurling. My mother played camogie. She was a good camogie player. And I used to knock about a bit with a stick. My son plays. He's a good hurler; he plays hurling. I've no problem supporting it <u>as games</u>. I don't like <u>the politics of it</u>, but as a pure game, yes, I think they are very good games. I used to go and watch them in Casement Park.

As we saw in Chapter 4, it was Dónal's grammar school that introduced him to the Irish language and enabled him to visit an Irish-language college in the Donegal Gaeltacht of *Teileann* (Teelin):

It was such an experience, you know, it was obviously all coming together: <u>the music</u>, the <u>beauty</u> of the place itself, the fact that I was having a lot of <u>freedom</u> for the first time in my life. There were <u>girls</u> there [as opposed to gender segregation in school], you know? It was a <u>whole experience</u> for me. And you know, it's something I, in my mind, would return to a lot, you know? I've been back to the places as an adult, and they are still absolutely beautiful. But, you know, it's not the same as when you were a child. Sort of rosy – golden – huge. And the summers were always wonderfully <u>bright</u>, and even the rain was <u>nice</u>, you know? [Dónal laughs] And the <u>food</u> was superb. You stayed in people's houses, you see, that was the idea in the Gaeltacht. You lived with a family. And they got the money for you staying there. So it was a good income for them. But they fed you phenomenally well. ... <u>Fantastic food, fresh milk from the cow, fresh butter, home-baked bread!</u> It was, you know, an experience! So, you see, my feelings, they are all interlinked with all of those things. It was a very romantic time for me, a very beautiful place to be in, very small group of people, all learning the same things, and you were doing lots of activities, sport, music and dancing.

Dancing invariably meant 'céilí dancing':

We did dancing in the evening, learnt céilí dancing three nights a week, and one night there would have been *céilí mór*. You know, 'a big céilí'. And they'd have brought in a céilí band, and we'd all be dancing, you know, the whole school would have danced. And you would be learning the dances as well, you know? So it was great.

The Gaeltacht stays induced in Dónal a great love for the Irish language and for the music in particular. Not that Dónal had not been in contact with Irish music before. As he remembered, 'there was lots of singing in my house. That's where I learnt my singing from'. And the 'big groups in the mid-sixties, early sixties would have been the Dubliners, the Clancy Brothers' performing 'what I would call stage Irish stuff, stage Irish singing'. However, the Irish music that Dónal came across in the Gaeltacht was 'distinctly different' and 'new, completely new for me and struck a really powerful feeling in me':

> I mean, I get moved by different types of music .... But certainly the Irish music was – so beautiful! Even though it was a very rough kind of version of it, do you know what I mean? It wasn't, we weren't polished. We were just a bunch of kids, and the teacher was just a teacher, you know? There was just the beauty on its own of the music and the language. And I was so struck by it, you know, so for me that was, erm, an important thing for me, a big driver for me.

However, while Dónal was falling in love with this Irish music, he apparently did not identify (with) it as distinctly 'Irish music':

> But for me, it was learning, you know, and being introduced to music that happened to be in the Irish language – as well. But I didn't say, I didn't feel it as, 'This is part of my roots; this is my culture; I need to learn it because it's my culture.' I didn't think that way. I just thought, 'God, it's beautiful. I need to, I want to learn; I want to sing that. I want to remember it because it is lovely.' Not because it was part of what I believed to be Irish. I didn't have that.

At the outbreak of the Troubles in 1969, Dónal was in his mid-teens and, as he told me, had up to that time 'never had any sense at all, whatsoever' of any local trouble. For example, in order to get to his Catholic grammar school every day, Dónal used to take the bus down the Falls Road and then walk straight across Protestant West Belfast, wearing a school uniform clearly indicating that he was pupil at a Catholic school and hence probably also a Catholic. Yet, as Dónal insisted, 'I don't remember ever a problem, ever!' But then, after the summer of 1969, there was one occasion:

> I was actually walking back from school across the other way, back to the Falls. And I remember somebody; he didn't actually stop me, but he looked at me as I walked across. And because the Troubles had broken out, I was conscious of it. And he didn't really do anything. He just kind of stared at me. ... I don't even think he said anything. He was young, but he was bigger than me. And I thought, 'This guy knows I'm a Catholic.' And that was the first time I really kind of thought about it. Hadn't really been aware of it up to that point. ... And I just ran. He didn't chase me or anything. I just got that fear. And I thought, 'I'm not gonna go this way anymore, too risky.' So I went into town and came out again instead of coming across. ... You know, routes that I felt were safe. So that was my kind of first feelings of change.

This event was soon followed by another that for Dónal exemplified 'a fundamental change'. Dónal recalled that there was a pupil at his school who was a cadet in the Parachute Regiment of the British Army. One day his class mates:

> pushed him in the toilet block, and they attacked him. He was a pupil at the school, in the classes that they were in. And up until this point in time, you know, when the British army first arrived in Belfast, they were welcomed on the streets in West Belfast, particularly around the Falls; cups of tea, whatever they wanted. It was only when the government changed tactics and started to oppress that things changed. And he wasn't even <u>serving</u> in the army; he was only a <u>cadet!</u> And these guys all attacked him. … I remember the incident very well, vividly. 'Cause I remember thinking, 'But these guys were all playing football last week! What's different?' I hadn't really appreciated the importance of the changes that were going on. So to me that was like a <u>fundamental change</u> that happened. Suddenly, somebody that they were playing with, somebody that had been part of their team was suddenly no longer part of the team, was an enemy! Somebody who had actually done nothing on an individual basis to deserve the attack was being attacked!

In the months to come, the issue of taking sides became ever more important. After the summer of 1969, as Dónal remembered:

> There was a fear of attack by Protestants because there had been attacks on parts of Catholic West Belfast in Bombay Street, Conway Street and so on, by parts of the police and Protestant mobs. And there was a fear in Catholic areas that this could happen again. So there was a whole defence mechanism based around local vigilante-type arrangements. … So every area formed what was called 'Citizens' Defence Committees'.

These committees used burnt-out vehicles, pieces of concrete and other materials to barricade their local areas, and then policed these barriers day and night. However, when the British Army imposed internment (i.e. imprisonment without trial) in August 1971, 'there was a feeling that Citizens' Defence Committees, barricades, barriers wasn't going to be enough. You needed to fight back with guns'. What followed were the beginnings of a recruitment drive for young people to join the Provisional IRA. As Dónal recalled, he once became part of this recruitment drive himself when 'the young people in our area were all called to a meeting in the house of a known Republican sympathizer'. So Dónal went, and while the whole issue was presented by an adult 'in a very reasonable, rational way', it was enough for Dónal to realize that this was 'a recruitment drive for something that I didn't want to be involved with'. Hence Dónal left and did not get involved.

However, he did become increasingly involved with playing Irish music, and this was related to the Troubles as well. Before the Troubles, the town centre was Belfast's entertainment hub, with its offering of dancehalls and pubs featuring live music. Dónal recalled, 'You would have had very, very little in your local area'. Yet once the bombing started, people tended to associate in their local areas. This led to a huge growth in local entertainment and shebeens (i.e. illegal drinking dens). It was at such shebeens and social clubs in West Belfast that Dónal ended up performing with Irish folk bands.

In these places, Dónal remembered, 'you would have been expected to do rebel music. That's what people wanted! And if you didn't want that, you were stuck with it anyway because everybody else wanted it!' Hence, Dónal and his mates often performed songs that he would have preferred not to sing. But 'the thing was if you didn't play those places you were very restricted as to where you could play, and you would probably not have earned very much money. So it was an economic decision, but it went against all my principles.' A typical night progressed as follows:

> Certainly the first half, you would do <u>better-quality</u> material. I mean there is some very beautiful rebel material. It's not necessarily all blood-and-guts. Some of it is superb, you know? And stuff that I would quite happily do anywhere, where people weren't offended by that. But in the first half, you would have done all your best material. Maybe traditional music, and whatever was going. Trying to get people to listen, you know? 'Cause anybody can get up and do rebel music once a crowd have got the blood up. Because it doesn't matter. They all sing with you anyway. So they drown you out. But if you want to distinguish you from the next band, you had to play your best material in the first half. So that's generally what you did. And the second half didn't matter. You just started playing the rebel stuff. And as the night progressively went on, you played more and more – outrageous, in my opinion, 'cause more blood-and-guts towards the end of the night. And you really got into the very heavy stuff. So people would be on their feet, standing on their tables, jumping up and down. Roaring and rambling, and smashing their bottles on the floor. That kind of thing. Quite <u>scary</u>, actually. Oh, it is. Imagine a crowd of people standing on their tables, shaking their bottles whenever you give a particular song. Puh! It's <u>abhorrent!</u> You know, and you're rising all these people <u>up</u>! God, when they leave the place, what are they gonna do? That's the sort of thing. I always kind of wonder. Like, what happened after they – It's very scary, thinking those thoughts, you know!

While – as Dónal put it – these nights 'were bad enough', 'other nights were worse' when the IRA would suddenly appear on stage wearing balaclavas and brandishing guns because they were going to make a statement, and 'you had no idea they were gonna be there':

> Most of them would have been masked, but the person making the speech might not have been masked. They may have been, you know, one of the political people [of Sinn Féin] as opposed to an actual [volunteer] … And they would have been reading out, 'This is what you have to do. And here

is what we're doing.' You know what I mean? Urging people to support them. … And, I mean, you were preaching to a group of people who were feeling that way <u>anyway!</u> It wasn't a difficult thing to do. And every time, 'Oh yeah', roared and stamping their feet. Quite a <u>frightening</u> thing to be in it, you know? Imagine if you [being a German – OZ] were back in the Third Reich? And standing there, and you got all of this stuff happening, and you don't wanna <u>be</u> there, but you are <u>there!</u> And you are not gonna be different, you gonna be banging the bottles as well and stamping your feet. You're standing on the stage, there is <u>no</u> <u>way</u> you gonna be sitting and saying, 'I don't wanna be here!' You gonna be saying, '<u>Yeah!</u>' You know, of course you are. You are only a human being.

After years of being involved in these events, Dónal chose not to play in the clubs anymore because he was not comfortable with such political enthusiasm. He was then part of another Irish folk band that 'played all over Northern Ireland at that time. In fact, we made a point of trying to stay away from West Belfast. It was hard work because the biggest opportunities were in West Belfast. But by and large, we worked outside that. … Just to get away from being connected with the rebel thing.' While Dónal thus managed to personally 'get away from being connected', his overall sense of ethnic identity did not cease to be affected by the persistent link between Irishness and 'the rebel thing'.

For the greater part of our series of interviews, Dónal hence described himself as having 'this identity crisis for a long time', being 'very torn' between wanting to be Irish and being unable to identify with this identity because Irishness had become so closely associated with Republican violence. As Dónal put it in one of numerous variations:

I recognize that I was born a Catholic and brought up as a Catholic. And I suppose, there's an expectation that I would automatically identify with an Irish culture. … While I was young, I went to the Gaeltacht, learnt Irish at school, very strongly had those – strong affiliations with the language and music. And <u>still</u> would have that! The actual identity of that with who I am, it didn't square up because of really the violence that occurred since 1969. And that was a formative time for me because I was fifteen, sixteen. And I'm not a violent person, and I can't, I couldn't connect the idea of being Irish with the violence of the IRA, irrespective of any justification; none of it ever justified itself to me. And so for people to declare themselves 'Irish' and kill people for it, you know, I just couldn't square that. So for me, I still have a <u>real</u> problem with it. I suppose underneath it all, I would <u>love</u> to say to people, 'I have a <u>real</u> <u>strong</u> <u>Irish</u> <u>identity!</u>' I mean, I have a strong affiliation with Irishness. But because, for me, it's been spoiled, tainted, ruined almost by the Troubles, I have a real problem <u>saying</u> <u>it</u>! … So I'm left in a very difficult position because I <u>want</u> to be Irish, but I've got a problem with all the violence. And that's really made it very difficult for me to overcome that. And I <u>don't</u> feel British at all! So what I <u>chose</u> to call myself was 'European'. I don't <u>really feel that</u> terribly strongly. But I feel that describes me better than – I can't call myself Irish, at the moment.

As Dónal thus clarified for me (and himself) on several occasions, 'If you had to be at war to be Irish, I didn't want that', even though 'at the core it's sad that I can't identify with, I suppose, what I feel strongest about'. Yet Dónal simply did not want 'to be lumped in with all that lot' who were 'killing people in my name'.

When extensively reflecting again on his position during our last interview, Dónal suddenly came to realize that his identity crisis did not actually consist in his Irishness being ruined by the Troubles but rather in being forced to answer a question that was important to others but not for him:

> I think this is what happens. This is really <u>the nub of</u> it. I think people <u>presume</u> that you need to have an identity, which is associated with, you know, a culture: Irishness or Britishness or something. So it's <u>other people</u> that I respond to when they say to me, 'What are you?' 'Cause I don't think about it. … I mean all the forms that you fill in as well say, 'Are you Irish or British or what are you?' You have to tick boxes if you fill in an application form, and you have to say what you are. So whether you liked it or not, you were confronted by something that to me wasn't important. It is important to other people but not important to me. So I suppose what I've been saying is, it's a crisis for me because if I have to answer a question, 'Are you Irish, are you British?' I have to answer the question! 'Where were you born?' 'Were you born in Britain; were you born in Ireland?' I've got to answer the question! So you are confronted by it because other people presume that it is important or <u>need to count it</u> for some reason. Because they need to know how many Irish people, how many British people they've got in their workforce or how many Catholics, how many Protestants they have. These things to me are not important. But I am confronted by them because other people expect me to have an answer. So, you know, it's a crisis in that sense. I'm only realizing that having this discussion because you go down to the core of it. … I'm just being confronted by these things, 'Shit, what am I? I don't wanna be Irish. I am certainly not feeling British, ah, ah, ah [Dónal acts out his decision] "European", that's the easiest thing to tick.' … To prevent them putting me in a box that I don't wanna be in. And I don't wanna be described by somebody else as being either on their side or against them because here that's what it means: if you are Irish you are against this; if you're British against that. And I don't want that!

During our last interview, Dónal developed this as a new position whereas I interpret(ed) it as an additional facet of his complex identity in which, to my mind, two things came together. First, Dónal actually did have a strong affiliation with Irishness even though this identity 'associated with, you know, a culture' might indeed have been much less important for him than for other people, who nevertheless made him self-classify in such terms. Second, the growing ethnicization in the course of the Troubles had become highly problematic for Dónal because the label 'Irish' had accumulated so many violent political implications in the context of the Republican 'armed struggle'. As Dónal strongly rejected these implications, he could no longer unproblematically call himself 'Irish'.

In sum, while it had been important after 1969 for other locals such as Mairéad 'to be able to identify the fact that I was Irish and opposed to what was happening and to stand up and be counted' (see Mairéad's section), Dónal apparently resented and opposed precisely this logic, according to which being counted as 'Irish' almost invariably also meant to be counted on as a supporter of the armed struggle. As Dónal said, this was simply 'a box that I don't wanna be in'.

Fíona, age 47

In contrast to Dónal, Fíona was one of my interlocutors who were not only unequivocal but assertive in their responses to my questions about ethnic and national identity: 'I'm Irish, very much so!' As Fíona recalled from her childhood in the late 1950s and 1960s in Belfast, her parents regarded themselves as Irish, although identity, culture and nationalism were not centrally important within her family, as her parents 'were too busy trying to make a living'. Given this rather low profile of Irishness at home, Fíona personally 'wouldn't have been aware' of being Irish prior to the outbreak of violence. This was the case also because – as she told me – 'I was still pretty young when the Troubles broke out'. Yet, Fíona insisted that becoming Irish was not only a question of just getting older but also and perhaps more importantly of personally having strong experiences related to the Troubles, which not only raised awareness but also the relevance of being Irish:

> Like when they brought internment in, I understood, I really got the gist of – how they were treating our people. That they were able to put so many of us behind bars for no reason, without any going to a court, whatever. They were able to just pick us off the streets and stick us into a jail. Not knowing how long you were gonna be there for. So that really made me – see how we were being treated. Plus I have personal experiences of things that happened. ... My home's being raided. Where they threw my mother, and knocked my baby brother's first tooth out! You know, I've seen all this happening! When they came in and they wrecked homes, in my own home and all. I'm saying, 'What right have they to do this?' ... When the Troubles came about, it _hit_ _me_ _then!_ I started to question and being able to say, 'Right, I'm Irish here; hold on a moment!' – I wouldn't say it was a slow process. I think it was something that was hitting me very quick! ... And it was only when I started to see things happening that I stopped and said, 'Right, hold on'; getting my own identity for myself; findin' out who I was or what I was!

Almost overnight, the Troubles foregrounded the issue of Fíona's identity. This personal transformation thereby not only fostered – as described in Chapter 4 – a desire to learn her 'native language' but also turned her (like many others) into a Republican and strong supporter of the armed struggle.

The Troubles were also a main cause of Fíona's increasing immersion into Irish music. Echoing Dónal's 'on-stage' report, while differing profoundly from his stance in actually wanting to be part of this development, Fíona described the Troubles-induced growth of entertainment in local clubs and shebeens, with a special emphasis on 'Irish traditional music' and 'ballads of the Troubles':

> During the Troubles when they [i.e. local clubs and shebeens] were at the heart of things, erm – that's where you went! You went to that type of clubs, you know? … And nearly every other club would have had the likes of that music, right? And quite a lot of it, even though it was Irish traditional music, a lot of it was brought in with the likes of the ballads of the Troubles. You know, songs about what was happening like [the internment song] 'Men Behind the Wire'; them type of songs. But at that time, that was the thing! You know what I mean? … And you wanted to be a part of it! … It fired your blood! It fired your blood!

According to Fíona, 'every club on the road really would have had at least one night a week' with Irish traditional music, sometimes even more because local Republican clubs such as 'the likes of the "Roddys" and the "Felons" and all had it every night of the week', given 'that's all you'd have got. That would have been all like Republican, traditional type of music!'

However, as Fíona told me, local entertainment changed quite fundamentally from the early 1990s onwards with the peace process when Irish traditional music both slowly moved into the city centre again and generally began to decline. Conversely, other forms of entertainment entered hitherto inaccessible local realms such as Republican clubs 'like the Felons. You would never have had a disco or anything in the Felons. That was all Republican and traditional. Now there are discos!' As Fíona generally interpreted this new situation:

> Everybody's going with the flow now, you see. And to be honest with you, I think, half of them is just going with the money! You're getting the money in, you see, from the younger crowd now. But they don't wanna hear this type of music! So if you were going to look for a night where there is going to be a [traditional] session, you'd have to go into the centre of town more. As I personally couldn't tell you a club on the road where I could turn round and say, 'Well, if you went in there on a Monday night, you'd guaranteed it!' I couldn't tell you one. Whereas a lot of years back, you'd have been able to say, 'Oh, yes, you can go in there tonight, and you're guaranteed it.' I couldn't tell you where now!

In the ethnographic present that Fíona and I shared, it was thus not 'like that anymore', when people had 'wanted to be part' of the Irish music as described above. Instead – Fíona argued – for 'the younger generation because they don't know what it was like during the Troubles, for to listen to traditional Irish music now, it's something that you have to like!'

Regarding Gaelic games, however, it was the younger generation that seemed to have encouraged Fíona to actually get involved more than she used to be. This was so, Fíona explained, because 'my son is in the "under-tens" like, of the GAA, in the hurling, and I'll go and watch his team, and I watch the senior teams in his club'. Fíona also watched Gaelic games on television 'anytime there would be a big match, the likes of the all-Irelands or whatever', and had been to the local stadium Casement Park in order to support Antrim, but – as she put it – 'I wouldn't think of travelling a long distance to go. I'm not that much into it'. As Fíona jokingly told me, she did not really understand the rules of Gaelic games, but then she did not understand soccer either and nevertheless watched Glasgow Celtic: 'I just like watching Celtic winning [Fíona laughs]. I think if you support something like, you have to go and see their matches. I wouldn't be that bad. ... It's like the Irish Republic playing the likes of another country. I like to see the Irish Republic win, you know, even in the soccer.'

While certain elements of 'Irish culture' such as the music and games thus figured in Fíona's daily life, and although being Irish obviously mattered very much to her (and not only when the Irish Republic played soccer), Fíona's Irishness generally seemed to only rarely be an object of reflection. On the contrary, and in stark contrast to Dónal, Fíona at one point summarized her sense of identity in an almost annoyed tone: 'My Irish identity is just something that I have and I wouldn't lose sleep over'.

Pól, age 47

As a Republican ex-prisoner who spent sixteen years of a life sentence in the H-Blocks at Long Kesh, unsurprisingly, Pól straightforwardly described himself to me as 'Irish'. When contemplating the genesis of his personal sense of Irishness, he emphasized that:

> I think it definitely came through the political struggle! The armed struggle, imprisonment, and probably I had to learn a bit about myself first. You know, about the community, or become more aware of what that community meant to me, and over the values of it. And the community, being a small community, you know, and then – sort of widening that out. And probably it's only in later years, did I think of then – you know, the bigger [community] – right, as Irish, what is it? What does it mean? – So I would have been through that!

From his childhood in the late 1950s and 1960s in a small town outside Belfast, Pól recalled that in his family he 'would have had some exposure to sort of Irish music and all the rest of it [i.e. Irish culture], that you were aware of it'. Yet there was never 'any big emphasis on, "This is Irish as opposed to British!" You know, there was never that element in the house, you know!' Pól also recalled that 'when the British anthem came on television, it was switched off, not in any aggressive way, but it was just like, you know; I don't know how many Protestants also probably switched it off, you know?' Generally speaking, however, his parents were not political in any way. To be Irish did not really matter at home, and his family was not particularly committed to any element of 'Irish culture'.

At school, Pól came into contact with Gaelic games as well as soccer, and in his local area, 'there was Gaelic football organized in way of [GAA] teams, which there wouldn't have been for soccer'. Yet – as Pól laconically observed – 'I wasn't a great sportsman, so I wasn't really into Gaelic football!'

All in all, Pól would not have become very concerned with questions of 'culture' and identity in his life had it not been for his growing experience of injustice during the Troubles, his increasing politicization and his eventual involvement with the armed struggle, which brought questions of Irishness very much to the fore:

> As I began more to become a teenager, and the whole sort of process that ended up me becoming involved in the struggle, erm – <u>yes</u>, you became aware of being <u>Irish</u>, or an Irish <u>Republican</u>. <u>But</u> it was as much to do with the sort of <u>injustice</u> that was going on at that particular time! So you were just wondering if the injustices had have been sorted out, would you have thought that that was okay then? So, was it about <u>being</u> <u>Irish</u> or was it about being treated <u>unjustly?</u> You know, that was the two options. And I think for Republicans, what they realized once the whole civil rights campaign started in '68 and '69 and got beaten off the ground and killed in Bloody Sunday in Derry, that really Nationalists weren't able to get <u>rights</u> within the Northern state! So it had to be 'National' rights; it had to be then like – all-Ireland, a whole political unification because the Northern state couldn't reform itself! So, it's probably <u>that</u> point when people started to see themselves <u>more</u> as being – <u>Irish</u> in a particular way! Or that being <u>Irish</u> was gonna have to mean – having a unified state and end of Partition. Because the Northern state couldn't just produce the goods, it couldn't!

In Chapter 4, I described at length how Pól's subsequent life unfolded once he had been caught and sentenced to life imprisonment in the H-Blocks at Long Kesh, paying particular attention to the protest period between 1976 and 1981 and the role that the Irish language came to play in this process. As was shown, for Pól the Irish language expanded from initially being primarily a strategic practice to eventually also embodying a significant dimension of both his identity and the political struggle. This sequence for the Irish language echoed the broader development of Pól's outlook on the whole conflict, which he seems to have interpreted first in rather localized terms of injustice, then in terms of colonialism and imperialism within a broader political analysis of nation-states and finally with regard to 'other cultural dimensions':

> The <u>starting</u> <u>point</u> was the injustice! It was <u>them</u> who had the guns and the power and all the rest of it. And then there was <u>us</u>, and we were <u>nobody</u>; we were <u>the</u> <u>second</u> <u>class!</u> ... So at the start, I'd have seen the conflict as

more localized, and as more – I mean, it's like a civil war, more local, more personal. I mean, you [personally] <u>know</u> the people, and all the rest of it! It's only as you get <u>involved</u> you see, this is something that is <u>a</u> <u>broader</u> <u>thing</u>. Like so, why were these people <u>armed</u> in the first place? Why has the Protestant community got weapons? It's because of, you know, colonialism, and then Partition, and the set-up of the Northern state. So you start to see it now in a <u>much</u> <u>wider</u> <u>way</u>, you know! So in terms of <u>politics</u>, as time goes on, you become much more aware that all of this started because of the whole politics and everything behind them. You know, the colonialism, imperialism and all the rest of it. And then, I think, as you grew older, then more of an awareness about <u>Ireland</u> <u>itself!</u> And other <u>cultural</u> dimensions of it! Erm – culture as the language and the [Gaelic] games and, you know, and all the rest of it! But I mean, it would have been up <u>late</u> that <u>I</u> would be more interested in Ireland, the GAA and watching their games. And again, because they became more modernized! It's on the TV more! Which it wasn't before! So it becomes more popular for kids to wear the GAA tops. So they start to wear the uniforms in the streets. So you start to <u>see</u> <u>it</u> much, much more! Again, because of politics! Because beforehand, Gaelic games were not shown on TV! You had to go to the pitch to actually see them, you know? Whereas <u>soccer</u> was shown on TV; <u>rugby</u> was shown on TV. So as that changes as a result of politics, then you start to see them more. So you start to become more interested in them!

Pádraigín, age 40

When discussing her ethnic identity, Pádraigín emphasized that for her personally there had never been any doubt about being Irish: 'I can't imagine thinking I was anything else, 'cause I was born in Ireland, I mean, really. And my parents are Irish and I grew up always knowing I was Irish, so how could I be anything else?' Although Pádraigín recalled from her childhood in North Belfast during the late 1960s and 1970s that 'you didn't think of being Irish when you were younger', she emphasized that the situation in the North of Ireland was special:

> Don't forget I was brought up <u>right</u> <u>through</u> <u>terrible</u> <u>times!</u> Like, bombs in the town centre. So, my parents would've had to explain things that they mightn't have explained normally. ... And there was bombs and terrible things happening. It was a terrible time to grow up! I mean, you can't imagine that now, living in Belfast now. ... [Now] there's no British soldiers marching down the road all the time and, 'What's your name, and where do you live, and what's your date of birth?' And really, explosions.

Within Pádraigín's family, 'Irish culture' generally seems to have formed an important part 'in all our life, you know, from a very early age', even though it was 'not so much talked about, it was just lived'. Irish music was a particularly prominent feature from early on:

Daddy would've listened to traditional music at home; it is <u>mostly</u> from Daddy, all this comes from, actually! Mummy was supportive, like. Erm, when I was <u>very young</u>, probably about seven or eight, Daddy came in one day with a tin whistle and a little booklet of how to put your fingers on it and what to do. And we taught ourselves how to play the tin whistle. And Daddy bought records. <u>Every week</u> he bought a new record! He used to go down to [the then still existent] Smithfield [market] and get a new traditional record. And then he would make compilation tapes, and he had a tape recorder in our car and made mixtures of things, and we'd sing along and, you know? And then he encouraged us, like I got a fiddle and my sister got a flute. And my brother got the mandolin, and Daddy went along to the mandolin classes with him, you know? And I don't know, we were just nurtured; we were very well nurtured, very privileged, really, like.

As Pádraigín repeatedly told me, within her immediate social world of mainly 'Castle Catholic' middle-class families in North Belfast (see Chapters 4 and 1), her family's commitment to 'Irish culture', including the Irish language, was actually quite unusual given that many others distanced themselves from anything Irish in order to avoid any possible appearance of being connected to Irish Republicanism and the armed struggle. This was not the case with Pádraigín – she laconically observed: 'I was listening to [the Irish traditional bands] Clannad and the Bothy Band, and my friends were listening to ABBA. You know, I was different, without a doubt!'

Pádraigín went to violin classes for classical music when she was about twelve years old and also played in the school orchestra. However, as she put it, 'I wasn't getting very far 'cause I was really into traditional music', which she was 'picking up by ear, rather than sheet music' and which 'was all self-taught then. There weren't really a lot of [Irish traditional music] classes around in Belfast at all'.

During the summer [stays] in Donegal we would have gone to sessions every weekend. When we were up there, you know? But I spent my teenage time really being completely involved in that. Like, if we were up for three weeks, we'd been out every night of the week. Daddy took us over, and, you know, we played in the pubs and enjoyed the craic [i.e. the fun and enjoyable time].

As Pádraigín recalled, when she later went to university in Coleraine, there were other musicians there. At the same time, her sister also went to Trinity College Dublin, and met musicians there, and 'there was plenty of music on the go then'. Together, the two sisters were away every weekend 'at different things', given that traditional music would have been 'very strong in the eighties'. When Pádraigín finished university and started working in Belfast in 1987, she continued to play traditional music regularly at sessions in pubs and bars:

When I came back to Belfast there was a session in the Rotterdam [Bar]. And there was always a tradition of music in Kelly's Cellars. As far back, even back to when I was at school, seventeen and eighteen – there would have been music in Kelly's Cellars. And, there was a place in the Short Strand [i.e. a small Catholic enclave in the predominantly Protestant eastern inner-city Belfast] that had music. I remember going to it once with a friend of mine. And like, it scared me! It was like a barricade around it. So there would have been sessions, when I came back in '87, there were sessions. I mean, I went to a regular session in the Rotterdam in Belfast. And then after that, we went to a bar called the Blackthorn. I mean, there's always music. Belfast is not bad for music, you know!

While Pádraigín's life-long interest in Irish music thus originated in her childhood and from her family, it was only through her grammar school that she was exposed to another domain of 'Irish culture', namely, Irish dancing. However, she encountered Irish dancing not in isolation but as part and parcel of a whole package that included both the Irish language and Irish music:

While we were at school, that's why, you know, I think the Irish teachers did well in our school. They didn't just teach Irish [language] in a vacuum. We would have had céilí dancing classes at lunchtime. So, we would know all the céilí dances. It wasn't just the language, it was, like, the teacher played Clannad records to us and played the traditional music to us as well, and we learned some of the songs, and we had a wee traditional music group in school. And then a lot of my generation went to the Irish colleges in the Gaeltacht areas. And that [i.e. céilí dancing] would have been your activity. And maybe that's why people learnt that as their culture as well. Because it was always; say if you went, as a youngster, like, people who were my age all went to Rannafast and Loch An Iúir to the Irish colleges. And you spent your mornings learning Irish and your afternoons learning the song and the céilí dances. And you had really good craic mixing with boys and girls.

Thus apart from Irish music, Pádraigín recalled that her teenage social life was 'all céilí and the youth club', the activities of which were not religious, although it was organized at the local Catholic parish church.

Later in life, when Pádraigín returned after studying in Coleraine, she also got involved with set dancing. As she recalled, 'There was a massive upsurge and interest in set dancing in, again when I came back from university, say '86, '87.'

I would say the first classes in Mandela Hall [i.e. the bar of the students' union at Queen's University Belfast] were around 1986. 'Cause I remember being jealous because my brother was living here. He was going to set dancing. And I was still in Coleraine. And then when I came home, I couldn't drive. And I remember getting the bus from where I was living at home. So it's definitely my first year home in 1987. Going over, heading over to Queen's for eight o'clock. And it was, like, a bit of a social life for you. Where you got to know Belfast people and young working people as well. You know, it was a mixture.

At that time, 'there would have been eighty people at those classes, really big interest in that', whereas now, 'there's still an interest in it and there's still the odd céilí [i.e. events, where sets are also danced], but you'd be lucky you get one set [with eight dancers] in the class, whereas then you had, you know, you had ten sets'. According to Pádraigín, these classes were also good for singles:

> You would go on your own and the girl who ran it was just like, 'Okay, I get you a partner for you now. You go here,' and then, 'Okay, you [i.e. another girl] have been dancing for a while, I put you down and you [i.e. Pádraigín] get up.' It was a really good community! And all mixtures of people doing that, you know? It wasn't just a Catholic interest at all! And it was very young! Now, the people who are interested in it are a wee bit older. Now, I don't go set dancing anymore, but it was a big part of my social life there, ten years ago.

Pádraigín told me that the general interest in set dancing somewhat diminished in the late 1990s, because – as she reckoned – 'a lot of those people who were attending set dancing classes are attending salsa dances now'. For her personally, being interested in and becoming involved with Irish dancing developed almost as a corollary of her strong identification with Irish music: 'having been a musician already, then I learnt to dance, and to the music that I had been playing, was a nice thing to add!'

Against the backdrop of Pádraigín's extensive involvement with Irish music, Irish dancing and, of course, the Irish language (see Chapter 4), it is not surprising that she did not really become active with Gaelic games, especially since she was 'not a sporty person; too lazy' and the ball was 'very hard, very scary'. Yet some contextual factors might have played a role as well:

> Actually, Gaelic games weren't all around me! You know, in North Belfast we didn't have [many GAA clubs]! You know, I am not aware of. But maybe my parents weren't that sporty. Mummy played camogie for County Derry. So, she was aware of it. But I went to a Catholic school that had a Protestant PE teacher and we didn't do camogie! We did hockey, you know! So, and I wasn't aware of any GAA clubs. And maybe my father wasn't sporty, you know? So it wasn't all around me! It was West Belfast; every flip's turn, there was a GAA club; it's very strong!

Another contextual factor for the lack of Gaelic games seems to have been a generally ambivalent ethos at Pádraigín's Catholic grammar school, where – despite the provision of the Irish language and céilí dancing – Irishness as such was viewed with suspicion:

It was a Catholic school, you know, a Catholic grammar school, yeah. They didn't push Gaelic games, no. They didn't push much for Irish identity. You know, we [i.e. Pádraigín's family] would have had a name in school for being 'Irish', you know, or 'a Republican family' as such. And 'Republican' meant not that we wanted a free, democratic society, but 'activist' [i.e. supporting the armed struggle], you know? We would have had a fairly strong name for that, you know? Just because they [i.e. other Catholic middle-class families related to that school] equated the interest in the language and in culture with that!

Sinéad, age 33

Thinking back on her childhood in the 1970s in West Belfast, Sinéad emphasized that Irishness in general and 'Irish culture' in particular did not matter at all in her family. The typical elements of 'Irish culture' described in this chapter thus did not figure in Sinéad's home, and this lack of 'Irish culture' apparently imprinted on Sinéad's later life as well. Thus, Gaelic games were never an issue within her family, and nobody ever played these sports or took any interest in following them. Sinéad also never played Gaelic games at school, where it was not part of her physical education.

Irish music did not play any role at home, as Sinéad's parents did not listen to traditional music, which Sinéad came into contact with primarily through school. As she recalled, 'just, you had normal music lessons' in which the pupils would have listened to some traditional music and through which Sinéad learned how to play the tin whistle. Outside school she had some friends who played in bands, and – as she told me – 'I would just ask thems to give me the notes' of some of their tunes. While Sinéad and her family were seemingly not into (local) politics at all, these tunes still happened to be partly associated with Republican songs, such as 'The Ballad of Billy Reid' and 'Séan South of Garryowen'.

At the time that I met Sinéad, she told me that she also sometimes listened to traditional music at home on the radio or on CDs: 'just, like Christy Moore and all thems!' Occasionally, she also co-organized and attended 'wee Irish nights', 'wee get-togethers for fund nights. We try and raise funds for the Irish-medium school' where (as described in Chapter 4) Sinéad helped out in the after-school club.

> These events are just, an Irish night! Well, sometimes not even an Irish night, actually! Sometimes, it's just like a disco where people would buy tickets, come in and; they'd get the money; the money would go into the school. But now we had one a couple of weeks ago. And we had a couple of Irish singers. … It was brilliant!

While Irish music thus still occasionally figured in Sinéad's life, this was not the case for Irish dancing, which had only briefly mattered to Sinéad in her school days. As she recalled, 'When I was at primary school, I took a couple of night classes in Irish dancing'. She did so because her parents sent her to Irish dancing, although – as she realized – 'I don't even know why they sent me because, I mean, they were not Irish-minded! Like, it was just something, "Now, there's something for you to do. Away, and do it!"' It thus apparently had little to do with consciously practising something 'Irish' but rather with the fact that when Sinéad was a young girl, 'it was a common thing that girls would go to this dancing' – 'you would have tried it!' However, after a while Sinéad stopped attending dance classes, never to return to Irish dancing again. She reasoned, 'I would say I was more of a tomboy when I was younger. I just wanted to go and do boy-things, so Irish dancing just didn't appeal to me'.

During our encounters, Sinéad told me how much she wanted to send her own daughter to Irish dancing. However, it seemed that this pastime had become far too expensive for her to be able to afford it:

> I'd have loved to put my wee girl in the Irish dancing now. But it's far too dear. The likes of one costume, it's 500 to 600 pounds! And each time they go into a different competition, you have to buy a new dress! … Different *feises* [i.e. competitions] want different costumes! So it's far too dear! And you can't say to the child, 'You're only going in to <u>learn</u> it; you <u>can't</u> <u>go</u> into any of the competitions!' Because what's the point in putting the child in, then?

Apart from this type of solo Irish dancing, Sinéad ended up attending a céilí only once in the mid-1980s when she went to a Donegal Gaeltacht for an Irish-language weekend with her class from the Springhill Community House (see Chapter 4). Aside from this incident, céilí dancing did not figure again in Sinéad's life. As she assured me with regard to céilís in West Belfast, 'They would have been advertised, but I never went looking!'

All in all, it became clear during our interviews that for Sinéad, participation in typical aspects of 'Irish culture' had generally not been important. While she had always self-ascribed as 'Irish', being Irish simply had not been relevant for her. This only changed once Sinéad started sending her son to the Irish-medium nursery and therefore revived her own capacity to speak the language, which she had not used since attending school. This seems to be the position that Sinéad put across in the following quotation, thereby providing a complementary comment to her final words in Chapter 4, where she merely reported (rather than identified with) the notion of the-Irish-language-as-the-essence-of-Irishness:

> I only <u>really</u> started seeing myself as being Irish when my son started coming into the [Irish-medium] nursery. And I started going <u>back</u> to learning my Irish! … [Before that] I'd say, even when I was filling in forms, when it came to 'Nationality', I just <u>stuck</u> 'Irish' to my son. I was like [Sinéad gestures as though checking off the box], 'Ach, stick with "Irish" to him. I'm not sticking nothing else to him!' But now that I am actually trying to learn the language, I can see myself as – now that I am writing 'Irish' [on the form] – I <u>am</u> an Irish person 'cause I'm trying to learn the language!

Caoimhín, age 17

Being born in Belfast in the mid-1980s, Caoimhín was still a pupil at a local grammar school in West Belfast at the time of my fieldwork and was one of my youngest contacts. Nevertheless, he had an explicit conception about what it meant to be Irish. When talking about this sense of identity, Caoimhín told me that in his experience several elements of 'Irish culture' had a considerable presence in contemporary West Belfast:

> I'd say Gaelic games is a very big thing. ... I'm not really into traditional music myself, but I know a lot of people who play it and are interested in it. I wouldn't say that it is as big as the Gaelic games or the [Irish] language or whatever, but it's not as if it's under threat or anything! There's people who, like, pay big money! – Irish dancing, as well, that's another thing I could imagine [as part of 'Irish culture']. That would be very big!

As mentioned in passing, Caoimhín himself was 'not really into traditional music', even though he would occasionally enjoy listening to such Irish music:

> I'm not a big, big fan of the music myself. It's just, I enjoy listening to the traditional music and stuff on Saturday nights in the Cluain Árd [i.e. during informal instrumental sessions]. I have a few CDs and stuff, but I don't play or anything. But I do enjoy listening to it, especially when it's live!

Caoimhín listened 'to all sorts of music' and to 'just whatever is on the radio, like pop music' and would 'go out and hit some bars' and discotheques on weekends with his mates, primarily heading for 'a couple of clubs around the local area' in West Belfast. He also occasionally went 'to the sessions down the Cluain Árd' and would 'go to someone like Christy Moore or "*Bréag*" ['Lie']', a local Irish-medium Reggae-band in West Belfast. Generally, however, he did not attend concerts and did not play music himself, given that – as Caoimhín put it – 'I haven't got a note in my head'. As Caoimhín recalled, he was in contact with Irish music from early on since his father had an interest in it:

> Irish music would have been around a lot, like. My Dad's into it. ... Every tape and CD that's lying around the house'd be played sometimes. It wasn't like it [i.e. traditional music] was on every day, all day. But you knew what type of music it was as soon as you heard it. You recognized it. ... You see, I was saying to you before, my sisters did the Irish dancing, so they had the CDs to the music that they danced to. Just the fiddling stuff, so all them CDs and all would've been about the house, and tapes.

As mentioned at the end of this quote, all of Caoimhín's sisters were involved in Irish dancing, as 'mostly girls, like, when they're young would do Irish dancing'. He himself attended one dance class when he was seven years old, but he did not like it at all:

> When I was younger I went up <u>one</u> day and just didn't enjoy it at all! One! My friend and my sister and all was going, and my friend's ma was taking them up. So I went up one day, and just – I knew I was never able to do it! … I couldn't do it. Didn't like it. Just wasn't for me. Same with the music, as well. I knew when we were playing [the tin whistle at school]. So it just wasn't for me.

However, Caoimhín did 'love the céilí dancing' since 'it's not that hard, it's just everybody together; some fun, so it is, especially, when you have all your friends and stuff, down in the Gaeltacht. Brilliant!' When he was younger, Caoimhín's mother occasionally attended céilí dances with friends, but it was only when he started going to Gaeltacht colleges that Caoimhín actually tried céilí dancing himself. As he recalled, his participation came about:

> just from going up to the Gaeltacht and the Gaeltacht college. They would have céilís most nights, and there you'd learn the dances. It's a good laugh and something different. You know, there wouldn't really be that many céilís on in Belfast for <u>young</u> people! Just be all discos and stuff. So it was a bit of a change! It was good fun as well. I really enjoyed 'em.

Apart from enjoying céilís in the Gaeltacht, overall Caoimhín was not overly enthusiastic about musical affairs. This was somewhat in contrast to his involvement with Gaelic games, which had started early on. When I asked Caoimhín how he became involved with Gaelic games, he explained that it was

> hard to say, really. Just 'cause it's all around you! I mean – it's hard to say – friends would be like, 'Oh, did you see [County] Antrim?' Just, it'd be something you'd talk about. 'Did you see [County] Antrim playing [County] Cork or whatever?' It's just, like, just something, sometimes you would talk about. … That would be more interesting than, like, most girls and stuff. So it would be something that you'd talk about and support.

According to Caoimhín, local children typically played Gaelic games in physical education classes at Catholic primary and secondary schools, which – in most cases – would have their best players on their own school teams. However, players that ended up playing for the school teams usually had played from an early age for local GAA clubs:

> People would be playing [in GAA clubs] since they were like five or six years old, playing all their life, them. By the time they get to secondary school, the PE coach or PE teacher would know that they play for such-and-such a team and that they're a good player. They would know. They

would know all good players before they even had one training session, you know what I mean?

Since Caoimhín had not played for a local GAA club, his career as an active player ended prematurely after being on the school team at primary school. As he explained to me, when he came to grammar school, 'it was like a mix from all the different [primary] schools, and I just wasn't good enough to get on the team'. He continued playing both Gaelic football and hurling in physical education but stopped playing these sports regularly and competitively when he stopped doing PE after fifth year.

Caoimhín's interests in sports were in fact more focused on soccer. As with Gaelic games, he found it difficult to pinpoint the exact context in which he had first come into contact with this sport, as 'it's just always been about. I played it since I was young and have seen it on TV. It's something that you do when you are younger'. Although Caoimhín played soccer at school in physical education, there were no school soccer teams. Caoimhín therefore played for two years for a local soccer club in Catholic West Belfast, which was 'actually the only Catholic team in the [local] League'.

Thus, Caoimhín was predominantly engaged with supporting Glasgow Celtic at the time of our interviews. With regard to Celtic matches, Caoimhín told me that 'everyone that's on TV, I'd definitely watch it, unless I'm working or something'. He was not a member of one of the many Glasgow Celtic fan clubs in Belfast because 'you have to pay money in, and you're expected to go to matches every week, and I wouldn't be able to go every week. It costs too much money'. However, one of his uncles was a member and hence supplied him with tickets for home matches at Celtic's Parkhead in Glasgow. Caoimhín would attend matches there 'about two or three times during the season'.

Caoimhín thought that many people in Catholic West Belfast who were into soccer would also take some interest in Celtic because of the club's 'big Irish connection' in originating from the Irish immigrant community in Glasgow during the late nineteenth century (see also Chapter 1). Given the rather low profile of soccer in Ireland generally, Glasgow Celtic was hence, within mainland U.K., 'the only real Irish team, and successful, like'.

Reflecting on how he had become what he was – namely, Irish – Caoimhín highlighted the dual character of both being moulded by 'the Irish influences' 'all around you' into becoming Irish and of subsequently becoming aware of precisely this process:

It was just growing up! Like, you don't really <u>know</u> you're Irish! You're just, like, you go, look around. Like, when I was younger we used to play Gaelic football, and you just – you were playing Gaelic football! … You were going to Gaelic matches and all. Your wee sisters were doing Irish dancing. And all that would have just come in. And then, like, when you're older, you can <u>think about it!</u> You just go, like, 'I never thought about it. I was just being Irish.' If you had've been born in France, or whatever, you would have been growing up doing different things, and then, you would have realized, 'Oh, I'm French.' Just, when you're growing up – all these, like, the Irish influences are all around you! – So it's not really your choice, you know what I mean? Just, how you're influenced by, well, your peers, and – it sort of just <u>moulds</u> you into being Irish!

Preliminary Observations

In this chapter, I have provided as diverse and saturated as possible insights into the pathways that led my primary informants (with the exception of Dónal) into becoming Irish. Tracing more than fifty years of history, I have described how these local Irishmen and Irishwomen were differently exposed to and variously engaged with the three cultural domains of Gaelic games (including soccer as its ambiguous 'other'), Irish music and Irish dancing that I identified in Chapter 7 as exemplary aspects of 'Irish culture'. In addressing the specific conditions and conditionalities that moulded the development of my informants' respective Irishness during the second half of the twentieth century, these reconstructed biographies thereby generated ethnographic material that is relevant for all three analytical dimensions of this book.

This observation is easily demonstrated by the example of Caoimhín's final quotation, which I cited in his biographical section. In this excerpt, Caoimhín explicitly addressed the dialectic between practical experiences of 'just being Irish', on the one hand, and self-reflexive representations of Irishness ('you can think about it'), on the other. In other words, Caoimhín himself highlighted the dual character of 'becoming who you are' through practically engaging with 'the Irish influences' 'all around you' – be it Gaelic games, Irish dancing or Irish music – and of 'becoming aware of who you are' through self-reflection and representations of Irishness. It is exactly this dynamic between variously representable but actually realized cultural practices and representational practices of 'culture' that constitutes the focal point of my first analytical dimension, and that is also emphasized in this chapter's title: 'Becoming (Aware of) Who You Are: Irish'.

A preliminary synopsis of the ten biographical sketches reveals their relevance for the second dimension of structure and agency, and this, again, is illustrated by Caoimhín's quote. As he put it, when growing up, 'the Irish influences are all around you! – So it's not really your choice'. Instead, 'how you're influenced by, well, your peers ... just moulds you into being Irish!' Caoimhín thus stressed the importance of various structural contexts for turning 'you into being Irish'. As we have seen throughout this chapter, these structural contexts were to a great extent the same as those that were relevant for the Irish language in Chapter 4. Such structural contexts in conjunction with the wider political context of the Troubles heavily influenced trajectories into local Irishness, but the ten actors (like others) were still also left to use their own agency. They did so in divergent ways, creating a spectrum in which some people – like Micheál – ended up playing Gaelic games, doing Irish dancing and getting into Irish music (besides also speaking Irish), whereas others – like Sinéad – did not really adopt as their own 'the Irish influences' of Gaelic games, Irish music or Irish dancing that were 'all around'.

Finally, the third dimension of biographical time also made its presence felt in Caoimhín's quotation. By constructing an opposition between, first, 'just growing up' and 'then, like, when you're older, you can think about it [i.e. Irishness]', Caoimhín emphasized a chronological sequence whereby the individual comes to have a self-reflexive stance as part of his or her maturation. This observation is important in referring to variously formative qualities of specific stages within life cycles such as childhood, formal education, working life and parenthood. However, Caoimhín's observation also needs to be qualified in two respects. First, self-reflexive, identity-related representations do not necessarily only follow practical experiences but can also occur at the same time or even before any such practical engagements (as was largely the case for the Irish language revival). Second, life stories emerge at the intersection of both more personalized developments within individual life cycles and broader trends in a more inter-subjective time. With the exception of Roibeárd, each of the above informants who personally experienced the outbreak of the Troubles clearly characterized this event as having had a profound impact on their subsequent development as an Irish person. The ups and downs of political conflict and localized violence as well as the eventual emergence of the peace process in the 1990s made their marks on these individuals' lives.

When describing how Caoimhín's quotation could be used to illustrate the relevance of a structure-agency perspective for the analysis of local Irishness, it became evident that Caoimhín did not seem to ascribe much importance to individual agency in shaping individual processes of identity formation. In Caoimhín's words, 'It's not really your choice'. On the contrary, Caoimhín saw structure as much more dominant in moulding 'you into being Irish' because 'the Irish influences are all around you' and 'you're influenced by, well, your peers'. In the next chapter, I will systematically pursue this issue by analysing the ways and extent to which present Irishness in Catholic West Belfast came about as the product of individual agency or instead, as Caoimhín seemed to suggest, 'the Irish influences' 'all around you'. It is to an investigation of this interplay between 'nets' of Irishness, that were cast in different structural contexts and variously 'netted', and 'free-floating' actors that I turn now.

Chapter 9
Casting Nets of Identity
A Contemporary History of Irishness in Catholic West Belfast

On a Tuesday evening in August 2004, I paid a visit to Maebh, who lived with her two daughters Bronagh and Catriona in Catholic West Belfast close to the Stewartstown Road, much further up and beyond the Falls Road from where I was staying. I initially met Maebh, her partner Daithi and a group of her friends at the Cultúrlann at the weekly rehearsals of the Irish-medium *Cór Loch Lao* (the 'Belfast Bay Choir'). Over time, I became friends with these middle-aged acquaintances, and I joined them for walks around Belfast, usually on Sundays. In this process, I also met relatives and friends of these people, who often got together casually at Maebh's home. Constituting an informal meeting place where relatives, friends and neighbours gathered for such social visits that used to be called 'céilís' in the Irish North (Vallely 1999e), Maebh's place was thus, in a way, what older people in Catholic West Belfast recalled as a typical 'céilí house'.

While my friends and I had thus been 'céilí-ing' for some time at Maebh's, in recent weeks I had not seen much of them, as it was the summer holiday season, and everybody seemed to be either in the Gaeltacht or in Spain. Since I knew that Daithi, Maebh and her two daughters were about to return from the Mediterranean, I gave them a call and learnt that Daithi planned to go and watch a hurling match at a local Gaelic Athletic Association (GAA) pitch close to Maebh's house that night. He invited me to join him, and proposed that we meet at Maebh's place at 7:00 p.m. When I arrived at around the agreed time and entered Maebh's red-brick, two-storey, semi-detached house, I first met eighteen-year-old Bronagh, who was having dinner in the kitchen with a friend. In the living room, Maebh, Daithi, his sister Fionnoula with her three-year-old son Cathal, as well as Mary (a Canadian living in Belfast and another good friend from the choir) were sitting on two armchairs and a sofa, while Maebh's younger daughter, thirteen-year-old Catriona, was running about the place with two friends from the neighbourhood. Shortly after I entered and greeted everybody, Marcas, another friend from the choir, arrived as well, adding yet another person to the already quite packed room in which everybody was engaging in noisy parallel conversations about their holidays and current affairs.

Looking around, I observed the interior of this orange-painted living room with parquet flooring where we usually spent most of the time during our visits to Maebh's. Opposite the broad window front facing the street were the two leather armchairs. To the right of the chairs was a sofa of the same material, while an electric fireplace with a large mirror above the mantelpiece was located to the left. In the far left corner, a television towered above a DVD player. The three walls (besides the window front) were covered with framed photos of family members, especially the two daughters at different ages and on various occasions, including their respective First Holy Communions in the Catholic Church.

Beside the fireplace, there was a framed depiction of 'The Sacred Heart of Jesus' showing the flaming heart shining with divine light, pierced by the lance-wound, surrounded by a crown of thorns, and bleeding over Jesus, who pointed with his wounded hands at the heart and looked heavenwards. As a Catholic devotion to Jesus' physical heart as the symbolic representation of his divine love for humanity, pictures of the Sacred Heart can be found in many Catholic homes, given that within the traditionally associated twelve promises of the Sacred Heart, the second and ninth blessing explicitly speak about the family and the home. These two promises were also printed on the depiction of the Sacred Heart in Maebh's house, stating, 'I will give peace in their families' (second promise) and 'I will bless the house in which the image of My Sacred Heart shall be exposed and honoured' (ninth promise).

The living room further accommodated an array of bric-à-brac including a collection of trophies, cups and medals won in recent years by Catriona in Irish step dancing competitions (formerly, both Maebh and her elder daughter Bronagh were involved in Irish step dancing as well). These trophies, decorated with typical Celtic ornaments and depictions of Irish solo dancers, shamrocks, Celtic crosses and Irish harps, were indicative of precisely that type of 'Nationalistic' or 'Irish-ish' home environment that Dónal evoked in his first quote in Chapter 8 in order to insist that such common emblems of Irishness were, in fact, conspicuously absent in his own home. Although Maebh's house did not feature Irish tricolours or pictures of James Connolly or President de Valera (Dónal's examples), it did exhibit numerous other emblems of Irishness, especially in the adjacent room, which made clear that this was indeed a home in which Irishness had a strong presence: decorative china plates with Celtic ornaments, brass-coloured Celtic crosses, plates with images of Irish harps, the Claddagh ring (an Irish symbol of love and friendship) and Irish step dancers, as well as a framed reprint of the 1916 Easter Proclamation of the Irish Republic, were all mounted on the walls.

Within this more general atmosphere, about half an hour after my arrival Daithi suggested that we move to the nearby GAA pitch, as the hurling match was about to start. As it turned out, most of the visitors did not want to join us, so in the end, only Daithi, his little nephew Cathal, Mary and I went over to the playing field, which was just around the corner. Daithi and Cathal took a *sliotar* ('hurling ball') and their hurling sticks with them, including a child's stick. When we arrived at the field, there were three adjacent pitches, and Daithi explained that they belonged to different local GAA clubs. Tonight, Daithi continued, we would see a hurling match in the under-18 County Antrim Hurling Club Championship with the local Patrick Sarsfields Gaelic Athletic Club (GAC) competing against a team from Ballycastle.

Funnily enough, although we had specifically come to watch this match, ultimately we paid little attention to the game. Having not seen each other for a while, we adults chatted amongst ourselves as Cathal played by himself. Soon, however, Daithi joined his small nephew, and the two went a bit further down the sideline, where they started knocking their own hurling ball back and forth. As became obvious, little Cathal very much enjoyed trying to hit the sliotar with his hurling stick, crowing when he succeeded. Daithi and Cathal were not alone in playing alongside the match, as a number of other youngsters and spectators did so as well, even venturing onto the corner of the pitch.

When the match was over, we headed back to Maebh's place. Maebh's younger daughter Catriona and her two female friends were outside the house, hanging around in front of the door. Catriona wore a Glasgow Celtic top, tracksuit trousers and sneakers. She had recently dyed her hair, although – as she would half-jokingly tell us later on – her mother disapproved. As we could see (and hear) when approaching the house, they had a little stereo with them. Some pop music was playing, and the girls danced a bit, with Catriona seamlessly switching between disco-style and Irish dancing steps. I followed Daithi, Cathal and Mary into the house, which constituted a structural context in which 'Irish culture' was evidently interwoven with many other facets of everyday life and where Irishness in general clearly had its place.

In this chapter I will focus more generally on the place that Irishness came to occupy in Catholic West Belfast in the second half of the twentieth century. I will argue that in order to better understand the Irishness of the local Gaeilgeoirí I encountered during my fieldwork in 2003–2004, it is necessary to investigate thoroughly the network of influences between several structural contexts – including the one of 'family and friends' as exemplified in the opening vignette on Maebh's house – that brought about and lived on in the present configuration of Irishness in Catholic West Belfast. Drawing on secondary literature and cross-referencing my own material such as the life stories in Chapter 8, I will trace a contemporary history of local Irishness by analysing the evolving interplay between individual agency and structural contexts (dimension 2) in my informants' biographies (dimension 3), that is to say from about the mid-twentieth century onwards.

For this purpose, I will first provide a short history of the broad structural contexts with some general relevance for Irishness as they emerged in the North of Ireland since Partition. I will then follow each of the three exemplary domains of 'Irish culture' identified in Chapter 7 – namely, Gaelic games, Irish music and Irish dancing. In each of these three sections, I will first provide some historical background before engaging with the specificities of Catholic West Belfast since the 1950s. Against this historical backdrop and despite some range of motivations that drove my local informants to varying extents into practical engagements with Gaelic games, Irish music and Irish dancing, I will ultimately argue that all three domains persistently exhibited a strong element of habituation or traditional motivation, in Weber's terminology. Many people in Catholic West Belfast – at least many within the local subset of Irish learners and speakers – were considerably predisposed to coming into contact and practically engaging with these three cultural domains because of the overlapping and interconnected influences of several structural contexts. In other words, as I will show, various structural contexts such as family and friends, schools, the GAA and the media were each independently casting a similar net of 'Irish culture and identity' into daily life in West Belfast – a fact that made it very likely for subsequent generations of local Catholics ultimately to become 'netted' or 'caught up' in Irishness.

'A constant counter-narrative to the dominant narrative of the society': Emerging Structural Contexts for/eclosing Irishness in Northern Ireland

In the course of providing a 'prehistory' for the Irish language up to the 1950s, I already referred to some of the general characteristics of daily life in the new 'Northern Ireland' since Partition (see Chapter 5), and numerous historical studies offer in-depth analyses of various aspects of Northern Irish life. In the following, I will thus concentrate on a few largely uncontroversial key features of everyday life in the North of Ireland, as it has developed from the 1920s onwards.

Deliberately established as a polity in which the overall Protestant minority within Ireland would reign as the local majority, Northern Ireland soon came to be dominated by a politics of control, which primarily aimed at securing the constitutional link with Britain (Douglas 1997: 156–62). The Local Government (NI) Act of 1922 introduced discriminatory measures into the voting system, allowing electoral boundaries to be redrawn and abolishing proportional representation in favour of single-seat constituencies, which de facto safeguarded Unionist majorities (Coohill 2000: 150). The Special Powers Act (1922) gave the state excessive powers like internment without trial and the banning of organizations, publications and meetings. Civil service employment came to strongly favour Protestant applicants, and '[m]irroring the public sector, informal social and economic structures also emerged in the private sector to make more complete the social, psychological and spatial divisions in Northern Ireland society' (Douglas 1997: 158). According to Coohill, this led to a 'complete' divide in society:

> The Northern Ireland government instituted a series of discriminatory measures against Catholics. Many Catholics responded by retreating into their own communities. This meant that both communities increasingly lived completely within their own communities .... Throughout Northern Ireland, there were two distinct, and *complete*, communities. 'Complete' is as important as 'distinct' here, because there were separate neighbourhoods, schools, shops, clubs and associations, professions and almost all aspects of daily life. Education was particularly segregated and there was a great deal of argument over how the funding of the Catholic and Protestant schools should be handled by the government. (Coohill 2000: 160 – emphasis in the original)

While these 'completely' separated lives of both communities evolved within a Northern Irish state that from early on was politically dominated by Protestant Unionism, the diminishing sense of ethnic Irishness among Northern Protestants additionally meant a growing 'cultural' hegemony of Britishness (Walker 1996: 119).

In Chapter 2, I analytically distinguished between four types of structural contexts vis-à-vis local Irish Gaeilgeoirí, depending on how the question of ethnicity is conceptualized. According to this distinction, the emerging Northern Irish state can be described – relative to local Irish Catholics – as an external structural context since it consisted of practices by other actors (politicians, civil servants, etc.) who were in agreement with the actors under focus that the latter were Irish and that they themselves were not (see Chapter 2). In this external structural context of the Northern Irish state, symbols of Britishness came to fill civic space with a lawful presence that embraced everybody, Protestant and Catholic: for instance, several of my informants – like Rónán, Micheál or Pól in Chapter 8 – recalled how in the 1950s and 1960s the British anthem would be played at communal events 'that were under the law such as cinemas and theatre plays' (Micheál), while this did not happen in the rest of the U.K. Apart from its presence during graduation ceremonies at university, the British anthem also regularly featured on television, leading Pól's parents to casually switch it off.

Furthermore, the Union Jack (i.e. the British) flag flew on public buildings; war memorials celebrating the British Empire stood in the centre of cities, towns and villages; and annual parades organized by the Orange Order, prominently celebrating the historical subjugation of Catholics on the Twelfth of July, were provided with public space that had also been cleared from work obligations, as 'the Twelfth' was made a public holiday in 1926 (Bryan 2007: 103–4; see also Jarman 1997 and Bryan 2000). It is against this background that Bryan aptly sums up the political and 'cultural' organization of Northern Irish public space up to the 1960s:

> To put this situation another way, into the 1960s civic space was dominated by the politics of Unionism, the symbols of Britishness and empire, and the rituals of Loyalism. There were moments of opposition, limited forms of resistance, and certain spaces when alternative identities made appearances, but in the main the Union flag dominated. It is within this context that the development of the Civil Rights movement from 1967 onwards needs to be seen. (Bryan 2007: 104)

As is well known, the violent oppression of this Civil Rights movement by Protestant mobs and the Northern Irish state led to the outbreak of the Troubles in 1969 that eventually brought about some late state recognition for the existence of Irishness in Northern Ireland, namely, within an evolving rhetoric of 'two cultural traditions' since the mid-1980s (Nic Craith 2003: 48–57).

Yet before expressions such as 'respect', 'tolerance', 'mutual understanding' and 'parity of esteem' officially made their presence felt during the final decades of the twentieth century, the structural context of the Northern Irish state had not only foregrounded political and 'cultural' Britishness but also had deliberately deemphasized and excluded Irishness from the public sphere. Walker provides a number of examples of such exclusion, situating them within the more general political climate:

What was happening in the north [after Partition]? Just as the independent Irish state developed its sense of Irishness in a largely exclusive way, so in Northern Ireland there was a retreat from a sense of Irishness and the development of a heightened sense of British identity embracing Ulster, or Northern Ireland, which denied increasingly a sense of Irishness. This other exclusive identity, based around unionism, was directed primarily at the protestant section of the population. The Northern Ireland prime minister Lord Craigavon in 1934 spoke of 'a protestant parliament and a protestant state', and this spirit affected strongly the new northern identity. British symbols and culture were emphasised and Irish symbols and culture were often ignored. For example, Irish history in the schools and the Irish language were downplayed. The government dropped its grant for the teaching of Irish in schools in 1933, a move welcomed by the Northern Whig which referred to 'moribund Gaelic'. In 1934, after complaints from various quarters, including Lord Craigavon himself, the B.B.C. stopped broadcasting Gaelic football results in Northern Ireland; it recommenced in 1946, but initially the results of matches played on Sunday were broadcast on Monday. (Walker 1996: 119–20)

In the first part of this book, I covered the various ways in which the Northern Irish state handled the Irish language with a mixture of neglect, suspicion and hostility. Here, I will illustrate this neglect of Irishness with regard to its limited media presence. Broadcasting in the region since 1924, BBC Northern Ireland in early decades favoured 'a consensus model', which, on the one hand, exhibited an ignorant metropolitanism that was rather out of touch with local divisions, hence provoking Unionist complaints during the 1930s that there was an excess of 'Gaelic football results' (see above) or 'too much of the Irish pipe, the Irish jig and the Irish atmosphere in the BBC programmes from Belfast' (quoted in McLoone 1996: 27). At the same time, however, the BBC also swiftly conformed with the majority culture of Unionism and in so doing discriminated against Irishness as the minority culture (Butler 1994: 456–57; Nic Craith 2003: 146–47). Hence, as indicated by Walker in the above quote, the results of GAA matches were no longer broadcast after 1934 and were only reported again after the Second World War, initially with a one-day delay. Up until the 1970s, a general indifference towards Irish sports would be 'reflected in the refusal by the mainstream media to allocate the same air-time and column inches to Gaelic games as were given to other local sports' (Fahy 2001: 47). According to Butler (1994: 457–58), local media agencies somewhat changed in the mid-1960s by trying to build up a more moderate, though largely fictive, 'middle ground' from which even Irish history as a whole could be portrayed. But the outbreak of the Troubles would soon lead to considerable restrictions for media coverage, ultimately giving way from the mid-1970s onwards to a recognition of the realities of two conflicting traditions through establishing an impartial (rather than a balanced) system of 'dissensus broadcasting' (Butler 1994: 460–68).

Against this backdrop of not only foregrounding Britishness but also intentionally deemphasizing local Irishness, the Northern Irish state might be interpreted as having not only neglected but actually denied the Irish identity of local Catholics, proclaiming them to be British. The state can thus also be seen as having constituted an internalizing structural context – one consisting of practices by other actors (politicians, civil servants etc.) who disagreed with the Catholics under focus in seeing the latter as part of their own and common identity, which was British, while local Catholics insisted that they were different, namely, Irish. This is at least how the behaviour of the Northern Irish state came to be interpreted by many of my Catholic informants. Several insisted that by preventing, for instance, Gaelic games from being broadcast and by discriminating against the Irish language, the establishment had actively tried to create the impression that 'Irish' people and 'Irish culture' did not exist, and that Northern Ireland was a purely 'British' place.

Having so far exclusively concentrated on the Northern Irish state, which – whether interpreted as an external or an internal structural context – in any case attempted to foreclose any form of Irishness in the 'British' North, I now turn to the other side of the great divide, namely, to the 'parallel universe' of 'Catholic Northern Ireland' (as Micheál called it in Chapters 5 and 8). Douglas succinctly describes how Northern Catholics reacted to the emerging hegemonic culture of British Protestant Unionism through 'tactics of defiance and non-recognition of the new state and abstention from involvement in its structures and processes' (Douglas 1997: 159). In political terms, this initially often meant a refusal to vote or – once participation in elections had become widespread – a refusal by successful Nationalist candidates to take their seats. In addition, the rejection of official Northern Ireland became substantiated by 'an alternative and opposing set of social and economic nationalist structures, often generated by, and focused on, the Catholic church'; this entailed not only separate educational and teacher-training facilities but also financial structures in Credit Unions and charities, 'sporting and cultural organizations such as the GAA' as well as 'a separate nationalist press, which highlighted the biased sectarian repression of the unionist state in its own partisan fashion' (Douglas 1997: 160).

Within this evolving parallel universe of Catholic Northern Ireland, resistance to British hegemony basically took on two forms. On the one hand, the established tradition of political resistance through armed rebellion ensured that the IRA would continue to engage in violent campaigns immediately after Partition, during the Second World War, and in the border campaign between 1956 and 1962 (Coohill 2000: 151, 161; Fraser 2000: 5–6, 34). On the other hand, more symbolic gestures of resistance like the refusal to participate in elections would emerge as well. This form of resistance also included a counter-hegemonic response to symbols such as the British anthem when exposed to it – as Rónán and Micheál recalled in Chapter 8 – in cinemas or during public ceremonies like university graduations.

Yet this parallel universe of Catholic Northern Ireland was not only integrated through a common insistence on not being British – through 'us-hood' – but also through a shared sense of Irishness and unifying activities within the community – through 'we-hood'. In other words, 'Catholic Northern Ireland' also constituted an internal structural context, comprising practices by other actors who agreed with the actors under focus (i.e. local Gaeilgeoirí) that they were all Irish. According to Micheál, this Catholic 'world apart' maintained 'a constant counter-narrative to the dominant narrative of the society', defiantly stressing its own Irishness. It is in this sense that Roibeárd only slightly overstated the point in Chapter 8 when claiming that Irishness 'may have been a political issue, but for the two sides it was no issue. It's the same today. One side's Irish, the other side believes themselves to be British. But the Irish have never questioned themselves as to what they are. Never.'

Before devoting the remainder of this chapter to an analysis of the three cultural domains of Gaelic games, Irish music and Irish dancing within the internal structural context of Catholic West Belfast, I must provide a final note on the overarching impact of the Troubles on local perceptions of Irishness. When reconstructing a contemporary history of the Irish language in Chapter 5, I emphasized how profoundly the outbreak of the Troubles impacted local actors, whatever their age at the time. I extensively quoted Stiofán, who – then a teenager – vividly recalled how Irishness suddenly lost its innocence. Stiofán (like everyone else) was forced to come to terms with, first, why there was a conflict at all and, second, how he personally wanted to respond to this new situation. As the reconstructed life stories of becoming Irish in Chapter 8 made clear, many locals – such as Mairéad, Fíona, Pól and Pádraigín – interpreted this situation in terms of Irish people being ethnically oppressed for centuries by an external agent, the British state. This, in turn, foregrounded people's sense of Irishness and made many think about what it actually meant to be Irish. Finally, locals were forced to take sides in either being for or against the armed struggle or, as Stiofán put it, in attempting 'to be neither for it nor against it, trying to ignore it'. In short, for many locals the outbreak of the Troubles profoundly ethnicized everyday life by generally raising the practical relevance of Irishness. For some people, like Mairéad, Fíona and Pól, this process was inextricably linked with the Nationalist or even Republican project of politically unifying Ireland; for others, such as Pádraigín and, in an ambiguous sense, Micheál, the heightened relevance of individual Irishness drove them into a more ethnicist direction.

However, there was another possible reaction to growing ethnicization during the Troubles other than increasingly identifying with one's own Irishness, namely, developing an (ethnic) identity crisis. The section on Dónal's life story in Chapter 8 provided a powerful example of such an 'identity crisis' – as Dónal himself called it – poignantly illustrating how the strong alignment of Irishness with a politics of violence produced much suffering for those who vehemently refused to take sides and be counted (on) as 'Irish'. Such a crisis in ethnic identity positioned people 'between the lines' in two ways: it made people read 'between the lines' of hegemonic trauma narratives that were forcefully backed up by those with the guns and thereby dangerously placed them 'between the (front-)lines' of political war; no wonder that people like Dónal felt silenced and generally did not dare to speak about their feelings with other locals (see Zenker 2010). Given this atmosphere of silence possibly causing other locals not to talk to me about similar feelings, I find it hard to say how widespread such an ethnic identity crisis actually was in Catholic West Belfast. Yet whatever their frequency, it is clear that such crises constituted the necessary flip-side of an ever stronger and unproblematic identification with growing ethnicization during the Troubles in precisely experiencing as problematic this increasingly important sense of Irishness.

No Games, Just Sports?
Gaelic Games and the Playground of Catholic West Belfast

I now turn towards the first of the three exemplary cultural domains of Irishness, namely, to Gaelic games. I can thereby draw on Chapter 7 in which I extensively described this cluster of sports that includes Gaelic football and its female equivalent, ladies' Gaelic football, hurling and its female variant 'camogie', as well as rounders and Gaelic handball.

These Gaelic games are played between different clubs of the *Cumann Lúthchleas Gael* ('Gaelic Athletic Association' [GAA]) as well as of sister associations for the female games. The clubs – more than 2,500 in Ireland in 2004 – form the basic units of the GAA and are usually organized on a parish basis. At the next organizational level, the thirty-two County Boards run GAA affairs and club competitions within their respective counties. The four Provincial Councils in Ireland organize the Provincial Championships for clubs and counties and administer disciplinary matters within their respective jurisdictions. Finally, the GAA is run at the national level by the Central Council and its Management Committee, implementing rule changes and organizing the all-Ireland stages of the inter-county and inter-club championships (Sweeney 2004: 17–19).

As I showed in Chapter 7, Gaelic games were highly popular at the time of my fieldwork in 2003–2004, both in the Irish Republic and among Catholics in the North of Ireland, with the annual All-Ireland Senior Championships in Gaelic football and hurling having developed into major sporting events and public displays of national identity – to such an extent that since Partition, religious as well as political leaders in the South 'had to be seen at Croke Park on All-Ireland final days or else their credibility would be dented' (Cronin 1999: 89).

When looking into the history of Gaelic games, the founding of the GAA in 1884 conveniently offers itself as a starting point. On Saturday 1 November 1884, seven men (some sources speak of fourteen) met at Hayes's Commercial Hotel in Thurles, County Tipperary in order to found an organization with the name 'the Gaelic Athletic Association for the Preservation and Cultivation of our National Pastimes (GAAPCNP)'; within weeks this was abbreviated to 'the Gaelic Athletic Association (GAA)' (Gaelic Athletic Association 2008d). The driving force behind this meeting was Michael Cusack, an amateur athlete, sports enthusiast and Irish nationalist, who had prefaced the meeting with two letters to newspapers in which he had argued for the necessity of substantiating Irish nationalism with a distinctive 'Irish culture', including revived national games. Thus explicitly propagating an ethnicist project from the outset, Cusack had found support with Maurice Davin, who was one of the leading athletes at the time. Together, they brought about the meeting, which established an association with the express purpose of drafting rules for revived Irish athletics and pastimes, to open these activities to the ordinary man on the street and to protect them against the overwhelming influence of foreign games imported from England. The initial aim of the GAA was thereby to take over 'athletics', hence the organization's name. Yet hurling and Gaelic football – subsequently reinvented as standardized and codified spectator sports – soon outstripped athletics in popularity, eventually leading the GAA in 1922 to farm out athletics to a separate organization (Cronin 1999: 72–83; Sweeney 2004: 8–12; Gaelic Athletic Association 2008d).

The foundation of the Gaelic Athletic Association is to be seen in the context of the general upsurge of Irish ethnicism and nationalism of the late nineteenth century, typically referred to as the 'Irish-Ireland' movement or 'the Gaelic revival' (Hutchinson 1987). Douglas Hyde (1986), the first president of the Gaelic League, concisely argued for 'the necessity for de-Anglicizing Ireland' in a pamphlet of the same name in 1892. Various strands within the Gaelic revival, which also prominently included the Gaelic League (see Chapter 5), agreed with Hyde's sentiment, recognizing the need to revive and maintain a distinctive 'Irish culture' and identity. And like other Irish-Ireland organizations at the time, most notably, again, the Gaelic League, the GAA soon experienced the tensions between Irish ethnicism and nationalism (particularly physical-force Republicanism) within its own ranks. According to Bairner:

> In the early years of the GAA's existence, despite attempts by Cusack and others to ensure the involvement of all of the main strands of Irish nationalist opinion, the association quickly came under the control of the most revolutionary group within the nationalist camp at the time, namely the Irish Republican Brotherhood. (Bairner 2005: 194–95)

After a massive initial expansion, the GAA experienced a considerable decline throughout the 1890s, when the predominance of the Irish Republican Brotherhood (IRB) within this sporting body was met with fierce opposition by the Catholic Church. However, the influence of the IRB prevailed, and the GAA substantially grew again during the first decade of the twentieth century, establishing clubs in all thirty-two counties of Ireland (Mandle 1987: 91–165). Hence, '[b]y 1914 the GAA could claim to be the single most important institution (outside the Church) in the country, its place in Irish life and Irish nationalism assured' (Mandle 1979: 107).

While it is clear that the leadership of the GAA was strongly connected to the IRB and that GAA members were also prominently implicated in the Easter Rising of 1916, there is some controversy over the extent to which the GAA as an organization was really involved. While Mandle sees the role of the GAA as crucial, concluding that 'no organisation had done more for Irish nationalism than the GAA' (Mandle 1987: 221), this position is contested by Cronin, who rejects the idea that the GAA was 'the mass-based spiritual home of physical-force nationalism', suggesting instead that '[i]t is nationalist history, which has decreed the rank-and-file of the G.A.A. and the I.R.B. were indivisible, rather than any hard evidence' (Cronin 1999: 86, 87). Similar controversies also surround the rationale behind the introduction in the 1880s and early twentieth century of several bans that prohibited participation in 'foreign games', GAA membership for pro-British security forces and the use of GAA grounds for non-Gaelic games. While some, such as MacLua (1967), see the introduction of the bans as strongly driven by Irish nationalism, others, like Cronin (1999: 84–85), cite the organization's need to establish and protect itself against the contemporary dominance of other sporting bodies.

Be that as it may, in 1971 the first ban to go was Rule 27, which had barred GAA members from playing 'foreign games' such as soccer, rugby, hockey or cricket (Sweeney 2004: 14–15; see also Chapter 7). Next, in 2001, came the abolition Rule 21, which banned members of the British Army and the Northern Irish police force – the former Royal Ulster Constabulary (RUC) – from joining the GAA (Sweeney 2004: 15–16). Finally, Rule 42, preventing the use of GAA grounds for non-Gaelic games, still remains in place, although it was amended in 2005 to allow soccer and rugby to be played at Croke Park under certain circumstances. These developments, and especially the decision to abandon Rule 21 in 2001 immediately after the former pro-British RUC was reformed into the Police Service of Northern Ireland (PSNI), are indicative of a certain fission that emerged after Partition between the GAA in the South (and especially its central administration) and the Northern GAA. In the South, by the late 1920s the GAA 'had become a vital part of the institutional infrastructure of the fledging Irish Free State' (Sugden and Bairner 1993: 33). In contrast, for many members in the North, the GAA as an all-Ireland entity continued to represent 'a sporting manifestation of their political utopia' (Hassan 2003: 99) that was yet to be fulfilled. What is more, given the close alignment of cultural preferences and political orientations in the North, GAA members also came to suffer disproportionately from harassment by Northern security forces (see Fahy 2001), as was still the case in the early 1990s when Sugden and Bairner wrote:

> Surveillance of individual G.A.A. members, along with their clubs, is based on the premise that although they may be meeting for the purpose of sport, by their membership of the G.A.A. they have proclaimed a nationalist political preference. In this way their sporting involvement is viewed as a political statement. Thus, while sports such as hockey, rugby and soccer are largely ignored by soldiers, the G.A.A. constantly finds its activities disrupted by them. Disruption includes stopping and searching G.A.A. members travelling to and from games and meetings, raiding games in progress and the establishment of more permanent structures of vigilance, often involving the construction of army and police barracks on or adjacent to Gaelic pitches. (Sugden and Bairner 1993: 36)

Given that, in 2001, many Northern Catholics viewed the allegedly reformed police force, PSNI, as nothing but old sectarian wine in new egalitarian bottles, it is not surprising that out of the six northern counties, only County Down voted together with virtually all southern counties in favour of removing Rule 21 (Sweeney 2004: 16). Thus, despite the recently emergent revisionist metropolitanism of Dublin 4 – the postal district housing Dublin's political and media elite – which has distanced itself altogether from what has been depicted as the reactionary nationalism characteristic of the GAA as a whole (Doak 1998), there is, in fact, considerable divergence within the association. As Hassan sums it up: 'In essence it is this apparent tension between the sporting and business postmodernism of the GAA's central operation [in the South] and the parochial, amateur and identity-ridden GAA of Northern Ireland that most clearly defines the organization in modern times' (Hassan 2003: 107).

The reference to the revisionism of Dublin 4 foreshadows another important debate, namely, the one surrounding the historical origins of the games themselves. When describing the origins of hurling and Gaelic football, many observers note that both historical and mythical records for hurling matches date back long before Christendom, whereas a precursor of Gaelic football was played in Ireland for centuries (e.g. Mandle 1987: 15–17; Sugden and Bairner 1993: 24–25; Sweeney 2004: 7–8). Such a depiction of historical continuity clearly forms the basis on which the GAA rests, or, to put it differently, the whole notion of an ethnicist sports 'revival' necessarily presupposes the idea of continuity with the past.

However, this continuity has recently been contested by historical revisionists who dispute the historicity of Gaelic games and, following Hobsbawm and Ranger (1983), speak of an 'invention of tradition' (Cronin 1999: 70–116; Bairner 2005: 195). Cronin is most detailed in this critique, arguing that both the GAA and traditionalist historians have created the impression that there is a clear linkage between the games of Ireland's mythical past and those of the modern GAA. This can be easily illustrated for the GAA, when looking at its representation of hurling that I quoted in Chapter 7:

> Hurling is a game similar to hockey, in that it is played with a small ball and a curved wooden stick. It is Europe's oldest field game. When the Celts came to Ireland as the last ice age was receding, they brought with them a unique culture, their own language, music, script and unique pastimes. One of these pastimes was a game now called hurling. It features in Irish folklore to illustrate the deeds of heroic mystical figures and it is chronicled as a distinct Irish pastime for at least 2,000 years. (Gaelic Athletic Association 2008c)

According to Cronin, such a pretence of historical continuity with Ireland's ancient, heroic and mythical past stands in stark contrast to the realities of the late nineteenth century, when contemporary (mainly English) influences such as muscular Christianity and the emergence of modern regulatory sporting bodies ensured that, as a matter of fact, 'Gaelic games, at the time of their very inception were an invention' (Cronin 1999: 112).

Such historical revisionism has surely provided valuable insights into the complexity and various interactions between historical processes throughout the late nineteenth century (and beyond), calling into question simplistic representations of Gaelic games as unproblematic continuations of the Irish past. However, at least for the case of Gaelic games, there are also three main objections to such a line of reasoning. First, historical revisionists such as Cronin criticize traditionalist historians for their one-sided emphasis on 'historical continuity' and thereby silent engagement with nationalist identity politics by authenticating and legitimating ethnicist/nationalist discourses that evoke an unchanged past. Yet revisionists are often equally one-sided in inversely overemphasizing 'historical discontinuity'. In doing so, they likewise engage in identity politics, namely, in the anti-nationalist project of undermining and deconstructing ethnicist/nationalist discourses (see Doak 1998: 30–32 and Hassan 2003: 98–99 for a similar criticism).

Second, the topos of an 'invention of tradition' – so widespread in studies of ethnicity and nationalism – has it that nationalist actors are duped into believing that their 'cultural traditions' are very old and continuous with the past, while, in fact, 'we' social scientists and historians know better: these traditions are only of recent origin (see also Chapter 2). Yet, at least in the case of Gaelic games in Catholic West Belfast, this topos seems considerably misplaced. Rather than elaborating on an 'ancient tradition' of Gaelic games handed down from 'time immemorial', several of my informants (themselves hurlers and Gaelic footballers) told me exactly what I have just summarized as 'revisionism', namely, that Gaelic games were actually nationalist inventions of the late nineteenth century. Contrary to the typical topos of 'invented traditions', an astonishing number of my informants had read the same body of literature as I had, and several of them were much more 'revisionist' in their attitudes towards Gaelic games (and other cultural domains) than I was, and still were dedicated Irish ethnicists/nationalists.

To my mind, this latter observation is quite fascinating and leads me to a third criticism, namely, that 'traditions' are primarily discussed as depersonalized, collective phenomena. This creates a number of ultimately unanswerable questions: Which empirical phenomena count as 'old' rather than 'invented traditions'? How old is 'old'? How much continuity is necessary and how much change is tolerable for a practice to still qualify as 'truly' traditional? Rather than treating 'traditions' at this depersonalized, collective level, I prefer adopting Weber's understanding of the term in his discussion of orientations of actions (see Chapter 2): in this sense, 'traditionally' motivated practices do not have to be 'old' but merely to be 'determined by ingrained habituation' (Weber 1978: 24–25). According to this understanding, practices are thus 'traditional' when they are strongly motivated by habit, and as I will show below, such 'traditions' actually add considerable credibility to any plausibly constructed ethnicity.

Based on this general background information, I now turn to the question of how locals in Catholic West Belfast came into contact and then engaged to differing extents with Gaelic games from the 1950s onwards. An important structural context to begin with is the one constituted by family and friends. The reconstructed life stories in Chapter 8 thereby show a persistent pattern: many of my informants first were exposed to Gaelic games through their relatives and friends. Thus during the 1940s, Roibeárd was encouraged by his family to 'be like Uncle Jimmy' and to 'play for Antrim'. In the 1950s, both Mairéad and Micheál were socialized in 'GAA families', in which a parent (or both) had played for the county. Throughout the 1960s and 1970s, Pádraigín grew up knowing that her mother had played for the county even though her family seemed too occupied with Irish music to also cultivate Irish sports. Caoimhín recalled from his childhood in the 1980s and 1990s that it was 'hard to say, really', where he had first come into contact with Gaelic games ''cause it's all around you', yet he could remember how casually talking with school friends about these sports would have been common (see Chapter 8). Finally turning towards the ethnographic present that I experienced in Catholic West Belfast in 2003–2004, situations like the one described in the opening scene – when Daithi and his three-year-old nephew Cathal informally knocked a hurling ball back and forth alongside a hurling match – showed that enculturation into Gaelic games through family and friends continued in the present.

Yet, obviously not every family in Catholic West Belfast was a 'GAA family'. For many of those who did not encounter Gaelic games at home, first contact occurred at school. According to Hassan (1998), who did research on the role of Catholic schools in the promotion of Gaelic games, opportunities for sports have tended to be quite limited in a great number of schools in the North of Ireland, and the choice of which sport to play has been further bifurcated according to religious background: whilst state-run (de facto Protestant) schools have primarily offered rugby and soccer, Catholic schools have mainly engaged with Gaelic games, with many also offering soccer, while only a few Catholic grammar schools have recently started teaching rugby as well.

Against this backdrop, it is hardly surprising that most of my key informants – including Roibeárd, Rónán, Mairéad, Micheál, Dónal, Pól and Caoimhín (see Chapter 8) – encountered Gaelic games at school throughout the second half of the twentieth century. While thus constituting a prevalent pattern, this was obviously not without exceptions: in Pádraigín's 'Castle Catholic' grammar school in North Belfast in the late 1970s, her Protestant PE teacher taught hockey rather than Gaelic games, and Sinéad claimed that Gaelic games had not formed part of the curriculum at her schools in Catholic West Belfast in the 1970s and 1980s.

Besides school, a third structural context in which local Catholics engaged with Gaelic games obviously consisted of local GAA clubs. At the time of my fieldwork in 2003–2004, there was a total of fifteen such clubs in Catholic West Belfast. Local histories of individual GAA clubs echoed the broader developments of the association as outlined above: in a rapid response to the newly founded Gaelic Athletic Association, the first GAA clubs were set up in Belfast from 1885 onwards, but subsequent turmoil in the 1890s led to their disintegration before efforts to reorganize the GAA in Antrim began to yield results again in the early twentieth century (Antrim GAA – CLG Aontroim 2008). Hence, of the fifteen GAA clubs in West Belfast in operation at the time of my fieldwork, John Mitchel's Gaelic Athletic Club (GAC) was founded as the first in 1900. Other clubs followed suit such as Lámh Dhearg GAC (1903), Patrick Sarsfield's GAC (1906), Michael Davitt's GAC (1912) and O'Donovan Rossa GAC (1916). Up to the early 1950s, these clubs were joined by Cardinal O'Donnell's GAC (1927), St John's GAC (1929), Éire Óg GAC (1932), St Paul's GAC (1941) and St Agnes' GAC (1951), which ensured that by the time my oldest informants started playing Gaelic games as youngsters, most of the local clubs were already established. This is not to say that new GAA clubs did not emerge afterwards. Similarly, GAA clubs that existed for some time disintegrated or merged with other local clubs. However, the overall number of local GAA clubs seems to have stayed fairly constant over the past fifty years, as I was told by several former players.

Within this overarching club infrastructure, many of my informants had for some years played Gaelic games at a local club, including Roibeárd, Mairéad and Micheál. It would be easy to add many more people such as Daithi, who began his career as an active player in the 1960s and continued to play for several decades, or Stiofán, who played for a local club in the late 1960s and early 1970s and continued to be a fanatical supporter. However, an important change occurred within the GAA in the 1970s when the association modified its orientation towards youngsters. As Stiofán remembered:

> I started playing in school first. Again, things are better organized nowadays. When I was at primary school, there were no clubs for primary school kids, you know? Like, all my children started playing for a club when they were five or six. But in those days you didn't do that until you were in your teens.

Thus in recent decades, the older pattern whereby people first encountered Gaelic games at school before playing for a local GAA club has become inverted, leading to the present situation as described by Caoimhín in Chapter 8: 'People would be playing [in GAA clubs] since they were like five or six years old, playing all their life, them', so that by the time they get to secondary school they are already known as good players.

A final structural context that brought together and kept local Catholics in contact with Gaelic games was provided by the media. On 29 August 1926, the All-Ireland hurling semi-final between Kilkenny and Galway became the first match ever to be broadcast by the newly founded Irish State radio station 2RN, constituting the first radio commentary outside America on a field game (De Búrca 1999: 143). From 1932 onwards, when the signal began to be transmitted from Athlone in the Irish midlands, this public service radio, soon to be called *Radio Éireann*, could be received across the entire island. Gaelic games had been being broadcast over the Southern sound waves for decades when the new television service in the Irish Republic, *Telefís Éireann*, began to broadcast matches in the early 1960s. Initially, the annual coverage of live matches was restricted to 'the two All-Ireland finals, the two football semi-finals and the St Patrick's Day games' (De Búrca 1999: 198), but even this limited live broadcasting, together with the advent of television generally, produced a considerable decline in attendance at GAA matches throughout the 1960s and 1970s. However, since the late 1970s, increased live tele-broadcasts on the programme 'The Sunday Game' together with massively expanding sponsorship, GAA-related advertisements (as exemplified in Chapter 7) and merchandising of GAA products like county jerseys have led to the growing visibility, publicity and popularity of the GAA (De Búrca 1999: 197–200, 223, 229). This process has been particularly pronounced in the North of Ireland, where – as described above – Gaelic games were rather neglected by the mainstream media up until the 1980s. It is hence not surprising that while active GAA members such as Daithi described Gaelic games as having more or less stayed on the same level over the past decades, other informants who had not been heavily involved with the GAA (such as Pól) claimed that Gaelic games had recently expanded.

Turning to the question of why local Catholics have engaged with Gaelic games in West Belfast since the 1950s, one obvious reason consists in the explicitly ethnicist/nationalist programme of the GAA, which continues to represent itself as 'a National organisation which has as its basic aim the strengthening of the National Identity in a 32 County Ireland through the preservation and promotion of Gaelic Games and pastimes' (Gaelic Athletic Association 2003: 4). In other words, a value-rational motivation for wanting to maintain a distinctive 'Irish culture' through playing the 'Gaelic game' of identity politics immediately suggests itself. I am sure that there were many people in Catholic West Belfast who were so motivated, and the wish among some parents that their children should participate in these Irish sports, as well as the fixation in Catholic schools on Gaelic football, hurling and camogie, point in this direction.

On the other hand, however, the way in which virtually all of my informants actually talked about how they had (or had not) engaged with these games often told quite another story. This story – as we have seen in Chapter 8 – spoke of divergent personal preferences that made locals choose between various sports that were all-round in Catholic West Belfast including Gaelic games but also soccer (e.g. Rónán, Dónal, Pól and Caoimhín), boxing (e.g. Roibeárd), tennis (e.g. Mairéad) and netball (e.g. Mairéad). This story further spoke of different interests and abilities, which prevented some from engaging with Gaelic games in the first place, while causing others to end their GAA careers early. This story finally also spoke of the ambitions of players to be as successful as their relatives in playing for the county in the All-Ireland Championship. The following statement by Roibeárd, already quoted in Chapter 8, nicely encapsulates this:

> My grandfather played Gaelic football, great-grandfather played Gaelic football and my great-uncles played for County Down. You know, it was the thing to do. I've a second cousin playing for Down at the minute. And his grandfather played for County Down. So, you know, it's <u>tradition</u>.

Instead of (mis)interpreting this talk of 'tradition' in the depersonalized, collective sense of an 'old' practice, exhibiting unspoiled historical continuity, I prefer to see it in the light of Roibeárd's insistence that 'it was the thing to do' – that is, in terms of Weber's traditional motivation. In other words, local engagements with Gaelic games were, to my mind, also greatly motivated by the mere fact that they were simply 'all around you' and had hence predisposed successive generations to play them as well. To put it yet another way, Gaelic games in Catholic West Belfast were to a considerable extent also 'just sports', which locals – depending on their personal interests, abilities and ambitions – were very likely to engage with habitually.

'If you feel like singing, do sing an Irish song': Irish Music in Catholic West Belfast

Through codifying and mass-popularizing Gaelic games, the GAA created a broad consensus as to what constituted 'Gaelic games' in the first place. In the absence of a single, equally accepted institution for 'Irish music', definitions of this musical genre are more diverse, varying not only between people but sometimes also over time for the same person. In Chapter 8, I described how Roibeárd, Rónán and Micheál initially came into contact with certain 'Irish songs' in the English language, only to later learn that 'true' Irish traditional music, both in Irish and in English, was 'actually' something different. In this section, I take a pragmatic stance, sidestepping such debates on authenticity and rather treating any music as 'Irish' that was represented as such by my informants.

This hence somewhat controversial cluster of songs and tunes usually referred to as 'Irish music' or 'traditional music' (Ó hAllmhuráin 1998: 9) exhibits a number of prototypical characteristics such as being largely inherited from the past, being aurally and orally transmitted by example rather than by formal teaching, originating from 'the people', especially in rural areas, rather than from identified authors, and comprising a multiplicity of versions for well-known tunes. Having said that, there are also rather recent pieces in this genre, much 'traditional music' has been transcribed by collectors since the eighteenth century, many songs and tunes have been deliberately composed by 'authors' and distributed as sheet music, broadsides and pamphlets, and much of 'Irish music' has also been disseminated through radio, records, stage performances and, later on, television and CDs (Irish Traditional Music Archive 1999; Ó hAllmhuráin 1998: 8). This observation highlights that the broad category of 'Irish music' includes both music that more or less displays the aforementioned prototypical characteristics of 'traditional music' and other pieces that simply conform to the musical style, idiom and aesthetics of this 'tradition' independently of their age, mode of transmission or origin (Ó Canainn 1978: 1).

Generally speaking, Irish music consists of 'three interlocking traditions', namely, instrumental music, songs in Irish and songs in English (Ó hAllmhuráin 1998: 9). According to the Irish Traditional Music Archive, the bulk of Irish instrumental music:

> is fast isometric dance music – jigs, reels and hornpipes for the most part; slower listening pieces composed for an instrument or adapted from song airs form only a small proportion. Melodies are generally played in one or two sharps, and belong to one of a number of melodic modes, which have mostly seven notes on the scale, but sometimes six or five. Their range does not frequently exceed two octaves, and they end on a variety of final notes. The dance music has associated solo and group dances. (Irish Traditional Music Archive 1999: 403)

Jigs are typically in 6/8 time, whereas reels and hornpipes are played in 4/4 time. These dance tunes usually comprise two eight-bar segments, each of which is played twice through, with the whole sequence being repeated twice (or thrice) before moving on to the next tune (Ó hAllmhuráin 1998: 10). Wind, string and free-reed instruments prevail, especially flute, tin whistle, uilleann pipes, fiddle, concertina and accordion, with percussion instruments being of only minor importance, while the guitar is considered somewhat controversial (Irish Traditional Music Archive 1999: 403).

Besides Irish instrumental music, which is sometimes (also derogatorily) called 'diddle-de-dee music', the Irish song tradition is characterized by Ireland's bilingual legacy. Irish songs in the Irish language are particularly associated with *sean-nós* ('old style') singing, a style developed over the centuries in Irish-speaking Ireland and Gaelic-speaking Scotland, persisting with stylistic variations in different Gaeltacht regions (Mac Con Iomaire 1999). Ó hAllmhuráin characterizes the art of sean-nós as:

> an unaccompanied form of singing which demands tremendous skill and artistic understanding. It derives in part from the bardic tradition of professional poetry which declined in the seventeenth century. There is no display of emotion or dramatics in *sean nós*. The singer is expected to vary each verse using improvisation, an implicit music skill which requires subtle changes in rhythm, ornamentation and timbre. (Ó hAllmhuráin 1998: 11–12)

While older than Irish songs in the English language, the latter have become more widespread (Irish Traditional Music Archive 1999: 403). Traces of the transition from Irish-medium to English-medium songs can still be found in bilingual macaronic songs that grew in popularity especially throughout the nineteenth century (Ó Muirithe 1999: 356). Songs in English were thereby introduced by English or Scottish settlers and Irish migrant workers, or written by local (Anglo-) Irish people whose mother tongue was English. Evoking a broad range of moods – sentimental, rabble-rousing, comical, etc. – these Irish songs in English cover numerous themes including love, courtship, emigration, praise of place, nationalist politics (especially in rebel songs) and many other topics of human interest (Ó hAllmhuráin 1998: 12).

A brief run through some of the history of Irish music may help to develop a clearer picture of its various subcategories and their respective historical interrelations. For this purpose, a convenient entry point seems to be the Belfast Harp Festival of 1792, as it constituted one of the first conscious antiquarian attempts to resuscitate as 'Irish music' the atrophying, patron-based harp music of the old Gaelic aristocracy. During this festival, a young organist from Armagh – Edward Bunting – was hired to notate tunes from the musicians. Deeply impressed by this experience, Bunting devoted much of his remaining life to collecting and publishing Irish music. These collections formed the basis of a subsequent introduction of the native repertoire into the Anglophone world, most prominently by Thomas Moore. Moore moved to Britain in the late eighteenth century and began to adapt tunes from Bunting to his own lyrics in English. His pieces were published as 'Irish Melodies' in ten volumes between 1808 and 1834. These parlour songs, performed in salons by singers and pianists, were tremendously successful in their romantic but politically harmless lamentations for a defeated culture and created an instantly recognizable Anglophone form of 'Irishness' (Ó Laoire 2005: 268–71; White 1999: 407).

During the 1840s, the political songwriters of the Young Ireland movement radicalized Moore's approach, producing vigorously political ballads (including the still popular rebel song 'A Nation Once Again'), which they published in their widely read newspaper *The Nation* (McCann 1995: 57; Ó Laoire 2005: 274). Besides such politicization, the new genre of Irish songs in English was further popularized from the mid-nineteenth century onwards on the stage. Many Irish popular songs – loved by some, disregarded by others – were specifically written for stock Irish characters in American 'vaudeville' theatrical entertainments and British 'music halls', the popularity of which only declined in the mid-twentieth century. These and many other Irish songs in English were disseminated, for instance, by the Walton Music Firm, which published sheet music in highly popular songsters and anthologies beginning in the 1920s. In 1952, this Dublin-based firm began recording singers for its new Glenside record label and broadcast these recording artists on Radio Éireann on the weekly fifteen-minute 'The Walton's Programme' on Saturday afternoons (Ó hAllmhuráin 1998: 101–8; Carolan 2004). Finally, the emergence in the USA of the Irish ballad-group The Clancy Brothers (and Tommy Makem), who – belting out Irish songs with gusto in their Aran sweaters – provided a fresh take on Irish music that was highly successful in the USA and then Ireland, further set the scene for Irish songs in English in Catholic West Belfast from the late 1950s onwards (Vallely 1999d).

During the nineteenth century, when Irish songs in English rapidly expanded, songs in Irish also continued to be written and performed by poet-singers. As Ó Laoire (2005: 272) observes, their work 'remained locally popular, surviving the Famine, but because of their lack of wide access to print culture, was largely unknown outside their own communities until the later Gaelic revival at the end of the century'. The low profile of songs in Irish was further due to the fact that the antiquarian interests of Bunting, Moore and others in 'Irish music' focused on old melodies but generally set them to new English texts. It was only from Patrick Weston Joyce's 'Irish song and music' (1888) onwards that both original tunes and lyrics were preserved (White 1999: 407–8).

Interest in songs in Irish was reinvigorated during the Gaelic revival of the late nineteenth century. The Gaelic League was here at the forefront, promoting not only the Irish language but also Irish music and dancing (McCarthy 1999: 72–78). The League celebrated the 'old Irish style' of singing in the Gaeltacht that soon came to be called *sean-nós*, while somewhat dismissing Moore's 'Irish melodies' as an Anglo-Irish embarrassment (Ó Laoire 2005: 275–76). In 1897, the Gaelic League was related to the establishment of two annual festivals, *An tOireachtas* ('The Assembly') and *Feis Cheoil* ('Festival of Music'). The Oireachtas has functioned since as the annual Gaelic League festival, featuring various competitions in the Irish language, instrumental music, song and dance, with *sean-nós* singing being the most prestigious competition today (Vallely 1999c). The Feis Cheoil also consisted of various musical competitions and continues to be open to non-traditional performers like it was in the beginning. The early emphasis on Irish instrumental music disappeared by the 1920s, however, thereafter turning this *feis* into a largely non-traditional festival (Vallely 1999a).

As we will see in the next section, the Gaelic League was also behind the reinvention of traditional Irish group dancing – the so-called céilí dances – that became very popular at the turn of the twentieth century (Ó hAllmhuráin 1998: 97). This had consequences for Irish traditional music as well: hitherto, Irish dance music was performed individually by a single musician, however, the new céilí dances were played for larger audiences, thus necessitating louder volume and hence ensemble playing. This was the birth of so-called 'céilí bands' that started to spread throughout Ireland from the 1920s onwards. Céilí bands reached their zenith in the 1950s and 1960s, when famous groups such as the McCuskers from Armagh or the McPeakes from West Belfast toured the USA and performed at New York's Carnegie Hall and the White House. But the emergence of semi-pop, electric-guitar-based 'showbands' in the 1960s as well as the outbreak of the Troubles in the North eclipsed this commercial form of ensemble playing, while a more recent idea, namely, playing instrumental music for listening rather than dancing, created another institution of Irish music: the pub 'session' (Vallely 1999g; Hamilton 1999).

This new idea of playing for listening was intimately bound up with yet another round of Irish music revival that has taken place since the mid-twentieth century. In prior decades, Irish instrumental music had somewhat fallen into neglect in the South, as the Public Dance Halls Act (1935) broke the link between local music-making and social dance (see next section), while non-traditional music was achieving a higher profile through records, radio and the above-mentioned Feis Cheoil. Against this backdrop, a group of traditional musicians set up *Comhaltas Ceoltóirí Éireann* ('Gathering of Ireland's Musicians') in 1951 as an organization promoting Irish traditional music, especially through its annual All-Ireland competition in instrumental music, song and dance – the *Fleadh Cheoil* ('Festival of Music') – which has subsequently developed into a premier event in Ireland's musical calendar (Ó hAllmhuráin 1998: 144–46).

This new impetus gained further momentum in the 1960s through Seán Ó Riada, who is 'widely regarded as one of the most influential figures in Irish music in the second half of the twentieth century in terms of public appeal' (Ó Laoire 2005: 279). As a composer, arranger, academic and musician, Ó Riada profoundly modernized the image of Irish music, through, amongst other things, composing highly acclaimed film scores that featured his orchestra *Ceoltóirí Chualann* ('Musicians of Cualann'). In contrast to contemporary céilí bands, Ó Riada introduced this group of traditional musicians 'to classical-style arrangements, harmonies, improvisation, and dress suits – all of which helped to place their rural art on a par with other "socially correct" art forms in urban Ireland' (Ó hAllmhuráin 1998: 148–49). Ceoltóirí Chualann became the Chieftains, which was to become one of the most successful Irish traditional bands worldwide. In addition, Ó Riada also broadcast a Radio Éireann series in 1962 entitled 'Our Musical Heritage', in which he renewed public interest in Irish music through situating it in an original 'world-music' context (Ó Laoire 2005: 279–80; Ó hAllmhuráin 1998: 147–50).

In the 1960s, Irish music thus generally experienced a revival of sorts, even though various strands within the music scene to some degree accused others of being 'unauthentic', 'vulgar' or 'snooty'. Irish instrumental music thrived within

Comhaltas Ceoltóirí Éireann, in Ó Riada's 'high art' performances and, though diminishingly so, through céilí bands. Irish ballads in the English language continued to be popular through radio and records, especially in the somewhat rejuvenated form of the Clancy Brothers and the Dubliners. At the same time, a more internationalized focus on 'folk music' within Great Britain and the USA spilled over to Ireland, including the North, creating a cross-community interest among younger Belfast generations in the 'pure' traditions of unaccompanied singing in English and Irish, which – while leaning to the political left – excluded rebel songs as 'unauthentic' and generally remained silent about local politics (McCann 1995; Vallely 1999b). This broad variety of musical strands was not only to provide a springboard for future artists such as the Chieftains, Planxty, Clannad, Enya, Christy Moore and Altan, but also set the scene for local Catholics in West Belfast to encounter and engage with Irish music from the mid-twentieth century onwards.

Turning towards the more specific question of how locals came into contact and engaged with Irish music in Catholic West Belfast, the structural context of family and friends is again of great importance. Virtually all of my informants recalled how they had come into contact with Irish music (in addition to other types of music) in their families. As we saw in Chapter 8, in many families it was a common thing to sing. Records and later CDs also constituted an important means of exposing subsequent generations to Irish and other varieties of music. Finally, several families – such as Roibeárd's and Pádraigín's (see Chapter 8) – themselves played instrumental music.

Another important structural context for the inculcation of Irish music consisted in the media. In the early 1950s, Radio Éireann in the South broadcast a number of successful series featuring traditional music collected in the field such as 'A Job of Journey Work' or 'The Long Note' (Ó Laoire 2005: 277). Yet, arguably the biggest impact in shaping people's sense of 'Irish music' was the above-mentioned 'Walton's Programme', which was broadcast on Saturday afternoons for twenty-nine years from 1952 until Radio Telefís Éireann (RTÉ) ended all externally sponsored programmes in 1981. According to Carolan:

> Many Irish people over 40, whether they live at home or abroad, will recognise with a certain ruefulness what was once the most famous sentence in Irish music: "And remember: if you feel like singing ... do sing an Irish song". From 1952 to 1981 it was the sign-off sentence of one of Ireland's best-known broadcasters, the late Leo Maguire of Dublin, who presented on Radio Éireann, Irish national radio, a weekly live programme of Irish popular music, "your weekly reminder of the grace and beauty that lie in our heritage of Irish song, the songs our fathers loved". ... In memory, the programmes are imbued with the Saturday afternoon lassitude of that placid, politically uncomplicated and far-off time, before weekends had been invented. ... The radio programme, the records, and the voice of their presenter Leo Maguire, soon became a fixed part of the round of the week in pre-television Ireland, embedded in the national consciousness. (Carolan 2004: 1, 2, 4)

After television was introduced, RTÉ continued to broadcast Irish traditional music and songs on weekly programmes like 'Céilí House', which has been on the air for more than forty years (Radio Telefís Éireann 2008). As previously mentioned, the situation was somewhat different in the North of Ireland, where the BBC avoided material that might be seen as challenging Britishness. But as Ó Laoire notes:

> Matters improved with the appointment of Andrew Stewart in 1948, a seasoned BBC broadcaster, who oversaw the broadcast of the legendary series "As I Roved Out" in 1951. By 1967, when a Clancy Brothers' concert heralding the arrival of BBC2 was held in the Ulster Hall, the reception was unanimously enthusiastic, leading to a series with the group. (Ó Laoire 2005: 277–78)

Nevertheless – as we saw in Chapter 4 – it was not yet possible even at that time for Roibeárd to perform songs in Irish on Northern television, whereas he did end up moderating (and singing on) a television programme in the South for three years, which featured all of the upcoming Irish traditional bands including the Chieftains and Clannad.

Schools provided a third structural context for Irish music. Many of my informants remembered how they learnt English-medium 'Irish songs', including rebel songs, in their primary and secondary schools. A persistent feature of music lessons also seems to have been the exposure to some instrumental music and the necessity of trying to play the tin whistle, as both Sinéad and Caoimhín could vividly remember, while certain schools – like Pádraigín's – even had their own 'traditional music groups'. Closely related was another structural context with some relevance for Irish music, namely, the Gaeltacht colleges. Many of my informants who attended such summer colleges as pupils, recalled that learning and singing songs in Irish formed an important part of their daily routine, especially in afternoon classes. Back in West Belfast, the structural context of Irish-language organizations, including the Árdscoil and the Cumann Chluain Árd, further ensured exposure to Irish music through the teaching and singing of Irish-medium songs in the Cluain Árd, as well as through weekly céilís that were danced to Irish instrumental music. This indirect contact with instrumental music through Irish dancing also took place – as we will see in the next section – in schools of Irish dancing and at céilís in local parish halls of the Catholic Church.

Another context in which instrumental music and especially Irish songs in the English language figured prominently was the GAA. As Roibeárd mentioned in Chapter 8, each county was associated with its own song in English, like 'The Green Glens of Antrim' for County Antrim (encompassing Belfast) – and 'you would be used to singing these county songs at matches'.

So far, I have concentrated on those structural contexts that, despite some internal variation, were fairly steady over the past several decades in bringing people into contact with Irish music. Yet wider developments in youth culture and politics also engendered specific changes within other structural contexts beginning in the 1960s. The upsurge of interest in 'Irish music' at that time has to be seen as part of a wider 'modernization' process that also brought about other forms of 'modern' entertainment like ballroom dancing, rock 'n' roll and jiving in big dancehalls such as the Plaza in the city centre or the Jig in West Belfast. This 'modernization' also meant – as Micheál put it – that some aspects of 'Irish culture' such as the Irish language became increasingly 'associated with very old-fashioned ideas about Irishness from the turn of the century'. Thus, when Micheál became interested in Anglo-Irish literature, the Irish language and Irish music in the 1960s, of these only traditional music was fashionable at the time. That Irish music was a fashion at all seems to be related to the fact that its image had become strongly modernized by Seán Ó Riada, by internationally acclaimed bands like the Clancy Brothers and by a globalizing folk scene that politically linked up with contemporary Civil Rights, workers' rights and peace movements in the USA and elsewhere.

While Irish music thus had its place in the 1960s in pubs and social clubs like the Pike Folk Club that Micheál frequented (see Chapter 8), this latter structural context was not left unchanged by the outbreak of the Troubles. In Chapters 4 and 8, Dónal described how the city centre had constituted Belfast's entertainment hub, whilst local areas hardly offered entertainment opportunities. This was to change dramatically once the violence began, as 'people tended to then associate with their own local areas rather than have to take the risk of walking into town or not getting home or maybe a bomb going off'. With people staying in their areas and lacking effective policing, numerous illegal drinking dens – so-called 'shebeens' (anglicized from the Irish word 'síbín') – sprang up in Catholic West Belfast, which together with Republican social clubs were 'at the heart of things', as Fíona put it in Chapter 8. In these places, Irish music became a dominant form of entertainment, yet in its rebel-song variety rather than in the recently popular 'folk' tradition:

> The emerging republican nationalist movement expressed its anger, sorrow, aspirations, and increasing resistance, in the traditional mode of political balladry. From Belfast and other affected areas, songs poured forth into the street and into the clubs and pubs. A whole nationalist repertoire dating back as far as the 1798 rebellion became available to those unfamiliar with it. New songs were written daily, about each news-worthy incident. The composers were often local people, more or less musically trained. Local groups sprang up to perform songs and the local recording studio produced recordings of those same people and groups. Performance venues was [sic] frequently dominated by floor-singers. (McCann 1995: 72)

Using the example of Dónal and Fíona, I described in Chapter 8 how such local performances of rebel songs by Irish folk bands looked during the Troubles, both on stage, where the IRA would regularly make sudden appearances, and from the auditorium, where 'you wanted to be part of it' as 'it fired your blood' (Fíona). At the same time, Irish instrumental music also continued to be played – be it in pub sessions in which Pádraigín became heavily involved in the 1980s or within the new structural context of schools of music in West Belfast such as the Francis McPeake School of Music, founded in 1977 by members of the McPeake family (Francis McPeake School of Music 2008).

Several of my informants noted that when Belfast opened up again in the course of the peace process in the 1990s, local entertainment both diversified and to some degree returned to the city centre, which led to some degree of decline in Irish music. As Fíona described in Chapter 8, other forms of entertainment such as discotheques entered the realm of Republican clubs like the Felons, which before this point was 'all Republican and traditional [music]'. This observation was confirmed by a leading figure in this Republican club, who told me that while there had been 'a lot of folk music, music of war, rebel songs' in the 1970s and 1980s, there was 'more disco, pop, more modern music' since around the mid-1990s. According to this informant, Irish music had since then 'run out', and if the Felons club had not changed to meet the tastes of its young clientele, it would have had to close down. Thus, during the ethnographic present of 2003–2004, teenagers like Caoimhín would go out on weekends and hit some local bars, clubs and discotheques, while Irish music – in the absence of violent conflict – had apparently turned mainly into an issue of personal taste.

Turning to the question of what had driven local Catholics over the past fifty years to variously engage with Irish music, a number of affectual motivations can be observed. As Dónal described it in Chapter 8, 'just the beauty on its own of the music' moved him emotionally and became 'a big driver' for his lifelong involvement. Others were captivated by the emotional bonding – the 'incredible atmosphere' and the 'real sense of belonging' of which Rónán spoke in Chapter 8 that was created through actually making this music together with relatives and friends, be it during sing-songs, sessions or band performances. Finally, many also had a strong emotional identification with the content of Irish songs (mostly in English) as locals 'knew the meaning of them' (Rónán) and since this type of music 'was about you, about your family, about your race, about your neighbours' (Mairéad).

Besides these emotional reasons for making (and listening to) Irish music, some locals were also motivated on more instrumentally rational grounds. Thus, Roibeárd had primarily wanted to improve his Irish language, and when he realized that 'the best Irish was in the poetry of Ireland, which was generally set to music', he decided to collect and learn songs in Irish. Another instrumentally rational motivation – namely, the need to earn money – was behind Dónal's initial decision to play 'rebel material' in clubs and shebeens in West Belfast, even though this went against his principles.

This leads to another quite specific cluster of affectual, value-rational and instrumentally rational motivations that were apparently relevant, especially at the height of the Troubles when rebel songs were a staple of local musical consumption. Within the context of ongoing conflict, these political songs (affectively) expressed and evoked strong feelings of anger, sorrow and hope; (value-rationally) represented – and thereby preserved, as a end in itself – knowledge about acts of injustice by the

British state and heroic deeds of Irish people; and could simultaneously be used (in an instrumentally rational way) as a means of mobilizing resistance among local Catholics.

These and other motivations evidently played a role. Yet it is my contention that underneath these variable reasons, there was also a strong traditional motivation for engaging with Irish music. Virtually all of my informants were heavily predisposed to some practical involvement through exposure to this music in numerous contexts: within their networks of relatives and friends, through the media, in schools, Gaeltacht colleges, Irish-language organizations, schools of Irish dancing, Catholic parish halls, the GAA, pubs and social clubs, as well as in schools of music. The practice of Irish music in Catholic West Belfast to my mind additionally entailed a strong element of habituation, or, to put it differently, various engagements with Irish music were to a considerable extent also a matter of taste – a taste based on a 'habitus' (Bourdieu 1984) prevalent for much of the second half of the twentieth century in Catholic West Belfast and ensuring that many people would often, though not always, sing an Irish song whenever they felt like singing.

Knowing How to Do your Sevens:
Dancing to the Tune of Irishness in Catholic West Belfast

Comparable to the field of Gaelic games and somewhat in contrast to the cultural domain of Irish music, there is some broad consensus as to what constitutes 'Irish dancing' in its several variants, and this relative conformity is largely due – as we will see below – to the Gaelic League. Irish dances can be divided, first, into solo and group dances. Irish solo dancing is typically referred to as 'step dancing', which – massively popularized worldwide through the show 'Riverdance' and its sequels – is typically learnt in schools of Irish dancing by children 'as young as 4 years of age but 6 or 7 is more the norm' (Whelan 2000: 31) and which is then primarily performed in competitions. Like all Irish dances, step dancing is done to Irish instrumental music usually comprising two eight-bar segments (see above). Each step dance consists of a number of movements strung together into an eight-bar choreographic structure that is asymmetrically repeated and called a 'step' – hence the name of this type of dancing (Brennan 1999: 63; Foley 1999: 380). In terms of body posture, step dancing is characterized by moving only from the hips downward, with quick, precise leg movements and an emphasis on elaborate footwork, while the upper body and the arms are kept straight and largely stationary (Breathnach 1971: 55–56). Step dancing is thereby either done as a light dance with soft shoes (e.g. the light jig) or as a heavy dance with hard shoes beating out the rhythm (e.g. the hornpipe) (Whelan 2000: 25). During competitions or public performances, Irish step dancers typically wear intricate costumes, especially the girls, with their ornately embroidered dresses, and wigs with 'bouncing curls' (Wulff 2007: 91), while boys wore kilts from about the 1920s until relatively recently, when dancing shows such as Riverdance turned black trousers into an accepted male costume (Brennan 1999: 151; Whelan 2000: 37–38).

Besides this form of solo dancing, there are also two types of Irish group dances, namely, 'céilí dances' and 'set dances'. The term 'céilí dancing' uses the Irish word '*céilí*', which now carries three different meanings: first, it denotes a social visit as described in the opening scene to this chapter; second, it indicates a social dance event, sometimes also involving songs and performances; and third, it refers to this specific type of dance (Vallely 1999e). Céilí dances are group dances that, being taught in schools of Irish dancing and in special céilí clubs, are performed in competitions as well as at céilís, the previously mentioned social dance events. They are somewhat 'formal and formulaic' (Ó hAllmhuráin 1998: 97) and structured on a few basic steps – the side step or 'the sevens' as described by Roibeárd in Chapter 8, the two short threes, the promenade step, the rising step, and the rise and grind – which combine into various figures that make up different formations such as round dances, long line dances and long column dances (Whelan 2000: 26–27).

The second type of Irish group dancing is called 'set dancing', which in its many localized forms ultimately derives from the French 'quadrille' and hence constitutes 'a combination of Irish dancing steps and French dance movements, danced to Irish music' (Murphy 1999: 346). According to Boullier:

> The Quadrilles were and still are danced by four couples facing each other in a square. This formation is called a 'set'. Each traditional set dance is arranged into a number of separate dances called figures. In the set of Quadrilles there are six figures. Each figure varies in length, usually three or four minutes. Modern set dancing is a continuation of the Quadrilles. (Boullier 1998: 21)

Set dances are usually performed by 'sets' of four couples, hence the name, but they can also be adapted into 'half sets' in which only two couples dance together (Breathnach 1971: 49). Since set dances are not part of the standardized curriculum in schools of Irish dancing, are not promoted by a single country-wide organization and prevail in social rather than competitive contexts, there is much regional variation in this less-rigidly performed dance style, and many sets are named after their local town or area of origin (Murphy 1999: 347).

A short excursion into the history of Irish dance may rightfully begin with the travelling dancing masters of the late eighteenth century, as all three of today's dancing types can be traced back to them. First mentioned by the English geographer Arthur Young in 1780 (Ó hAllmhuráin 1998: 57), these dancing masters formed part of everyday life in Ireland up until the mid-twentieth century, and even some of my informants recalled how they had still come across the travelling dancing master Ducky Mallon at céilís in the 1960s. Back in the eighteenth century, such dancing masters used to travel in the company of a piper or a fiddler in somewhat circumscribed territories, staying in different communities, typically for six weeks at a time. Lodging in a farmer's house and using a barn or the kitchen for teaching the steps, the host's children were usually not charged, while other participants from the local community had to pay. Often somewhat whimsical figures, teaching not only native and foreign dances but sometimes also deportment and fencing, the dancing masters created their own steps for solo dances, which they taught to their best pupils for virtuoso performances, as well as for group dances that required less disciplined footwork (Breathnach 1971: 51–56; Brennan 1999: 45–62).

During the early nineteenth century, soldiers returning from the Napoleonic Wars brought the French quadrille sets to Ireland, yet it was again the dancing masters who not only adopted these dances but also adapted them to local tunes, musical tempo and steps. Breathnach provides a nice summary of this transformation:

> Quadrilles were tremendously popular in the Paris of Napoleon. The victorious armies of Wellington became familiar with them and later introduced them to England and Ireland. The then Knight of Glin, it is said, ordered the dancing masters of the district to teach the new dances as they were performed in France and Spain. The dancing masters, however, adapted these dances by substituting native steps for the ballroom steps and by speeding up the time to that of the jig and common reel. Thus naturalised, the sets of quadrilles … spread throughout the country and maintained their popularity for over a hundred years. (Breathnach 1971: 48–49)

Besides these sets as well as other locally invented or absorbed figure dances, the most popular forms to emerge in the nineteenth century were 'the ballroom dances such as the schottische, the barndance, the military two-step and the waltz, which became part of the dance practice of all classes of society' (Brennan 1999: 28).

However, this bricolage-type appropriation of many different influences into the culture of dancing in Ireland was to become problematic during the Gaelic revival of the late nineteenth century when the ethnicist preservation of 'Irish culture' and hence the 'Irishness' of dancing suddenly became a primary concern. Like with Irish music, again the Gaelic League could not confine itself to matters of the Irish language, additionally becoming a key player in 'Irish dancing'. Initially though, this was a rather coincidental development that evolved in London, where a Gaelic League branch soon flourished after the foundation of the organization in 1893. Besides offering language classes, some of its members felt that their activities lacked a social dimension, especially after attending Scottish evenings in London that were run under the name 'céilí'. They decided to use the same term for a London social evening based on the structure of the Scottish evenings, and the first Irish 'céilí' was held on 30 October 1897 (Vallely 1999e). As the knowledge of 'truly' Irish dances was limited among attendees, sets, quadrilles and waltzes were danced. In order to change this deplorable situation, Patrick Reidy, a London dance master familiar with non-quadrille figure dances from his native County Kerry, was subsequently employed. Members of the London branch also travelled to West Cork and Kerry in order to collect such figure dances, which were published in two books, *A Handbook of Irish Dances* by O'Keefe and O'Brien

(1902) and *A Guide to Irish Dancing* by Sheehan (1902). These new 'céilí dances' were performed by the London branch at the 1901 Oireachtas of the Gaelic League and soon were being taught in other branches in conjunction with Irish step dance. However, enthusiasm for these céilí dances, which were propagated as 'truly Irish' whilst sets came to be seen as 'foreign' and improper, was not shared by all members of the Gaelic League. In the early 1900s, a fierce debate raged within the organization as to which dances were acceptable as 'Irish', thus leading to the establishment of a committee responsible for investigating the origins of various dances. Ultimately, however, céilí dances prevailed, and 'un-Irish' dances including the sets were progressively banned at Gaelic League céilís (Ó hAllmhuráin 1998: 96–98; Brennan 1999: 29–43; Cullinane 1999).

By the late 1920s, the Gaelic League was involved not only in running Irish dance competitions but had also set up its own schools of Irish dancing. However, there were still many irregularities in competitions, which led the Gaelic League to establish *An Coimisiún le Rincí Gaelacha* ('The Irish Dancing Commission') (Brennan 1999: 38–39; Whelan 2000: 43–44). According to Ó hAllmuráin:

> The Commission formally codified Irish dancing as a competitive process in 1930. It was formed to exercise control over local as well as national competitions. It also sanctioned all open competitions, authenticated students, certified teachers and authorised adjudicators, so that the same standards were adhered to throughout the Irish dancing world. As well as regulating solo and group dances, the Commission laid down precise rules for national dance costumes, along with the 'proper' type of music and rhythm required for its dancers. Inevitably, set dancers continued to sin in their limbo of 'foreign dancing', well beyond the fold of this new commission. (Ó hAllmhuráin 1998: 125–26)

The commission, which continues to operate under the auspices of the Gaelic League, also collected and standardized céilí dances in *Ár Rinncídhe Fóirne* ('Our Figure Dances'), which was published in three parts in 1939, 1943 and 1969, and defines the movements permissible in céilí dance competitions (Cullinane 1999; Foley 1999: 380).

Given 'the Ban' in the Gaelic League and its Irish Dancing Commission, according to which anyone caught participating in dancing other than Irish could be expelled from an Irish dance class or barred from attending Gaelic League céilís (Vallely 1999f: 101; Whelan 2000: 29), it is not surprising that set dancing experienced a considerable blow during the first half of the twentieth century. The situation for set dancing was further aggravated by the fact that informal social dances in rural areas, which had been held as 'house dances' in people's kitchens and barns, or open-air at crossroads during summer (Brennan 1999: 103–19), became increasingly suppressed in the Irish Free State when the Catholic Church and the state joined forces. For a long time, the clergy had been implacably opposed to gatherings of mixed gender for the purpose of dancing, as these meetings were seen as leading to the occasion of sin. During the heyday of clerical opposition in the 1920s, massive condemnations focused particularly on privately run dance halls and non-Irish dances – partly out of nationalism but partly also because the latter involved more permanent physical contact than step and céilí dancing (Brennan 1999: 121–33; Whelan 2000: 15–17). After strong pressure from the clergy, the Southern state introduced the Public Dance Halls Act (1935):

> which confined the holding of dances to halls licensed for such a purpose and which imposed a government tax on the admission price. All over rural Ireland, the clergy organised the construction of parochial halls, and thereafter Church and state combined to eliminate the organisation of any dances outside these halls. (Brennan 1999: 125–26)

This law had the effect of not only nearly wiping out informal house dances and crossroad céilís but also of severing the link between local music-making and social dance (see above), as professional céilí bands came to perform at licensed halls, whilst other instrumental musicians could no longer play at private dances (Whelan 2000: 16–17). Allegedly 'foreign' dances such as sets together with their informal dance events hence went into decline, while céilí dancing in licensed dance halls became very popular in most parts of Ireland, with some massive venues in Dublin and Belfast attracting more than a thousand dancers per night (McCann 1983: 63; Ó hAllmhuráin 1998: 137; Whelan 2000: 27). As described above in the music section, céilí dancing has also declined since the late 1960s, a development related to the emergence of showbands and alternative, more 'modern' forms of entertainment as well as, in the North, the outbreak of the Troubles (Whelan 2000: 27).

Around the same time, however, there were also the first signs of a set-dancing revival, which was facilitated, somewhat surprisingly, by the GAA. As mentioned in Chapter 5, the GAA from early on supported 'the Irish language, traditional Irish dancing, music, song, and other aspects of Irish culture', as the 'additional aims' of the organization still read in the 'Official Guide' (Gaelic Athletic Association 2003: 4). For many decades, the GAA thereby followed the lead of the Gaelic League and banned 'foreign' dances – including set dancing – in its clubs (McCann 1983: 59). However, in 1971 the GAA included set dancing into *Scór* ('Score'), its annual series of competitions between different GAA clubs in various 'Irish-cultural' activities. This 'was the first serious attempt to create any kind of national forum for set dancers' (Ó hAllmhuráin 1998: 173–74). During the late 1970s, Comhaltas Ceoltóirí Éireann (CCÉ) also integrated set dancing into its annual Fleadh competitions (Murphy 1999: 347). In 1982, the well-known Willie Clancy Summer School in County Clare offered its first set-dance class, introducing many dancers for the first time to sets (Whelan 2000: 29). Throughout the 1980s, the set-dancing revival reached urban Ireland as set-dance classes began to mushroom in pubs, social clubs, public halls and leisure centres (Brennan 1999: 158–63).

In 1970, Irish step dancing also experienced a boost when the Irish Dancing Commission instigated the annual *Oireachtas Rince na Cruinne* (the 'World Irish

Dancing Championships'). During the 1990s, Irish step dancing got an even greater boost after 'Riverdance', an intermission piece of seven minutes during the Eurovision Song Contest 1994, mesmerized millions of television viewers (Whelan 2000: 24). Due to critical acclaim, it was extended into a full stage show that, touring the world, has become 'the single most successful production using Irish dance as its centrepiece' (Brennan 1999: 155). This show, as well as sequels such as 'Lord of the Dance', ensured that registration at schools of Irish dancing subsequently 'more than doubled' (Brennan 1999: 156).

Having briefly sketched a historical framework for Irish dancing, I can now turn to the question of how local Catholics in West Belfast actually moved within this framework in getting in contact and variously engaging with these three Irish dancing types since the 1950s. First of all, the structural context of family and friends seems again crucial, as many if not most of my informants recalled how they initially learnt about Irish dancing through their parents, siblings and friends who were already involved in these dances. Reflecting broader developments in Ireland, 'Irish dancing' initially meant only céilí dancing and step dancing, as set dancing generally became popular among Northern Catholics from only the 1980s onward. Within their families, some of my informants (like Roibeárd) learnt their first Irish dancing steps. During the 1980s, others – including Mairéad and Pádraigín – were encouraged by relatives and friends to participate in set-dancing classes like the one in Mandela Hall, the students' hall at Queen's University Belfast described by Pádraigín.

Many of my informants also recalled how their parents had encouraged or even explicitly sent them to local schools of Irish dancing. Hence, Roibeárd remembered laconically from his childhood in the 1940s that he was given the choice to 'go to boxing or to go to Irish dancing'. In the 1950s when she was about seven years old, Mairéad was also sent to such a dancing school. In the 1960s, Micheál was less fortunate than Roibeárd in having no choice, at least initially, being made to do Irish step dancing.

But a strong 'Irish-cultural' family background was apparently no prerequisite for being sent to a school of Irish dancing, as the case of Sinéad shows. She was sent to step dancing in the 1970s, not because her parents were Irish-minded but rather because 'it was a common thing that girls would go to this dancing'. Caoimhín also observed for the 1990s that 'mostly girls, like, when they're young would do Irish dancing', even though he himself had also tried it once. Finally, at the time of my fieldwork in 2003–2004, Catriona – who we encountered in the opening scene to this chapter – was also attending a school of Irish dancing and had evidently been encouraged to do so by the example of her mother and older sister. The transient moment described in the vignette at the beginning of this chapter, when Catriona seamlessly switched between disco-style and a couple of Irish dancing steps, was thereby emblematic of how Irish dancing formed part of daily life in Catholic West Belfast (rather than merely constituting a museum piece of 'Irish culture'). Moreover, this moment can also be interpreted as a juncture at which such Irish dancing was both the outcome of structural predispositions and itself the medium for 'transmitting' this type of dancing to others – to her two female friends, to little Cathal, to me – and thereby possibly predisposing them to follow suit. As this anecdotal coverage of the past decades suggests, Irish step dancing has been a rather common pastime in Catholic West Belfast for girls, while – as Whelan observes – 'having to wear a kilt was responsible for putting the majority of boys off learning Irish dancing' (Whelan 2000: 38).

A third structural context with some relevance for exposing people to Irish dancing was the media. For instance, as Micheál recalled from the 1960s, on the above-mentioned radio programme 'Céilí House', 'they used to dance. It actually works with hard dances 'cause you get the syncopation of the feet dropping to the music'. And Caoimhín also mentioned how he had been familiar with céilí dancing, as he had seen it on television. Schools also seem to have formed a structural context in which Irish dancing occasionally figured. Some informants mentioned how céilí dances were taught in physical education; others recalled that their schools had special structures in place for teaching and dancing céilís, be it the Irish-language club at Micheál's grammar school in the 1960s, which had céilís every month, the lunch-time céilís in Pádraigín's school in North Belfast during the 1970s or the organization of public céilís that Mairéad recalled as taking place in school halls. Finally, schools also provided the venue for independent Irish step dancing classes. In fact, this has been a common feature throughout Ireland according to Whelan, who claims that '[m]ost dance teachers use the local school halls' (Whelan 2000: 31).

Turning our attention towards the céilí dancing that was still very popular in Catholic West Belfast in the 1950s and 1960s, and even partly into the 1970s, it is astonishing how much of McCann's (1983) observations about Belfast céilís in the 1930s and 1940s applies to these later decades. Like before, the Catholic Church was opposed to most forms of dancing – especially to so-called 'English dances' – while approving of céilí dances often organized under the control of the clergy in local parish halls, like, for instance, Roibeárd and Mairéad recalled (see Chapter 8). Another structural context for such céilís consisted in local Irish-language organizations like the Árdscoil and the Cumann Chluain Árd, which unsurprisingly adhered to the ban on 'foreign dances' by the Gaelic League and were well known for their regular céilís far into the 1970s. Although it introduced set dancing into *Scór* competitions in 1971 (see above), the GAA equally figured in the memory of informants like Mairéad and Micheál rather as a context for céilí dancing – no wonder, as any dances other than céilís continued to be banned from club premises until 1973 (McCann 1983: 63). Micheál's description in Chapter 8 of the weekly céilís that the GAA organized during the 1960s in the Fiesta Ballroom in the centre of Belfast thereby leads to another important context for céilí dancing during that period, namely, to pubs, halls and social clubs. Like in the preceding decades described by McCann (1983: 59), 'a whole range of Belfast dance halls and restaurants' were frequently rented for big céilí events, especially at festive times like Christmas, Easter or St Patrick's Night, but sometimes also for specific fundraising campaigns. As we saw in Rónán's section in Chapter 8, such benefit céilís also figured prominently later in the 1970s and 1980s, when funds for the local Irish-medium primary school Bunscoil Phobal Feirste had to be raised. In recent decades, such céilís in Belfast pubs, halls and clubs have been joined by set-dancing events as well.

As mentioned before, céilí dancing was already somewhat in decline by the late 1960s, when other, more 'modern' entertainment opportunities like ballroom dancing in big dancehalls in the centre of Belfast became very attractive. Yet once the Troubles began, céilís went further into decline, and this was apparently so for two reasons: first, given the level of violence, people preferred to stay in their local areas and did not dare travel to big céilí venues; and second, as Mairéad aptly put it in Chapter 8, 'there was new entertainments as well. I'm saying this tongue in cheek because there was rioting. It was much more fun than céilí dancing'. This ultimately produced a situation in the ethnographic present of this study in which – as Caoimhín described it in Chapter 8 – 'there wouldn't really be that many céilís on in Belfast for young people! Just be all discos and stuff'.

However, there has been one final structural context that has persistently kept up and maintained céilí dancing over the past fifty years, and this has been the Gaeltacht colleges. All of my informants who had successively attended these summer colleges from the 1950s onwards emphasized how they had engaged in céilí dances in afternoon classes and during social dances at night. Even after céilí dancing was in general decline in and beyond Belfast, Gaeltacht colleges continued to put a special emphasis on this dancing form. Pádraigín thus evidently hit the nail right on the head when observing in Chapter 8 that in Gaeltacht colleges céilí dancing would have been 'your activity. And maybe that's why people learnt that as their culture as well'. In other words, Gaeltacht colleges have been paramount in recent decades in transmitting céilí dances as 'Irish dances' to younger generations.

Ultimately, turning to the question of what has driven local Catholics since the 1950s to practise some form of Irish dancing, a number of affectual motivations suggest themselves. Apart from the fact that dancing in general is a joyful activity that many people experience as positively contributing to their well-being, the various forms of Irish dances also allowed successive generations of males and females in Catholic West Belfast to meet and engage with each other in a morally acceptable way. In a nutshell, as Roibeárd summarized the main attraction of céilís during the 1950s and 1960s, 'That was "boy meets girl"'. With regard to Irish step dancing, personal ambitions and issues of pride when winning competitions surely also played an important role.

Furthermore, until recently, Irish dancing could be little more than a hobby, the only available profession being the dance teacher. Yet 'Riverdance' and other stage shows turned step dancing into a much broader profession with a potentially glamorous career, which suddenly also opened this pastime for a new instrumentally rational motivation, namely, the possibility of earning a lot of money. Value-rational considerations along familiar ethnicist lines – such as the desire to maintain and protect these dances as part of 'Irish culture' against the eroding influences of 'foreign dances' (controversially including set dances) – also clearly played some role when parents sent their children to Irish dancing schools; Micheál's family might serve as a prime example of this motivation.

However, like with Gaelic games and Irish music, there has evidently also been a strong element of habituation involved, which predisposed locals to engage with Irish step, céilí or set dancing in Catholic West Belfast. In Roibeárd's words in Chapter 8, it 'was part of your upbringing to dance'. Initially, such habitually motivated dancing often took the form of céilí dances, which subsequently went into decline as circumstances changed during the Troubles. New circumstances, especially an official recognition through GAA competitions and the Fleadh Cheoil, produced a 'fashion' of set dancing since the 1980s – as such a habitually motivated social practice par excellence. Meanwhile, Irish step dancing has been handed down from (female) generation to (female) generation in such a seemingly comprehensive way that Mairéad rightfully claimed in Chapter 8 that 'I suppose it's nearly like a tradition, you know?' As with Roibeárd's use of the term 'tradition' when talking about Gaelic games, I think that this last quote should be understood as referring to a traditional motivation in the Weberian sense. It is in this sense that Catholics in West Belfast have been likely to know how to do 'their sevens' in céilís and beyond, inasmuch as these very dancing steps were all around them throughout the past fifty years.

Conclusions

In this chapter, I have reconstructed a contemporary history of Irishness in Catholic West Belfast from about the mid-twentieth century onwards. First, I generally clarified the place that Irishness has come to occupy in Northern Ireland since Partition. As I showed, local society soon bifurcated into the officially acknowledged and state-supported sphere of British Protestant Unionism, which, at best, neglected and, at worst, excluded local Irishness from public space. Under these conditions, the parallel universe of Irish Catholic Nationalism emerged as an overarching structural context, which not only maintained an ethnic self-ascription as 'Irish' but also established many internal structural contexts such as largely Catholic families and social networks, Catholic schools, the Catholic Church itself, some form of internal economy, its own Nationalist/Republican parties, social clubs, sporting bodies, 'cultural' organizations and many more.

Against this backdrop, I turned towards the three exemplary cultural domains of Gaelic games, Irish music and Irish dancing, identified in Chapter 7 as being typically represented in Catholic West Belfast as part of 'Irish culture'. Each of the subsequent three sections began with a historical overview of the respective field, which allowed me to more appropriately situate the specific developments in Catholic West Belfast since the 1950s. Trying to explain these respective developments in Catholic West Belfast since the mid-twentieth century from a structure-agency perspective, I have shown how all four ideal-typical motivations, as suggested by Max Weber, played some role. Affectual motivations were clearly important such as the need for emotional bonding and the experience of unity created when making music or dancing together, particularly in the face of a war raging on the streets. Sexual desires for meeting potential partners at social dances were evidently also a primary driver, as were personal ambitions in sporting and dancing competitions, besides – of course – simply enjoying the fun of participating in Gaelic games, Irish music or Irish dancing. Instrumentally rational motivations also played their part in, for instance, driving some towards an engagement with songs in Irish in order to improve their language skills, while others performed music for money in order to make ends meet. Others, again, used such musical events as a means of political mobilization. Value-rational motives in the form of an ethnicism aimed at the preservation, as an end in itself, of Gaelic games, Irish music and Irish dancing as parts of a distinctive 'Irish culture' – a motivation that strongly prevailed with regard to the Irish language (see Part I) – evidently had its place as well.

Yet in addition, I have shown that all three cultural domains persistently exhibited a strong element of habituation or traditional motivation. Many people in Catholic West Belfast, at least within the subset of local Irish learners and speakers, were considerably predisposed to get in contact and practically engage with Gaelic games, Irish music and Irish dancing, simply because these cultural practices were all around them. As I have tried to show in much detail, these influences were not simply 'there'; instead, the repeated and repetitive exposure to each of these three cultural domains was *systematic* – 'collectively orchestrated without being the product of the orchestrating action of a conductor' (Bourdieu 1977: 72) – as numerous internal structural contexts independently cast a similar 'net of Irish culture and identity' into everyday life in Catholic West Belfast. This produced a net-like structure of predispositions that made it very likely for subsequent generations of local Catholics ultimately to become 'netted' and 'caught up' in Irishness.

Thus without negating the relevance of agency, I argue with regard to the three exemplary cultural domains of Gaelic games, Irish music and Irish dancing that the pole of 'structure', through traditional motivation, has also been of considerable importance in bringing about the state of Irishness that I experienced during my fieldwork in 2003–2004. The vignette at the beginning of this chapter, sketching an everyday-life scene from the structural context of family and friends, nicely illustrates this net-like structure of multifaceted predispositions: apart from generally inculcating a sense of Irishness through the visual display of many 'identity containers' (Irish step-dancing trophies, Celtic ornaments, an Irish harp, a Claddagh ring, the 1916 Easter Proclamation), this structural context also provided the space for practically engaging with, and thereby transmitting, both Gaelic games and Irish dancing. The episode in which Daithi and his little nephew Cathal knocked a hurling ball back and forth alongside an ongoing hurling match, to my mind, illustrates this particularly well.

So far, I have only concentrated on the interplay and 'networking' between those internal structural contexts that directly exposed subsequent generations in Catholic West Belfast to Gaelic games, Irish music and Irish dancing, and thereby made it likely that Irishness was reproduced in local practice. Yet taking one retrograde step, it becomes possible to see that this entire process of the reproduction of 'Irish culture and identity' was itself stabilized by the overarching internal structural context of Catholicism. As described in the first section of this chapter, a distinct and almost complete community of Catholics emerged in the North after Partition, and this 'Catholic Northern Ireland' provided the overarching structural context that, cut off through segregation, encompassed and thereby facilitated the continued existence of all the other internal structural contexts that, in turn, helped to reproduce Irishness. In other words, Catholicism – in practice – 'meta-structured' everyday life in Catholic West Belfast and beyond, thereby directly stabilizing the internal structural contexts of Catholic families and social networks, Catholic schools, the GAA, Catholic pubs and social clubs, schools of music, schools of Irish dancing, Catholic parish halls, Irish-language organizations and, to some degree, the media, which – in turn – has facilitated the continuation of 'Irish culture and identity'.

When finally taking yet another retrograde step, the external/internalizing structural context of the Northern Irish state can be interpreted as having additionally and unintentionally stabilized this internal reproduction of Irishness from the outside, namely, by continuously marking and enacting religion as the root cultural difference. This allowed Northern Irish society to become polarized according to religious background, as described at the beginning of this chapter (and in Chapter 1). And, ironically, this profoundly stabilized Catholicism as, in turn, the stabilizing force behind those internal structural contexts that ultimately orchestrated the probable reproduction of Irishness in everyday practice, without being the product – to a great extent at least – of any consciously orchestrating action.

Chapter 10

'Something inside so strong'

Local Representations and Practices of Irishness

Close to where I lived in Catholic West Belfast, at the junction of the Falls Road and Broadway, there were two pubs facing each other across the Falls, namely, Caffrey's and the Red Devil Bar. During my time in Belfast, I would often stop by either pub for a couple of pints, and so I ended up at the Red Devil on a Sunday night in early February 2004. Generally speaking, the Red Devil presented itself as a supporters bar for the English football club with the nickname 'The Red Devils', Manchester United, and regularly showed live football matches from the English Premier and Scottish League as well as from European competitions, in addition to offering disco nights and quiz evenings. However, as I knew, Sunday night was the Devil's 'folk night'.

On that particular Sunday night, I entered the Red Devil at around 9:30 p.m. The pub had been recently refurbished with ochre-yellow painted walls and red columns. The bar itself was completely new, as were the benches, chairs and tables, and the general atmosphere of the pub was much brighter than before. I could see four television screens on the upper walls and columns, all showing the same programme, as the music had not yet started. There were about fifty people present, most of them middle-aged men with the somewhat typical working-class attire that I have described in Chapter 1: very short hair (some almost bald); some with golden earrings and necklaces; a few with tattoos on the forearms; most wearing shirts or T-shirts, white being the prevailing colour. There were only about ten women, who also appeared to be working class: mostly with long hair (dyed in some cases); many with big golden earrings; heavy make-up and tight clothes, some wearing short skirts.

I ordered a pint and sat down at a table where I soon ended up chatting with four young men and a girl, all in their late teenage years, who had come to listen to the young musician with a boyish face, blue sunglasses and black Che Guevara T-shirt, and who had begun to set up some equipment in a corner close to the bar. One of the young men at my table claimed that this musician was really 'unique' in that he was the only local singer who was still 'singing Republican and truly socialist songs', while others, he claimed, had turned into Republican singers only and had left socialism behind. That this singer had not done so I knew from previous performances – an impression that was to be reinforced soon.

As the place became packed (evidently, some people had specifically come for this gig), the televisions were switched off and the young man in the corner began his performance. First, he asked everybody to stand up, as he was going to sing the Irish national anthem. Everybody stood, most holding their hands behind their backs, and some people sang along. After the musician had finished, the audience applauded and took their seats. The musician then started his programme.

As became clear, most of the songs were not written by the artist himself. Instead, several were cover versions of songs by Christy Moore, others were popular Irish ballads, many of them with a strong Republican leaning, while others rather carried an internationalist and socialist message. Similar to Christy Moore in his style of performance, the musician accompanied most of his songs with a guitar, and for a few played the Bodhrán (an Irish frame drum). He also played one tune on a large tin whistle. Among the songs that I knew were 'Back Home in Derry', written by Bobby Sands in the H-Blocks, Christie Moore's 'Viva La Quince Brigada', commemorating those Irishmen who fought against Franco during the Spanish civil war, as well as various Irish folk songs, some of which the performer also sang in Irish. Between the pieces he usually commented on the next song. These short monologues often referred to the political context of the songs, which were typically Republican or socialist. The latter applied to a song he sang about Victor Jara, a famous musician who supported Allende's socialist government in Chile and who was subsequently killed alongside many others during the political putsch by Pinochet in 1973.

While the singer was performing, the audience continued chatting and drinking beer, cider and wine, and empty bottles and glasses piled up on the tables. However, many people also listened to the songs and clearly took them as highly appreciated background music, with virtually everybody applauding after each piece. Occasionally, some people also joined in and sang parts of the songs along with the musician. Evidently, they did so when they liked the tune or supported the political content of a ballad. This political dimension became particularly clear when a number of males got up during certain songs, lifted their clenched fists as a symbol of leftist resistance and joined in the singing. This was especially the case with songs that poignantly expressed and evoked strong feelings of anger, sorrow and hope in relation to the Northern Irish situation, and I could sense how these powerful emotions were increasingly building up in the audience. One such song was the ballad 'Joe McDonnell', which – written by Brian Warfield, the lead songwriter with the longstanding Irish band The Wolfe Tones – movingly tells the story of this West Belfast Catholic. The song is a narration of how Joe McDonnell grew up in West Belfast, was interned without trial, subsequently joined the IRA, and eventually ended up dying in the H-Blocks as one of the ten Republican hunger strikers in 1981. Between the narrative verses, the chorus forcefully makes clear who is regarded as the 'actual' terrorist in the longstanding war between the Irish people and the British state:

> And you dare to call me a terrorist, while you look down your gun
> When I think of all the deeds that you have done

You have plundered many nations, divided many lands
You have terrorized their peoples, you ruled with an iron hand
And you brought this reign of terror to my land

Another song that aroused equally strong if not stronger emotions in the audience was the performance of 'Something Inside So Strong'. Written in the mid-1980s by the British African Caribbean singer and songwriter Labi Siffre as an anti-Apartheid anthem for the South African liberation struggle, this song was adopted by Irish Republicans, partly out of solidarity with the anti-colonial struggle in South Africa, but partly also because the meaning of Siffre's powerful lyrics was locally reinterpreted in terms of the Northern Irish conflict (Rolston 2001: 55). This might go some way to explaining why it was such a haunting experience to be present on that night in the Red Devil with more than fifty others, most of whom were moved quite strongly, when the musician in the corner, together with an increasing number of people from the audience standing with raised fists, began to sing:

The higher you build your barriers, the taller I become
The farther you take my rights away, the faster I will run
You can deny me, you can decide to turn your face away
No matter, 'cause there's …

Something inside so strong, I know that I can make it
Though you're doing me wrong, so wrong,
you thought that my pride was gone
Oh no, something inside so strong, oh – something inside so strong

The more you refuse to hear my voice, the louder I will sing
You hide behind walls of Jericho, your lies will come tumbling
Deny my place in time, you squander wealth that's mine
My light will shine so brightly, it will blind you, 'cause there's …

Something inside so strong, I know that I can make it
Though you're doing me wrong, so wrong,
you thought that my pride was gone
Oh no, something inside so strong, oh – something inside so strong

Brothers and sisters, when they insist we're just not good enough
Well we know better, just look 'em in the eyes and say
We're gonna do it anyway, we're gonna do it anyway!

Because there's something inside so strong, and I know that I can make it
Though you're doing me wrong, so wrong,
you thought that my pride was gone
Oh no, something inside so strong, oh –
Something inside so strong! (Siffre 2012)

In this chapter, I will address the complex interrelations between representations and practices of 'being Irish' in Catholic West Belfast (dimension 1) as powerfully exemplified in this vignette, in which 'Irish(ized) songs' not only served as a means of representing and thereby stirring people's sense of identity as 'something inside so strong' but in which the very performance of these songs themselves constituted a variously representable but actually realized cultural practice to be reckoned with. In other words, the 'Irish songs' of that night could simultaneously pass for both representations and practices of Irishness.

Building on the preceding chapters, I will first reconstruct prevailing notions among Irish Gaeilgeoirí in Catholic West Belfast about what it actually takes to make somebody Irish. As will be shown, three criteria were usually mentioned, namely, self-identification as Irish; having some connection to 'Irish culture'; and, finally, place of birth. Subsequently, I will focus on how Protestants were seen by local Catholics in terms of ethnicity, given that Protestants constituted a 'classificatory anomaly' in sharing with Irish Catholics the same place of birth, while usually lacking practical engagements with 'Irish culture'. As I will demonstrate, many Catholics ultimately regarded local Protestants as Irish despite the additional fact that the latter usually did not identify themselves as Irish and often even explicitly rejected such an ethnic ascription. This discussion will further suggest that the criterion of 'place of birth' was surprisingly seen by many Gaeilgeoirí as more important than the criterion of 'Irish culture', which necessitates a re-evaluation of the model of ethnicity that has been used thus far in this study.

This conceptual reconsideration of ethnicity is the subject of the third section of this chapter, where I will suggest an expanded model of ethnicity that also encompasses my earlier distinction between representational practices of 'culture' and variously representable cultural practices. This model conceptualizes the causal logic that underlies the (re)production of ethnicity in terms of 'autochthony', entailing a triad in which three components – 'individual', 'territory' and 'group' – are situated in time and causally linked through place of birth and/or residence, membership with land rights and shared culture and/or descent. As I will argue, this causal logic can thereby take two inverse directions, corresponding to two different ideal-types: 'individualized autochthony' links the individual, territory and group in such a way that shared culture and/or descent are the likely consequences of place of birth and/or residence, whereas 'collectivized autochthony' inverts this causality. Against this backdrop, I will show that local representations of Irishness in Catholic West Belfast can be characterized as largely conforming to individualized autochthony whereby common cultural practices – locally represented as 'Irish culture' – were typically seen as the outcome of a shared place of birth, namely, (the whole of) 'Ireland'.

Ultimately interpreting these findings with regard to the first dimension of my analytical framework, I will argue that many Gaeilgeoirí in Catholic West Belfast regarded the relationship between local representations of 'Irish culture' and actually realized cultural practices as clearly a case of *selection*, at least as concerns the exemplary domains of Gaelic games, Irish music and Irish dancing.

What it Takes to be Irish

During my stay in West Belfast, it soon became evident that virtually every local
Catholic I talked to seemed to view him- or herself as Irish. However, with the
exception of the realm of the Irish language in which – as described in the first
part of this study – ethnicist evocations of Irish as 'our own native language'
loomed large, questions of 'Irish culture and identity' were actually only
rarely addressed in public discourse and did not play a significant role in daily
conversation. By and large, people's sense of Irishness thus 'went without saying'.
Yet, when I specifically asked locals in informal conversations and with open-
ended questions in formal interviews, Irish learners and speakers in Catholic
West Belfast typically described their Irishness as a clear, if not the principal,
element of their identity. Irishness thereby formed the basis for their frequently
strong political convictions, aspirations and actions as Irish Nationalists or
Republicans. Yet what did being Irish mean to them? Take, for instance, the
following extract from an interview with Máire, a woman in her fifties, who I had
seen twice a week at a local Irish-language class for months before we began our
series of formal interviews:

OZ: The last time you told me that you see yourself as being Irish. So what
         makes somebody Irish in your opinion?
Máire: What makes somebody Irish? Being born in Ireland. Erm. Being part
         of the Irish culture. Just that they always identify themselves as Irish
         and never ever as British – it's a natural thing to feel Irish. Like you,
         probably, you're German.
OZ: Alright. And when you say 'being part of the Irish culture', what do
         you mean by that?
Máire: Well, when we were young, we played camogie. I would be interested
         in Gaelic football. Irish dancing, we all did, when we were young.

Within this short extract, Máire mentioned three aspects of Irish identity that I
frequently encountered in conversations with locals about their Irishness, namely,
'being born in Ireland', 'being part of Irish culture' and, finally, self-identification
as Irish. Let us look at them separately.

Although conversations with many local Gaeilgeoirí about their sense
of Irishness obviously varied and while people also differed and sometimes
contradicted each other (and, at times, themselves), 'being born in Ireland' was
often the first thing that came to people's mind when asked about what made
somebody Irish. So, for instance, the immediate response by Roibeárd was,
'Basically, if you are born in Ireland'. Rónán made the same point plain and
simple when asked what it took for Irish people to actually be Irish: 'I think the
fact they're born in Ireland, just. I don't think there's any other great qualities to
that, you know?' Marcas, who we met briefly at Maebh's house in the opening of
Chapter 9, echoed this position as well but then went on to discuss the status of
the Irish diaspora and the role of descent, using the example of some relatives:

> Well, simply to be born in Ireland makes you Irish. Yet I have a sister, all
> their children were born in London; her husband was born in England
> as well. And they all say 'We're Irish'. So I would actually say anybody is
> Irish who identifies with Ireland. I don't believe in such a thing such as an
> 'Irish race', only Irish people living in Ireland. They are made up of lots of
> waves of ethnic groups, waves of migrants coming into Ireland over many
> centuries. So I see 'Irish' not in racial terms. You just have to identify with
> Ireland in some ways.

This quote is particularly interesting, as it rejects the notion of an 'Irish race' and
argues that Irish people born abroad are actually also 'Irish' because of their self-
identification 'with Ireland' rather than because of any biological link through
shared descent (which was my default expectation). I will come back to these two
points below.

It would be easy to enumerate many more informants who emphasized the
criterion of 'place of birth' for turning anyone born in Ireland into an Irish person.
Thus, while arguing that people could also adopt an Irish identity later on in their
lives, Roise – the second Republican ex-prisoner among my key informants – still
proclaimed that 'in order to be Irish full stop, you need to be born in Ireland'.
Fíona also emphasized that she 'was born here' when asked why she was Irish. In
explaining what she meant by 'here', she said, 'In Ireland. I don't class myself as
British because I was happen to be born this side of the border. It all comes down
to, I think, what is on the map: on the island of Ireland'. This illustrates what, in
my experience, was a largely uniform pattern in Catholic West Belfast: 'Ireland'
was construed in Catholics' geography of ethnic identity as the whole of the island
of Ireland. It was the seemingly self-evident natural givenness of geographical
unity to which people's sense of place of birth referred, rather than to political
units on the island, which were seen as artificial.

The following excerpt from an interview with Dónal nicely links up with the
second of the three aspects of Irishness enumerated by Máire, namely, 'being part
of Irish culture'. Like others before him, Dónal first underlined that, 'for a lot of
people', it would be 'the first and most natural reason to be called Irish' because
they 'were born here'. However, Dónal then went on to emphasize that 'it has to
go a bit further than that', as 'it's also what happens to you when you, when you
grow up':

> The normal thing would be if you live in a particular piece of land,
> you know, whatever that land is called, you know, for example, we're
> in Ireland, whether North or South; you'd expect to be classified as
> an Irish person because you were born here. And I suppose for a lot of
> people, if there wasn't any other reason to be called Irish, that would be
> the first and most natural reason to be called Irish, as simply because
> you're born in that land. Erm, but I guess it has to go a bit further than
> that. You need to have lived in the place for a while as well. Because you
> can be born in America and then lived there for three months and then

live all of your life in Germany, and, technically, then you're probably American, but, you know, who you are really is; you are much more German because you are involved in the German culture. So I suppose even though it's about where you're born, and so it's also what happens to you when you, when you grow up.

In Chapter 7, I quoted and analysed three long citations by Caoimhín, Rónán and Micheál in order to show what was commonly represented in Catholic West Belfast as typical elements of 'Irish culture'. In the following description, Micheál again enumerated various activities (including the practice of Hiberno-English) as 'ineluctably and inescapably Irish':

> There are some activities that are ineluctably and inescapably Irish. If, for example, you speak the Irish language, then you are doing something that, essentially, is not done anywhere else. You know, except by, sort of, linguists and academics. But if you speak the Irish language, you're doing something that belongs to the culture of this country and doesn't belong anywhere else. And – if you sing a particular style of singing, even the same song will not be sung the same way in other places. There's also overlaps in the song tradition, but there's – a repertoire that belongs to here and doesn't belong elsewhere. If you speak English in a certain way, if you use the present habitual tense of the verb 'to be', if you say, 'Sometimes he does be very good and sometimes he does be very bad', which is the present habitual; it's a substratum of the Irish language; that is something that belongs to Ireland and hasn't transferred anywhere else. So there's some activities that – are inescapably – that are more Irish than others. ... The game of hurling, for example, has Irish roots. Doesn't seem to have come from anywhere else and is largely played here. ... It's an activity that mainly happens in Ireland or in the satellite communities around the world, is something that is Irish merely because other people don't do it. But that doesn't necessarily mean that because you're doing something that the other [non-Irish] people don't do, that you're more Irish than [other Irish] people who do things that other [non-Irish] people also do.

As we will see below, Micheál's final observation (echoed by many local Gaeilgeoirí) that active engagements with 'Irish culture' did not actually make one 'more Irish' had profound implications for Irishness in general and the ethnicity of Protestants in particular.

The third aspect of Irish identity enumerated above, namely, self-identification as Irish, was mentioned already in Chapter 7 as a relevant criterion of Irishness when Micheál insisted, 'You need to identify with the island or with the culture or the people in some way'. In the same interview, he elaborated that for an outsider to become Irish, it required 'some kind of a conscious commitment to the country'. Many other informants also told me that it was important – as one Irish speaker from the Cluain Árd put it – 'what you believe yourself to be'. Thus, Mairéad, after mentioning place of birth and the relevance of 'Irish culture' also told me, 'And obviously it's a choice. … It's really a very individual thing for people, how they feel about themselves'. Marcas also stressed in the above-quoted excerpt, 'You just have to identify with Ireland in some ways'. Finally, Máire insisted in the short dialogue I cited at the beginning of this section that besides place of birth and 'Irish culture', locals were Irish given the fact '[j]ust that they always identify themselves as Irish'.

Besides these three aspects, and contrary to what I had expected before coming to Belfast, 'shared descent' did not really figure much as a criterion when local Gaeilgeoirí explained to me what made somebody Irish. In most cases, people did not mention 'descent' and would only elaborate on it when I specifically enquired about its relevance. This is not to say that it was not mentioned at all. For instance, after explaining that it made you Irish '[b]asically, if you are born in Ireland' (see above), Roibeárd went on to argue with regard to the Irish diaspora that 'the case could be made that if someone was born somewhere else but had both parents Irish, then he could also claim to be Irish because then there is no confusion'. Pádraigín also provided a sweeping statement in which she cited 'Irish parentage', amongst other factors, when characterizing Irishness as being defined through 'probably being born in Ireland, and having Irish parentage and living in the country and living the culture'. However, I find it hard to say whether this and similar accounts really enumerated preconditions for making somebody Irish or whether they merely described empirical features that were simply given for (prototypically) Irish people.

This is not to say that I did not meet anybody who explicitly mentioned 'descent' as a proper criterion of Irishness. For instance, Daithi made quite clear that, as he phrased it, 'I think there is something Irish which is innate and not taught, you know? There's something, what do you say? It's in your blood. There's something in the blood, d'you understand?' Others like Stiofán also explicitly took 'parentage or grand-parentage' to be a criterion when providing their own definition of Irishness. Yet, I think that from the point of view of Stiofán at least, descent figured as a means for the Irish diaspora to link up to the actually relevant 'root' criterion of place of birth in order to 'take as wide a definition as possible':

> There's no easy, no short answer to the question about identity. And there's no short answer on the connection between identity and language and culture, all that sort of stuff. … Being born in Ireland should make you Irish, in my opinion. If you're born in Ireland, you're Irish. … Many Irish people were born in London to Irish parents, so some parentage or grand-parentage could mean you're Irish. So I think, to be honest, I would tend to take as wide a definition as possible. And up until the recent referendum [in 2004], I would have said that the qualification for Irish citizenship and Irish passport was a fair definition of being Irish. That if you're not born in Ireland, your parents are born in Ireland, your grandparents are born in Ireland, that meant you're Irish. Now that's been changed, or that's going to be changed

following the referendum. Being born in Ireland won't necessarily mean Irish citizenship. But as far as I am concerned, being born in Ireland or your parents being born in Ireland or your grandparents being born in Ireland entitles you to be Irish.

In the above quotation, Stiofán also mentioned the referendum that took place in the Irish Republic on 11 June 2004. The electorate voted on whether or not to insert a more restrictive citizenship clause into the Irish Constitution. This clause was to ensure that, from then on, a person born in the island of Ireland without 'at least one parent who is an Irish citizen or entitled to be an Irish citizen is not entitled to Irish citizenship or nationality, unless provided for by law' (The Referendum Commission – An Coimisiún Reifrinn 2004). Almost 80 per cent voted in favour of this citizenship restriction, and this fact was often angrily mentioned to me as being disgraceful by many informants who strongly rejected 'shared descent' as a meaningful criterion for Irishness. Thus, Séamus – a nineteen-year-old man from a strongly Republican family who I regularly met at the Cultúrlann – responded to my question about whether one had to have Irish parents in order to be Irish, 'No, no, no! That's the whole thing about this damn referendum in Dublin, which said if your parents aren't Irish, you can't be'. Marcas was quoted above, explaining that, in his words, 'I don't believe in such a thing, such as an "Irish race"'. Similarly, Ciarán – my very first Irish teacher and subsequent key informant – argued that '"descent" is not important to qualify for an Irish identity'. When hypothetically discussing the ethnicity of children born to Filipino migrant workers in Belfast, Roise also insisted that 'if you're born in Ireland, you're Irish, disregarding of your parents', thus turning the Belfast-born offspring of immigrants into Irish persons as well. Following this territorial logic, Roise went on to explain that 'if Irish parents give birth to a child in England, it would be English'. Finally, one of the four pupils at the local Irish-medium secondary school interviewed as a key informant when I was doing participant observation at this institution quite aptly summarized what, to my mind, was in fact the prevailing position among Irish Gaeilgeoirí in West Belfast on this issue of descent: 'You don't need Irish parents in order to be Irish, but usually, it is just like that.'

   Even more surprising to me than the widespread rejection of 'shared descent' as a criterion for Irishness was the complete absence of any reference to religion when my informants talked about their sense of identity. No one referred spontaneously to 'religious background' as a possible criterion, and when I specifically enquired about Catholicism as a prerequisite for being Irish, each and every one of my informants stridently rejected such an idea. So Roise told me, for instance, 'You don't have to be a Catholic in order to be Irish, absolutely not, preferably not!' Marcus made the same point, emphasizing that being Irish did 'certainly not' require having a Catholic background. Micheál as well echoed what I take to be a surprisingly uniform pattern in Catholic West Belfast, at least among the many Gaeilgeoirí with whom I spoke, when I asked him whether one had to be a Catholic to be Irish. He answered, 'Most definitely not!'

As Walker (1996: 110–27) shows, representations of 'Irish identity' have varied widely over the past centuries with regard to the question of whether or not the 'Irish people' were seen as consisting of only Catholics, only Protestants or as being independent from any religious affiliations. Even in the late nineteenth and early twentieth century, all three positions could still be discerned (ibid.: 112–18). However, after Partition, in the Irish Free State in the South 'the new Irish national character was often closely associated with Catholicism. For example, on St Patrick's Day 1935, de Valera broadcast that Ireland had been a Christian and [C]atholic nation since the time of St Patrick. "She remains a [C]atholic nation"' (ibid.: 119). In contrast (as we saw in Chapter 9), Protestants in the North decreasingly viewed themselves as 'culturally' Irish and increasingly opted for an ethnic Britishness, especially after the outbreak of the Troubles (ibid.: 119–24).

Within the academic literature addressing the Northern Irish conflict of recent decades, there has been a common insistence – Hayes and McAllister (1999) speak of an 'academic consensus' – that the Catholic–Protestant divide should be interpreted in ethnic terms (Boal et al. 1976), with the two groups 'being seen as ethnic ones socially marked by religion' (Brewer 1992: 356). Wallis, Bruce and Taylor (1986: 3) proclaim that there can be 'no real doubt as to Catholic and Protestant communities constituting ethnic groups'. Such representations are echoed by Mitchell, who also speaks of 'religion as an ethnic marker' (Mitchell 2005: 8), whilst Nic Craith (2002: 142) claims that 'Catholicism is regarded by many Northern nationalists as the primary focal point of their identity'.

My point is not so much that these commentators are mistaken when it comes to contemporary Irishness within Catholic West Belfast; I am rather arguing that their statements are imprecise in failing to distinguish between conceptual representations of 'Irish culture and identity' and actually realized cultural practices. In other words, while a Catholic religious background, in practice, evidently had everything to do with (re)producing Irishness in Catholic West Belfast, constituting a meta-structural context from which virtually everything else followed (see Chapter 9), it was still possible for Catholicism to have nothing to do with Irishness in terms of how this sense of identity was actually conceptualized by the actors themselves. To put it differently: the fact that religious and ethnic identities only rarely cross-cut each other in practice in the Irish North did not mean that they were not conceptualized within locally prevailing representations as cross-cutting ties of affiliation. Thus, while there was a shared consensus in Northern Ireland about who has a Catholic or Protestant religious background, Catholics and Protestants have tended to disagree in terms of the ethnic identities they respectively ascribe to themselves and to members of the other faith (and also about what political aspirations should follow from these ascribed ethnic identities) – an observation that I will attend to in the next section.

First, however, it is necessary to distinguish between 'those aspects of culture which are self-consciously worn as identity labels' and 'those aspects which are quietly reproduced without forming part of self-identity' (Eriksen 2000: 196) – Schlee (2008: 61–74) speaks of 'identity markers' and 'diacritical features' in this context – in order to be able to observe more appropriately that Catholicism was actually strongly rejected as an 'ethnic marker' within 'local representations of Irishness' in Catholic West Belfast, while constituting one of those ethnically unmarked 'diacritical features' that were still highly relevant *in practice*, even when 'not consciously "made relevant"' within local representations (Eriksen 2000: 199; see also Chapter 2). It is to precisely this dynamic that Ciarán referred when stating:

> I have never argued that one has to be Catholic in order to be Irish, but the reality of the situation is that most Irish are Catholics. But I strongly oppose the assertion that being Catholic is a prerequisite for being Irish. I see being Irish as distinct from being Catholic. But in reality, when I look around me, I have to admit that the two things are virtually identical.

To sum up, in representations of Irishness in Catholic West Belfast, many local Gaeilgeoirí repeatedly mentioned the three criteria of place of birth, connection to 'Irish culture' and self-ascription as Irish as making somebody Irish. At the same time, most people I talked to did not conceive shared descent or a Catholic religious background as relevant preconditions, and many explicitly objected to such ideas. The three approved criteria of Irishness thereby coincided in the individual biographies of virtually all of my informants, which makes it difficult to tell from their life stories alone whether these criteria were seen as equally important or whether some took conceptual precedence over others. To answer this question, it is more helpful to focus on how local Protestants were actually seen in terms of ethnicity by my Catholic informants, given that the former shared with Catholics the same place of birth, while being only rarely involved with 'Irish culture' and typically not identifying themselves as Irish. It is to this 'classificatory anomaly' that I now turn.

The Irishness of Protestants and the Politics of a Classificatory Anomaly

As I have already mentioned, among the three locally approved criteria of Irishness, 'place of birth' evidently provided a discourse of inclusion under the common denominator of Irishness for both children of immigrants born in Ireland and for local Protestants. However, the second aspect of Irishness – being part of 'Irish culture' – seemed to have rather exclusionary effects for descendants of immigrants and for Protestants in particular. While many local Catholics emphasized that these elements of 'Irish culture' were not restricted to Catholics but also rightfully belonged to local Protestants as fellow Irishmen, and while a number of Catholics highlighted some Protestant involvement, few denied that 'Irish culture' was predominantly practiced by Catholics, especially Gaelic games and the Irish language. In practice, 'Irish culture' thus seemed to exclude Protestants from a common Irishness. However, a second look at the perceived relationship between practising 'Irish culture' and 'the Irish people' among Catholics reveals a much weaker connection.

Many of my informants – and it should not be forgotten that as Gaeilgeoirí they were all heavily involved in 'Irish culture' – emphasized to my initial astonishment that they actually did not see 'cultural' practice as a precondition for being Irish. Take for example the following statement by Peadar, an Irish speaker in his thirties, who had been a language activist for all of his professional life:

> I don't want to be snobbish, but the ability to speak Irish surely reinforces one's Irishness. But it is not a prerequisite to being Irish. Just because I speak Irish makes me not more Irish, but personally I undoubtedly feel more Irish. Do I feel that others do need to speak Irish to be wholeheartedly Irish? Definitely not! I don't see that as a contradiction. For me personally, to have the ability to speak Irish enriches my Irishness.

This quotation reveals a very typical pattern of argumentation among local Catholics: practical involvement with some form of 'Irish culture' was seen as making one personally feel 'more Irish', but such involvement was rejected as either 'actually' making one more Irish or as a general precondition of Irishness. At a personal level, practising 'Irish culture' could enrich one's Irishness, or, as many locals suggested, it could help reassure one of one's own Irish identity in times of conflict, during which questions of identity became both salient and contested. Practising 'Irish culture' could be helpful as a 'decolonizing weapon' in demonstrating one's own 'cultural' distinctiveness vis-à-vis what was seen as an ethnically different oppressor, or it could be seen as something that Irish people should do in order to maintain their valuable and distinctive 'culture', which was threatened with destruction, with those Irish people who did not seem to care being frowned upon, but such apathetic individuals remained 'Irish' nevertheless. They were generally not seen as being 'less Irish' but only as (regrettably) less interested in 'their own' culture. In short, while the actual practice of 'Irish culture' could thus potentially provide a basis for the exclusion of Protestants from Irishness – something Protestants often emphasized – this was usually not the point of view of local Catholics.

Against this backdrop, it is not surprising that many local Catholics insisted that Protestants were actually also Irish. This position was concisely expressed by Liam, a sixteen-year-old pupil from the local Irish-medium secondary school who we already encountered in Chapter 6. In an interview, I asked him about the ethnic identity of local Protestants. He stated:

> Protestants just have a different religion. It would be Unionists. Unionists claim to be British and want to be part of the British Isles. They claim to be British. But I would say, no, they are Irish. They were born in Ireland. They have an Irish background. Their parents were born in Ireland as well. They follow a different culture, but they are still Irish.

Inclusion based on birth location thus dominated for Liam over the potentially exclusionary element of 'Irish cultural' practice in ascriptions of Irishness. Another example of this line of reasoning was provided by Pádraigín in the following quote in which she argued that since involvement with 'Irish culture' – here in the form of the language – was not necessary for being Irish, local Protestants were also Irish:

> Protestants are just as Irish as I am. They don't necessarily have to speak Irish to be Irish 'cause life didn't work out for them that they got Irish. They weren't lucky enough. Nobody told them that they were allowed that culture like everybody else. There wasn't that, you know? I know how hard it was to find a school that taught Irish here for Catholics. But it's even bloody harder to find a Protestant school who teaches that. It's not their fault. The state has dictated to them, you know?

Yet this fairly widespread position sat uneasily with the third aspect of Irishness characterized in the previous section, namely, self-identification as Irish. Many local Catholics emphasized that they were Irish and continued to identify themselves as Irish 'and never ever as British' (as Máire insisted), although they were for a long time denied public expression of their ethnic identity by the state (see Chapter 9). For such individuals, it seemed, a persisting self-identification as Irish had been a crucial element of their identity. When discussing the ethnic identity of immigrants' children born in Ireland – for instance regarding the Filipino community in West Belfast – it was often highlighted, like Roibeárd did, that 'it's also a matter of choice. A Filipino who is born in Belfast can be Irish if he wants'. However, when talking about Protestants' choice to be British, the situation was apparently different.

In trying to come to terms with this somewhat special treatment of Protestants' self-identification by local Catholics, the following extract from an interview with Stiofán provides some orientation. After stressing that he would see anybody in terms of the identities of *their* choosing, Stiofán, himself a declared Irish Republican, went on:

> Yeah, I accept what anybody would say about their sense of national identity. But I know there was a school of thought within Republicanism especially, you know, for many years that said, 'Well if they call themselves Protestants, they call themselves British. But under the surface they are really Irish.' I wouldn't follow that type of people. … Just, I never believed in it.

While this statement shows that there also existed a position in Catholic West Belfast that explicitly put individual self-identification above the principle of inclusion based on place of birth – a position that will ultimately be shown below to be only a refinement of this same principle – it also points to the fundamental reason of the persistent notion of Protestants' Irishness, namely, the centrality of this notion in local political discourses of Irish Nationalism and Republicanism.

Since the emergence of the United Irishmen in the 1790s, the first Irish liberation movement aiming at establishing an independent Irish republic by 'unity of Protestant, Catholic and Dissenter', Irish Nationalism and Republicanism have taken various forms and routes. Disagreements have focused on goals, ranging from various degrees of autonomy from Great Britain to total independence, as well as regarding the future political system – be it a monarchy or a republic. Conservative, more Catholic-oriented forces have been opposed by distinctly left-wing Republicans, who have sought to combine their struggle for national liberation with various socialist aspirations. The question of the appropriate means by which to achieve national self-determination has been another area of dissent. While constitutional Nationalists have propagated the use of exclusively peaceful means, more radical Republicans have justified their 'armed struggle' as the only way to move forward. In the North of Ireland, a more moderate and purely constitutional 'Nationalist' position has become associated with the Social Democratic and Labour Party (SDLP), whereas Sinn Féin and the IRA have been regarded as the proponents of a more radical 'Republican' position, advocating the use of violence. Since the beginnings of the peace process in the early 1990s and the subsequent IRA ceasefire, however, Sinn Féin has made considerable strides towards a more 'constitutional' position, abandoning violent means. This development reached a peak in 2005 when the IRA declared its armed campaign to be over and apparently put their weapons beyond use.[1]

Despite these variations, there has been a core of Irish Nationalist and Republican thinking, at least during the twentieth century, which can be characterized as follows: the island of Ireland is the homeland of one nation, the Irish people. Proponents of this view argue that after centuries of oppression by an external agent – the British state – this nation should be granted its entire territory in accordance with the principle of national self-determination. They claim the Irish national revolution of 1918–1921 remains incomplete. What became 'Northern Ireland' was artificially held back within the United Kingdom, and subsequently developed into a place where Catholics were treated like second-class citizens by the local Protestant majority and its state apparatus. However, according to this position, neither Partition nor local sectarian discrimination were ultimately the fault of local Protestants. Instead the British state was to blame, with its 'colonial' and 'imperialist' interest in retaining control over this part of the island. For this purpose, the British state artificially divided the Irish nation, fostering the sectarian divide by granting privileges to local Protestants. The British state thereby succeeded in blinding Protestants to their 'true interests' as co-members of the secular Irish nation through the creation of a false sense of Britishness, as well as of an allegiance to the Union (McGarry and O'Leary 1995: 21–35; Patterson 1997: 101). The popular base for Britishness and Unionism among Protestants was thus not to be taken at face value but rather to be explained by state-incited sectarianism and economic incentives. As Patterson convincingly argues, there has been an 'unbroken thread of analysis' in twentieth-century Irish Nationalist/Republican thinking that claims 'that Unionism's substance is the British "guarantee"; if British support is removed,

---

1. For detailed discussions of the various strands in the development of Irish Nationalism and Republicanism, see Rumpf and Hepburn (1977), Cronin (1980), Bean (1994), McGarry and O'Leary (1995: 13–91) and Patterson (1997).

Ulster Protestants will wake up to their real interests' (Patterson 1997: 112). Against this backdrop, it does not come as a surprise that Protestant self-identification as British found little resonance in Catholic West Belfast: the inclusion of Protestants into the Irish nation based on place of birth was simply too crucial a part in the whole discursive field of local identity and politics.

While I would argue that this inclusivist approach was still a dominant way of making sense of identity and politics in Catholic West Belfast at the time of my fieldwork, a relatively recent refinement could also be observed. Traditionally, there was no need for Republicans to engage with self-declared 'British Unionists' on questions of identity; it was assumed that 'Unionists' would soon rediscover their Irishness after British withdrawal anyway. However, intensive talks between Republican and Nationalist leaders and the British and Irish governments in the course of the peace process led to some rethinking within Republicanism, especially when it became evident during the 1990s that Irish national self-determination was not to be achieved without the consent of the entire population of Northern Ireland (Patterson 1997: 225–76). As Bean (1994: 18) notes, this led to intensified attempts by Republicans to 'empathise with and explore the identity and real fears of the Unionist population'. At the annual party conference in 1995, a senior member of Sinn Féin from West Belfast emphasized that Republicans had to approach Protestants in a 'language of invitation' because 'in our vision of a united and independent Ireland there must be a place for those who consider themselves British and who wish to stay British' (quoted in Patterson 1997: 260).

While such statements suggest that Irish Republicans had started to question their fundamental assumption that British Unionists were actually Irish, this was probably not the case. Consider, for example, the following statements by Séamus – the young Republican who so strongly reacted against 'descent' and the 2004 referendum in the previous section – when talking about the identity of local Protestants:

> They're British. They see themselves as British. Like, I'd say they're Irish who refuse to believe that they're Irish. And I'm not trying to be disrespectful by telling them that they're Irish, but if they want to believe that they're British, if they want to get on like the British, fair enough. It doesn't bother me, anyway. ... I mean, for me to try and tell them that they're Irish would be exactly – to do exactly on them what they've been doing on us, which I'm against. ... Let them believe they're British. I don't care. But – let them believe they're British in an All-Ireland.

What seems different in Séamus' account as compared to the earlier quotations by Liam or Pádraigín is his acknowledgement that telling Protestants what they 'really' are would be treating them in the same 'disrespectful' way in which Catholics were treated by the former Protestant ascendancy. This does not mean, however, that Séamus actually accepted the self-identification of Protestants as British; he merely tolerated it, provided that it had no political consequences in terms of legitimate claims to national self-determination: 'Let them believe they're British', but 'in an

All-Ireland'. This conforms to Patterson's (1997: 261) observation that while Sinn Féin may well have been preparing for peace during the 1990s, 'it was a peace that was seen, by Republicans, necessarily to involve only respect for the individual and communal rights of Protestants. There was little evidence that they were prepared to accommodate significantly Unionism as a political identity.'

What this suggests is that the above-mentioned refinement in local political discourse in Catholic West Belfast basically comprised two acknowledgements. First, forcing an 'Irish' identity on Protestants was acknowledged to be disrespectful, morally unacceptable and strategically counter-productive if Protestant consent was needed in an agreed All-Ireland. Second, everyone could legitimately claim whatever identity he or she believed him or herself to have (as misconceived as this was from the 'true' Irish viewpoint) as long as only the Irish had a legitimate claim to national self-determination. In other words, it was increasingly realized among Catholics that Protestants did not necessarily have to and might not recognize their 'true' Irish identity for an All-Ireland to occur. Local Catholics could thus – and mostly seemed able to – afford to tolerate the individual right of self-identification, provided the collective right of national self-determination was only granted to the Irish. The privileged position of Irish national self-determination thereby continued to be legitimized by a notion of Irishness based on 'being born in Ireland', which still encompassed Protestants as 'actually' Irish. The only thing that seemed to have been refined in Catholic West Belfast was that Protestants were no longer necessarily required to realize the 'true nature' of their identity.

As I have shown, the prevailing notion of Irishness in Catholic West Belfast as ultimately rooted in a common place of birth offered inclusion to local Protestants. Yet this offer has rarely been accepted. On the contrary, since the outbreak of the Troubles in 1969, Protestants' self-identification as 'Irish' has drastically diminished, while their self-characterization as 'British' has almost doubled: while in 1968, 20 per cent of Protestants saw themselves as 'Irish' and 39 per cent as 'British', by 1994 merely 4 per cent of Protestants chose the label 'Irish' as opposed to 71 per cent 'British' (Trew 1996: 142).

That the predominantly Unionist Protestant population should be increasingly hostile to the Catholic offer of inclusion in a shared sense of Irishness is to be expected, given their outlook on questions of identity and politics. From a Unionist perspective, as McGarry and O'Leary (1995: 97) concisely argue:

> There is not one nation in Ireland – which is a sentimental, irrationalist myth, sustained by fallacious geographical determinism. Unionists insist that they differ decisively from the other people in Ireland in religion, ethnic origin, economic interests, and sense of national identity. They are not Catholics. They are ethnically linked to Scotland and England. Their economic interests are connected with Britain. They regard themselves as either British or Ulsterfolk. … Although some unionists insist that they are Irish, i.e. culturally Irish, and even ethnically Irish, this identity is, they say, consistent with their British national or political identity and allegiance. They have a dual identity, they are politically British but culturally Irish.

It is hard to imagine a position that could be more opposed to the outlined representations of Irishness in Catholic West Belfast: where local Irish Nationalists emphasized one nation linked with the whole of Ireland, Unionists proclaimed the existence of (at least) two peoples and denounced Irish political geography as a simplistic insular attitude. While mutually recognized cultural differences in practice as well as the role of self-identification were downplayed by the Irish Nationalists, they were highlighted by Unionists, who emphasized religious differences in particular. Whereas Catholics propounded inclusion, Protestants put forward exclusion: they separated themselves from local Irish by deliberately stressing their latecomer status as descendants of Scottish and English settlers, while simultaneously arguing that they had lived for long enough in the area of 'Northern Ireland' to claim legitimate self-determination as a group (McGarry and O'Leary 1995: 92–93).

However, one remark by McGarry and O'Leary deserves further attention, namely, their observation that some Unionists separated their ethnic from their political identity by identifying themselves as ethnically Irish, while politically supporting the Union with Great Britain. This conforms to an observation by one of my few Catholic interlocutors from West Belfast who had regular and intimate contact with Unionists due to his cross-community work:

> Whereas Unionists will be quite happy, if they trust you, to identify themselves as Irish, they won't do it if there's a Nationalist in the company. They tend not to. Because the Nationalist will read something into that that they don't want to be read into. Something which is not true, and which they do not want to happen. So they're – they're under pressure from Nationalists to adopt an Irish identity. Nationalists expect that an Irish cultural identity will immediately lead to an Irish political identity and nationalism. And the Unionists react to that. So what they actually can say out loud is kind of limited.

This clearly corresponds to the more traditional approach of inclusion: Protestants will realize that they have 'actually' also been Irish all along, and will then inevitably support a united Ireland. The more refined approach remains based on the same premise yet does not require the insight of Protestants into their 'true' identity anymore, as long as they politically support an All-Ireland. 'Be Irish or be whatever you want, but in either case be in support of a united Ireland' was thus the plain message that was communicated by local Catholics through their offer of inclusion based on place of birth. Since accepting this invitation invariably entailed a journey to a political destination that most Protestants had repeatedly made clear they had no wish to reach, the offer could not but fall short. By inseparably linking Irish identity and Irish nationalism, and by ultimately failing to take the political aspirations of most Protestants seriously, the offer of inclusion thus led, in practice, to the alienation and de facto exclusion of Protestants from a shared sense of Irishness. Or, to use the terminology provided when distinguishing between four different types of structural contexts in Chapter 2, Protestants in the North of Ireland largely constituted an externalizing structural context relative to local Catholics – a context consisting of practices by other actors who disagreed with the actors under focus in seeing themselves as having a different identity, while the latter insisted that they were all Irish.

Leaving this strongly politicized dissent on the alleged Irishness of Protestants behind, it is time to realize that most observations in this chapter have so far been rather unexpected: instead of demonstrating (as the model of ethnicity presented in Chapter 2 seemed to suggest) that Irishness in Catholic West Belfast was solely defined through self-representation as 'Irish' and through some involvement with a distinctive 'Irish culture', the local situation was shown to be more complicated because of the additional criterion of 'place of birth'. What is more, the whole discussion in this section of the 'classificatory anomaly' of Protestants – viewed as 'Irish' because of birth location even though they usually lacked 'Irish culture' and a corresponding self-identification – has further made clear that the criterion 'place of birth' was actually viewed as more important than involvement with 'Irish culture'. But does this not go against everything I have assumed so far in this study? If an involvement with 'Irish culture' was apparently not necessary to be Irish, why should local Catholics have been bothered at all about whether or not they practised Gaelic games, Irish music or Irish dancing – let alone the Irish language?

Autochthony as the Causal Logic behind Ethnicity

In order to answer such questions, the original model of ethnicity as construed in Chapter 2, focusing only on the relationship between representational practices of 'culture' and variously representable cultural practices, needs to be refined and expanded to include territorial criteria (i.e. place of birth and/or residence) as well as the potential criterion of 'shared descent', even though the latter was only of minor importance in Catholic West Belfast. I will do this by first critically discussing some analytical distinctions as developed within two crucial bodies of literature – studies of nationalism, on the one hand, and of autochthony, on the other – in order to then synthesize insights from both fields into an expanded model of ethnicity. This model will suggest that 'autochthony' is the causal logic underlying ethnic identity, entailing a triad in which three components – 'individual', 'territory' and 'group' – are situated in time and causally linked through place of birth and/or residence, membership with land(ed) rights and shared culture and/or descent.

Within the study of nationalism, there is a long history of differentiating and analysing empirical cases of nationhood and national identity according to basic classifications. While some authors have developed quite elaborate typologies – for example, Smith in his *Theories of Nationalism* (1983: 211–29) – most have been content with using one of several root dichotomies such as 'political–cultural', 'liberal–illiberal', 'universalistic–particularistic', 'inclusive–exclusive' and so on. A cursory list of such dichotomous distinctions provided by Spencer and Wollman (2005: 199) mentions fourteen such dualisms, many of which overlap. Moving back in time, the genealogy of such dichotomies notably includes an early distinction between 'voluntarist' and 'organic' nationalisms in the late nineteenth century (Smith

2001: 36), Meinecke's (1919) opposition between the largely passive '*Kulturnation*' and the rather politically active '*Staatsnation*' and – most prominently perhaps – Kohn's (1944) argument around the mid-twentieth century contrasting 'Western' with 'Eastern' forms of nationalism.

Kohn's basic distinction between 'Western' and 'Eastern' nationalisms has proven to be highly influential within the study of nationalism. In recent years, this dichotomy has gained further prominence (not only within but also outside academia) through a terminological distinction between 'civic' and 'ethnic' nationalism. As Smith puts it, the 'civic' or Western model is 'predominantly a spatial or territorial conception', whereas the distinguishing feature of the 'ethnic' or non-Western nation is 'its emphasis on a community of birth and native culture' (Smith 1991: 9, 11). Within this framework, civic nationalism has typically been discussed positively as liberal, voluntarist and inclusive, whereas ethnic nationalism has been viewed negatively as illiberal, organic and exclusive.

Such broad and fundamental conceptions of nationalisms – 'East' and 'West', 'ethnic' and 'civic' – have not passed, of course, without criticism. Kohn's conceptual regionalism has been widely criticized for being crude, grossly exaggerating and displaying a somewhat neo-orientalist flavour (e.g. Spencer and Wollman 2005: 200). Thus instead of denoting whole world regions, the civic–ethnic opposition has been increasingly used as a means of differentiating concrete states. However, as Brubaker (2004: 135) notes, many scholars of nationalism have lately 'grown uncomfortable with the unequivocal sorting of cases into "civic" and "ethnic" categories' and with characterizing 'an entire state, or an entire national movement, simply as civic or ethnic'. Instead, it has become, in a way, a mainstream position within studies of nationalism to regard 'civic' and 'ethnic' primarily as ideal-type positions and to analyse – as Smith (1991: 13) phrases it – all concrete cases as containing 'civic and ethnic elements in varying degrees and different forms. Sometimes civic and territorial elements predominate; at other times it is the ethnic and vernacular components that are emphasized'. In fact, Smith's own work, most notably *The Ethnic Origins of Nations* (1986), has been central in bringing about this approach of investigating empirical elements of concrete cases according to the civic–ethnic distinction in the first place.

Despite these more nuanced usages of the civic–ethnic divide, several observers have highlighted the inherent analytical and normative ambiguities of this master dichotomy. For my current purposes, Brubaker's (2004) succinct discussion provides a satisfactory summary of the primary contentious issues. As Brubaker (ibid.: 136–40) shows, the civic–ethnic distinction is analytically ambiguous in that both terms can be defined either broadly or narrowly, leading to fundamental problems in the concrete application of the dichotomy. If the term 'ethnic' is defined narrowly as only rooted in (assumed) descent, too many heterogeneous cases end up being classified as 'civic', while a broad notion of 'ethnic' as based on shared culture leaves hardly any cases in the 'civic' box. Conversely, a narrow concept of 'civic' as acultural, ahistorical and universalist 'has never been instantiated' (ibid.: 137), whereas a broad definition also entailing a civic culture incorporates virtually all 'ethnic' cases as well. Finally, even if a definition of the 'civic' and 'ethnic' could be agreed upon, it is often very difficult to decide – even for single elements within a given nation, as Brubaker convincingly shows with regard to language policies – in which box they actually belong.

Apart from these analytical uncertainties, Brubaker's (2004: 140–44) discussion also shows the civic–ethnic distinction to be haunted by normative ambiguities. As was mentioned before, 'civic' nationalism has typically been viewed as being positively inclusive, whereas 'ethnic' nationalism has been criticized for being dangerously exclusive. Yet, apart from highlighting that inclusion is nothing inherently positive, Brubaker (ibid.: 141) aptly states that 'in fact all understandings of nationhood and all forms of nationalism are simultaneously inclusive and exclusive. What varies is not the fact or even the degree of inclusiveness or exclusiveness, but the bases or criteria of inclusion and exclusion'. Against this backdrop, Brubaker (ibid.: 144–46) argues for the dissolution of the ambiguous and overburdened civic–ethnic dichotomy and suggests, as a modest alternative, a distinction between 'state-framed' and 'counter-state' understandings of nationhood.

While I endorse Brubaker's criticism of the civic–ethnic divide and have advocated replacing this master dichotomy by several, more nuanced analytical dimensions (see Zenker 2009), I still think that the analytical distinction between 'civic' and 'ethnic' nationalism has been valuable in enumerating most of the basic elements that typically seem to play some role in the (re)production of ethnicity and – when combined with demands for a state – nationality (see Chapter 6). However, as I will argue below, these basic elements need to be conceptualized differently with regard to their various interrelations, and for this purpose a critical discussion of a second body of literature, namely, the recent ethnography of autochthony, may be instructive.

According to the Oxford Dictionary of English, the term 'autochthon' is derived from the Greek *autos* ('self') and *khthōn* ('earth'), literally meaning 'sprung from the earth', and designates 'an original or indigenous inhabitant of a place' (Soanes and Stevenson 2003: 107). Against this backdrop, autochthony can be provisionally defined as referring to a proclaimed 'original' link between an individual, territory and group, which typically presents itself as 'self-evident', profoundly 'authentic', 'primordial' and/or 'natural'.[2] In a recent literature review of the current upsurge of autochthony discourses in African and European countries, Ceuppens and Geschiere (2005) observe that the closely related term 'indigenous peoples' has gained a somewhat broader appeal, especially since the establishment of the United Nations Working Group on Indigenous Populations in 1982. However, 'indigenous peoples' are usually conceived of as marginalized 'others' in need of protection in 'their own lands', whilst the 'autochthon' is typically conceived of as an 'in-group'

---

2. This apparent 'immediateness' has been variously noted, for instance by Jean and John Comaroff (2001: 648, 649, 651), who characterize autochthony as 'a naturalising allegory of collective being-in-the-world', which – in self-styling itself as 'the most "authentic", the most essential of all modes of connection' – 'natures the nation'. Ceuppens and Geschiere (2005: 385, 402) also highlight the 'apparently self-evident nature and "naturalness"' of autochthony claims, while Geschiere and Jackson (2006: 6) speak of autochthony as allegedly based 'on some sort of primordial truth-claim about belonging to the land'.

in need of protection from scrounging strangers – the 'allochthons' – who have immigrated into 'one's own homeland' (Ceuppens and Geschiere 2005: 386).[3]

Since the 1990s, 'autochthony' has become a violently contested issue in many African countries. This development can be seen as an unexpected corollary of democratization in the form of reintroduced multipartyism as well as decentralized development policies that increasingly by-pass the state (Ceuppens and Geschiere 2005: 385, 389–90; Bayart et al. 2001). Being a crucial mode within the new politics of belonging that has emerged as the flip-side of globalization, autochthony discourses thereby take various forms (Ceuppens and Geschiere 2005; Geschiere and Jackson 2006). As a fascinating new body of literature on various African and European countries shows,[4] autochthony is typically used as a means of specifying, with regard to the state, both which level within a segmentary identity structure is the relevant one for a given context and which identity definition on that level is appropriate. In some contexts autochthony thereby functions as an alternative to national citizenship; in other settings, it operates rather as its redefinition.

As these observations suggest, this new ethnography explicitly addresses the relationship between autochthony and other forms of belonging like ethnicity, nationality and citizenship. Yet it is interesting to note that these texts typically engage this relationship empirically rather than conceptually. In other words, the authors often use terms such as 'ethnic groups', 'national citizenship' or 'the nation' as conventional labels for specific levels within the segmentary identity structure without sufficiently addressing the question as to what analytically distinguishes these different forms of belonging.[5] In instances in which the concept of autochthony is actually specified in some way, this is usually done ambiguously through a characterization of autochthony, on the one hand, as 'a new form of ethnicity' equally capable of 'creating an us-them opposition' and 'arousing strong emotions regarding the defense of home and of ancestral lands' (Geschiere and Nyamnjoh 2000: 424; see also Ceuppens 2006: 151; Geschiere and Jackson 2006: 5–6). On the other hand, however, autochthony is also represented as different from ethnicity (Ceuppens 2006: 149; Geschiere and Jackson 2006: 5–6) since the latter term 'evokes the existence of a more or less clearly defined ethnic group with its own substance and a specific name and history', whereas autochthony is 'less specific' (Geschiere and Nyamnjoh 2000: 424), 'empty' (Ceuppens and Geschiere 2005: 387) and 'contentless' (Jackson 2006: 100): 'an identity with no particular

---

3. While this bifurcation between autochthony and indigeneity might indeed occur in the popular imagination, I argue elsewhere (Zenker 2011) that, analytically speaking, indigeneity should be rather understood as constituting a particular version of autochthony.

4. So far, autochthony research in Africa has primarily focused on Cameroon (Geschiere and Nyamnjoh 2000; Konings and Nyamnjoh 2003; Geschiere 2004; Leonhardt 2006; Socpa 2006); Ivory Coast (Dozon 2000; Chauveau 2006; Marshall-Fratani 2006), Eastern Congo (Jackson 2006), the Black Volta region (Lentz 2003, 2006a, 2006b), and South Africa (Comaroff and Comaroff 2001; Landau 2006). In Europe, Belgian Flanders has been studied in much detail (Ceuppens and Geschiere 2005: 397–402; Ceuppens 2006).

5. Jackson (2006: 100–9) is most explicit in this regard when he equates 'ethnicity' with the local, 'nationality' with the national [sic] (i.e. with the state) and 'megaethnicity' with the regional level.

name and no specified history, only expressing the claim to have come first, which is always open to contest' (Ceuppens and Geschiere 2005: 387).

These definitions by Geschiere and other authors seem to suggest that autochthony should ultimately be treated as distinct from ethnicity. But a second look at the above-mentioned empirical cases from Africa and Europe shows, first, that almost all described 'autochthonous' identities below the level of (nation-)states actually do refer to named ethnic groups, which not only have specifiable histories but in fact specify them (among others) through claims of having been the first to arrive in 'their own territory'. Second, even when the nation and its citizenry are reclassified through autochthony at the state level, this smaller-scale redefinition is typically 'ethnic' rather than 'civic' in nature. In fact, the replacement of 'civic' citizenship with a more restrictive 'ethnic' citizenship is usually the very *raison d'être* behind the evocation of a rhetoric of autochthony in the first place. In the end, this all seems to suggest that, despite some proclamations to the contrary, within this new ethnography of autochthony it is usually the 'ethnic' that legitimizes privileged access to land (and other territorialized resources) through autochthonous first-comer claims rooted in the past.

It is thus somewhat ironic that when comparing these observations from the new research on autochthony with the civic–ethnic distinction within studies of nationalism, it is evident that both bodies of literature provide rather contradictory accounts as to how identity formations of individuals and groups literally 'take place': within studies of nationalism, it is generally the 'non-ethnic' ('the civic') that is associated with territory through place of birth and/or residence (the 'ethnic' being mainly linked to descent and/or culture), whereas in research on autochthony, it is typically the 'ethnic' that interconnects an individual, territory and group in such an allegedly 'original' way that land rights follow from first-comer claims linked to a 'pivotal event' in the past.

Against the backdrop of this critical discussion, I argue for a synthesis of insights from both fields by conceptualizing the causal logic that underlies the (re)production of ethnicity in terms of 'autochthony'. In this sense, 'autochthony' can be seen as a triad in which its three components – 'individual', 'territory' and 'group' – are simultaneously situated in time and causally linked through the interconnections of place of birth/residence, group membership with land rights (in a broad sense, possibly including the political right to national self-determination) and shared culture/descent. Against this backdrop, the previously mentioned differences between studies of nationalism, on the one hand, and studies of autochthony, on the other, can be reinterpreted as complementary in addressing two alternative ideal-typical modes of this very same causal logic – modes distinguished only by their respective causal directions and the way in which they handle time.

Within such an approach, 'civic' nationalism turns out to be based on 'individualized autochthony' (see Figure 10.1) in which an individual – through his or her place of birth and/or residence – first causally links up with a territory, which – through land(ed) rights embedded in membership titles – is connected to a group, which, in turn, is likely to link up again with the individual through the possible though not necessary connection of a shared culture and/or descent. This type of autochthony is 'individualized' in the sense that the proclaimed original link between an individual, territory and group is essentially produced through the 'present continuous' of individuals – that is through their individual place of birth and/or residence in their respective 'presents'. Commonality of place of birth and/or residence thereby simultaneously connects to and constitutes both 'the territory' and, then, 'the group'. Over time, this pattern is likely ultimately also to effect commonalities of culture and/or descent among these individuals (unless, of course, these individuals migrate or they are the progeny of migrant parents).

In contrast, cases typically characterized in terms of 'ethnic' nationalism (or, in fact, 'autochthony')[6] can be interpreted as based on another autochthonous mode that inverts the causal direction of individualized autochthony (see Figure 10.2): within 'collectivized autochthony', an individual – through shared culture and/or descent – first causally links up with a group, which at some point in its proclaimed past connected itself – through the establishment of land(ed) rights for its members – to a territory, which now in the present is likely to link up again with the individual through the possible though not necessary connection of placing the birth and/or residence of this individual within its own confines. This mode of autochthony is 'collectivized' since the proclaimed original link between an individual, territory and group is essentially established through the 'passé simple' of groups, distinguishing between 'earlier-comers' and 'later-comers' to that territory based on alleged 'collective pasts'.[7] Shared culture and/or

---

6. Within the recent literature, the empirical cases discussed under the label 'autochthony' invariably fall only into this second type. However, there are passages within this body of texts that already point to the necessity or at least the possibility of distinguishing between two opposed modes of autochthony. For instance, Geschiere and Nyamnjoh (2000: 442) observe how (this mode of) autochthony typically fetishizes the collective at the expense of the individual, without realizing, however, that this situation could also be inverse. Similarly, Geschiere and Jackson (2006: 7) note as 'an interesting catch' that autochthony literally means 'from the soil itself', while most present-day autochthony movements claim to be first-*comers*, which implies a movement in the past. Yet the authors fail to acknowledge that this catch might indicate that one cannot only be 'from the soil itself' through a past movement of one's own group, but also through one's own individual birth 'from' and/or residence within the present territory.

7. The new ethnography of autochthony usually insists that the contested pasts of groups are typically discussed in terms of which group has 'come first' and what this 'pivotal historical event' of 'coming first' actually means, namely, possession through discovery or labour (e.g. Lentz 2006b: 48–52). However, even though in many cases of collectivized autochthony these contests about first-comer claims surely prevail, they are not necessarily the only option for this autochthonous mode to be operative. In other words, collectivized autochthony is based on the claim that in the past of one's own group, a pivotal event such as discovery, labour or conquest turned the group and its future members into the legitimate 'owners' of the land, either because the group was (allegedly) first, because the group was (allegedly) there before rival groups (yet after irrelevant others) or because the group has been there for a sufficient length of time to be on equal footing with even more 'indigenous peoples'. The first case refers to the typical 'first-comer' situation. The second case solves the apparent paradox mentioned by some observers (e.g. Jackson 2006: 113) in which several groups claim to have arrived before some other rival group but after another first-comer group (like pygmies) that are usually so marginalized and so different in terms of social, political and economic organization as not

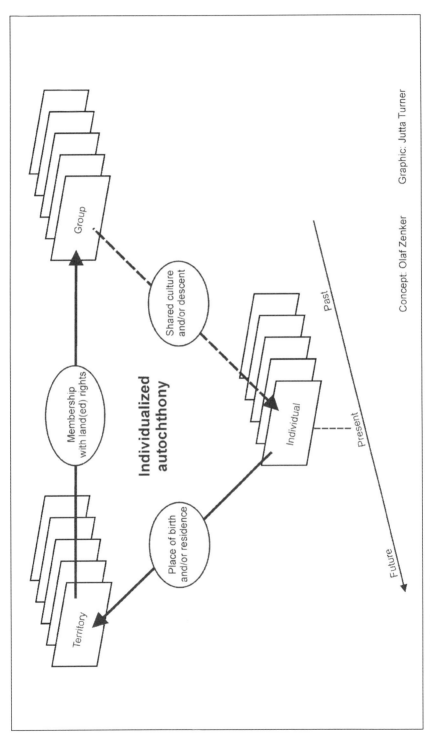

Figure 10.1 Individualized autochthony

descent serve as the necessary link for an individual to be connected, first to 'the group' and then to 'the territory', but group, territory and their interconnection are conceived of as being independent from and prior to the individual. In many cases, this nexus is likely ultimately also to cause the individual to be born and/ or to reside within the territory to which his or her community of culture and/or descent proclaims entitlement. Yet this is not necessarily so, as the prototypical case of diasporas illustrates.

Within this expanded and refined model of ethnicity based on the causal logic of autochthony, not only 'shared culture' but also all the other causal links – namely, 'shared descent', 'membership with land(ed) rights' and 'place of birth and/or residence' – are located on the level of representations, in which they are projected as being internally shared, while making members different from non-members. Each of these interconnecting mechanisms can thus be analysed individually with regard to the respective relationship between what is proclaimed in representations and what is actually experienced in practice by the involved actors. In other words, each of these causal links has its own empirical interrelation of representations and practices, moving between 'selection' and 'pretension' (see Chapter 2). In this study, it so happens that I am particularly interested in 'culture' given that I am trying to explain how and why the local Irish language revival fits into Irishness in Catholic West Belfast. But, generally speaking, it is equally possible to analyse the dynamics of 'selection' and 'pretension' with regards to (alleged) descent, membership with land(ed) rights, place of birth and/or place of residence.

Furthermore, the suggested ideal-typical distinction between individualized and collectivized autochthony can be used to explain why 'place of birth and/ or residence' and 'shared culture and/or descent' are often ambiguously coupled together within discussions of civic and ethnic nationalisms, even though there is no obvious reason for doing so, especially with regard to 'shared culture and/ or descent' (see Chapter 2). Against the background of this analytical model, however, these couplings do make sense since 'place of birth' and 'place of residence' are truly interchangeable when it comes to evoking the individualized-autochthonous logic behind ethnicity, whilst 'shared culture' and 'shared descent' equally actuate the very same logic of collectivized autochthony. In other words, whether ethnicity discourses emphasize place of birth *or* place of residence as a necessary condition for group membership, *both* set into motion the same causal logic of individualized autochthony; by contrast, whether identity discourses demand as a prerequisite 'shared culture' *or* 'shared descent', in *both* cases the same causal logic of collectivized autochthony is activated.

Another ambiguity built into the civic–ethnic divide can also be avoided by using this model of autochthony: on the one hand, the 'civic' and the 'ethnic' are

---

to constitute any serious challenge within state politics (see also Leonhardt 2006). The third case applies to many Northern Irish Protestants, who often stress their late-comer status as descendants of Scottish and English settlers during the seventeenth century Plantations, while simultaneously arguing that they have lived in the region long enough to claim legitimate self-determination (see the previous section of this chapter).

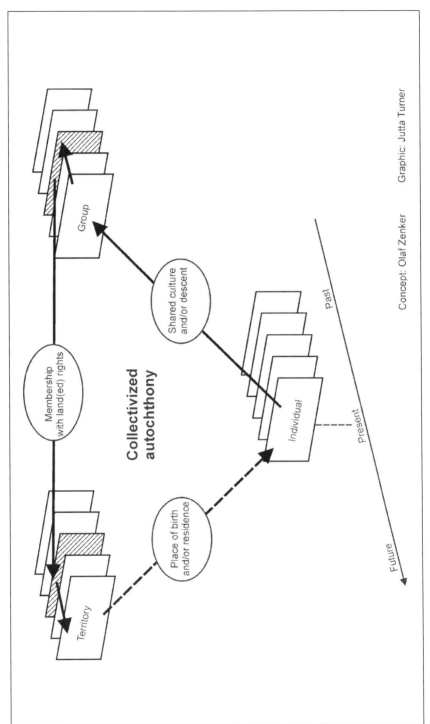

Figure 10.2 Collectivized autochthony

typically distinguished by different ingredients. As the above quote from Smith indicates, the 'civic' is typically a 'territorial conception', whilst the 'ethnic' rather emphasizes the 'community of birth and native culture' (Smith 1991: 9, 11). Yet, only a few pages later in the same text, Smith (ibid.: 13–14) insists that both models also share 'certain common beliefs about what constitutes a nation', and goes on to enumerate these defining ingredients in a way that largely conflates the earlier distinction between 'civic' and 'ethnic' nations.[8] This ambiguity is dissolved within the dichotomy of individualized and collectivized autochthony since this distinction is not based on different ingredients, but on different causal directions in which the same elements are prototypically linked: individualized autochthony sees shared culture and/or descent as likely consequences following from place of birth and/or residence, while collectivized autochthony inverts this causality. In other words, no less than collectivized autochthons do individualized autochthons prototypically envision a shared culture (and/or shared descent) within the territory of the ethnie. Both only differ in the causal logic they utilize to explain this coincidence. While shared culture (and/or descent) is the independent variable – the prerequisite of ethnicity – for the collectivized autochthon, it is the likely but not necessary outcome for the individualized autochthon. This also means, however, that for both groups, 'shared culture' is not simply given but is instead either the independent cause of the ethnie (in collectivized autochthony) or merely a potential effect about which one can never be sure (in individualized autochthony). This turns an ethnicist revival of a 'distinctive culture' into a potential necessity for both the collectivized and individualized autochthon, thus constituting a crucial difference between the suggested model of ethnicity based on autochthony and the classical civic–ethnic divide: for the textbook 'civic nationalist', a shared culture is truly negligible, whereas for the ideal-typical 'individualized autochthon', a 'distinctive culture' is not only likely but actually desirable within his/her quest to come closer to a prototypical ethnicity that – to spin further the metaphorical language of the model – ideally consists of a 'closed causal triangle'.

Against the backdrop of this analytical discussion, let us finally return to the situation in Catholic West Belfast. As I have described in previous sections, virtually all of my informants within the local language scene gave priority to 'place of birth' rather than to 'shared culture' when asked about their Irishness. Many if not most held the view that Protestants were thus also Irish, whatever else the latter might say themselves. Only few of my informants mentioned 'shared descent' as a relevant criterion; in fact, the vast majority objected to my explicit inquiries as to whether one had to be of Irish descent or a Catholic in order to be Irish, some even rejecting such positions as 'racist' or 'sectarian'. This was surely not representative of Irish Nationalists throughout the North or down South in

---

8. Smith (1991: 14) defines the nation as 'a named human population sharing an historic territory, common myths and historical memories, a mass, public culture, a common economy and common legal rights and duties for all members'. Apart from 'shared descent', which is ambiguously left out, all nations – 'civic' and 'ethnic' – thus seem to share, amongst other things, a territory and a culture.

the Irish Republic, but within the radicalized, considerably leftist and strongly Republican heartland of Catholic West Belfast, I experienced such statements as sufficiently 'authentic'. Therefore, when reinterpreting the case of Irish identity in Catholic West Belfast in terms of 'autochthony', most of my informants were without much doubt propagating a notion of Irishness that was based on individualized autochthony.

Conclusions

Having analysed in previous chapters 'Irish-cultural' practices within the three exemplary domains of Gaelic games, Irish music and Irish dancing over the past fifty years in Catholic West Belfast, this chapter has addressed the complexities of representations of Irishness as they made sense of the relative presence or absence of such practices within Northern Ireland. I therefore concentrated first on the question of what it actually took to be Irish from the point of view of my informants. I argued that despite variations, there were typically three criteria for Irishness that were mentioned again and again: first, being born in Ireland (i.e. place of birth); second, being part of 'Irish culture' (i.e. shared culture); and, third, self-identification as Irish. I showed that both the criteria of 'shared descent' and of a common Catholic background did not actually play an important role in local conceptions of Irishness. With regard to Catholicism, I argued for the necessity of distinguishing more precisely between the conceptual and practical level: constituting – as a 'diacritical feature' – a crucial meta-structural context, Catholicism obviously had everything to do with (re)producing Irishness in practice (see Chapter 9), yet in terms of an 'ethnic marker' that specified what made somebody Irish, Catholicism had absolutely nothing to do with Irishness in terms of how local Catholics actually conceptualized it in their representations.

This final observation seamlessly led to a discussion in the second section of this chapter of how Northern Irish Protestants were seen by my Catholic informants in terms of their ethnic identity. Most of my informants insisted that local Protestants were actually Irish since the latter were equally entitled to 'Irish culture' and also because a practical involvement with Irish culture did not actually 'make' one more Irish but only made one personally 'feel' more Irish.

Against the backdrop of this discussion, I acknowledged the necessity of expanding the model of ethnicity that I presented in Chapter 2. I suggested an extended model of ethnicity based on the causal logic of 'autochthony', entailing a triad in which three components – 'individual', 'territory' and 'group' – are situated in time and causally linked through place of birth and/or residence, membership with land(ed) rights and shared culture and/or descent. All of these causal links can thereby be analysed with regards to their individual dynamics between representations and practices like I have done for 'shared culture' within this book.

With regard to the situation in Catholic West Belfast, a practical involvement with 'Irish culture' was generally not viewed by my informants as constituting a necessity for making somebody Irish. In accordance with the locally prevailing causal logic of individualized autochthony, this 'culture' was instead seen as typically following from simply living within the community of Irish people. As we saw in Chapter 9, this was to a great extent really the case in Catholic West Belfast for the three exemplary domains of Gaelic games, Irish music and Irish dancing: instead of being practised because of an ethnicist value-rational motivation (as was the case for the Irish language), these 'ineluctably and inescapably Irish' activities (Micheál's phrase) were rather engaged with for various other reasons – mostly unrelated to questions of identity and including a strong element of habituation (or traditional motivation, in Weber's terminology) rooted in structural predisposition.

However, as suggested by the model of individualized autochthony, this 'shared Irish culture' was only a likely, though not necessary, consequence of being born in Ireland, and my informants were acutely aware of two crucial exceptions. First, local Protestants were as Irish as any local Catholic because of their common place of birth, but they usually did not practise 'Irish culture' simply because 'life didn't work out for them that they got [e.g.] Irish', as Pádraigín put it. Second, among Irish Catholics, the 'Irish-cultural' element of the Irish language largely disappeared in practice due to the centuries-long pressures of Anglicization; hence, a common and distinctive language was no longer a likely consequence of sharing the same place of birth.

Bearing these last qualifications in mind, I can finally interpret my findings on local Irishness in Catholic West Belfast in terms of the first analytical dimension of this study – that is to say by placing local dynamics between representations and practices within a continuum between *selection* and *pretension*. Seen in this light, all three locally propagated criteria of self-identification, 'being born in Ireland' and 'being part of Irish culture' were thereby clearly experienced by my informants as obvious cases of *selection* – at least regarding their own identifications, birth locations and personal involvements with the three exemplary domains of Gaelic games, Irish music and Irish dancing – in that these representations merely selected as 'ethnic markers' from what was sufficiently and independently realized in cultural practice anyway.

To my mind, it is this considerable independence between the genesis of each of these cultural practices ('to be born' also has, of course, a cultural dimension, as I will illustrate momentarily) and acts of representation, which then selected from these practices in order to instantiate a self-identification, a 'place of birth' and a distinctive 'Irish culture' that formed the ultimate ground on which a frequently strong sense of Irishness as 'something inside so strong' could build up in Catholic West Belfast. Or, to make the same point in an *ex negativo* way, it is my suspicion that many people in the Republic of Ireland voted in favour of the 2004 referendum restricting citizenship regulations in order to prevent what was described by the Irish government as the scare of '"citizenship tourism", where pregnant women from other countries … could come to Ireland to have their babies and acquire Irish citizenship for them' (Coulter 2004). Whatever one might think about this issue in moral terms, to my mind it shows that many people felt that those children born in Ireland to women who had (allegedly) come to Ireland purely in order to give birth were not 'authentically' Irish precisely because the act of giving birth and the subsequent 'selection' of this practice as an ethnic marker constituting Irishness were not causally independent.

Within the second part of this book, my analysis of exemplary domains of 'Irish culture' has shown that, following the logic of individualized autochthony, this distinctive 'culture' was locally seen largely as a consequence of being born in Ireland; in other words, as an effect of already being Irish rather than as something that one first had to practise or even revive in order only then to become Irish in the first place (as would be the case with collectivized autochthony). However, the first part of this study seemed to show that this was exactly what was going on in Catholic West Belfast with regard to the local Irish language revival. So, then, how does this all fit together? And, as I asked at the end of Chapter 6, why, how and under which circumstances should it be plausible that in order to be what you already are (i.e. Irish), you have to become what you yourself agree you are not (i.e. an Irish speaker)? It is time, it seems, finally to try and make sense of it all.

Epilogue

Chapter 11

'Trying to make sense of it all'

Identity Matters in Catholic West Belfast

We were in our teenage years in the 1970s. So the whole situation here was, you know, it was an evolving situation. There was murder and mayhem in the streets; there was internment; there was all the arrests; bombs went off all over the place. But it was also people trying to make sense of it all! And of course, we were teenagers, you know; we looked at our teenage years for some sense in life.

Stiofán, explaining how he became involved with the Irish language

Ultimately 'trying to make sense of it all', it is helpful to remember that sense-making practices are as much part of 'what's going on' in an ethnographic setting as are those practices to which such interpretative representations (including my own) aim to refer. I have persistently argued throughout this book that it is this interplay between representational practices and therein represented practices that needs to be refocused within studies of ethnicity in general, and regarding the interrelation of the Irish language and Irishness in Catholic West Belfast in particular. Now attempting to integrate my findings in this respect, it is not only necessary to summarize my intermediate results but also to recapitulate how I started.

The starting point of this study consisted in a combination of a certain theoretical dissatisfaction with the 'basic social anthropological model of ethnicity' (Jenkins 1997: 3–15) and an empirical observation concerning local Irishness in Catholic West Belfast. As I argued at length in Chapter 2 with regard to theories of ethnicity, this basic social anthropological model is dominated by what I called 'constructivism in a narrow sense' – a position most prominently associated with Barth's introduction (1969b) to his edited volume *Ethnic Groups and Boundaries* (1969a) in which he argues that actors construct their ethnic identities in interaction with members and non-members by selecting and representing a limited number of their cultural practices as ethnic boundary markers and only those that are shared within while differentiating members from non-members. Barth thus not only suggests that ethnic identities are primarily the product of social practices (a position I referred to as 'constructivism in a broad sense') but additionally claims that the crucial processes lie at the level of representational practices producing 'the ethnic boundary' rather than at the level of therein represented practices, 'the cultural stuff'. As I showed, this narrow constructivism developed into the dominant paradigm within anthropological studies of ethnicity and was subsequently radicalized into a position in which it was suggested that only narrowly constructed representations of difference, whether 'real or imagined', actually matter. Within this spectrum of narrow constructivist positions, culture is effectively theorized as negligible, with Barth conceptualizing 'the cultural stuff' as unproblematic, simply constituting a given repertoire from which actors select their ethnic markers, and more radical constructivists declaring (by to some degree drawing on the Thomas theorem) that actual culture is irrelevant, as all that counts is what people (pretend to) believe.

However, as I argued, the theoretical neglect of actual culture for the (broadly understood) construction of ethnicity seems premature, as the state of culture might influence what people believe to be the case; in other words, the relationship between representations and practices should be determined empirically rather than predefined theoretically. Furthermore, there is a broader spectrum of propositional attitudes that actors maintain vis-à-vis their identity-related representations than just 'belief/conviction', and this is an observation for which neither Barth nor more radical constructivists can account. Barth's actors simply select and represent cultural practices and are thereby obviously convinced that what they represent is what they do; for more radical constructivists, the appearance of 'belief' is, by definition, at the heart of ethnicity. (This is actually also the case for instrumentalists, even though they argue that political elites merely pretend to believe in certain ethnic representations in order to mobilize 'the masses', because for such mobilization to be effective, at least 'the masses' must believe.)

Dissatisfied with the neglect of actual culture within the prevailing paradigm of narrow constructivism, I came across the empirical case of the local Irish language revival in Catholic West Belfast. The Irish language caught my attention not only because it was locally represented as being related to Irishness while constituting a cultural practice, the actual realization of which could be investigated in everyday life; but the local language revival was even more compelling to me precisely because – as an ethnicist revival of actual cultural practices – it cannot, in fact, be explained by the standard model of narrow constructivism. To put it differently, given that within narrow constructivism cultural practices are assumed to be either unproblematically 'given' (according to Barth) or in themselves irrelevant (as more radical constructivists would have it), the basic social anthropological model of ethnicity simply does not offer a theoretically founded answer to the question as to why (and how) actors should bother to change their actual cultural practices for identity-related reasons rather than merely modifying their representations. This is not to say, of course, that explanations of revivalist behaviour are in principle incompatible with narrow constructivism. But such explanations necessarily remain external to the basic model, as the latter fails to theorize explicitly in the first place the relationship between representational practices of 'culture' and variously representable cultural practices in terms other than 'selection'.

This becomes evident when trying to situate the case of the Irish language revival within a typology of relationships between language, as one dimension of identification (Schlee 2008: 25), and ethnicity: such a relationship typically moves within a continuum defined, on the one extreme, by cases in which 'an ethnic group is completely coterminous and identified with the community of speakers of a certain language', whereas the other extreme consists of 'a total lack of such a congruence and the absence of any association between an ethnic group and the language(s) spoken by it' (Schlee 2001: 8287). Given that this typology is based on the factual presence or absence of a common language that thus either can or cannot be selected as an ethnic marker, the case of the Irish language revivalists does not fit in here: while being unable to select a factually present language, these Gaeilgeoirí still insisted that Irish people should be able to speak their 'own native language', thereby highlighting a counter-factual representation they themselves acknowledged as constituting a pretention. In registering this deviation, which made the local Irish language revival (like, in fact, all ethnicist revivals) a rather special case, this study set out explicitly to analyse the empirical interplay between representations and practices with regard to the interrelation between the Irish language and Irishness in Catholic West Belfast in order not only to explain this particular case but also to thereby learn something more general about the mechanisms at work in the (broadly defined) social construction of ethnic identity.

In this spirit, the study analytically isolated the language and Irishness and, in each of the two main parts of the book, concentrated on one phenomenon at a time, analysing it with regard to its respective research question: how had the Irish language/Irishness been practically experienced and represented by and to Irish Gaeilgeoirí in their respective interactions with various structural contexts, creating the present configuration of 2003–2004 in Catholic West Belfast, and why had their experiences and representations taken on these particular forms? Now bringing together the results of the first main part, a compact answer to this overarching research question concerning the Irish language reads as follows: in Catholic West Belfast, many Irish people came to adhere to the representation of Irish as 'our own native language'. Yet in people's own perception, this notion did not sufficiently correspond to their actual practices, which turned this self-acknowledged case of pretension into a strong identity-related driving force behind a local Irish language revival that was value-rationally motivated for all, and instrumentally rational for some. This revival had to operate within the dynamics of structure and agency that were crucially shaped by the external structural context of the Northern Irish state, which treated Catholics as second-class citizens and handled the language with a combination of neglect, suspicion and hostility. This generally unfavourable context was profoundly affected by the Troubles, which for many brought their sense of Irishness to the fore and thereby created a desire to turn the hitherto rather pretentious representation of Irish as 'our own native language' into one of 'selection' by actually learning and speaking Irish. Given the heavy power asymmetries between the state and the local language scene, this revival had to build on equally powerful actions, and this it could do, given the emerging interplay between strongly committed language activists who produced a growing supply of Irish and equally committed Republicans in and beyond the prisons who more and more accelerated the demand for Irish, which ultimately brought about the present Irish language scene in Catholic West Belfast. This ethnographic present was populated by numerous local Gaeilgeoirí whose respective biographies not only constituted the medium in which these developments had taken place; rather, these biographies also provided emergent repertoires of experience that were used as objects of representations in the ongoing process of reworking positionalities that actors had already been developing throughout their lives. All in all, this whole process had effectively led to the actual expansion of Irish as a practised language, even though Gaeilgeoirí in Catholic West Belfast continued to exist only as a local minority.

Integrating my findings from the second main part, a compressed answer to the overarching research question regarding Irishness can be given in the following way: within Catholic West Belfast, many of my informants from the local Irish language scene represented their own sense of Irishness in terms of three main criteria, namely, being born in Ireland, having some connection to a distinctive 'Irish culture' and identifying themselves as Irish. With regard to their own situation, it was evident that local Irish Catholics experienced these representations as simply selecting as 'ethnic markers' from what was sufficiently and independently realized in actual cultural practices anyway. However, local Gaeilgeoirí also weighted these criteria, conceiving 'place of birth' as more important than practical engagements with 'Irish culture'. While for political reasons violating their third criterion of self-ascription, this causal logic enabled Catholics to see local Protestants as 'actually' being Irish. I suggested that we should interpret this as a case of ethnicity based on individualized autochthony, in which 'shared culture' is seen as the likely and desirable (though not necessary) consequence of 'place of birth (and/or residence)'. At least with regard to the three exemplary domains of Gaelic games, Irish music and Irish dancing, such a distinctive 'Irish culture' was thereby indeed simply 'given' in Catholic West Belfast; in other words, the practical (re)production of this 'culture' was not generally based on the identity-related motivation of a value-rational ethnicism.

This is not to say that value-rational ethnicism was not at all a driving force for engaging with Gaelic games, Irish music and Irish dancing in Catholic West Belfast. All in all, however, other motivations prevailed, most notably a traditional motivation for engaging with 'Irish culture' resulting from a net-like structure of predispositions that had been cast in complex and overlapping ways by various internal structural contexts. Within the local dynamics of structure and agency, this multifaceted structural predisposition was stabilized over the past decades by the meta-structural context of Catholicism, which was itself ironically put in (its) place by the Northern Irish state. In the biographies of my informants, the outbreak of the Troubles engendered an ever-expanding ethnicization of everyday life to which many locals reacted by increasingly identifying with being Irish, while others felt incapable of reconciling their sense of belonging with what they experienced as a by then 'violated' Irishness. These tensions lived on in the ethnographic present of 2003–2004, which was not only the product of such past events but additionally provided an arena in which these and other past experiences were reworked as actors continuously made sense of themselves, of fellow Irish people – whether Catholic, Protestant or Dissenter – and of the non-Irish world beyond.

Having summarized the intermediate results of this study, I can now turn towards the final task of integrating these findings from the first and second part, which at first glance seem to be somewhat at odds with one another: whereas the first part suggested that Irish Gaeilgeoirí in Catholic West Belfast felt they had to learn and speak Irish *in order to become more or 'truly' Irish*, the second part on Irishness suggested the opposite, namely, that following the logic of individualized autochthony, a distinctive 'Irish culture' was seen largely as a consequence of being born in Ireland – in other words, as *an effect of already being Irish* rather than as something that one first had to practise or even revive in order to only then become Irish. To put it bluntly, my informants apparently contradicted themselves when proclaiming, on the one hand, that being born in Ireland unambiguously made somebody Irish, that a practical involvement with 'Irish culture' was not needed and that such an actual practice also did not make one 'more' Irish, whilst, on the other hand, expressing and indeed actuating precisely this desire to practise 'Irish culture', and the Irish language in particular, in order to personally feel 'more' Irish.

This seemingly inconsistent attitude among many of my informants can be easily demonstrated with regard to a few exemplary quotes, including the following statement by Peadar that appeared in Chapter 10:

> I don't want to be snobbish, but the ability to speak Irish surely reinforces one's Irishness. But it is not a prerequisite to being Irish. Just because I speak Irish makes me not more Irish, but personally I undoubtedly feel more Irish. Do I feel that others do need to speak Irish to be wholeheartedly Irish? Definitely not! I don't see that as a contradiction. For me personally, to have the ability to speak Irish enriches my Irishness.

A variation on this same attitude can be found in Micheál's account presented in Chapter 4:

> On a personal level, and that's just speaking about myself, it solves some problems to be involved in activities that are very clearly identifiable markers. So that one solution to a dilemma, 'What does it mean to be Irish?' – one possible solution to that dilemma is to learn the language and speak the language. … You need to know what it means to be Irish. And the Irish language and games and songs are ways of dealing with that problem!

Other informants also repeatedly expressed this fundamental viewpoint, even though people obviously used different words. Thus, reflecting on why she had been so strongly involved with the Irish language, Pádraigín argued that although

Irish meant a lot to her personally, this was not to say – as she put it – 'that all English speakers who don't speak Irish in Ireland are not Irish, but I think they're really missing out!' Another way of getting the same point across was provided by Siobhán, a mother of several children attending local Irish-medium schools, when she stated, 'I do have to say that having the Irish language helps 'cause you feel more Irish, but it does not make you less Irish if you don't have the language!' Finally, Mairéad also argued that practical involvement with one's 'own culture' was not necessary but helpful in that 'it gives you that sense of identity, that you know exactly who you are and where you're coming from; otherwise you can flounder around, you know?'

Towards the end of both parts (i.e. in Chapters 6 and 10), I asked the following question, which was related to my initial irritation about this apparent inconsistency: why, how and under which circumstances should it be plausible that in order to be what you already are (i.e. Irish), you have to become what you yourself agree you aren't (i.e. an Irish speaker)? By providing a combination of a general and specific answer to this question, I will ultimately integrate my results from both parts of this book into an explanation of the Irish language revival in Catholic West Belfast, which can simultaneously be read as specifying more generally the logic behind ethnicist revivals.

To my mind, the general answer to this question is to be found in acknowledging that the suggested model of ethnicity based on the causal logic of autochthony simultaneously establishes any ethnic identity in both categorical and prototypical terms. In the case of individualized autochthony – which clearly prevailed for Irishness in Catholic West Belfast – categorical ethnicity is established through the prerequisite of place of birth (and/or residence), and anyone fulfilling this condition is unconditionally seen as having this particular identity. At the same time, however, an ethnic identity based on individualized autochthony is also seen in prototypical terms as furthermore exhibiting a 'shared culture' (and/or descent) as a consequence of sharing a place of birth/residence, and it is only such a prototypical ethnicity that is ultimately perceived as being 'whole'. (This duality of categorical and prototypical ethnicity applies also, of course, to collectivized autochthony, although the causal direction is here inverted.)

This distinction between categorical and prototypical ethnicity is reminiscent of Dahl's discussion of Oromo identity, addressing particularly the Boraan variety (Dahl 1996). Dahl argues that the western folk model of ethnicity builds on a categorical 'container metaphor', according to which one either belongs to a clearly bounded category defined by common properties or one does not. By contrast, Boraan identity is presented as following a gradual 'centre-periphery schema' in that boundaries are less important than prototypical core values, according to which one can be more or less Boraan (Dahl 1996: 162–65). While Dahl thus argues that different models of ethnicity either follow the 'container principle' or the 'centripetal principle', as Schlee characterizes these two modes in his critical discussion (Schlee 2003: 353–54), it is suggested here that ethnicity based on the causal logic of autochthony rather distinguishes *and* combines categorical and prototypical identities within a more comprehensive model.

Thus combining categorical and prototypical Irishness, it was indeed possible for Irish Gaeilgeoirí in Catholic West Belfast to feel that in order to be prototypically 'whole' as the Irish persons they already were in categorical terms (due mainly to their place of birth in Ireland), they had to become what they themselves agreed they were not, namely, Irish speakers. The actual desire to move closer to such a prototypically 'whole' Irishness was linked to the extent to which these matters of identity actually mattered in everyday life. In other words, when daily life in Catholic West Belfast became increasingly ethnicized in the course of the Troubles, more and more people came to feel that they should repossess their 'own native language' in order to personally feel 'whole' as Irish prototypes. Such a change in actual cultural practices thereby not only diminished psychological insecurities about what it meant to be Irish at a personal level (see Micheál's quote above) but also had further practical value for nationalism in facilitating the instrumentally rational communication of cultural distinctiveness towards what was perceived as an ethnically different oppressor.

But even against the backdrop of this general answer concerning the how and why of the local Irish language revival, the idea of Irish as people's 'own native language' remains somewhat strange. Why was it compelling in the first place for locals to identify Irish as their 'own' even though it evidently was not and had not been their 'own'? In other words, how exactly had the Irish language been integrated into local Irishness to plausibly set in motion an ethnicist revival of actual cultural practices? In order to provide a specific answer to this question, it may be helpful to conceive the logic behind the revival in terms of a chain of interlinked conceptual steps.

Beginning with the final stage within this logic behind the revival, a considerable minority of people in Catholic West Belfast have begun to learn and speak the Irish language in recent decades. As I have shown, this expansion of actual language practices was linked – through an emically acknowledged case of evident pretension – to the locally prevailing representation of Irish as people's 'own native language'. As I argued in the first part of this book, it was precisely this pretentious relationship between representations and practices that had been the dominant value-rational driving force behind the local revival in Catholic West Belfast, which occurred throughout and partly because of the Troubles. For this to be actually operative, however, people not only had to believe they were already Irish, they also had to perceive the representation of Irish as Ireland's truly 'native language' as a plausible extension of other crucial representations of Irishness that they also held; based on accepted historical knowledge about linguistic development on the island of Ireland, people perceived this extension in such a way. As we learnt in the second part of this study, other such crucial representations of Irishness referred, first and foremost, to 'self-identification as Irish', to 'being born in Ireland' and to a distinctive 'Irish culture', including – amongst other things – Gaelic games, Irish music and Irish dancing. I argued that from the point of view of my informants such representations clearly constituted a case of selection, at least when it came to their own case as Irish Gaeilgeoirí in Catholic West Belfast. This was so because most of my informants experienced these cultural practices of identifying with being Irish, of being born in Ireland and of engaging, for instance, with Gaelic games, Irish music and Irish dancing as sufficiently given. These sufficiently realized cultural practices were based on a variety of motivations, which were by and large independent from the identity-related motivation of value-rational ethnicism (so central for the Irish language). It was precisely this considerable independence of such cultural practices from identity matters that allowed them to be experienced as the 'authentic' matters of this very identity. The fact that these practices were thereby to a large extent also based on traditional motivations – rooted in structural predispositions resulting from the practices of fellow Irish people in numerous internal structural contexts – further provided this 'authentic' experience with a doxic quality that naturalized what people as social actors could actually also have done quite differently.

Interpreted in such terms, the logic behind the revival can ultimately be refocused concerning the three analytical dimensions of this study. With regard to time, it is evident that in order to revive Irish as one's 'own native language', one already must view oneself as Irish. In other words, the logic of the language revival presupposed the anteriority of Irishness. However, as we have seen in this study (and especially in the biographical chapters 4 and 8), the actual acquisition of Irish did not necessarily happen only after the practice of other elements of 'Irish culture' had been engaged. It was (and is) thus possible to engage simultaneously in two different practices, one perceived as simply expressing prior Irishness (e.g. learning Irish step dancing), while another can be experienced as, in a prototypical sense, actually only making oneself more Irish now (e.g. learning Irish). What I am getting at is that the logic behind the local language revival in fact conceptualized the relative anteriority of Irishness with regard to revivalist practices in 'tempo-logical' rather than 'chrono-logical' terms: instead of actually succeeding the establishment of Irishness in real time, the revival only had to build on a temporal logic which projected itself *as if* it followed prior Irishness in time (this I call 'logical time').

Turning towards the relationship between representations and practices, the above explications reveal that within the logic of the revival, selection dominated pretension in tempo-logical terms. To put it differently, for the pretension of Irish as people's 'own native language' to become an actual driving force behind a language revival, it had to be plausibly rooted – within logical time, as just described – in 'prior' cases of selection. It is at this point that the lack of comprehensiveness in this book concerning 'Irish culture' can be shown to be irrelevant for the revivalist logic to still be functional: a revival can occur as long as it can draw on some cases of selection, irrespective of the relationship adhering between representational and therein represented practices for the remainder of an allegedly distinctive 'culture', and as I have shown, this was indeed the case locally for self-identification as Irish, for being born in Ireland, Gaelic games, Irish music and Irish dancing.

Finally, addressing the interplay between structure and agency, I argued that for a value-rational ethnicism to become a powerful and convincing motivation, it had to, again tempo-logically, build on 'prior' practices based on motivations that were largely independent of such ethnicist values: in order to intentionally become more Irish, one had to have 'earlier' become Irish largely as an unintended consequence and by-product of one's own activities. The more these latter activities were thereby rooted in structural predispositions, engendering traditionally motivated actions, the better, given that such traditional practices were not only experienced as 'authentically' Irish but also as 'naturally' and 'self-evidently' so.

It is in this sense that the logic behind the revival, constituting the specific answer to the question concerning the how and why of the local Irish language revival, can be summarized: the representation of Irish as people's 'own native language' – an evident case of pretension – could become the dominant value-rational driving force behind the revival because it was plausibly integrated into other representations of Irishness that evidently selected other given elements of local Irishness, which, in turn, were perceived as having made people Irish *prior* to their engagement with this revival; these other cultural elements, largely based on non-identity-related motivations (especially traditional motivations), were thus experienced as constituting the authentic matters of categorical Irishness, on which attempts to 'repossess' a more prototypical Irishness could build. Rephrased in the terminology of this book, the specific logic behind the revival can hence be characterized as being based on a pretension tempo-logically dominated by a selection, itself experienced as 'natural' when rooted in the 'tradition' of structural predispositions. While I believe this to be the case for all ethnicist revivals, I am convinced that this specific logic, combined with the general answer given above, emphasizing both the categorical and prototypical nature of autochthonous ethnicity, sufficiently accounts for the empirical case of the Irish language revival in Catholic West Belfast. Against this backdrop, I thus conclude that over the past decades, the Irish language could indeed be actively transformed into something that – from the point of view of local Gaeilgeoirí – was increasingly 'all around us', precisely because in a tempo-logical rather than chronological sense, Irishness had already been 'all around us'.

Post Scriptum

Bibliography

Adams, Gerry. 1986. *The Politics of Irish Freedom*. Wolfeboro, NH: Brandon.

Anderson, Benedict. (1983) 1991. *Imagined Communities: Reflections on the Origin and Spread of Nationalism*. Revised and extended. London and New York: Verso.

Andersonstown News. 2004. 'Fermanagh Looking to Regain the Finishing Touch in Replay'. Belfast. 23 August 2004: 57.

Andrews, Liam S. 1997. 'The very dogs in Belfast will bark in Irish: The Unionist Government and the Irish Language 1921–43', in Aodán Mac Póilin (ed.), *The Irish Language in Northern Ireland*. Belfast: Ultach Trust, pp. 49–94.

———. 2000. 'Unionism and Nationalism and the Irish language, 1893–1933', Ph.D. thesis. Belfast: Queen's University Belfast.

Antrim GAA – CLG Aontroim. 2008. 'History of the GAA in Antrim'. Retrieved 19 August 2008 from http://www.antrimgaa.net/history/

Appadurai, Arjun. 1996. *Modernity at Large: Cultural Dimensions of Globalization*. Minneapolis: University of Minnesota Press.

Austin, John L. 1962. *How to Do Things with Words*. Oxford: Clarendon Press.

Bailey, Benjamin. 2001. 'Switching', in Alessandro Duranti (ed.), *Key Terms in Language and Culture*. Malden and Oxford: Blackwell Publishers, pp. 238–40.

Bairner, Alan. 2005. 'Irish Sport', in Joe Cleary and Claire Connolly (eds), *The Cambridge Companion to Modern Irish Culture*. Cambridge and New York: Cambridge University Press, pp. 190–205.

Barth, Fredrik (ed.). 1969a. *Ethnic Groups and Boundaries: The Social Organization of Culture Difference*. Oslo, Bergen, London: Universitetsforlaget and George Allen & Unwin.

———. 1969b. 'Introduction', in Fredrik Barth (ed.), *Ethnic Groups and Boundaries: The Social Organization of Culture Difference*. Oslo, Bergen, London: Universitetsforlaget and George Allen & Unwin, pp. 9–38.

———. 1998. 'Preface 1998', in Fredrik Barth (ed.), *Ethnic Groups and Boundaries: The Social Organization of Culture Difference*. Prospect Heights, IL: Waveland Press, pp. 5–7.

Bayart, Jean-François, Peter Geschiere and Francis B. Nyamnjoh. 2001. 'Autochthonie, démocratie et citoyenneté en Afrique', *Critique Internationale* 10: 177–94.

BBC 2000. 'Maze Prison'. Retrieved 01 February 2006 from http://news.bbc.co.uk/hi/english/static/in_depth/northern_ireland/2000/maze_prison/default.stm

Bean, Kevin. 1994. *The New Departure: Recent Developments in Irish Republican Ideology and Strategy*. Liverpool: University of Liverpool, Institute of Irish Studies.

Billig, Michael. 1995. *Banal Nationalism*. London and Thousand Oaks, CA: Sage.

Blom, Jan-Petter and John J. Gumperz. 1972. 'Social Meaning in Linguistic Structure: Code-switching in Norway', in John J. Gumperz and Dell H. Hymes (eds), *Directions in Sociolinguistics: The Ethnography of Communication*. New York: Holt, Rinehart and Winston, pp. 407–34.

Blumer, Herbert. 1969. *Symbolic Interactionism: Perspective and Method*. Englewood Cliffs, NJ: Prentice-Hall.

Boal, Frederick Wilgar, Russell C. Murray and Michael A. Poole. 1976. 'Belfast: The Urban Encapsulation of a National Conflict', in Susan E. Clarke and Jeffrey L. Obler (eds), *Urban Ethnic Conflict: A Comparative Perspective*. Chapel Hill, NC: Institute for Research in Social Science, University of North Carolina at Chapel Hill, pp. 77–131.

Boullier, Dianna. 1998. *Exploring Irish Music and Dance*. Dublin: O'Brien Press.

Bourdieu, Pierre. 1977. *Outline of a Theory of Practice*. Cambridge and New York: Cambridge University Press.

———. 1984. *Distinction: A Social Critique of the Judgement of Taste*. Cambridge, MA: Harvard University Press.

———. 1990. *In Other Words: Essays towards a Reflexive Sociology*. Cambridge: Polity.

Breathnach, Breandán. 1971. *Folk Music and Dances of Ireland*. Dublin: Talbot Press.

Brennan, Helen. 1999. *The Story of Irish Dance*. Dingle: Brandon.

Brewer, John D. 1992. 'Sectarianism and Racism, and their Parallels and Differences', *Ethnic and Racial Studies* 15(3): 352–64.

———. 2002. 'Are there any Christians in Northern Ireland?', in Ann Marie Gray, Katrina Lloyd, Paula Devine, Gillian Robinson and Deirdre Heenan (eds), *Social Attitudes in Northern Ireland: The Eighth Report*. London: Pluto Press.

Brubaker, Rogers. 2004. '"Civic" and "Ethnic" Nationalism', in Rogers Brubaker (ed.), *Ethnicity without Groups*. Cambridge, MA and London: Harvard University Press, pp. 132–46.

Bryan, Dominic. 2000. *Orange Parades: The Politics of Ritual, Tradition and Control*. London and Sterling: Pluto Press.

———. 2007. 'Between the National and the Civic: Flagging Peace in, or a Piece of, Northern Ireland?', in Thomas Hylland Eriksen and Richard Jenkins (eds), *Flag, Nation and Symbolism in Europe and America*. London and New York: Routledge, pp. 102–14.

Buckley, Anthony D. 1982. *A Gentle People: A Study of a Peaceful Community in Ulster*. Holywood: Ulster Folk and Transport Museum.

———. 1998. *Symbols in Northern Ireland*. Belfast: Institute of Irish Studies, Queen's University of Belfast.

Buckley, Anthony D. and Mary Catherine Kenney. 1995. *Negotiating Identity: Rhetoric, Metaphor and Social Drama in Northern Ireland*. Washington, DC: Smithsonian Institution Press.

Bufwack, M.S. 1982. *Village without Violence: An Examination of a Northern Irish Community*. Cambridge, MA: Schenkman.

Burton, Frank. 1978. *The Politics of Legitimacy: Struggles in a Belfast Community.* London and Boston: Routledge and K. Paul.

Butler, David E. 1994. 'British Broadcasting in Northern Ireland: A Contradiction in Terms?', in Jürgen Elvert (ed.), *Nordirland in Geschichte und Gegenwart = Northern Ireland, Past and Present.* Stuttgart: F. Steiner, pp. 453–68.

Carey, Tim. 2004. *Croke Park: A History.* Wilton: Collins Press.

Carolan, Nicholas. 2004. 'Glenside – Irish Classics': Booklet Text to the CD 'Glenside: Irish Classics'. Dublin: Glenside, a division of Waltons Music.

Cavalli-Sforza, L.L., Paolo Menozzi and Alberto Piazza. 1994. *The History and Geography of Human Genes.* Princeton: Princeton University Press.

Central Statistics Office – An Phríomh-Oifig Staidrimh (CSO). 2003. *Census 2002: Principal Demographic Results.* Retrieved 21 July 2008 from http://www.cso.ie/census/documents/pdr_2002.pdf

Ceuppens, Bambi. 2006. 'Allochthons, Colonizers, and Scroungers: Exclusionary Populism in Belgium', *African Studies Review* 49(2): 147–86.

Ceuppens, Bambi and Peter Geschiere. 2005. 'Autochthony: Local or Global? New Modes in the Struggle over Citizenship and Belonging in Africa and Europe', *Annual Review of Anthropology* 34: 385–407.

Chauveau, Jean-Pierre. 2006. 'How does an Institution Evolve? Land, Politics, Intergenerational Relations and the Institution of the "Tutorat" amongst Autochthones and Immigrants (Gban Region, Côte d'Ivoire)', in Richard Kuba and Carola Lentz (eds), *Land and the Politics of Belonging in West Africa.* Leiden and Boston: Brill, pp. 213–40.

Clifford, James and George E. Marcus (eds). 1986. *Writing Culture: The Poetics and Politics of Ethnography.* Berkeley, Los Angeles, London: University of California Press.

Coakley, John. 2007. 'National Identity in Northern Ireland: Stability or Change?', *Nations and Nationalism* 13(4): 573–97.

Comaroff, Jean. 1985. *Body of Power, Spirit of Resistance: The Culture and History of a South African People.* Chicago: University of Chicago Press.

Comaroff, Jean and John L. Comaroff. 2001. 'Naturing the Nation: Aliens, Apocalypse and the Postcolonial State', *Journal of Southern African Studies* 27(3): 627–51.

Comhairle na Gaelscolaíochta. 2004. *Bunachar sonraí gaelscoileanna 2003–04 / Irish-medium School Database 2003–04.* Belfast: Comhairle na Gaelscolaíochta.

———. 2007. *Comhairle na Gaelscolaíochta.* Retrieved 16 January 2007 from http://www.comhairle.org/english/index.asp

Conradh na Gaeilge. 2005. *Conradh na Gaeilge.* Retrieved 17 January 2007 from http://www.cnag.ie/

Coogan, Tim Pat. 1996. *The Troubles: Ireland's Ordeal 1966–1996 and the Search for Peace.* London: Arrow Books.

———. 2002. *On the Blanket: The Inside Story of the IRA Prisoners' 'Dirty' Protest.* New York: Palgrave MacMillan.

Coohill, Joseph. 2000. *Ireland: A Short History.* Oxford and Boston: Oneworld.

Cormack, R.J. and R.D. Osborne. 1994. 'The Evolution of a Catholic Middle Class', in Adrian Guelke (ed.), *New Perspectives on the Northern Ireland Conflict*. Aldershot and Brookfield: Avebury, pp. 65–85.

Coulter, Carol. 2004. *Referendum 2004 – An Irish Times' Guide*. Retrieved 18 September 2008 from http://www.irishtimes.com/focus/referendum2004/guide.html

Coulter, Colin. 1999. *Contemporary Northern Irish Society: An Introduction*. London and Sterling: Pluto Press.

Croke Park Stadium – Páirc an Chrócaigh. 2008a. *Croke Park Stadium – History and Development*. Retrieved 25 July 2008 from http://www.crokepark.ie/page/history__development1.html

———. 2008b. *Welcome to Croke Park*. Retrieved 25 July 2008 from http://www.crokepark.ie/index.html

Cronin, Mike. 1999. *Sport and Nationalism in Ireland: Gaelic Games, Soccer and Irish Identity since 1884*. Dublin: Four Courts Press.

Cronin, Sean. 1980. *Irish Nationalism: A History of its Roots and Ideology*. Dublin: The Academy Press.

Cullinane, John P. 1999. 'Céilí Dance', in Fintan Vallely (ed.), *The Companion to Irish Traditional Music*. Cork: Cork University Press, pp. 64.

Cultúrlann McAdam Ó Fiaich. 2006. *Cultúrlann McAdam Ó Fiaich – Fáilte, Welcome, Bienvenue, Bern Vinda, Bienvenido, Willkommen, Bienvenuto*. Retrieved 12 December 2006 from http://www.culturlann.ie/

Dahl, Gudrun. 1996. 'Sources of Life and Identity', in P.T.W. Baxter, Jan Hultin and Alessandro Triulzi (eds), *Being and Becoming Oromo: Historical and Anthropological Enquiries*. Lawrenceville, NJ: Red Sea Press, pp. 162–77.

De Brún, Fionntán. 2006. 'Introduction', in Fionntán De Brún (ed.), *Belfast and the Irish Language*. Dublin: Four Courts, pp. 7–14.

De Búrca, Marcus. 1999. *The GAA: A History*, 2nd edn. Dublin: Gill and Macmillan.

Delaney, Liam and Tony Fahey. 2005. *The Social and Economic Value of Sport in Ireland*. Dublin: ESRI.

DENI 2006. *Pupil Religion by School Management Type 2000/01 – 2005/06 Excel*. Retrieved 26 May 2006 from http://www.deni.gov.uk/pupil_religion_series_2005_06-2.xls

Dinneen, Patrick S. 1927. *Foclóir Gaedhilge agus Béarla: An Irish-English Dictionary*. Dublin: The Irish Texts Society.

Doak, Richard. 1998. '(De)constructing Irishness in the 1990s: The Gaelic Athletic Association and Cultural Nationalist Discourse Reconsidered', *Irish Journal of Sociology* 8: 25–48.

Doherty, Paul and Michael Poole. 2000. 'Living Apart in Belfast: Residential Segregation in a Context of Ethnic Conflict', in Frederick Wilgar Boal (ed.), *Ethnicity and Housing: Accommodating Differences*. Aldershot: Ashgate, pp. 179–89.

Douglas, Neville. 1997. 'Political Structures, Social Interaction and Identity Change in Northern Ireland', in Brian Graham (ed.), *In Search of Ireland: A Cultural Geography*. London: Routledge, pp. 151–73.

Dozon, Jean-Pierre. 2000. 'La Côte d'Ivoire entre démocratie, nationalisme et ethnonationalisme', *Politique Africaine* 78: 45–63.

Duffy, Mary and Geoffrey Evans. 1997. 'Class, Community Polarisation and Politics', in Lizanne Dowds, Paula Devine and Richard Breen (eds), *Social Attitudes in Northern Ireland. The Sixth Report 1996–1997*. Belfast: Appletree Press, pp. 102–37.

Eriksen, Thomas Hylland. 1991. 'The Cultural Contexts of Ethnic Differences', *Man* 26(1): 127–44.

———. 2000. 'Ethnicity and Culture: A Second Look', in Regina Bendix and Herman Roodenburg (eds), *Managing Ethnicity: Perspectives from Folklore Studies, History and Anthropology*. Amsterdam: Het Spinhuis, pp. 185–205.

———. 2002. *Ethnicity and Nationalism: Anthropological Perspectives*, 2nd edn. London and Sterling: Pluto Press.

Fahy, Desmond. 2001. *How the GAA Survived the Troubles*. Dublin: Wolfhound Press.

Feldman, Allen. 1991. *Formations of Violence: The Narrative of the Body and Political Terror in Northern Ireland*. Chicago: University of Chicago Press.

Fenton, Steve. 2003. *Ethnicity*. Cambridge: Polity.

Foley, Catherine. 1999. 'Step Dance', in Fintan Vallely (ed.), *The Companion to Irish Traditional Music*. Cork: Cork University Press, pp. 380–81.

Foras na Gaeilge. 2007. *Foras na Gaeilge – Fáilte / Welcome*. Retrieved 16 July 2007 from http://www.gaeilge.ie/

Forbairt Feirste. 2006. *About Us*. Retrieved 13 June 2006 from http://www.forbairtfeirste.com/site/home.htm

Francis McPeake School of Music. 2008. *History*. Retrieved 08 August 2008 from http://www.francismcpeake.com/

Frank, Gelya. 1995. 'Anthropology and the Individual Lives: The Story of the Life History and the History of the Life Story', *American Anthropologist* 97(1): 145–48.

Fraser, T.G. 2000. *Ireland in Conflict, 1922–1998*. London and New York: Routledge.

Friel, Brian. 1981. *Translations*. London: Faber.

Gaelic Athletic Association. 2003. *Official Guide 2003*. Dublin: The Gaelic Athletic Association.

———. 2005. *An chomhdháil bhliantúil 2005: Tuarascáil, cuntas airgid agus rúin don chomhdháil*. Dublin: Gaelic Athletic Association.

———. 2008a. *All about Football*. Retrieved 22 July 2008 from http://www.gaa.ie/page/all_about_football.html

———. 2008b. *GAA – Cumann Lúthchleas Gael: Official Website*. Retrieved 22 July 2008 from http://www.gaa.ie/index.html

———. 2008c. *All about Hurling*. Retrieved 22 July 2008 from http://www.gaa.ie/page/all_about_hurling.html

———. 2008d. *General History – The Birth of Cumann Luthcleas Gael*. Retrieved 22 July 2008 from http://www.gaa.ie/page/the_birth_of_cumann_luthcleas_gael.html

Gardner-Chloros, Penelope. 2003. 'Code-switching', in William J. Frawley (ed.), *International Encyclopedia of Linguistics*. Volume 1: AAVE-Esperanto, 2nd edn. Oxford: Oxford University Press, pp. 331–33.

Garfinkel, Harold. 1967. *Studies in Ethnomethodology*. Englewood Cliffs, NJ: Prentice-Hall.

Geschiere, Peter. 2004. 'Ecology, Belonging and Xenophobia: The 1994 Forest Law in Cameroon and the Issue of "Community"', in Harri Englund and Francis B. Nyamnjoh (eds), *Rights and the Politics of Recognition in Africa*. London and New York: Zed Books, pp. 237–61.

Geschiere, Peter and Stephen Jackson. 2006. 'Autochthony and the Crisis of Citizenship: Democratization, Decentralization, and the Politics of Belonging', *African Studies Review* 49(2): 1–7.

Geschiere, Peter and Francis B. Nyamnjoh. 2000. 'Capitalism and Autochthony: The Seesaw of Mobility and Belonging', *Public Culture* 12(2): 423–52.

Giddens, Anthony. 1984. *The Constitution of Society: Outline of the Theory of Structuration*. Berkeley, Los Angeles: University of California Press.

Glór na nGael. 2006. *Fáilte/Welcome*. Retrieved 13 June 2006 from http://www.glornangael.ie/

Gramsci, Antonio. 1971. *Selections from the Prison Notebooks of Antonio Gramsci*. London: Lawrence & Wishart.

Gumperz, John J. 1982. *Discourse Strategies*. Cambridge: Cambridge University Press.

Hall, Stuart. 1997. 'The Work of Representation', in Stuart Hall (ed.), *Representation. Cultural Representations and Signifying Practices*. London and Thousand Oaks, CA: Sage, The Open University, pp. 13–74.

Hamilton, Colin. 1999. 'Session', in Fintan Vallely (ed.), *The Companion to Irish Traditional Music*. Cork: Cork University Press, pp. 345–46.

Harrington, John P. and Elizabeth J. Mitchell (eds). 1999. *Politics and Performance in Contemporary Northern Ireland*. Amherst: University of Massachusetts Press.

Hassan, David. 1998. 'The Role of Catholic Secondary Schools in the Promotion of Gaelic Games as an Expression of Irish Nationalism', Masters thesis. University of Ulster.

———. 2003. 'Still Hibernia Irredenta? The Gaelic Athletic Association, Northern Nationalists and Modern Ireland', *Culture, Sport, Society* 6(1): 92–110.

Hayes, Bernadette C. and Ian McAllister. 1999. 'Ethnonationalism, Public Opinion and the Good Friday Agreement', in Joseph Ruane and Jennifer Todd (eds), *After the Good Friday Agreement: Analysing Political Change in Northern Ireland*. Dublin: University College Dublin Press, pp. 30–48.

Hindley, Reg. 1990. *The Death of the Irish Language: A Qualified Obituary*. London and New York: Routledge.

Hobsbawm, Eric. 1983. 'Introduction: Inventing Traditions', in Eric Hobsbawm and Terence Ranger (eds), *The Invention of Tradition*. Cambridge and New York: Cambridge University Press, pp. 1–14.

Hobsbawm, Eric and Terence Ranger. 1983. *The Invention of Tradition*. Cambridge and New York: Cambridge University Press.

Holy, Ladislav and Milan Stuchlik. 1983. *Actions, Norms and Representations: Foundations of Anthropological Inquiry*. Cambridge and New York: Cambridge University Press.

Howe, Leo. 1990. *Being Unemployed in Northern Ireland: An Ethnographic Study*. Cambridge and New York: Cambridge University Press.

Hutchinson, John. 1987. *The Dynamics of Cultural Nationalism: The Gaelic Revival and the Creation of the Irish Nation State*. London and Boston: Allen & Unwin.

Hyde, Douglas. (1892) 1986. 'The Necessity for de-Anglicising Ireland', in Douglas Hyde and Breandán Ó Conaire (eds), *Language, Lore, and Lyrics: Essays and Lectures*. Blackrock: Irish Academic Press, pp. 153–70.

IICD 2005. 'Report of the Independent International Commission on Decommissioning'.

Irish Traditional Music Archive. 1999. 'Traditional Music, ITMA Definitions', in Fintan Vallely (ed.), *The Companion to Irish Traditional Music*. Cork: Cork University Press, pp. 402–3.

Jackson, Stephen. 2006. 'Sons of which Soil? The Language and Politics of Autochthony in Eastern D.R. Congo', *African Studies Review* 49(2): 95–123.

Jarman, Neil. 1997. *Material Conflicts: Parades and Visual Displays in Northern Ireland*. Oxford and New York: Berg.

———. 2007. 'Pride and Possession, Display and Destruction', in Thomas Hylland Eriksen and Richard Jenkins (eds), *Flag, Nation and Symbolism in Europe and America*. London and New York: Routledge, pp. 88–101.

Jenkins, Richard. 1983. *Lads, Citizens, and Ordinary Kids: Working-class Youth Life-styles in Belfast*. London and Boston: Routledge & Kegan Paul.

———. 1993. 'Beyond Ethnography: Primary Data Sources in the Urban Anthropology of Northern Ireland', in Chris Curtin, Hastings Donnan and Thomas M. Wilson (eds), *Irish Urban Cultures*. Belfast: Institute of Irish Studies, pp. 243–62.

———. 1997. *Rethinking Ethnicity: Arguments and Explorations*. London and Thousand Oaks, CA: Sage.

———. 2002. *Pierre Bourdieu. Revised Edition*. London and New York: Routledge.

———. 2004. *Social Identity. Second Edition*. London and New York: Routledge.

Kabel, Lars. 2000a. 'Irish Language Enthusiasts and Native Speakers: An Uneasy Relationship', in Gordon McCoy and Maolcholaim Scott (eds), *Gaelic Identities = Aithne na nGael*. Belfast: Institute of Irish Studies – Queen's University Belfast/Iontaobhas ULTACH / ULTACH Trust, pp. 133–38.

———. 2000b. 'The Irish Language in Northern Ireland: Moving Interpretations of Language as a Symbol of Ethnicity', in Ton Dekker, John Hesloot and Carla Wijers (eds), *Roots and Rituals: The Construction of Ethnic Identities*. Amsterdam: Het Spinhuis, pp. 644–52.

Kachuk, Patricia Mary Catherine. 1993. 'Irish Language Activism in West Belfast: A Resistance to British Cultural Hegemony'. Ph.D. thesis. University of British Columbia.

Kirkland, Richard. 2002. *Identity Parades: Northern Irish Culture and Dissident Subjects*. Liverpool: Liverpool University Press.

Kohn, Hans. 1944. *The Idea of Nationalism: A Study in its Origins and Background*. New York: MacMillan Company.

Konings, Piet and Francis B. Nyamnjoh. 2003. *Negotiating an Anglophone Identity: A Study of the Politics of Recognition and Representation in Cameroon*. Leiden: Brill.

Landau, Loren B. 2006. 'Transplants and Transients; Idioms of Belonging and Dislocation in Inner-city Johannesburg', *African Studies Review* 49(2): 125–45.

Latour, Bruno. 2005. *Reassembling the Social: An Introduction to Actor-Network-Theory*. Oxford: Oxford University Press.

Lentz, Carola. 2003. '"Premiers arrivés" et "nouveaux-venus" discours sur l'autochtonie dans la savane ouest-africaine', in Richard Kuba, Carola Lentz and Claude Nurukyor Somda (eds), *Histoire du peuplement et relations interethniques au Burkina Faso*. Paris: Karthala, pp. 113–34.

———. 2006a. 'Land Rights and the Politics of Belonging in Africa: An Introduction', in Richard Kuba and Carola Lentz (eds), *Land and the Politics of Belonging in West Africa*. Leiden and Boston: Brill, pp. 1–34.

———. 2006b. 'First-comers and Late-comers: Indigenous Theories of Landownership in West Africa', in Richard Kuba and Carola Lentz (eds), *Land and the Politics of Belonging in West Africa*. Leiden and Boston: Brill, pp. 35–56.

Leonhardt, Alec. 2006. 'Baka and the Magic of the State: between Autochthony and Citizenship', *African Studies Review* 49(2): 69–94.

McCall, Cathal. 1999. *Identity in Northern Ireland: Communities, Politics and Change*. New York: St Martin's Press.

McCann, May. 1983. 'Belfast Ceilidhes – The Hey-day', *Ulster Folklife* 29: 55–69.

———. 1995. 'Music and Politics in Ireland: The Specificity of the Folk Revival in Belfast', *British Journal of Ethnomusicology* 4: 51–75.

McCarthy, Marie. 1999. *Passing It On: The Transmission of Music in Irish Culture*. Cork: Cork University Press.

Mac Con Iomaire, Liam. 1999. 'Sean-nós', in Fintan Vallely (ed.), *The Companion to Irish Traditional Music*. Cork: Cork University Press, p. 336.

Mac Corraidh, Seán. 2006. 'Irish-medium Education in Belfast', in Fionntán De Brún (ed.), *Belfast and the Irish Language*. Dublin: Four Courts, pp. 177–83.

McCoy, Gordon. 1997. 'Protestants and the Irish Language in Northern Ireland', Ph.D. thesis. Belfast: Queen's University Belfast.

———. 2006. 'Protestants and the Irish Language in Belfast', in Fionntán De Brún (ed.), *Belfast and the Irish Language*. Dublin: Four Courts, pp. 147–76.

McDermott, Philip. 2007. 'Broadcasting for Minorities: The Case of the Celtic Languages', in Máiréad Nic Craith (ed.), *Language, Power and Identity Politics*. New York: Palgrave Macmillan, pp. 101–22.

———. 2011. '"Irish Isn't Spoken Here?" Language Policy and Planning in Ireland', *English Today* 27(2): 25–31.

McGarry, John and Brendan O'Leary. 1995. *Explaining Northern Ireland: Broken Images*. Oxford and Cambridge, MA: Blackwell.

Mac Giolla Chríost, Diarmait. 2005. *The Irish Language in Ireland: From Goídel to Globalisation*. New York: Routledge.

McGrath, Grace. 2000. *A History of the Department of Education in Northern Ireland 1921–2000*. http://www.proni.gov.uk/Education/history.htm.

McKeown, Laurence. 2001. *Out of Time: Irish Republican Prisoners, Long Kesh, 1972–2000*. Belfast: Beyond the Pale.

McLoone, Martin. 1996. *Broadcasting in a Divided Community: Seventy Years of the BBC in Northern Ireland*. Belfast: Institute of Irish Studies, Queen's University Belfast.

MacLua, Brendan. 1967. *The Steadfast Rule: A History of the GAA Ban*. Dublin: Cuchalainn.

McManus, Antonia. 2002. *The Irish Hedge School and its Books, 1695–1831*. Dublin: Four Courts Press.

McMonagle, Sarah. 2010. 'Deliberating the Irish Language in Northern Ireland: From Conflict to Multiculturalism?', *Journal of Multilingual and Multicultural Development* 31(3): 253–70.

Mac Póilin, Aodán. 1997a. 'Plus ça change: The Irish Language and Politics', in Aodán Mac Póilin (ed.), *The Irish Language in Northern Ireland*. Belfast: Ultach Trust, pp. 31–48.

———. (ed.) 1997b. *The Irish Language in Northern Ireland*. Belfast: Ultach Trust.

———. 1997c. 'Aspects of the Irish Language Movement', in Aodán Mac Póilin (ed.), *The Irish Language in Northern Ireland*. Belfast: Ultach Trust, pp. 171–89.

———. 2006. 'Irish in Belfast, 1892–1960: From the Gaelic League to *Cumann Chluain Ard*', in Fionntán De Brún (ed.), *Belfast and the Irish Language*. Dublin: Four Courts, pp. 114–35.

Maguire, Gabrielle. 1991. *Our Own Language: An Irish Initiative*. Clevedon: Multilingual Matters.

Mahootian, Shahrzad. 2006. 'Code Switching and Mixing', in Keith Brown (ed.), *Encyclopedia of Language and Linguistics. Volume 2*. 2nd edn. Amsterdam, Boston, Heidelberg: Elsevier, pp. 511–27.

Mandle, William F. 1979. 'Sport as Politics: The Gaelic Athletic Association, 1884–1916', in Richard I. Cashman and Michael McKernan (eds), *Sport in History: The Making of Modern Sporting History*. St Lucia: University of Queensland Press, pp. 99–123.

———. 1987. *The Gaelic Athletic Association and Irish Nationalist Politics, 1884–1924*. London and Dublin: C. Helm/Gill and Macmillan.

Marshall-Fratani, Ruth. 2006. 'The War of "Who is Who": Autochthony, Nationalism, and Citizenship in the Ivorian Crisis', *African Studies Review* 49(2): 9–43.

Meeuwis, Michael and Jan Blommaert. 1998. 'A Monolectal View of Code-switching: Layered Code-switching among Zairians in Belgium', in Peter Auer (ed.), *Code-switching in Conversation*. London: Routledge, pp. 76–98.

Meinecke, Friedrich. 1919. *Weltbürgertum und Nationalstaat: Studien zur Genesis des deutschen Nationalstaats*. Munich and Berlin: R. Oldenbourg.

Mitchell, Claire. 2005. 'Behind the Ethnic Marker: Religion and Social Identification in Northern Ireland', *Sociology of Religion* 66(1): 3–21.

Muller, Janet. 2010. *Language and Conflict in Northern Ireland and Canada: A Silent War*. New York: Palgrave Macmillan.

Murchú, Máirtín Ó. 2000. 'Irish', in Glanville Price (ed.), *Encyclopedia of the Languages of Europe*. Oxford: Blackwell, pp. 243–50.

Murphy, Pat. 1999. '"Set" dance', in Fintan Vallely (ed.), *The Companion to Irish Traditional Music*. Cork: Cork University Press, pp. 346–47.

Murtagh, Brendan. 1996. 'Peace Line Communities: Implications for the Fountain', in Marie Smyth (ed.), *A Report of a Series of Public Discussions on Aspects of Sectarian Division in Derry Londonderry*. Derry Londonderry: Templegrove Action Research Limited.

Nic Craith, Máiréad. 1999. 'Irish Speakers in Northern Ireland, and the Good Friday Agreement', *Journal of Multilingual and Multicultural Development* 20(6): 494–507.

———. 2002. *Plural Identities – Singular Narratives: The Case of Northern Ireland*. New York: Berghahn.

———. 2003. *Culture and Identity Politics in Northern Ireland*. New York: Palgrave Macmillan.

———. 2007. *Language, Power and Identity Politics*. New York: Palgrave Macmillan.

Nig Uidhir, Gabrielle. 2006. 'The Shaw's Road Urban Gaeltacht: Role and Impact', in Fionntán De Brún (ed.), *Belfast and the Irish Language*. Dublin: Four Courts, pp. 136–46.

Northern Ireland Office, Great Britain. 1998. *The Agreement: Text of the Agreement Reached in the Multi-Party Negotiations on Northern Ireland*. Cmnd. 3883. Good Friday Agreement/Belfast Agreement. Belfast: HMSO.

Northern Ireland Statistics and Research Agency (NISRA). 2003. *Community Background and Religion*. Retrieved 06 June 2006 from http://www.nisra.gov.uk/archive/census/2001/standard%20tables/standard/Communitybgrel.pdf

———. 2004. *Specimen of the Household Census form 2001*. Retrieved 17 January 2007 from http://www.nisranew.nisra.gov.uk/Census/pdf/Householdform.pdf

———. 2006. *Northern Ireland Census 2001 Output*. Retrieved 06 June 2006 from http://www.nisranew.nisra.gov.uk/Census/Census2001Output/index.html

Ó Cadhain, Máirtín. 1964. *Mr Hill: Mr Tara*. Dublin: J.B. Houston.

Ó Canainn, Tomás. 1978. *Traditional Music in Ireland*. London and Boston: Routledge & K. Paul.

O'Connor, Fionnuala. 1993. *In Search of a State. Catholics in Northern Ireland*. Belfast: Blackstaff Press.

Ó Grianna, Séamus. 1986. *Nuair a bhí mé óg*. Dublin and Cork: Mercier Press.

Ó hAdhmaill, Feilim. 1985. 'Report of a Survey Carried Out on the Irish Language in West Belfast in the Winter of 1984/5'. Coleraine: Department of Social Administration. University of Ulster.

Ó hAllmhuráin, Gearóid. 1998. *Pocket History of Irish Traditional Music*. Dublin: The O'Brien Press.

O'Keefe, J.G. and Art O'Brien. 1902. *A Handbook of Irish Dances*. Dublin: O'Donochue.

Ó Laoire, Lillis. 2005. 'Irish Music', in Joe Cleary and Claire Connolly (eds), *The Cambridge Companion to Modern Irish Culture*. Cambridge and New York: Cambridge University Press, pp. 267–84.

Ó Muilleoir, Máirtín. 1986. 'The Necessity for Cultural Liberation', in Sinn Féin (ed.), *The Role of the Language in Ireland's Cultural Revival*. Belfast: AP/RN, pp. 20–23.

Ó Muirithe, Diarmuid. 1999. 'Song, Macaronic Song', in Fintan Vallely (ed.), *The Companion to Irish Taditional Music*. Cork: Cork University Press, pp. 354–56.

Ó Néill, Réamann. (n.d.). 'Teampall Shlí Leathan / The Protestant Broadway Church'. Unpublished manuscript.

O'Reilly, Camille. 1997. 'Nationalists and the Irish Language in Northern Ireland: Competing Perspectives', in Aodán Mac Póilin (ed.), *The Irish Language in Northern Ireland*. Belfast: Ultach Trust, pp. 95–130.

————. 1999. *The Irish Language in Northern Ireland: The Politics of Culture and Identity*. Basingstoke, Hampshire, New York: Macmillan Press and St Martin's Press.

Office for National Statistics (ONS). 2005. *The National Statistics Socio-economic Classification: User Manual*. Basingstoke: Palgrave Macmillan.

Ong, Aihwa. 1987. *Spirits of Resistance and Capitalist Discipline: Factory Women in Malaysia*. Albany: State University of New York Press.

Ortner, Sherry B. 1984. 'Theory in Anthropology since the Sixties', in *Comparative Studies in Society and History* 26(1): 126–66.

Patterson, Henry. 1997. *The Politics of Illusion: A Political History of the IRA*. London: Serif.

Peacock, James L. and Dorothy C. Holland. 1993. 'The Narrated Self: Life Stories in Process', *Ethos* 21(4): 367–83.

Peel, J.D.Y. 1989. 'The Cultural Work of Yoruba Ethnogenesis', in Elizabeth Tonkin, Maryon McDonald and Malcolm Chapman (eds), *History and Ethnicity*. London and New York: Routledge, pp. 198–215.

Pobal. 2006. *Scátheagras phobal na Gaeilge / The Umbrella Organisation for the Irish Language Community*. Retrieved 12 December 2006 from http://www.pobal. org/

Price, Glanville. 2000. 'Celtic Languages', in Glanville Price (ed.), *Encyclopedia of the Languages of Europe*. Oxford: Blackwell, pp. 83–84.

Purdon, Edward. 1999. *The Story of the Irish Language*. Dublin: Mercier Press.

Radio Telefís Éireann. 2008. *Céilí House*. Retrieved 26 August 2008 from http://www.rte.ie/radio1/ceilihouse/

Rolston, Bill. 2001. '"This is not a rebel song": The Irish Conflict and Popular Music', *Race and Class* 42(3): 49–67.

Rose, Richard. 1971. *Governing without Consensus: An Irish Perspective*. London: Faber and Faber.

Royce, Anya Peterson. 1982. *Ethnic Identity: Strategies of Diversity*. Bloomington: Indiana University Press.

Rumpf, Erhard and A.C. Hepburn. 1977. *Nationalism and Socialism in Twentieth-Century Ireland*. Liverpool: Liverpool University Press.

Runyan, William McKinley. 1996. 'Life History', in Adam Kuper and Jessica Kuper (eds), *The Social Science Encyclopedia*, 2nd edn. London and New York: Routledge, pp. 472–73.

Sartre, Jean-Paul. 1943. *L'être et le néant: essai d'ontologie phénoménologique*. Paris: Gallimard.

Schlee, Günther. 2001. 'Language and Ethnicity', in Neil J. Smelser and Paul B. Baltes (eds), *International Encyclopedia of the Social & Behavioral Sciences, Volume 12*. Amsterdam: Elsevier, pp. 8285–88.

———. 2003. 'Redrawing the Map of the Horn: The Politics of Difference', *Africa* 73(3): 343–68.

———. 2004. 'Taking Sides and Constructing Identities: Reflections on Conflict Theory', *The Journal of the Royal Anthropological Institute* 10(1): 135–56.

———. 2008. *How Enemies are Made: Towards a Theory of Ethnic and Religious Conflicts*. Oxford and New York: Berghahn Books.

Schrijver, Peter. 2000. 'Indo-European Languages', in Glanville Price (ed.), *Encyclopedia of the Languages of Europe*. Oxford: Blackwell, pp. 239–42.

Schütz, Alfred. 1967. *The Phenomenology of the Social World*. Evanston, IL: Northwestern University Press.

Scott, James C. 1985. *Weapons of the Weak: Everyday Forms of Peasant Resistance*. New Haven, CT: Yale University Press.

———. 1990. *Domination and the Arts of Resistance: Hidden Transcripts*. New Haven, CT: Yale University Press.

Searle, John R. 1969. *Speech Acts: An Essay in the Philosophy of Language*. London: Cambridge University Press.

Sheehan, J.J. 1902. *A Guide to Irish Dancing*. Dublin and New York: John Denvir.

Siedler, Reinhard. 1998. 'Erzählungen analysieren – Analysen erzählen: narrativ-biographisches Interview, Textanalyse und Falldarstellung', in Karl R. Wernhart and Werner Zips (eds), *Ethnohistorie: Rekonstruktion und Kulturkritik. Eine Einführung*. Vienna: Promedia, pp. 145–72.

Siffre, Labi. 2012. *Labi Siffre Lyrics Into the Light*. Retrieved 20 August 2012 from *http://lyrics.intothelight.info/*

Sinn Féin. 2007. *Irish Language*. Retrieved 16 January 2007 from http://www.sinnfein.ie/policies/irish_language

Sluka, Jeffrey A. 1989. *Hearts and Minds, Water and Fish: Support for the IRA and INLA in a Northern Irish Ghetto*. Greenwich, CT: JAI Press.

Smith, Anthony D. 1983. *Theories of Nationalism*, 2nd edn. London: Duckworth.

———. 1986. *The Ethnic Origins of Nations*. Oxford and New York: Blackwell.

———. 1991. *National Identity*. Harmondsworth: Penguin.

———. 2001. *Nationalism: Theory, Ideology, History*. Cambridge: Polity.

Soanes, Catherine and Angus Stevenson. 2003. *Oxford Dictionary of English*. Oxford: Oxford University Press.

Socpa, Antoine. 2006. 'Bailleurs autochtones et locataires allogènes: enjeu foncier et participation politique au Cameroun', *African Studies Review* 49(2): 45–67.

Spencer, Jonathan. 1996. 'Resistance', in Alan Barnard and Jonathan Spencer (eds), *Encyclopedia of Social and Cultural Anthropology*. London and New York: Routledge, pp. 488–89.

Spencer, Philip and Howard Wollman. 2005. 'Good and Bad Nationalisms', in Philip Spencer and Howard Wollman (eds), *Nations and Nationalism: A Reader*. Edinburgh: Edinburgh University Press, pp. 197–217.

Sugden, John Peter and Alan Bairner. 1993. *Sport, Sectarianism, and Society in a Divided Ireland*. Leicester and New York: Leicester University Press and St Martin's Press.

Sweeney, Eamonn. 2004. *Pocket History of Gaelic Sports*. Dublin: The O'Brien Press.

The Referendum Commission – An Coimisiún Reifrinn 2004. *The Referendum on Irish Citizenship*. Retrieved 08 September 2008 from http://www.refcom.ie/RefCom/RefComWebSite.nsf/0/C037F0ECB8CEAFC980256EA5005B0572

Trew, Karen. 1996. 'National Identity', in Richard Breen, Paula Devine and Lizanne Dowds (eds), *Social Attitudes in Northern Ireland: The Fifth Report*. Belfast: Appletree Press, pp. 140–52.

———. 1998. 'The Northern Irish Identity', in Anne J. Kershen (ed.), *A Question of Identity*. Aldershot et al.: Ashgate, pp. 60–76.

ULTACH Trust. 2006. *Iontaobhas ULTACH / ULTACH Trust*. Retrieved 12 December 2006 from http://www.ultach.org/

Vallely, Fintan. 1999a. 'Feis cheoil', in Fintan Vallely (ed.), *The Companion to Irish Traditional Music*. Cork: Cork University Press, pp. 121–22.

———. 1999b. 'Folk Club', in Fintan Vallely (ed.), *The Companion to Irish Traditional Music*. Cork: Cork University Press, p. 141.

———. 1999c. 'Oireachtas, An t-', in Fintan Vallely (ed.), *The Companion to Irish Traditional Music*. Cork: Cork University Press, p. 279.

———. 1999d. 'Clancy Brothers and Tommy Makem', in Fintan Vallely (ed.), *The Companion to Irish Traditional Music*. Cork: Cork University Press, p. 71.

———. 1999e. 'Céilí', in Fintan Vallely (ed.), *The Companion to Irish Traditional Music*. Cork: Cork University Press, p. 60.

———. 1999f. 'Dance', in Fintan Vallely (ed.), *The Companion to Irish Traditional Music*. Cork: Cork University Press, pp. 99–101.

———. 1999g. 'Céilí Bands', in Fintan Vallely (ed.), *The Companion to Irish Traditional Music*. Cork: Cork University Press, pp. 60–61.

Wacquant, Loïc J.D. 1989. 'Towards a Reflexive Sociology: A Workshop with Pierre Bourdieu', *Sociological Theory* 7(1): 26–63.

Walker, Brian Mercer. 1996. *Dancing to History's Tune: History, Myth, and Politics in Ireland*. Belfast: Institute of Irish Studies Queen's University of Belfast.

Wallis, Roy, Steve Bruce and David Taylor. 1986. *'No surrender!': Paisleyism and the Politics of Ethnic Identity in Northern Ireland*. Belfast: Department of Social Studies, Queen's University Belfast.

Weber, Max. 1978. *Economy and Society: An Outline of Interpretive Sociology*. Berkeley: University of California Press.

Whelan, Frank. 2000. *The Complete Guide to Irish Dance*. Belfast: Appletree.

Whitaker, Robin Gwendolyn. 2001. 'Talking Politics: Gender and Political Culture in the Northern Ireland Peace Process', Ph.D. thesis. University of California.

White, Harry. 1999. 'Music: History and Performance, 1700–1990s', in W.J. McCormack (ed.), *The Blackwell Companion to Modern Irish Culture*. Oxford and Malden: Blackwell Publishers, pp. 405–11.

Williams, Raymond. 1977. *Marxism and Literature*. Oxford: Oxford University Press.

———. 1980. *Problems in Materialism and Culture: Selected Essays*. London: Verso.

Wittgenstein, Ludwig. 1953. *Philosophical Investigations*. Oxford: Blackwell.

Woolard, Kathryn A. 2006. 'Codeswitching', in Alessandro Duranti (ed.), *A Companion to Linguistic Anthropology*. Malden and Oxford: Blackwell, pp. 73–94.

Wulff, Helena. 2007. *Dancing at the Crossroads: Memory and Mobility in Ireland*. New York: Berghahn Books.

Zenker, Olaf 2006. 'De Facto Exclusion through Discursive Inclusion: Autochthony in Discourses on Irishness and Politics in Catholic West Belfast', *Paideuma* 52: 183–95.

———. 2009. 'Autochthony and Activism among Contemporary Irish Nationalists in Northern Ireland, or: If "civic" nationalists are "ethno"-cultural revivalists, what remains of the civic/ethnic divide?' (and postscript by Joep Leerssen and reply), *Nations and Nationalism* 15(4): 696–722.

———. 2010. 'Between the Lines: Republicanism, Dissenters and the Politics of Meta-trauma in the Northern Irish Conflict', *Social Science & Medicine* 71(2): 236–43.

———. 2011. 'Autochthony, Ethnicity, Indigeneity and Nationalism: Time-honouring and State-oriented Modes of Rooting Individual-territory-group-triads in a Globalising World', *Critique of Anthropology* 31(1): 63–81.

———. 2012. 'On Prophets, Godfathers, Rebels, and Prostitutes: Distributed Agency in the Irish Language Revival of Northern Ireland', *Zeitschrift für Ethnologie* 137(1): 23–45.

Zenker, Olaf and Karsten Kumoll. 2010. 'Prologue: Opening Doors beyond Writing Culture', in Olaf Zenker and Karsten Kumoll (eds), *Beyond Writing Culture: Current Intersections of Epistemologies and Representational Practices*. New York and Oxford: Berghahn Books, pp. 1–38.

Index